Using Qualitative Methods in Action Research:
How Librarians Can Get to the Why of Data

Douglas Cook and Lesley Farmer, Editors

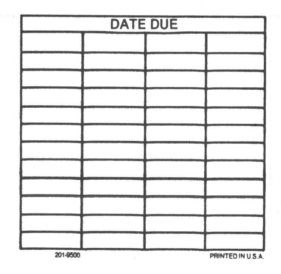

DATE DUE

201-9500   PRINTED IN U.S.A.

Association of College and Research Libraries

The paper used in this publication meets the minimum requirements of American National Standard for Information Sciences–Permanence of Paper for Printed Library Materials, ANSI Z39.48-1992. ∞

Library of Congress Cataloging-in-Publication Data

Using qualitative methods in action research : how librarians can get to the why of data / Douglas Cook and Lesley Farmer, editors.
     p.   cm.
  Includes bibliographical references and index.
  ISBN 978-0-8389-8576-2 (pbk. : alk. paper) 1. Public services (Libraries)—Evaluation. 2. Library administration—Decision making. 3. Academic libraries—Administration—Decision making. 4. Library science—Research—Methodology. 5. Action research. I. Cook, Douglas. II. Farmer, Lesley S. J.
  Z678.85.U85 2011
  025.5'877—dc22

                                     2011000967

Printed in the United States of America.

14 13 12 11 10   5 4 3 2 1

Contents

PART 1 QUALITATIVE RESEARCH IN THE LIBRARY

PART 2 USEFUL METHODOLOGIES OF QUALITATIVE RESEARCH

PART 3 ISSUES ADDRESSED THROUGH QUALITATIVE RESEARCH

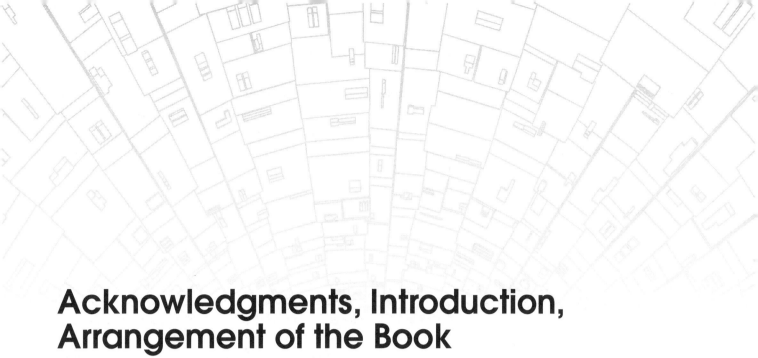

Acknowledgments, Introduction, Arrangement of the Book

Douglas Cook and Lesley Farmer

Acknowledgments

This book would never have happened without Pat Libutti. Pat laid the basic foundation for this project, getting it approved to be published, lining up many of the authors, and keeping it alive through several difficult situations. Unfortunately, because of health reasons, Pat had to finally give up the project. She chose us to bring it to life.

Pat was a true mentor to Doug in his early involvement in ACRL. As one small example, Pat advised and encouraged the EBSS Instruction for Educators committee to write a book on collaborating with classroom faculty. That project eventually became *The Collaborative Imperative*.[1] Pat's mentorship through the writing of that book was very typical of her contributions to ACRL. Many librarians, including Doug, became published authors as a result of her guidance, encouragement, and tremendous energy. Librarianship is a richer place because of Pat's caring involvement. Lesley too thanks Pat for her expert advice as well as her faith in recommending Lesley as a second editor for this book.

Doug would also like to thank Lesley for being so flexible as we took over this project. Although we had never met before, Doug and Lesley found out through this process that we have much in common as editors. We both like clean prose. We both are

willing to cut out all narrative that doesn't belong. And both of us insist that the narrative must hang together in a cohesive fashion. It has been a pleasure for Doug to work with Lesley. Likewise, Lesley has appreciated Doug's organizational and communications professionalism, which fostered a positive community of contributors. His editing background is renowned, and his graciousness is endless.

Many thanks go to our chapter authors, without whom this would be a very thin volume. We also need to thank our editor at ACRL, Kathryn Deiss, for her enduring patience as this book has moved through its various stages of development.

Introduction

Although qualitative research is increasingly being reported in the library literature, few books have yet been published for librarians about such research. Although qualitative research methodologies have been practiced for many years by anthropologists and ethnographers, only recently have they become academically acceptable for use in the other social sciences, including librarianship. K–12 educators were among the first to embrace qualitative research methods to determine such factors as the health of a media center or the way to solve a particular problem. Indeed

Lesley, as a professor of librarianship, saw the importance of this type of research for her students and consequently published a book on the topic in 2003.[2]

Quantitative research in the social sciences uses numbers and related statistical analysis to represent the perceptions or achievements of those under study. Quantitative research also allows the researcher to tease out causal relationships among variables numerated. Qualitative research, on the other hand, records and analyzes the actual words and actions of the people under study. These data are analyzed thematically to ascertain and represent the perceptions of the group.

As librarians usually enter the field because we are "people people," the actual words of the patron have an attraction to us that numerical representations cannot match. We want to know what our patrons want. We want to know how they feel about our services. And we would like the answers in words rather than numbers. Qualitative research methodology makes this possible. Content analysis, as an example, can be used to thematically get to the heart of the perceptions of a number of patrons, allowing us to report results with descriptive narrative rather than numbers. Such results give us the satisfaction of using the words of the patrons themselves to report our findings.

We trust that qualitative research and the sharing of results will delight you as much as it has us. We encourage you to undertake a qualitative research project and subsequently submit it for publication, or at the very least present your findings at a conference. We hope that the following chapters will present to you, in an easily understandable fashion, the basic tenets of qualitative research. And at the same time, we want these chapters to generate numerous ideas for action research projects that you can undertake with your patrons.

Arrangement of the Book

We kept the basic outline of Pat's original idea primarily intact. Part 1 provides a theoretical and practical overview of the process of qualitative and action research. Part 2 includes reports of a number of research projects on fairly common problems found in libraries. The final section of the book includes examples of qualitative research and/or assessment focused on such topics of the day as information literacy. A foreword and an afterword place the book within the larger context of library science.

Foreword

Marie L. Radford begins with a reminder that current lean budgets are fueling a push for more assessment of the programs that occur in libraries. She defines qualitative research as a potential program assessment tool that meets the requirements of gathering data for evaluation. Qualitative research also provides a greater opportunity for in-depth analysis than does quantitative research methodology.

Part 1

Part 1, "Qualitative Research in the Library," is divided into three chapters, which provide an overview of qualitative and action research.

Chapter 1: Qualitative Research and the Librarian. Lesley Farmer provides a theoretical basis for the use of qualitative research to assist librarians in solving problems met in their daily workplace. She also provides definitions of action research and closes with some very practical suggestions for its use.

Chapter 2: The Recursive Cycle of Qualitative Action Research. Douglas Cook builds upon the foundation laid in chapter 1. He begins by describing the detailed process of problem-based qualitative action research. A checklist for the process provides a practical framework for undertaking an action research project. The second part of the chapter focuses on the complex undertaking of gathering, analyzing, and validating data. Cook uses examples from the remainder of the book to illustrate the framework.

Chapter 3: Getting Ready to Turn Your Everyday Work into Meaningful Inquiry: Foundational Literature in Qualitative and Action Research. Cordelia Zinskie and Judi Repman provide an annotated bibliography of potentially useful scholarly resources related to qualitative and action research. They include basic books and journal articles from the social sciences as well as books from the sciences dealing with qualitative research. They also review journals that currently publish qualitative research. They close with some discussion of the various Web sites that provide scholarly assistance in the qualitative research realm.

Part 2

Part 2, "Useful Methodologies of Qualitative Research," includes chapters that provide examples of qualitative research methodologies typically used in the library environment.

Chapter 4: Teaching Alone and Together: A Narrative Inquiry. Roberta Tipton and Patricia Bender successfully collaborated for several semesters on providing research instruction to undergraduates. In an attempt to pinpoint the reasons for their success, they decided to record and then analyze an autobiographical discussion. They used content analysis to formulate themes, which represented the methods that most strongly supported their success. For example, they discovered that providing students with a context for their research resulted in essays that had greater relevance to the students.

Chapter 5: Understanding Social Networking: The Benefit of Discourse Analysis. Mariaelena Bartesaghi and Ardis Hanson combine efforts to explain how discourse analysis can be used to further refine an understanding of information literacy as it is played out within an online course. They used discourse analysis to analyze a group of graduate students discussing some problems with finding good information. The conversation occurred online via Skype. Their findings challenge the skill-based notions of information literacy commonly held by librarians today.

Chapter 6: Remote and Rural Voices: Using Interviews to Understand the Information Literacy Experience of Alaskan Special Educators. Jennifer Diane Ward and Thomas Scott Duke team-teach several online courses to practicing teachers pursuing a master's degree in education. They used focused individual exit interviews to determine if their students felt that their information-seeking and research skills were strong enough for them to maintain a research agenda after graduating. They found that the students felt positively about the skills they had learned but were concerned that they would no longer have access to scholarly resources after they graduated.

Chapter 7: Observing Relationship Building in the Library Instruction Classroom: Peer Observation and Consultation. Carolyn L. Cook and Karla M. Schmit collaborated to help Schmit fine-tune her instruction skills. They used classroom observation and diary keeping as a basis for content analysis. They found that Schmit displayed a number of positive actions, which helped her make individual connections with students that lasted outside her instruction sessions.

Chapter 8: Content Analysis: Deconstructing Intellectual Packages. Penny M. Beile used content analysis to analyze existing syllabi in an elementary education program. She discovered that faculty-assigned library or research-related assignments did become more complex in higher level classes at her institution. These findings helped librarians to fine-tune the sequential library instruction provided to the education department.

Chapter 9: Using Focus Groups to Understand User Needs and Forge New Directions. Michael Weber and Robert Flatley used a series of focus groups to gather authentic data from students using the library. A content analysis of their field notes provided a wide range of findings related to student satisfaction with the library. They were able to use their results immediately to make some needed changes. Their results also provided rich data for their long-term planning process.

Chapter 10: Performance-based Self-assessment of a Library Liaison Program Using a Rubric. Aaron Dobbs and Douglas Cook used a focused literature review to create a checklist of ideal library liaison responsibilities, which they then used to formulate a rubric. An analysis of individual librarian self-reports of recent liaison activities using the rubric allowed them to pinpoint areas of liaison collaboration being ignored, as well as the amount of attention being provided to specific faculty departments. These data are being used to refine the concept of liaison librarian at their institution.

Part 3

Part 3, "Issues Addressed through Qualitative Research," highlights a number of functions that librarians address daily. Each chapter defines a topic and then discusses how qualitative research methodologies can be used to examine this issue more closely.

Chapter 11: Analyzing LibQUAL+ Comments to Inform Library Decision Making. David A. Nolfi and Laverna M. Saunders discuss library decision making within the larger context of strategic planning. They used content analysis to thematically massage the open-ended comments that students made on the LibQUAL+ survey. Their findings informed their larger strategic planning process. They also discovered immediate changes that needed to be made to library services.

Chapter 12: Design and Analysis Challenges in a Multicampus Research Study. Robin Brown and Willis C. Walker report on an analysis of the success of a Web-based library tutorial. Their participation as interviewers was a part of a larger multimethod plan to evaluate the research skills of current students. A number of students were interviewed using a fixed list of questions and search tasks they were asked to perform. Because the larger multimethod evaluation was cancelled due to the retirement of the project's coordinator, the authors discuss some of the potential outcomes that could have occurred.

Chapter 13: Approaching Information Literacy Qualitatively. Janice Krueger, during a recent master's course on library instruction, introduced students to a lesson-planning strategy called *backward design*. She used content analysis of student comments at the end of the semester to determine their perceptions of the viability of backward design as an approach to planning information literacy instruction.

Chapter 14: The Reference Interview in Real Time and in Virtual Time. Isabelle Flemming and Lesley Farmer collaborated on a review of the current state of the reference interview as it has been influenced by Internet technology. They reported on a recent study undertaken to ascertain the success of the virtual reference service extant in Southern California as a viable option for answering homework questions for K–12 students. An analysis of the logs of online reference chats with children during four busy months from one year revealed that the service was being underused by K–12 students.

Chapter 15: Seeing Is Learning: The Synergy of Visual Literacy. Alessia Zanin-Yost defines visual literacy and compares it with current definitions of information literacy. She discusses the need for including visual literacy instruction with information literacy instruction. She concludes with the description of a content analysis of a number of post–visual literacy instruction interviews with students.

Chapter 16: Collective Action: Qualitative Methods for Library Collection Development. LeRoy Jason LaFleur outlines the need for qualitative methodologies of assessment for collection development. He provides numerous examples of qualitative methods that can be used to obtain information to inform successful collection building.

Afterword: An Enduring Epistemology of Practice

David Carr eloquently describes the current fluid state of library practice and the need for constantly approaching professional daily work with an open and questioning mind.

—*Doug Cook, Shippensburg, PA, 2010*
—*Lesley Farmer, Long Beach, CA, 2010*

Notes

1. Richard Raspa and Dane Ward, *The Collaborative Imperative: Librarians and Faculty Working Together in the Information Universe* (Chicago: Association of College and Research Libraries, 2000).
2. Lesley S. J. Farmer, *How to Conduct Action Research: A Guide for Library Media Specialists* (Chicago: American Association of School Librarians, 2003).

Foreword

Marie L. Radford

Without a doubt, these times of ongoing economic upheaval and escalating competition have resulted in a greatly increased emphasis on assessment of services and collections for all librarians, regardless of the type of institution they represent. This book is making a critically important contribution by providing a relevant, practical, and engaging guide to using qualitative methods in library assessment, especially within the context of action research.

All librarians are currently facing the challenge of an exciting yet daunting period of protracted rapid and revolutionary change. This shift has been brought on by technological developments in digitization of collections and demand for Web-based services that have had dramatic impact on every aspect of our profession. Added to this upheaval is the intensifying sophistication of systems, sources, and society that form the environment surrounding our institutions. It has thus become essential for librarians to respond appropriately by conducting, analyzing, and implementing the results of empirical investigations designed to determine the right mode and mix of services, programs, and resources (print and online) for their specific user communities.

Librarians are undergoing greater scrutiny as budgets have gotten tighter; staffing has gotten leaner, resulting in growing pressure to engage in research-based strategic planning and decision making. It is no longer valid to proceed by one's intuition or by a firm belief that the way things have always been done in the past is the correct way to forge a vital future for libraries. Sustainability of resources and funding, as well as maintaining and expanding relevance to our users, has evolved as an ongoing concern, perhaps to an even greater degree than previously.

The subtitle of this book, *How Librarians Can Get to the Why of Data*, highlights an important role of qualitative data methods. Statistical and quantitative methods are of ongoing importance, but frequently these numerical results can be difficult to interpret. For example, how *specifically* can services be improved when people have consistently rated library service as *Excellent* when asked by quantitative surveys? What does this *Excellent* rating mean? Why has it been chosen by the respondent? What factors were most important in selecting this *Excellent* rating? Especially when one is seeking to get in-depth, nuanced data, a combination of qualitative and quantitative methods (such as conducting a series of focus group interviews to inform survey development or developing a survey that poses some open-ended questions in addition to five- or seven-point Likert scales) or a purely qualitative approach (such as observations, interviews, or discourse analysis) can provide rich results that do get to this critically important aspect of unveiling the *Why of Data*.

In my scholarly work, I have been drawn to qualitative methods because I am interested in exploring and unraveling the complexities of human interaction in library encounters. I have used a variety of qualitative approaches to gain a greater understanding of such inquiries as what makes for successful face-to-face and virtual reference interactions, how users decide whether to approach or avoid librarians at service points, and what the generational differences are in information-seeking behaviors. In addition, I have successfully used qualitative methods to evaluate large-scale grant-funded public, academic, and consortial library projects, including programs, services, and management training initiatives, as well as to inform strategic planning initiatives.

It has been my experience that librarians have been intrigued and often excited by qualitative methods. The professional literature shows that many research studies have embraced these approaches, yet lack of training and, perhaps, the perceived subjective nature of these methods have continued to be barriers for library practitioners. Qualitative methods often involve collection of a large amount of text-based data for analysis that can seem daunting to the inexperienced (or even to the experienced) researcher. The time commitment for analysis of qualitative data is, in reality, much greater than that for many quantitative techniques. For example, a Web-based survey using SurveyMonkey, Zoomerang, or a comparable product can be inexpensive, and results are quickly obtained, with tables of numerical data ready to be cut and pasted into a report. However, a few open-ended, qualitative questions added to the survey can be extremely helpful in contextualizing the results and in producing illustrative and often telling quotations in the respondent's voice. As can be seen in the chapters and examples presented in this book, the extra effort needed for qualitative inquiry is certainly well worth the investment in terms of the richness of the results.

Action research initiatives are usually undertaken by professionals who are engaged in strategic planning, have important decisions to make, or have questions about the effectiveness or efficiency of decisions that have been already made. This book provides an opportunity for librarians interested in undertaking action research to expand their knowledge of the numerous types of qualitative methods and to read well-documented examples of the use of these methods in a variety of library settings to address a range of research questions. This volume can also be seen as an enticement, an invitation to try qualitative methods, even in an exploratory way, in the reader's next foray into research. Difficult times result in creativity and innovation in problem solving. Qualitative approaches to action research will help to provide the depth of understanding and critical insights to enable us to implement these innovations and respond effectively as library leaders and change agents.

PART 1
Qualitative Research
in the Library

Qualitative Research and the Librarian

Lesley Farmer

Abstract. This chapter lays the foundation for the remainder of the book by emphasizing the need for librarians to continually assess their programs. Theoretically, research could be considered as an extension of problem solving, a practice that librarians do routinely: identifying a problem, identifying significant factors, brainstorming possible solutions, determining possible consequences, choosing and implementing one solution, and evaluating its effectiveness. Thus, qualitative action research—systematically examining the work environment, formulating a problem, gathering data about it, analyzing the facts, drawing conclusions about ways to solve the problem, and then acting on the recommendations—is recommended as the methodology that comes closest to meeting the assessment needs of the profession. Such qualitative research methods are vital as they focus on the why of data rather than the what.

How often do librarians say, "There must be a better way to explain citation style"? When a research workshop is cancelled for lack of interest, do librarians try to figure out the problem? How do librarians decide which subscriptions should be renewed or dropped?

Librarians want to do the best job they can to carry out their library's mission. And they want to work smarter, not harder. Librarians routinely self-evaluate their efforts and try to make changes to improve. Yet their efforts do not always pan out.

Library improvement pressure also arises from constituents and other outside entities. In this age of accountability, librarians have to demonstrate their value to their users and decision makers. Being available and friendly is not enough. Circulation figures, class visit attendance sheets, and workload figures no longer suffice. Librarians have a habit of focusing on what they provide in terms of material and human resources, working hard on activities to serve their populations. Yet even the best collections and services are of little benefit if not used. Librarians need to incorporate assessment throughout their work and systematically structure efforts to make significant valid and reliable claims about the library program's offerings and their importance.

Description—A First Step to Research

At the very least, librarians need to describe the library program accurately and thoroughly in alignment with their institution *and* the profession. One of the most obvious but sometimes overlooked first steps is to document what is happening. Sometimes librarians get so busy doing things that they forget to write down the details. Yet the time devoted to careful documentation is well spent since the data can be used for further research.

Thinking in terms of a system can help clarify expectations and create a baseline set of data that can be used to facilitate effective assessment and improvement. Each element lends itself to distinct measurements.

- *Input products:* collection statistics, staff demographics, facilities dimensions and layout, hours of access, analysis of library documents
- *Input actions:* circulation statistics, instruction design and recording, scheduling
- *Output actions:* library visit statistics, reading statistics, researching statistics and analysis, production observations, library site and database hits
- *Output products:* student and faculty work analysis, test results, grades, promotion statistics

Some of these measurements are easy to use, such as volume number and circulation records. They are quantifiable. Even the number of class visits can be a simple source of data, although the *quality* of that class visit also needs to be considered. For example, one teacher might send a small group of students to the library to *look up facts about Brazil,* while another teacher might preplan with the librarian to help students identify the key periodicals for a specific academic domain, the result being a hands-on interactive class workshop using relevant database aggregators.

Measuring the quality of a process or product requires careful analysis of the critical features that distinguish *good* or *effective* and *bad* or *ineffective.* Several contributing factors need to be identified and assessed according to their relative importance as well as their impact on each other factor. Nevertheless, one cannot state that student B is twice as satisfied as student A, assigning a scalar measurement that can at best be ordinal in nature. Furthermore, each source of data might have unique characteristics that cannot be standardized for all similar data points. Where such quantitative research methods are limited, qualitative data can fill in the gaps and put flesh on the bones of numbers.

In any case, the documentation should be accurate and clear. Description captures *what is,* be it a person, a product, or a process; therefore, it should be valid: stating the critical features and not introducing extraneous information. By knowing the true status of the library program, the librarian can then have a sound base on which to improve that program.

What Is Research?

At its most basic level, research is a systematic process of investigating a topic and its context by strategically gathering data and analyzing them and then sharing findings and recommendations. The strategy or method used needs to be valid, measuring the intended factor, and reliable, that is, capable of being replicated with the same results.

In its simplest form, research enables librarians to systematically describe an issue or phenomenon, such as collection development or instruction. The researcher has to determine what critical features characterize the topic at hand. For instance, collection development needs to measure the number of resources added and withdrawn, the basis for acquisition decision (e.g., user request, book review, collection gap, etc.), the choice of vendor, turnaround time from order to shelf-ready, the cost of processing, as well as the properties of each resource (i.e., content subject and treatment, language, reading level, format, cost, etc.). The relative importance of each factor depends on the objective of the description: writing a "what's new" column for the library newsletter versus determining what subject areas need more resources versus identifying the bottleneck in acquisitions procedures.

The latter two objectives involve assessment: evaluating a situation, usually in comparison with some kind of standard or expectation. In the former instance, the librarian might compare the number and date of titles in different curricular areas, as well as check circulation or usage records to determine the demand for specific materials. Even checkout numbers might need further investigation in that low figures might mean that there is little interest in that subject or that the current collection does not meet users' needs. Likewise, high circulation statistics might mean that the collection is very relevant to users or that the collection needs additional titles to meet the demand. Thus, numbers—quantitative data—might not be sufficient in themselves. Depending on the research objective, those numbers might need to be informed by qualitative data, which can be generated via surveys, interviews, and clinical observation, in order to ferret out the reasons or rationale for the situation and make an informed decision. It should be noted that the research data collected result in findings that can be analyzed, but they do not necessarily lead to action; the researcher can stick with the status quo.

Consuming Research

A starting point in engaging in research is to consume it competently. Reading the professional literature, not only in information science but also in associated fields of study that the librarian might encounter, keeps librarians current about trends and research-based practice. Good reviews of the literature help librarians determine the contributing factors that impact library services and resources. Understanding the methodologies help librarians match research approaches and problems. Instruments that have been validated can be adapted for local issues, cutting down on research development time. Even reading the data discussion and conclusions helps librarians know how to manage data to make meaningful decisions.

Identifying Problems

While librarians regularly face problems, they have to decide which problems are worth researching systematically. Librarians need to identify as least some of the variables contributing to the problem and have an idea of how those variables are related. They need to determine which variables are under their control (for a problem outside of librarian influence, the locus of control needs to be identified in order to determine how to influence decision makers). Similarly, librarians should determine if the solution is feasible in terms of available resources and time. In the final analysis, the problem needs to be worth

the effort: that is, the return on investment should be apparent.

Using Data Methodically

In order to solve problems or make decisions, relevant and accurate data need to be collected and analyzed. Trying to determine an effective method to measure contributing variables can be difficult. For instance, do library users perform better than library nonusers in searching for scholarly articles in a database aggregator, if all other variables are held constant? The latter condition is a daunting task for librarians, who have little control of variables such as the users' environments. Users might get additional help from their teachers or peers. Users might frequent other libraries. Users might have poor time management and not produce the desired product. Facing this situation, librarians are apt to use pre- and posttests during one teaching session in order to measure impact of library instruction and use of library resources. With these tight constraints, the significance of learning is short-term at best. Too many outside variables would muddle regression analysis results.

Occasionally, librarians might analyze student work over time, but they cannot insure that lasting change is caused by the library. Students might self-report that the library program influenced their academic growth, but this kind of measure is understandably subjective. Quantitative measures are likely to be invalid when scrutinized carefully, particularly if perception data are labeled as scalar variables.

In the face of such challenges, librarians are apt to use qualitative research methodologies, reflecting a social science perspective. Even though qualitative research has sometimes been given short shrift, it generates a rich set of nuanced data that more accurately reflects the reality of users' interaction with the library, and the reason for that interaction, than any quantitative measure could capture.

The most common research methodology is action research: systematically examining the work environment, formulating a problem, gathering data about it, analyzing the facts, drawing conclusions about ways to solve the problem, and then acting on the recommendations. The action research librarian is an active participant in the research process, providing inside information while being able to contextualize the issue. That contextualization is often the basis for qualitative action research, gathering data about the underlying factors leading to the problem. While action research usually cannot be generalized to other settings, if the local interventions work, librarians are satisfied.

Making Generalizations

The next level of research tries to generalize conclusions and even possible theories from the data gathered. The population needs to represent different settings or demographics in order to determine whether a phenomenon exists across environments or situational conditions. The researcher analyzes potentially significant factors to see if certain behaviors or consequences arise when those factors are compared. Qualitative data can still be used to measure those occurrences. If the same motifs emerge in different settings, the researcher might be able to predict actions in general when certain conditions occur. When the predictability can be trusted across various populations, then theories can start to be built to explain these phenomena.

Another way to generalize from the particular is to identify a number of qualitative studies of similar phenomena, to determine common variables with similar outcomes. Taking into account varying settings or demographics of the participating populations, the researcher can build a case that holds for many situations. This kind of research is called meta-analysis and can still reflect qualitative perspectives, as the data arise from natural settings. Examples of such meta-analysis would be characteristics of good readers or strategies of effective information seekers.

Few librarians pursue these higher, more generalized levels of research. Their scope is usually their work setting. Nevertheless, their unique case studies can contribute to the body of knowledge within librarianship, particularly when considered as one data point for meta-analysis.

Research Paradigms

Theoretically, research could be considered as an extension of problem solving, a practice that librarians do routinely: identifying a problem, identifying significant factors, brainstorming possible solutions, determining possible consequences, choosing and implementing one solution, and evaluating its effectiveness. The depth of knowledge and analysis, the acuity of methodology, and the thoroughness of the processes differentiate research from day-to-day practice. Nevertheless, research approaches might be placed on a continuum from small-scale structured problem solving to large-scale empirical longitudinal research. Another dimension is the continuum from specific applied research to theoretical research.

Historically, research has been divided into quantitative and qualitative methods, the differentiation having as much to do with philosophical stance as the instruments used. Merriam clearly explains the difference between the theoretical basis of quantitative and qualitative research "as positivism [reality exists out there and is observable, stable, and measurable] vs. interpretive constructivism [reality is socially constructed; there is no single observable reality]."[1]

Quantitative research methods tend to build on controlled experimental scientific method, focusing on objective norms and abstractions of reality. Data tend to measure *what is happening*. Quantitative researchers often work from a theoretical basis called positivism; they assume that their study is completely objective, replicable, and therefore generalizable to other situations.[2]

Qualitative methodologies derive from a theoretical basis called constructivism: a belief that the world is very complex and relativistic. Too many variables exist in everyday situations to imagine that the results of a study could ever be replicated exactly. Furthermore, no researcher can truly be objective; it is impossible to take the humanity out of reflection upon a situation. Qualitative action research is phenomenological (focusing on people's actual lived experiences and realities), interpretive (focusing on people's interpretation of their acts and activities);, and hermeneutic (incorporating the meaning people make of events in their lives). Merriam states that "qualitative researchers are interested in understanding how people interpret their experiences, how they construct their worlds, and what meaning they attribute to their experience."[3]

The research question often dictates the type of methodology; for instance, "Is there a significant difference in the percentage of males and females who use library databases?" can be investigated using quantitative methods, while "Why do males prefer using Google instead of library databases?" would tend to employ qualitative methods. If qualitative research can be said to look at the *what*, then qualitative research methods may be said to focus on the *why*, interpreting subjective meanings of rich naturalistic data sets. At this time, particularly in the social sciences such as library science, a mixed-methods approach is usually the most effective since it can examine those factors that can be controlled while considering possible contextual and intervening factors that rest outside the scope of the researcher's control.

Action Research

Practitioners in many fields have long had an interest in studying their work environment to provide clues for making changes to better performance. Using methodologies first used by sociologists in the 1940s to improve workplace productivity and interpersonal relationships,[4] these reflective professionals began to study what they did, what their clients did, and what occurred in the clients' environment itself. A seminal feature was the active involvement of the stakeholders themselves in finding effective solutions. This kind of participatory and practical-based action was labeled action research.

Action research has since been described as a localized and quasi-experimental research method. Stringer defines action research as "a systematic approach to investigation that enables people to find effective solutions to problems they confront in their everyday lives."[5] It involves examining one's own practice with the intent of improving it. So, action research, as we are defining it, is a type of research that focuses on questions or problems in the workplace and attempts to find answers that solve, or shed light on, the specific problem under study.

Basically, researchers examine their immediate setting and define a problem to investigate. Then they review and synthesize the research and theory on the topic. From their reading, research questions are developed. Researchers identify contributing factors and assessment instruments to measure those factors and collect valid and reliable baseline data. The resulting data are analyzed and reported. At this point, action research may be considered completed, but usually action research goes on to design an action plan, or intervention, based on the data analysis. That action is implemented and evaluated. As a result of this action research, new questions often emerge, which starts a cycle of inquiry.

Action research can involve quantitative or qualitative data collection methods. The context shapes the organization and therefore the research methodology. Numerical data such as circulation records use quantitative measurement tools such as library management software and checklists. To get at user perceptions, on the other hand, qualitative data-gathering methods such as interviews and focus groups are more appropriate. Typically, a mixed-method approach is used so that contributing factors can be accurately described (quantitative) and the basis for their impact can be discerned (qualitative).

Philosophy of Action Research

Grundy posits three types of action research: technical, practical, and emancipatory.[6] Each reflects a philosophy about research and the role stakeholders.

Technical action research starts with a defined problem. On the basis of a theoretical framework, the researcher tests an intervention. Researchers and practitioners collaborate, thus optimizing effective practice and refining theory. For example, the library's circulation process results in long lines. Based on workflow analysis, an efficiency expert researcher might suggest a different way to place the circulation equipment and a more efficient checkout process. The intervention is implemented and tested, with data from the new arrangement and procedures (e.g., length of lines, speed of checkout) measured against the baseline data.

Practical action research begins with practitioner-researcher dialogue about a situation. They then identify a problem, search for underlying causes, and identify possible interventions. For instance, with increased numbers of computers being placed in the reference area, librarians may feel overwhelmed with queries at the reference desk. Should more librarians be allocated? Can staff resources be reallocated? The researcher and library staff collect baseline data about the reference questions and find that a third of the questions are technical. Some librarians do not feel equipped to answer these questions, nor do they think that these questions draw upon their reference expertise. The researcher and librarians review the literature about technology-related reference desk practices and ask their counterparts at other universities how they handle similar situations. Group representatives consult with the campus's technology office and find that they could use trained tech desk students. The library sets up a technical help desk, staffed by trained students, near the reference desk. The two desks collect follow-up data about their services, and a student survey measures customer satisfaction.

Emancipatory action research promotes social critical consciousness as reflection on theory leads to enlightenment, which is transformed into action. For example, reference librarians might be frustrated with the high number of students asking for help on how to cite resources. The researcher and librarians would discuss possible underlying factors such as student lack of knowledge, teacher lack of knowledge, lack of standardized citation styles across the campus, lack of instruction, and lack of information or guides about citation styles. The reference librarians might talk with the academic faculty and find that faculty assume that students know how to cite resources. The faculty discussions also reveal underlying attitudes about the value of citations and the role of the librarian in instruction. The researcher and librarians together decide on a three-pronged

intervention: a series of library workshops on citation styles, Web tutorials on citation styles, and citation guides embedded in the library Web portal. They also decide to assign one specific librarian for each college as a liaison to improve communication and cooperation. Librarians would inform the campus community about the workshops, the citation aids, and the liaison program. Follow-up data would include the frequency of reference questions about citing sources, the number of library Web portal citation guide hits, and a questionnaire to faculty about student citing quality and the library's instructional role.

In any case, action research is site-specific, and its conclusions cannot be automatically generalized because the setting is naturalistic and not all the factors can be controlled for. In addition, the researcher is usually a participant in the study and so cannot be strictly objective. Nevertheless, the rich data set generated from action research is a valuable source of information and investigation.

Qualitative Action Research

Before defining qualitative action research, it is necessary to describe its various characteristics, which Merriam systematically explains.[7]

- *Search for meaning* Qualitative action researchers, working from a constructionist theoretical foundation, are primarily interested in how people interpret and attribute meaning to their realities. Such an approach assumes that students, for example, are able to describe why they do or do not take a certain action. Qualitative researchers attempt to understand the human experience.
- *The researcher as instrument.* In direct contrast to quantitative research, qualitative research relies on the researcher as the main instrument for gathering data. Since human experience is the topic of qualitative research, a human researcher is best able to respond and adapt to the data being gathered.

- *Induction.* Rather than starting with a broad theory that must be proven with a particular study, qualitative researchers start with an individual situation that may eventually become the basis for a theory.
- *Context.* Quantitative researchers are concerned with generalizability and reliability of results and therefore conduct research in a sterile, controlled laboratory environment. In contrast, qualitative researchers conduct studies in their everyday settings. Looking at a problem as it actually occurs is more important than concerns about standardization.
- *Telling the story.* Words rather than numbers are used to portray what the researcher has discovered about a particular situation,

Beginning with Stringer's definition of action research—"a systematic approach to investigation that enables people to find effective solutions to problems they confront in their everyday lives"[8]—and refining it with a strict adherence to qualitative characteristics, we define qualitative action research within the library environment as follows:

> a systematic approach to investigation of a problem encountered in the daily library work environment, using methodologies that foster creating a detailed description of the context as reflected in the words and actions of the stakeholders and the librarian involved and that lead to effective solutions to the specific problem under study

Benefits of Research

At the very least, research can be considered as knowledge-based assessment. Effective library management involves ongoing monitoring and improvement through thoughtful problem identification and solutions. Systematically examining an issue, reviewing the relevant literature, gathering and analyzing significant factors, testing, and evaluating results all help solve crises. By documenting this process, librarians have more control of their efforts, can replicate the efforts more easily, and have the evidence needed to convince decision makers to allocate the resources necessary to solve the problem.

The most immediate impact is library service, with the intent of greater customer satisfaction. Hopefully, research efforts are conducted in consort with affected staff so that they feel like part of the solution, making a positive difference at their site. Especially when research processes, results, and recommended interventions are done as a transparent, shared governance action, staff morale can improve as well.

The research process constitutes authentic professional development as the librarian research self-identifies pressing issues and searches for best practice and underlying concepts and theories to ground understanding and appropriate action. As the librarian processes the new information and reflects on it in light of local needs, he or she adds to a personal repertoire of knowledge and skills that can be applied meaningfully and immediately, thus reinforcing the benefits of the effort.

More globally, by sharing the research with the larger professional community, librarians contribute to the body of knowledge in the field as well as help their colleagues who might have similar issues to confront.

Qualitative Action Research in This Book

This book provides librarians, largely in higher education, with the tools to engage in successful action research. It is not our intention to write an academic treatise on the process of conducting qualitative action research. Instead, it is our goal to encourage you to apply these pragmatic methodologies to your everyday library environment. It is also our goal to provide those of you who are not familiar with this type of research with enough information to help you understand how to interpret the remaining chapters of this book.

Notes

1. Sharan B. Merriam. *Qualitative Research: A Guide to Design and Implementation* (San Francisco: Jossey-Bass, 2009), 8.

2. Davydd Greenwood and Morten Levin, "Reform of the Social Sciences and of Universities through Action Research," in *The SAGE Handbook of Qualitative Research*, ed. Norman K. Denzin and Yvonna S. Lincoln (Thousand Oaks, CA: Sage, 2005), 53.

3. Merriam, *Qualitative Research*, 5.

4. Geoffrey E. Mills, *Action Research: A Guide for the Teacher Researcher*, 2nd ed. (Upper Saddle River, NJ: Merrill, Prentice Hall, 2003), 5.

5. Ernest T. Stringer, *Action Research*, 3rd ed. (Los Angeles: Sage, 2007), 1.

6. Shirley Grundy. *Curriculum: Product of Praxis* (Lewes, UK: Falmer, 1987).

7. Merriam, *Qualitative Research*, 14.

8. Stringer, *Action Research*, 1.

The Recursive Cycle of Qualitative Action Research

Douglas Cook

This chapter focuses on the process of how a librarian could approach a qualitative action research project. Specific steps to be undertaken are discussed and illustrated with examples from the remaining chapters of this book. Action research is described as recursive in that attention given to solving one problem typically uncovers other problems, which need to undergo similar study. In the second part of the chapter, the author focuses on several research processes relating to qualitative data, which need more explanation. For example, data chosen must enhance the researcher's understanding of what the people involved do, say, or think about the research question. Secondly, qualitative action research has specific data collection methodologies that will guide the process. In addition, adhering strictly to accepted methodologies will increase the validity of a study.

The Process of Action Research

This chapter will discuss the more pragmatic issues of how a librarian could approach a qualitative action research project. Steps to be undertaken will be discussed and illustrated with examples from the remaining chapters of this book.[1] The second part of the chapter will focus on several research processes relating to qualitative data, which are more complex and need more explanation. Regardless of the type of research undertaken, it is important to go about your exploration in a systematic fashion. One of the primary reasons for this approach, especially in qualitative research, is that the strength of research findings is primarily validated by a strict adherence to accepted procedures. A research check-list or plan will assist in reminding the librarian to complete each step. This adherence is especially important if you plan to share your results via an article in the library literature. Chapter 3 of this book (Zinskie and Repman) details the most important texts regarding action research. These texts espouse various plans to organize such a project; however, one of the clearest that has been adapted to the library situation is that created by Farmer.[2]

Before moving on to the detail of the process, I must mention two things:

1. Although this process is being presented in a logical, step-by-step fashion, reality does not always allow these steps to be

undertaken in the order in which they are presented here. Some librarians will feel most comfortable starting at the beginning and ending with the last step. Others, who are less likely to tackle projects in a linear fashion, may use this list as reminder regarding all the processes that must be addressed. At either extreme, it is good to remember that qualitative research is like the rest of life—rather chaotic.[3]

2. As another word of wisdom, depending upon the particular situation you find yourself in, you may or may not have need of every step in this checklist. You will find numerous examples of fine qualitative inquiry in the rest of this book that do not engage in all the steps in this checklist. Depending upon why a particular project is undertaken, not all the steps may be needed. One of the most complete examples of this process can be found in chapter 11 of this book. Nolfi and Saunders use a content analysis of the open-ended patron comments from a LibQUAL+ survey as a part of a much larger project of strategic assessment. Reading their chapter carefully will provide you with a good example of how a large, organized action research project unfolds. On the other hand, LaFleur, in chapter 16, under a completely different set of research requirements shares his methodologies with us, but does not, rightly so for his circumstance, organize his chapter under the linear fashion that the following checklist might bring you to expect.

Read on, but make the checklist fit your own circumstances.

Checklist

The multifaceted process of undertaking a qualitative action research project can be understood by discussing the steps in table 2.1.

TABLE 2.1
Action Research Checklist[a]
1. Focus on an issue.
2. Review theory.
3. Develop questions.
4. Collect data.
5. Analyze data.
6. Report results.
7. Design action plan.
8. Take action.
9. Evaluate action.

a. Lesley Farmer, How to Conduct Action Research: A Guide for Library Media Specialists (Chicago: American Association of School Librarians, 2003), 3. For a similar checklist, see Richard Sagor, Guiding School Improvement with Action Research (Alexandria, VA: Association for Supervision and Curriculum Development, 2000), 12–22.

Focus on an Issue

If your library experience is typical, finding an issue that causes you anguish should not be difficult. The library environment has changed so rapidly in the past few years that each day seems to bring with it a new challenge. Trying to decide how to meet these challenges is the stuff of qualitative action research. As an example, my library colleagues and I turned to action research out of a need to solve a problem (see chapter 10, Dobbs and Cook) where the solution needed to be workable, but more importantly, the solution and the trail that led to the solution had to be able to be described in an outcome-based narrative. We were charged with creating a process by which we could describe and evaluate the collaborative efforts of our liaison program. We chose to create a rubric to measure our liaison activity. Other chapter authors in this book report different problems or circumstances that prompted the need for qualitative research. We librarians always seem to have plenty of problems looking for a solution.

As a first step toward actually preparing for an action research project, Sagor suggests keeping a reflective journal to help identify issues that are problematic and yet have the potential to be solved.[4] A further collaborative technique is to talk reflectively with colleagues to focus specifically on a shared problematic issue. This practice might become a part of regular department meetings. Twentieth-century educator and reformer John Dewey said, "...a problem well stated is on its way to solution..."[5]

Review Theory

The step of reviewing theory provides you with the opportunity to examine the literature that may have some application to the specific problem about which you are concerned. In fact, it may be that a study has been published that provides you with the solution to your problem. Reviewing what others have written about the problem you are facing also helps you to specify the exact nature of your concern. It also gives you insight into how you might approach a study of the issue you face. You should organize your research along several lines.

1. Tap various fields of literature. Begin with the literature of library and information science. Particularly if the problem you are addressing is contemporary, other librarians have probably written on the issue. Creating a body of knowledge is a societal venture. Every discovery is based on the discovery of another researcher. You are participating in the process of making meaning from experience when you use the information provided by others interested in your problem.

   It will behoove you to then broaden your field of search to related areas. Often the literature in the field of the social sciences is pertinent to library situations. Education, in particular, has spawned numerous research projects very similar to those we face in the library. As an appropriate example from this book, Nolfi and Saunders (chapter 11) reviewed previous research in the field of management because they saw their project as a part of strategic decision making regarding their library.

2. Look at various types of information. As we often discuss with our students in library instruction sessions, there is a sharp difference between informative articles or essays about a topic and actual research that has been undertaken about the same issue. Both types of information are valuable for different parts of an action research project. Occasionally one will begin study of an issue that has not been researched before in the library field. As a part of their research on peer observation (chapter 7), for example, Cook and Schmit grounded their research in the theoretical literature of communities of practice, which proposes that strong relationships must be built between faculty and students before learning can occur. They also report doing an Internet search for an observation form. Their chapter is replete with references to previous research done regarding peer observation, but they also found that theoretical essays and an Internet search were important.

3. Research the methodologies you will be using. Depending upon your experience with research, you may need to include potential methodologies in your literature review. For example, content analysis is a qualitative methodology whereby themes are systematically uncovered in a transcript of an interview or an existing document. In this book, Tipton and Bender (chapter 4), Ward and Duke (chapter 6), Cook and Schmit (chapter 7), Beile (chapter 8), Weber and Flatley (chapter 9), Nolfi and Saunders (chapter 11), Krueger (chapter 13), and Flemming and Farmer (chapter 14) each relied on content analysis as a part of their qualitative research projects. Beile includes an excellent overview of content analysis in her chapter.

4. A final note: The literature review often occurs toward the beginning of a project, but it never stops there. As you uncover

anomalies or try to make sense of what you find, it is natural to dip back into to the literature to answer these needs.

Develop Questions

All rigorous qualitative action research projects are defined by a question to be answered. In particular, if you are required to report your data in the literature (as we recommend), the research question will focus the narrative. Merriam suggests that you "translate your general curiosity into a problem that can be addressed through research."[6] The question, in essence, provides the parameters within which you will be conducting your study. Your question will dictate participants, methodologies, and so on.

The majority of the chapters in the rest of this book include their research questions as a part of their narrative. A good example is that of Tipton and Bender (chapter 4). Tipton is a librarian, and Bender is an instructor of English composition. They had been successfully collaborating for several years on teaching research skills to students. As a method of discovery, they used an autobiographical interview to help them strengthen their past efforts. They state their research questions clearly as follows:

1. Which aspects of our class, both academic and social, allowed some students who had performed poorly in other writing classes to succeed in ours? Why did the students perform even better with the librarian added to the class?
2. What factors made our collaboration work so well even though we came from two different fields of study and taught different material to our students?
3. "Which elements of our collaboration, if any, could be scaled up or transferred to other classes?"

These questions came after much discussion and reading of the literature on the part of the researchers and served to focus their autobiographical interview as well as the resultant content analysis of the transcript of the interview. These questions also orga-nized the resultant narrative. Answering these questions became the focus of their action research.

Collect Data

Data come in many flavors; however, qualitative action research methodology has an accepted set of procedures by which data should be collected. The data of qualitative action research are the words, actions, and thoughts of your participants. The following data types and collection methods are used most often in qualitative action research. Sagor organizes these into three broad types[7] that make a useful categorization when it comes time to determine which to choose. These methodologies will be explained in more detail later in this chapter.

1. Existing data, for example, documents or artifacts. Examining existing data is often the realm of the historical researcher or the researcher interested in the current policy of an organization. Syllabi, transcripts of online reference interviews, and inter-library loan data are examples of existing data discussed in later chapters.
2. Nonobtrusive observation data, for example, recordings (audio and video), diaries, field notes, rubrics, and so on. Authors in this book make use of each of these types of observation.
3. Probes—data-gathering techniques that provide the researcher with participant experiences or expectations. Probes can include interviews, focus groups, or surveys. Individual interviews, focus groups, and surveys are made use of as data-gathering techniques in the chapters of this book.

Analyze Data

Data analysis is a difficult and recursive task, which requires much reflection and much more intense labor than you would assume. Data from the various methodologies used in qualitative research require specialized analytical techniques. Broadly speaking, however, data analysis consists of uncovering what people think, say, and do regarding the issue under study—and finding out the reasons for those perspectives and behaviors. You should be sifting through the data looking for recurring themes, which when compared become the basis for your solution. Merriam suggests, "Data analysis is the process of making sense out of the data. And making sense out of the data involves consolidating, reducing, and interpreting what people have said and what the researcher has seen and read—it is the process of making meaning."[8]

The method of analysis is dependent upon the research question being posed and the type of data that have been gathered. As mentioned previously, content analysis is a very common form of examination used in qualitative research studies. The findings of your research project will become the basis for making conclusions based upon your data.

Report Results

Reporting data can take many forms, from a simple memo explaining recommended changes based on data analysis to a published article. As authors, we would like to encourage you as a library practitioner to publish your research in the scholarly literature. Most published reports of qualitative action research include at least the following sections:[9]

1. Nature of the problem investigated
   a. Statement of the problem
   b. Context of the study
   c. References to the literature
   d. Theoretical framework of the study
   e. Research question(s) that shaped the study
2. The way the investigation was conducted
   a. Population studied
   b. How data were collected and analyzed
   c. Measures taken to ensure validity and reliability
3. The findings that resulted: outcome of the inquiry, organized according to the themes uncovered
4. Discussion of the findings as they related to the question: interpretations, connections to other data

5. Conclusions
   a. Solutions to the problem
   b. Recommended actions
   c. Implications

Numerous chapters in this book follow this outline, particularly those in part 2, which are cases of qualitative research projects using different analytic methodologies. As the chapters in part 3 of this book are more concerned with the qualitative examination of a particular issue, many of these chapters did not have the need to adhere as rigidly to this structure. Depending upon the reason for a study's genesis, reports are organized along different lines.

Design Action Plan

Of course, the entire reason behind your study is to make a change to your work environment. The plan and resulting action taken is shaped by the reason for the study. Stringer suggests that more formal action plans should include the following:[10]

1. Goal. Why should the action suggested be taken?
2. Objective. What actions are to be taken?
3. Tasks. How should these actions be taken?
4. Persons. Who should take the actions suggested?
5. Place. Where will the actions take place?
6. Timeline. When will the actions be accomplished?
7. Resources. What resources will be required to meet your stated goal?

Depending upon the size and nature of your issue under study, it may or may not be necessary to create a complete action plan to correct a problem. Weber and Flatley (chapter 9), for example, reported to their dean and department that students perceived building signage to be confusing. This problem was promptly remedied with physical changes. Their data-rich study also disclosed many other difficulties that could not be resolved so easily. For example, it was necessary for them to set long-term goals for revising their Web site, which students found ineffective.

Take Action; Evaluate Action

Most action researchers describe the process as a cycle. The action taken as a result of one study could easily uncover issues that also need to be researched with a second study. Dobbs and Cook (chapter 10), for example, spent an academic year creating and using a self-assessment rubric. The first reporting of their findings to library managers raised the issue of perspective—Would faculty agree with their assessment of themselves as subject liaisons? As a result of that report, their first qualitative assessment will be followed up with a probe to find out what faculty departments expect from them as librarians.

Gathering and Analyzing Qualitative Data

Certain parts of the qualitative research project seem to be more difficult to grasp than others. As librarians, we each have problems we can identify in our work environment that need solutions. Creating literature reviews is also a large part of our skill set. Since many of us were not trained in the perspective of qualitative research, it is typically the methodology-related decisions that cause us the most difficulty. The second half of this chapter will provide more specific information regarding gathering and analyzing qualitative data.

One of the most difficult questions to answer in the action research process is "What data should I collect to address my research question?" Those librarians who have conducted any type of formal research project know that this is a difficult question in any type of analysis. In the case of qualitative action research, this question can be partially answered in two ways. First, researchers are looking for the essence of people's experiences. Data chosen must enhance the researchers' understanding of what the people involved do, say, or think about the research question. Solutions will lie within the realities of the participants. Secondly, qualitative action research has specific data collection methodologies that will guide the process. Adhering strictly to accepted methodologies will increase the validity of a study as well.

Basic Types of Data

Data are the basis for any action research study. After deciding what to study, deciding how to collect data (and what data to collect) is a vital part of an effective study.[11] Data from the collection methodologies of action research take many forms—notes, transcripts, recordings, e-mails, policy statements, surveys, and so on.

Data Collection Methods Appropriate to Action Research

As mentioned above, qualitative action research most often involves three broad types of data and collection methods: existing data, nonobtrusive observation data, and probes. As an important aside, these categories help to clarify data collection; however, it soon becomes evident that data types do not fit neatly into categories. For example, we have included recordings as a nonobtrusive observation data source, which it certainly is. However, recordings are equally valuable for providing a record of an interview, which is an example of a probe. In addition, some research projects will include data collected within all three categories of methodologies.

1. Existing Data. Before observing activities under study or conducting interviews, it is wise to check to see if any relevant data already exist. As librarians, we have been trained to collect counts of virtually everything we do, such as circulation records and reference interviews.

Documents can broadly be defined as records that currently exist as a part of the activity or the environment under study.[12] One example of a document that may apply to a library situation is the written policy about a particular service under study. This documentation may exist in paper form or more likely on the Web. Any written document in any format could be included in an action research study. For example, Beile (chapter 8) made use of existing syllabi from education courses to determine if librarians were providing instruction that matched the needs of education students. LaFleur (chapter 16) discusses existing interlibrary loan data as a source for decision making regarding collection development. Flemming and Farmer (chapter 14) report the use of archived server transcripts of online reference questions as a basis for analysis.

Artifacts[13] can be any physical object that is related to your research question. For example, the reference desk would be an important artifact to study if research questions concerned student-librarian transactions at the reference desk. Library signage could fall into this category.

2. Nonobtrusive Observation Data. Nonobtrusive observations are those undertaken in some fashion to gain information about a question under study.[14] A librarian undertaking nonobtrusive observation, which is based on theoretical underpinnings of long-term ethnographic studies of cultures, would not interact in any way with the people under study. One typical example might be the observation of a colleague's teaching session for the purpose of that colleague's professional development. Cook and Schmit (chapter 7) provide a clear use of nonobtrusive observation. Indeed, the reason for the study was for Cook, a faculty member, to help Schmit, a librarian, improve her instructional skills. Cook observed Schmit's instruction. Cook took extensive field notes, and Schmit kept a diary for the semester-long study. Other examples might include an observation of where students sit in the library or of the number of students working in groups as opposed to the number working individually to inform the plans for a renovation. Participants themselves could undertake observations that could become data for a study. A creative example of this approach might be to ask students to use their cell phones to take pictures of the places they study during a typical week.[15] These visual records, along with the student's narrative, would be an example of an observation that could also be classified as a probe. As mentioned earlier, observations can take many forms, including recordings (audio and video), diaries, field notes, checklists, or rubrics, which will be discussed in more detail later.

Before we leave the topic of observation, it is important to discuss typical methodologies that might be used to capture viable data. Notes can take the place of a recording if the note taker is skilled and can take notes quickly.[16] Note takers should write down precisely what is said, using the interviewee's language, terms, and concepts, trying not to summarize in their own words at this point. At the end of the interview, notes should be read back to the interviewee to ensure that they reflect the conversation accurately. This type of note taking can also be done by a second researcher who acts as an observer, thus leaving the interviewer free to concentrate on the interview. Often, recordings take the place of, or supplement, note taking. Weber and Flatley (chapter 9) recorded their focus group sessions; however, their initial analysis was based on their field notes. They used the recording for fact checking and for obtaining exact quotes from their participants to use in their reporting.

Note taking can also take the form of an observational journal. Mills calls this type of note taking "anecdotal records."[17] In qualitative action research, the interviewer becomes the main instrument of research. What is written during observation is typically tied to the research question. If, for example, a colleague's instruction session is under observation with the final purpose being to increase the interaction between the students and the librarian, the observer would primarily record who is speaking and for how long. Cook and Schmit (chapter 7) used field notes in this fashion. As Cook was observing Schmit, she kept anecdotal notes that included the number of times that students spoke during the instruction session.

There are situations when the types of activities under consideration can be specified before the observation begins. An observational checklist can assist the observer in focusing on the activities under study. These types of checklists[18] should be carefully thought through to define each item on the list. The creation of such a checklist can often become a part of the research process itself. For example, an initial list of student behaviors as they use the library's Web page to find a scholarly research article could be recorded first using field notes. Afterwards, those student activity notes could be categorized and formulated into an observational checklist.

Checklists can be furthered refined into evaluative scales, typically called rubrics.[19] Rather than merely observing if an activity has or has not been performed, a rubric adds another dimension by allowing the observer to judge how well or how poorly an activity, such as Internet searching strategies, has been performed. Dobbs and Cook (chapter 10) created a rubric that they subsequently used to assess the self-reported collaborative efforts of all librarians in their department. They include details of creating a rubric in their narrative.

It is very common to make an audio or video recording of an observation. These recordings often take the place of detailed field notes in work-based action research. Very often verbatim transcripts are made of these recordings. As you will see in the next section, in order to work with the actual words spoken by the participants, it is easier to have a transcript, although it must be noted that the transcription process itself is time-consuming. Researchers planning to write a formal report of their findings will find it is important for the sake of veracity to quote the actual words spoken by participants. Very complex coding schemes have been devised for use by researchers who need to transcribe voice inflections and so on.[20] Bartesaghi and Hanson (chapter 5), for example, used the complex language of discourse analysis to describe the meaning making that occurred within a group of students discussing the importance of finding valid information when doing a literature review.

3. Probes. When research is considered, probes often come to mind first. These methods have been the type of research we have typically used to gain information about our patrons: interviews, focus groups, surveys, and questionnaires. Social science quantitative researchers have used surveys as a basis for statistical analysis for many years. Nolfi and Saunders (chapter 11) discuss LibQUAL+, which is a current example of a survey with which most academic librarians are familiar. Gathering data as a probe into the realities of patrons often takes much more preparation on the part of the researcher than do the other two categories of data gathering. This type of research is based on the questions asked or activities required of the participants. Merriam states it well when she says, "The key to getting good data from interviewing is to ask good ques-

tions."[21] Questions asked, particularly if in a survey that allows no researcher follow-up, should be in language that is simple and clear to the participant. Questions should be piloted on a similar sample group of patrons as those being probed. Each question should have a specific reason for being asked. Interviews and focus groups often require less formal questions than would a survey or questionnaire, as the researcher is present during the participants' responses and can follow up if a response is not clear. Weber and Flatley (chapter 9), for example, used focus group techniques to gauge the participant satisfaction of their students. This open-ended approach allowed students to bring up both positive and negative issues regarding the library that the researchers had not anticipated at the beginning of the study. Ward and Duke (chapter 6) used long and very focused individual exit interviews of their graduate students, who were P–12 special education teachers, to determine if the research instruction they were receiving was adequate to meet their after-graduation needs in their own classrooms. These researchers spent more effort in identifying specific questions that would get at student's opinions. They also used the same set of questions for each student interview.

There are six types of questions that Merriam suggests be considered when using a probe to gather data from patrons:[22]

1. *Experience and behavior questions.* This type of question would allow interviewees to relate in their own words how they think about a particular activity. An example of this type of question might be, "Tell me about what you do when you have to write a research paper. What is the first thing you are likely to do as you begin?" Ward and Duke (chapter 6) used a question of this type to discover if the research skills taught in their class were being used in the students' current life. They asked, "Do you find you are using any of these skills currently? In your teaching? In your personal life?"

2. *Opinion and values questions.* In this type of probe, the researcher is interested in the

beliefs of the patron. Student expectations about library service, for example, would be important to a researcher looking at a series of complaints. A typical question of this type might be, "Do you think that the library is open late enough in the evening for you to get your work done?" Zanin-Yost (chapter 15) used a question of this type to gauge her students' belief and understanding of the place of images in writing a formal research paper. She asked, "Do you think it is necessary to cite images when used for a presentation?"

3. *Feeling questions.* Particularly in personal interviews, topics often arise that bring with them strong feelings. In such a case, it would be important for the researcher to probe this response by asking, "Tell me how you feel about that." Ward and Duke (chapter 6) questioned their master's students in special education about the potential usefulness of the research skills they had learned. They asked, "What is your opinion about the importance of these skills to you as a teacher in a remote place?" As they report, this question elicited strong feelings, as the majority of their students were teachers in remote parts of Alaska with very little access to research databases and the like. The interviewees were justifiably concerned that after leaving the university setting, they would no longer have easy access to scholarly research.

4. *Knowledge questions.* These questions are important if there is a need to gauge the actual knowledge of students. An interview of a student in relation to the design of the library's Web site might include the question, "Show me how you would use the library's Web site to find a scholarly article for a research paper you are writing." Brown and Walker (chapter 12) reported their use of this type of question. Part of their student interviews involved asking a student to complete a task on a computer. They report, "For the first task, the student

was presented with a card with the citation for *Freaks: Myths and Images of the Secret Shelf* by Leslie Fiedler in both APA and MLA styles. They were asked to find it among the library resources using the most efficient search they knew of; they were further directed to talk the interviewer through the steps they employed."

5. *Sensory questions.* Questions probing sensory data of the participant could be very important to a research project investigating how students use the signage clues you have provided for them to find things. A researcher might ask, "When you want to find a book in the library, how can you tell where it is in the building? What things do you look at in order to track it down?" Weber and Flatley (chapter 9) reported that as a response to a relatively open-ended question—"In your opinion, how can the library be improved?"—one student who was visually impaired explained how difficult it was for her to navigate the book stacks because the signage was too high and thus too far away for her to read.

6. *Demographic questions.* These types of questions are particularly important if the researcher will be creating a formal report. When it is necessary to describe the participants involved in a study, this type of information is vital. Nolfi and Saunders (chapter 11) were able to report demographic data as the LibQUAL+ survey asks and tracks numerous facts about each participant. In addition, demographic information might well explain the participants' behaviors.

What Are Good Data?[23]

One reason that academic librarians have only recently begun taking advantage of the methodologies of qualitative action research is that for many years quantitative methodologies were judged to be more valuable. Much of this debate was centered on the definition of *good data*. Quantitatively defined, good data are more objective, valid, reliable, and generalizable.[24] Although the major question is the same—"Are your data trustworthy?"—different evaluative criteria are used in the judgment of the trustworthiness of qualitative data, as follows.

1. *Reliability.* According to Sagor, "Reliability relates to researchers' claims regarding the accuracy of their data."[25] Farmer further defines reliability when she explains that data that have been gathered by one researcher should be similar to the data gathered by another researcher in a similar situation.[26] Reliability is ensured in qualitative action research by a strict adherence to accepted methodologies and by tracking and being able to report the collection methodologies used. Beile (chapter 8) provides a good example of this practice. She carefully built a case, based upon previous studies, that content analysis was the best methodology for her to use in a thematic study of course syllabi.

2. *Validity.* Sagor writes that "*validity* refers to the essential truthfulness of a piece of data."[27] Validity also implies that the researcher has chosen the correct data to answer the research question.[28] Validity, particularly in a written report, is displayed by a description of how data were chosen in light of the research question. In addition, validity can be strengthened by making use of the actual words of the participants. If information-seeking behaviors are under study, having the participants talk aloud their strategies while the observer copies down their terms optimizes those terms' validity. Again, a strict adherence to accepted methodology is a final test of the validity of your results. Bartesaghi and Hanson (chapter 5) based their entire study on a short conversation held among a number of graduate students engaged in a Skype discussion of valid information. As a result, it was vital to their argument to quote and interpret the actual words spoken. In one such example, Bill spoke as follows:

21   Bill: I teach an undergraduate class and every semester I get people citing
22   sources that I'll go look at and find out they are actually drug company
23   websites and they'll - they'll present information as fact

The inclusion of this conversation in the final report supports the validity of their conclusions and adds to the authenticity of the narrative.

3. *Triangulation of data.* One valuable method for increasing the trustworthiness of your study is to triangulate data. Sagor defines triangulation as "the use of multiple independent data sources to corroborate findings."[29] Using different observers at different times, using different students completing the same task, having more than one person analyzing a piece of data, or using different collection methods to gather data on the same subject are all examples of triangulation. Nolfi and Saunders's analysis (chapter 11) of open-ended responses to the LibQUAL+ survey began with several librarians coding student responses independently. This technique reduced the amount of individual bias that might have occurred with a single coder.

Analyzing Data

As has been mentioned, it is primarily the goal of the qualitative researcher to turn data into text, as the goal is to describe what participants do, see, and think. All data need to be transformed into text, ensuring that the authentic words of the participants are intact. Audio and video recordings need transcribing. Field notes need to be readable. Survey data need to be compiled. Fortunately, computers can aid in this task. If data can be portrayed in digital text, they are much easier to manipulate and to include in the final report. A number of software programs have become available (see Nolfi and Saunders, chapter 11, for a discussion of these programs) to aid the researcher in analyzing data.

Farmer describes the basic process for analyzing data after it is collected.[30] Pragmatically, the librarian is looking for a solution to a problem—an answer to a research question; however, this information will be found by analyzing the words, actions, and thoughts of the people under study.

It is good to constantly keep in mind the research question under consideration. It is easy to become distracted by interesting tidbits of information discovered and therefore wander away from the main question. (It is, however, a good idea to record these ideas, as they may become the subject of a later project.)

The major idea behind data analysis is to summarize what has been found, to synthesize the information into a workable conclusion, while keeping as close as possible to the words, actions, and thoughts of the people involved. Although the researchers' thoughts are valuable, at the beginning stages it is important to limit observations to the data.

Coding and categorizing are methodologies that have a solid history in the literature of qualitative action research. Although each type of data is approached a bit differently, the general idea is to note, in some fashion, any themes or similarities in the data and then to begin to create categories from those data.

Noting similarities can be done in many ways. Many researchers prefer to work on paper, marking up the transcripts with numbers, words, colors, and so on, that represent important words, activities, or thoughts of the people involved. Other researchers prefer to do the same thing by color-coding noted items in a spreadsheet or word processing program. Regardless of format, this part of the analysis is an intensive reading and rereading of the data, coupled with noting similarities in some fashion.

As Tipton and Bender (chapter 4) began to analyze the transcript of their autobiographical discussion, they identified in the transcript frequencies of words that they felt were important. Following is a partial list of their frequency table:

> writing (105)
> writer or writers (39)
> research (61)
> together (17)

common or collaborative (7)
free or freeing (19)
aware or awareness (24)
context or contexts (21)
process or processes (19)

Categorizing, the next step, is a difficult task that is nicely conceptualized by Sagor, who suggests that we think of categorizing by imagining *piles* or *bins* into which a bit of data is placed.[31] Tipton and Bender (chapter 4) concluded their content analysis by uncovering the following themes, under which their data could be categorized:

> Metacognition
> Context
> Inclusion
> Affect
> Mentoring
> Standards

Farmer recommends another look at the research question to make sure that the librarian has not strayed from the question and the underlying research in the literature review.[32] How do the categorized and synthesized data help to begin answering the research question?

Summary and Conclusion

Stringer calls action research a spiral of activity.[33] Research is typically never done just for the joys of becoming involved in complex projects. Qualitative action research is done in reaction to a particular problem that has been noted in the everyday environment of the library. Merely studying and reporting on a problematic situation is not the final result of action research. As Farmer says so nicely, we need to remember to "[put] the action in action research. The real power of data lies in its use."[34] Doing the research is only part of the process. Reporting the research is only a part of the process. It is necessary to close the loop by using research conclusions to initiate changes in the library. Furthermore, those interventions need to be evaluated to see if they do, in fact, improve the situation. The process should also lead to new questions that can lead to further investigation. So rather than a completely closed loop, action research can be considered a recursive cycle of inquiry.

This chapter began by presenting an overview of the process of planning and enacting a qualitative action research project. A checklist of steps involved were presented. The chapter concluded with a discussion of gathering and analyzing data. Keeping these steps in mind as you read the cases in parts 2 and 3 of this book will help you to better understand the processes described in each chapter.

Notes

1. In order to add to the value of this casebook, we thought it expedient to use actual examples from this book to elucidate the process of research. You will find that some of our chapter authors focus on very specific steps of the process, whereas others have provided a complete record of the process in which they engaged. Further study of these chapters along with this chapter on process will enhance your ability to understand the complexity of qualitative research.
2. Lesley Farmer, *How to Conduct Action Research: A Guide for Library Media Specialists* (Chicago: American Association of School Librarians, 2003).
3. Einstein actually said, "Science is the attempt to make the chaotic diversity of our sense experience correspond to a logically uniform system of thought." Albert Einstein, *Out of My Later Years* (London: Thames and Hudson, 1950), 95.
4. Richard Sagor, *Guiding School Improvement with Action Research* (Alexandria, VA: Association for Supervision and Curriculum Development, 2000), 12.
5. John Dewey, *Logic: The Theory of Inquiry* (New York: Henry Holt and Co., 1938), 108.
6. Sharan B. Merriam, *Qualitative Research: A Guide to Design and Implementation* (San Francisco: Jossey-Bass, 2009), 59.
7. Sagor, *Guiding School Improvement*, 19.
8. Merriam, *Qualitative Research*, 175–76.
9. Ibid., 246.
10. Ernest T. Stringer, *Action Research*, 3rd ed. (Los Angeles: Sage, 2007), 128–29.
11. Merriam, *Qualitative Research*, 86.
12. Ibid., 139.
13. Nancy Fried Foster and Susan Gibbons, *Studying Students: The Undergraduate Research Project at the University of Rochester* (Chicago: Association of College and Research Libraries, 2007).
14. Merriam, *Qualitative Research*, 117.
15. Foster and Gibbons, *Studying Students*.
16. Stringer, *Action Research*, 72.
17. Geoffrey E. Mills, *Action Research: A Guide for the Teacher Researcher*, 2nd ed. (Upper Saddle River, NJ: Prentice Hall, 2003), 55.
18. Sagor, *Guiding School Improvement*, 83.
19. Ibid., 88.
20. David Silverman, *Interpreting Qualitative Data: Methods for Analysing Talk, Text and Interaction*, 2nd ed. (London: Sage, 2004), 177–79.
21. Merriam, *Qualitative Research*, 95.
22. Ibid., 96.
23. Stringer, *Action Research*, 57–62.
24. Mills, *Action Research*, 77.
25. Sagor, *Guiding School Improvement*, 111.

26. Farmer, *How to Conduct Action Research*, 9.

27. Sagor, *Guiding School Improvement*, 110.

28. Farmer, *How to Conduct Action Research*, 9.

29. Sagor, *Guiding School Improvement*, 19.

30. Farmer, *How to Conduct Action Research*, 17.

31. Sagor, *Guiding School Improvement*, 124.

32. Farmer, *How to Conduct Action Research*, 17.

33. Stringer, *Action Research*, 9.

34. Farmer, *How to Conduct Action Research*, 18.

Getting Ready to Turn Your Everyday Work into Meaningful Inquiry: Foundational Literature in Qualitative and Action Research

Cordelia Zinskie and Judi Repman

Abstract. Conducting meaningful research that is grounded in everyday practice is an area of increased emphasis for library and information professionals. This chapter provides an annotated list of foundational qualitative and action research resources that will allow librarians to develop valid research designs and identify appropriate analytical techniques. Emphasis is placed on books and journal articles, journals, and Web resources that provide both a general qualitative research methods perspective and a specific focus on library and information science inquiry.

Conducting meaningful research that is grounded in everyday practice is an area of an increased emphasis for library and information professionals. This chapter provides an annotated list of foundational qualitative and action research resources that will allow these individuals to develop valid research designs and identify appropriate analytical techniques. Emphasis is placed on books and journal articles, journals, and Web resources that provide both a general research methods perspective and a specific focus on library and information science inquiry.

Locating the Foundational Literature

The publication of this book is one indication of both the rapid growth of the use of qualitative research techniques in library and information science and interest in the use of techniques that provide insight into our practice beyond *the numbers*. As professionals in higher education settings, we know that quantitative data tell only part of the story about the work that we do. In comparison to quantitative researchers who are interested in designing studies that produce generalizable solutions to complex problems, qualitative researchers want to know "how research can generate useful, informational, and thought-provoking feedback or knowledge to relevant and interested communities of scholars and practitioners."[1]

Given that "librarianship and library practice can be advanced through the application of quality research,"[2] the first step of the research process is to identify the goals or questions that will be addressed by the study. These questions will then guide the selection of a research approach. Qualitative research can be used to answer exploration or *why* questions that emerge from one's own professional observations and reflections.[3] As *practitioner-researchers*, librarians should address problems that are grounded in their everyday work experiences.[4] *Action research* is the label most frequently applied to research designed to answer questions based on practice. Several items also link the use of both qualitative and action research methodologies to evidence-based practice (EBP). The basic tenet of EBP links the use of data gathered through a variety of research methodologies to professional decision making.[5]

This chapter provides an annotated list of foundational qualitative and action research resources useful in designing studies that investigate and analyze your everyday work. While each of the chapters in this book includes bibliographical references, this chapter has been designed to highlight key qualitative and action research literature. The chapter is organized into three categories: books and journal articles, journals, and Web resources. Each category includes two sections. The first includes items from a wide variety of fields by the most widely known authorities in qualitative and action research. The second section identifies resources specific to library and information science. Our goal has been to be selective rather than comprehensive, with a particular focus on items published within the past fifteen years.

The foundational resources identified here are widely used by qualitative and action researchers to develop valid research designs and identify appropriate analytical techniques. Key words such as *qualitative research, action research,* and *evidence-based practice* were used to identify journal articles and Web-based resources. The most commonly used Library of Congress Subject Headings include *qualitative research; action research; evidence-based practice; library science—research—methodology;* and *information science—research—methodology*. Bibliographies in published journal articles and qualitative research textbooks were also used to identify these key sources and resources.

Books and Journal Articles
General Treatment

Agee, Jane. "Developing Qualitative Research Questions: A Reflective Process." *International Journal of Qualitative Studies in Education* 22 (2009): 431–47. This article provides excellent coverage of a step that is critical in the design of a successful research project.

Berg, Bruce L. *Qualitative Research Methods for the Social Sciences*. 7th ed. Boston: Pearson Education, 2009. This qualitative methods textbook, which focuses on collecting and analyzing qualitative data, is designed for beginning researchers; it is written in a very user-friendly manner and contains concrete examples for each of the mainstream methodological strategies addressed.

Craig, Dorothy Valcarcel. *Action Research Essentials*. San Francisco: Jossey-Bass, 2009. Specific examples of research concepts drawn from actual action research studies are a highlight of this publication.

Creswell, John W. *Qualitative Inquiry and Research Design: Choosing among Five Traditions*. 2nd ed. Thousand Oaks, CA: Sage, 2007. Designed to assist researchers in identifying the appropriate qualitative research approach, this book provides basic information about narrative research, phenomenology, grounded theory, ethnography, and case study.

Creswell, John W. *Research Design: Qualitative, Quantitative, and Mixed Methods Approaches*. 3rd ed. Thousand Oaks, CA: Sage, 2009. Individuals interested in developing a research proposal for a project or grant should definitely have a copy of this book. Its chapters on use of theory, writing strategies, ethical considerations, purpose statements, and research questions include a side-by-side comparison of quantitative, qualitative, and mixed-method approaches, and the book concludes with three chapters focused on each of these methodological approaches.

deMarrais, Kathleen B., and Stephen D. Lapan, eds. *Foundations for Research: Methods of Inquiry in Education and the Social Sciences*. Mahwah, NJ: Lawrence Erlbaum Associates, 2004. This foundational text for researchers in education and the social sciences is significant for its presentation of research approaches without the traditional classifications of quantitative versus qualitative. Each chapter first addresses the theoretical orientation of the approach and then transitions into application of the method; topics of interest to qualitative researchers include qualitative interview studies, focus groups, narrative inquiry, ethnomethodological and conversation analytic studies, critical inquiry, and case study research.

Denzin, Norman K., and Yvonna S. Lincoln, eds. *The Landscape of Qualitative Research: Theories and Issues*. 3rd ed. Thousand Oaks, CA: Sage, 2007.

———, eds. *Strategies of Qualitative Inquiry*. 3rd ed. Thousand Oaks, CA: Sage, 2007.

———, eds. *Collecting and Interpreting Qualitative Materials*. 3rd ed. Thousand Oaks, CA: Sage, 2007. The third edition of the *Handbook of Qualitative Research* was published in 2005 as a 1,200+ page hardbound volume. This state-of-the-art work on qualitative research was later published in 2007 in the three paperback volumes listed here. The first volume, *Landscape of Qualitative Research*, addresses the current and future state of the field, the responsibilities of qualitative researchers, and issues affecting the major qualitative research paradigms. The second and third volumes focus more on methodological aspects and include chapters on narrative inquiry, interviews, observational methods, online ethnography, discourse analysis, focus groups, program evaluation, and the ethics and politics of interpretation. This handbook is suitable for practicing researchers or advanced-level graduate students. Helpful features of these texts are a glossary of terms and a list of recommended readings included at the end of each volume.

Given, Lisa M., ed. *The SAGE Encyclopedia of Qualitative Research Methods*. Thousand Oaks, CA: Sage, 2008. From action research to visual narrative inquiry, this two-volume reference text covers a wide range of qualitative methodological approaches. Additional categories of entries include history, data collection and analysis, computer software, and dissemination. Designed to appeal to a variety of disciplines, this text is available as a Sage eReference.

Marshall, Catherine, and Gretchen B. Rossman. *Designing Qualitative Research*. 4th ed. Thousand Oaks, CA: Sage, 2006. A practical guide for developing qualitative research proposals, this book contains vignettes that provide insight into the methodological challenges often faced by researchers during qualitative inquiry. This updated edition also includes information on electronic data collection via e-mail interviews and online discussion groups.

McNiff, Jean, and Jack Whitehead. *You and Your Action Research Project*. 3rd ed. London: Routledge, 2009. This recent update of a classic title in the field of action research covers all of the basic details of conducting an action research project. The focus reaches beyond education to include examples from many professional settings. These examples might be very helpful for library professionals who want to conduct collaborative action research with colleagues from other teaching fields.

Merriam, Sharan. *Qualitative Research: A Guide to Design and Implementation*. San Francisco: Jossey-Bass, 2009. This book provides an understandable and complete overview of qualitative research. Part 1 discusses the philosophical basis for qualitative research, as well as numerous formats that can be used. Part 2 discusses data collection, emphasizing interviewing, observation, and content analysis. Part 3 deals with analyzing and reporting qualitative data.

Patton, Michael Quinn. *Qualitative Research and Evaluation Methods*. 3rd ed. Thousand Oaks, CA: Sage, 2002. This comprehensive guide to designing and conducting qualitative research pays attention to topics often overlooked in other texts, including sampling, analysis, and interpretation. The emphasis on evaluation from a qualitative perspective is also valuable.

Rubin, Herbert J., and Irene S. Rubin. *Qualitative Interviewing: The Art of Hearing Data.* 2nd ed. Thousand Oaks, CA: Sage, 2005. Perfect for novice researchers, this publication models the interview research process, from selecting a topic, identifying participants, and developing the questions to coding and analyzing data and reporting results.

Sagor, Richard. *The Action Research Guidebook: A Four-step Process for Educators and School Teams.* Thousand Oaks, CA: Corwin Press, 2005. This useful basic guide describes methods for conducting action research in a school setting, focusing on a team approach to action research. The chapter "Turning Findings into Action Plans" emphasizes the use of action research in data-based decision making.

Stringer, Ernest T. *Action Research.* 3rd ed. Thousand Oaks, CA: Sage, 2007. This author describes the purpose and application of action research and provides tools to assist researchers with all stages of the action research process—from planning the study to writing the report.

Yin, Robert. *Case Study Research: Design and Methods.* 4th ed. London: Sage, 2009. This classic text for case study design is appropriate for researchers in a variety of professional fields and contains a number of examples from real-life case study research. Researchers interested in the case study approach may also want to refer to books authored by Stake and Merriam.

Subject-specific Treatment

Afzal, Waseem. "An Argument for the Increased Use of Qualitative Research in LIS." *Emporia State Research Studies* 43, no.1 (2006): 22–25. http://www.emporia.edu/esrs/vol43/afzal.pdf. This short article provides an excellent rationale to support the use of qualitative techniques along with a comprehensive bibliography of resources.

Baker, Lynda M., ed. *Library Trends* 55, no. 1 (2006). http://www.ideals.uiuc.edu/handle/2142/3654. The Summer 2006 issue of *Library Trends* is devoted to research methods; each article focuses on a specific research method and provides an example of the use of the method in library and information science studies. Research methods addressed include case study, content analysis, discourse analysis, ethnography, life history, and observation studies. All articles are available online.

Beck, Susan E., and Kate Manuel. *Practical Research Methods for Library and Information Professionals.* New York: Neal-Schuman, 2008. A comprehensive and current overview of relevant research techniques focusing specifically on library and information science, this volume includes strong chapters on action research and classroom research.

Booth, Andrew, and Anne Brice, eds. *Evidence-based Practice for Information Professionals: A Handbook.* London: Facet, 2004. As the title implies, this book provides a detailed overview and rationale for use of evidence-based practice methodologies in library and information science practice. Building on the extensive use of these techniques in health science librarianship, the *Handbook* clearly demonstrates how to apply the same techniques to a wide range of practice, including reference, collection management, and user instruction. While qualitative research design is not the focus on this volume, it is included as an option for certain kinds of research questions. The articles listed below provide additional perspectives and resources related to EBP, particularly in terms of the use of qualitative research techniques.

Booth, Andrew. "Bridging the Research-practice Gap? The Role of Evidence Based Librarianship." *New Review of Library & Information Science Research* 9 (2003): 3–23.

Booth, Andrew. "Clear and Present Questions: Formulating Questions for Evidence Based Practice." *Library Hi Tech* 24 (2006): 355–68.

Eldredge, Jonathan. "Evidence-based Librarianship: The EBL Process." *Library Hi Tech* 24 (2006): 341–54.

Given, Lisa. "Qualitative Research in Evidence-based Practice: A Valuable Partnership." *Library Hi Tech* 24 (2006): 376–86.

Connaway, Lynn Silipigni, and Ronald Powell. *Basic Research Methods for Librarians*. 5th ed. Westport, CT: Libraries Unlimited, 2010. Designed to be a basic textbook covering quantitative and qualitative techniques, this volume includes a particularly helpful guide to publishing your research in library and information science journals.

Curry, Ann. "Action Research in Action: Involving Students and Professionals." Paper presented at the World Library and Information Congress: 71st IFLA General Conference and Council, Oslo, Norway, Aug. 14–18, 2005. http://archive.ifla.org/IV/ifla71/papers/046e-Curry.pdf. This paper, presented by a library and information science faculty member, provides a good basic introduction to the action research process and includes several examples of sample projects.

Farmer, Lesley S. J. *How to Conduct Action Research: A Guide for Library Media Specialists*. Chicago: American Association of School Librarians, 2003. This is one of the few library-oriented works that discuss action research in the library realm. Although it is geared toward K–12 librarians, it is very applicable to other types of libraries as well.

Glazier, Jack D., and Ronald R. Powell. *Qualitative Research in Information Management*. Englewood, CO: Libraries Unlimited, 1992. Although much in the profession (and particularly in the realm of information management) has changed since the publication of this volume, the basic framework and detailed description of techniques such as visualization and structured participant observation remain useful. The majority of chapters were contributed by other authors, increasing the range of perspectives included.

Gorman, G. E., and Peter Clayton. *Qualitative Research for the Information Professional: A Practical Handbook* . 2nd ed. London: Facet, 2005. An excellent starting point for designing and developing a qualitative study, the chapters in this volume address a wide range of techniques with thorough coverage of observation, interviewing, group discussion and historical investigations. The research scenarios included in each chapter show how qualitative methodologies can be used in real-world library settings.

Koufogiannakis, Denise, and Ellen Crumley. "Research in Librarianship: Issues to Consider." *Library Hi Tech* 24 (2006): 324–40. Although this article is set in the framework of evidence-based librarianship, the comprehensive overview of research available at the time the article was published will be useful in identifying areas of research focus. Librarians interested in undertaking a research project may find the section on obstacles to conducting research particularly helpful.

Marzano, Robert J. *What Works in Schools: Translating Research into Action*. Alexandria, VA: Association for Supervision and Curriculum Development, 2003. Although not specifically a guide to action research, this widely known title provides an excellent summary of the research base in effective educational practices. Marzano is the author of similar titles such *as Classroom Assessment and Grading That Work* (ASCD, 2006) and *Classroom Instruction That Works* (ASCD, 2004), which provide the necessary foundation for action research projects.

McCombs, Gillian M., and Theresa M. Maylone, eds. *Library Trends* 46, no. 4 (1998). http://www.ideals .uiuc.edu/handle/2142/5416. This Spring issue of *Library Trends*, edited by Gillian M. McCombs and Theresa M. Maylone, was devoted to a review of qualitative research. All of the articles are available online.

Mellon, Constance Ann. *Naturalistic Inquiry for Library Science: Methods and Applications for Research, Evaluation, and Teaching*. New York: Greenwood Press, 1990. This title remains a classic source, although new resources will need to be consulted for data analysis tools.

Pickard, Alison Jane. *Research Methods in Information.* London: Facet, 2007. Designed to be a basic manual for research design and methodology, this volume includes chapters devoted to case studies, ethnography, action research, and grounded theory. Extensive description is provided for data collection techniques and analysis. With its coverage of quantitative and qualitative perspectives, this volume would be very useful for a mixed-methods study.

Thomas, Nancy P., and James M. Nyce. "Context as Category: Opportunities for Ethnographic Analysis in Library and Information Science Research." *The New Review of Information Behaviour Research* 2 (2001): 1–7. Another good basic review of techniques, this article is very useful for generating ideas for research projects.

Walden, Graham. R. "Focus Group Interviewing in the Library Literature: A Selective Annotated Bibliography 1996–2005." *Reference Services Review* 34 (2006): 222–41. This article presents an overview of the use of the focus group method in previous library research studies.

Watson-Boone, Rebecca. "Academic Librarians as Practitioner-researchers." *The Journal of Academic Librarianship* 26 (2000): 85–93. This article is a helpful starting point for anyone interested in action research in a library setting. Watson-Boone reviewed twenty-four published studies to identify seven common steps in the process of conducting practitioner (action) research and provides clear definitions of various categories of research studies such as case studies, evaluation, secondary data analysis, and survey research.

Wildemuth, Barbara M. *Applications of Social Research Methods to Questions in Information and Library Science.* Westport, CT: Libraries Unlimited, 2009. One of the newest publications geared toward research in library and information science, this text presents examples of typical research questions in the field and describes the research process for addressing those questions. Qualitative research topics covered in the book include case studies, naturalistic research, interviews, historical and documentary studies, and participant observation.

Journals
General Treatment

Action Research. http://arj.sagepub.com. This international, interdisciplinary, peer-reviewed journal publishes not only action research studies, but also includes articles on the philosophy and methodology of action research. This journal requires a fee-based subscription.

International Journal of Qualitative Methods. http://ejournals.library.ualberta.ca/index.php/IJQM/index. This peer-reviewed journal is published quarterly by the International Institute for Qualitative Methodology at the University of Alberta, Canada. Articles in this journal are designed to enhance knowledge of qualitative research methods for professionals and students in diverse academic fields. Registration (free at the time this chapter was written) is required to access the journal online.

International Journal of Qualitative Studies in Education. http://www.tandf.co.uk/journals/tf/09518398 .html. Focusing on education in a broad sense, i.e., P–12, higher education, nonschool settings, etc., this journal publishes empirical research that utilizes a variety of qualitative methods and approaches. A fee-based subscription is required.

Qualitative Inquiry. http://qix.sagepub.com. The emphasis of articles published in this journal is on methodological issues in qualitative research rather than on the outcomes of qualitative research studies. A fee-based subscription is required.

The Qualitative Report. http://www.nova.edu/ssss/QR/index.html. In addition to publishing empirical research studies, this peer-reviewed, online journal also is a forum for discussion and commentary on qualitative research. Articles are accessible online as PDF files with no fee or registration required.

Qualitative Research. http://qrj.sagepub.com. This journal has a multidisciplinary focus and publishes original research and reviews of research that highlight a diversity of methodological approaches. A fee-based subscription is required.

Subject-specific Treatment

College and Research Libraries. http://www.ala.org/ala/mgrps/divs/acrl/publications/crljournal/ collegeresearch.cfm. This is the peer-reviewed research journal published by the Association of College and Research Libraries. Research using a variety of methodologies is included in this quarterly publication. Access is free to members of the American Library Association's College and Research Libraries Division; a fee-based subscription is required for others.

D-Lib Magazine. http://www.dlib.org. Produced by the Corporation for National Research Initiatives, *D-Lib* is published online six times per year. The focus of the articles published is on research and development in digital libraries. This scope is broader than just research, but it is an excellent source for current awareness for research projects and initiatives. *Ariadne* (http://www.ariadne.ac.uk) would be a similar source for current awareness of research in the area of digital archives and libraries. Both of these publications are available online without a fee.

E-JASL: Electronic Journal of Academic and Special Librarianship. http://southernlibrarianship.icaap.org. This refereed, online journal is published by the International Consortium for the Advancement of Academic Publication, Athabasca, Canada. Coverage includes academic and special librarianship and many articles report research using qualitative methodologies. No fee or registration is required to access the journal online.

Evidence Based Library and Information Practice. http://ejournals.library.ualberta.ca/index.php/EBLIP. This quarterly online journal is peer-reviewed and open access. In addition to reporting original research, articles also provide reviews and commentaries on previously published research. The focus is on "research that may contribute to decision making in professional practice." Full text of the contents is available as PDF files without requiring a fee or registration.

Information Research: An International Electronic Journal. http://informationr.net/ir. This peer-reviewed journal is published online and is open access. Issues are published quarterly, and the journal is published privately by Professor Tom Wilson. The scope of research published includes any information-related discipline, and the range of research methodologies represented is correspondingly broad. No registration or fees are required to access the contents of the journal.

Library and Information Science Research. http://www.sciencedirect.com/science/journal/07408188. Published quarterly by Elsevier, this peer-reviewed journal publishes qualitative, quantitative and mixed-methods research in library and information science. A fee-based subscription is required.

Libres: Library and Information Science Electronic Journal. http://libres.curtin.edu.au. Published online by the Department of Information Studies Curtin University of Technology, Perth, Western Australia, one section of each biannual issue is peer-reviewed and addresses "Research and Applications." No registration or fee is required to access the full text of the contents as PDF files.

Web Resources
General Treatment

ActionResearch.net. http://www.actionresearch.net. This Web site provides access to a variety of resources centered around the living theory view of action research developed by Professor Jack Whitehead of Liverpool Hope University. The text of the 2002 edition of *Action Research for Professional Development: Concise Advice for New Action Researchers* by Jean McNiff is available at this site.

CARN: The Collaborative Action Research Network. http://www.did.stu.mmu.ac.uk/carnnew. Access to some components of CARN requires a membership fee, but the Web site does host some useful accessible resources, including a blog and a list of conferences related to action research.

DiRT: Digital Research Tools. http://digitalresearchtools.pbworks.com. This very useful wiki provides extensive resources about the use of digital tools in conducting research. The basic list is organized by research activity, such as collaboration, analyzing qualitative data, and transcribing handwritten or spoken texts.

International Institute for Qualitative Methodology. http://www.iiqm.ualberta.ca. This institute sponsors the Advances in Qualitative Methods conference; in addition, the Web site provides links to key resources in qualitative research.

Qual Page. http://www.qualitativeresearch.uga.edu/QualPage. This Web site is a repository of online resources for qualitative researchers, including organizations, conferences and workshops, journals, research methods, and data analysis software.

Research Methods Knowledge Base. http://www.socialresearchmethods.net/kb. Although this Web site is designed to support an undergraduate course in basic research techniques, many researchers will find this concise and focused treatment useful. The site highlights the design of quantitative research, which will assist in the creation of a mixed-methods study.

Subject-specific Treatment

American Library Association Library Research Roundtable. http://www.ala.org/ala/mgrps/rts/lrrt/index.cfm. One purpose of the roundtable is to promote library research using mentors, and this Web site provides links for participation. The home page for the mentor program (http://lrrtmentor.ci.fsu.edu/home.html) provides additional resources.

Qualitative Research in Information Systems. http://www.qual.auckland.ac.nz. This is the Web site for the ISWorld Section on Qualitative Research in Information Systems (IS) of the Association for Information Systems. The site provides an excellent overview of qualitative research with links to many key resources. A list of software tools is also included.

Notes

1. Melissa Freeman et al., "Standards of Evidence in Qualitative Research: An Incitement to Discourse," *Educational Researcher* 36 (2007): 30.
2. Lisa Given, "Qualitative Research in Evidence-based Practice: A Valuable Partnership," *Library Hi Tech* 24 (2006): 385.
3. See Andrew Booth, "Clear and Present Questions: Formulating Questions for Evidence Based Practice," *Library Hi Tech* 24 (2006): 355–68; or Denise Koufogiannakis and Ellen Crumley, "Research in Librarianship: Issues to Consider," *Library Hi Tech* 24 (2006): 324–40.
4. Rebecca Watson-Boone, "Academic Librarians as Practitioner-researchers," *The Journal of Academic Librarianship* 26, no. 2 (2000): 85–93.
5. Jonathan Eldredge, "Evidence-based Librarianship: The EBL Process," *Library Hi Tech* 24 (2006): 341–54.

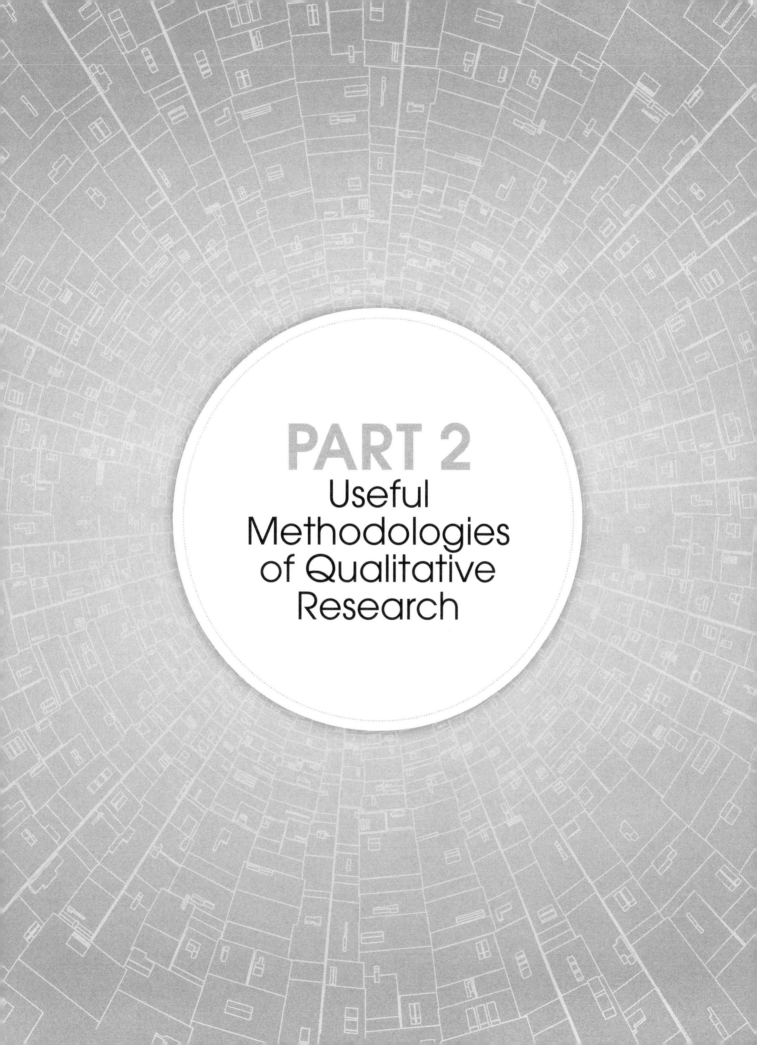

PART 2
Useful
Methodologies
of Qualitative
Research

Teaching Alone and Together:
A Narrative Inquiry

Roberta Tipton and Patricia Bender

Abstract. This chapter uses narrative inquiry to examine a teaching collaboration between a writing instructor/writing center director and an instruction librarian. Their field text was the edited transcription of an unstructured recorded conversation between the two. Three research questions were addressed: (1) Which aspects of the collaboration allowed some students who had performed poorly in other writing classes to succeed? (2) What factors made this collaboration work so well even though the researchers came from two different fields of study and taught different material to the students? (3) Which successful elements of the collaboration could be scaled up or transferred to other classes? The authors analyzed the transcribed text by extracting themes and by looking at word frequencies. They found that some of the factors in their success included modeling research and writing behavior for students, building a common vocabulary, and using targeted autobiographical writing as a tool for exploring the research/writing process. Their discussion implied that some of their findings could be transferred to other collaborations and scaled up into online environments.

Introduction

Rutgers–Newark is a unit of Rutgers, the State University of New Jersey, located in New Jersey's largest city. An urban campus of some 11,500 students, 7,307 of them undergraduates,[1] Rutgers–Newark takes pride in providing educational opportunities for underprepared and nontraditional students as well as multilanguage learners. *U.S. News & World Report* has named Rutgers–Newark the most diverse national doctorate-granting university in the country for over a decade.[2] Many of the undergraduate students transfer in from two-year schools in the area.

At the time of our study in 2004, Roberta Tipton had been the information literacy coordinator at the John Cotton Dana Library at Rutgers–Newark for nearly twelve years. Dana Library was and is the main campus library for undergraduates and most of the graduate students, with the exception of those majoring in law and criminal justice. Patricia Bender was then director of the Newark Writing Center, which provided tutoring and instruction for students in the Newark Writing Program. Bender also taught composition courses, and Tipton provided information literacy instruction for those courses. Much of the information literacy instruction on our campus is limited to the classic *one-shot* library class, but our collaboration for English 122, a course for underprepared transfer students, was very different. Bender explains the course in this excerpt from our autobiographical narrative inquiry.[3]

> **Bender:** I should say a little bit about English 122. It's a class for students who have some college credit and, in fact, have taken writing courses elsewhere. They have not placed into our English 101 or 102 here on the campus. So, rather than make them take a course again that they've had elsewhere and not get credit for it, we have an English 122 class. It is a credit-bearing, college-level class for students whose writing is weak. . . . Part of English 122 is a research component, and it is extremely important for students who come in with credit. Some of them may be second semester sophomores going into their junior year. So this course is not just a writing course for them, but a course in which they need to figure out how to do research and how to present that research. And those two things were both equally daunting: how to do research, and how to present the research. What became, for me, most important was how to help them do research and find their voice at the same time.

Tipton visited the English 122 class several times during the semester, teaching customized information literacy sessions and sometimes serving as an audience for student presentations. Our intention was to teach research and writing as a single, intertwined process, a principle that informs collaborations between the Dana librarians and the writing program to this day:

> **Tipton:** We want to talk about the way that we're approaching teaching English 122 and how we're working together and also trying to find common vocabulary, common approaches, some kind of common vision so that the students get a single way of learning or a single group of messages about how they can approach this class.

When we decided to record a dialogue about English 122 in January 2004, we were recording our thoughts after teaching two successful composition classes together so that we could evaluate where we had been and move forward by building on our common base of information. We were also thinking of writing an article in the future and needed a way to get into our first draft. We had created the English 122 writing course for underprepared students, as well as a number of other projects, including a number of writing/research workshops for graduate students, through a series of both structured planning experiences and collaborative dialogues over several years. Talking together for a microphone just seemed like a logical way of documenting our progress and identifying the main issues still to be faced.

At the time we recorded our talk, we already had objective evidence that our class had been successful because of student behavior changes we had observed during the class as well as the pass rate our students achieved on the departmental examination at the end of the course. Furthermore, the pass rate for the students we taught collaboratively was even higher than the pass rate for Bender's solo classes in past semesters. We wanted to know the following:

1. Which aspects of our class, both academic and social, allowed some students who had performed poorly in other writing classes to succeed in ours? Why did the students perform even better with the librarian added to the class?
2. What factors made our collaboration work so well even though we came from two different fields of study and taught different material to our students?
3. Which elements of our collaboration, if any, could be scaled up or transferred to other classes?

In this chapter we use narrative inquiry to examine a teaching collaboration between a writing instructor/writing center director and an instruction librarian. Our field text was the edited transcription of an unstructured recorded conversation between us. We used no software more complicated than a word processor and no audiovisual equipment more sophisticated than a tape recorder and a personal computer to create and analyze our field text.

Literature Review

In addition to the library literature, we explored literature on teaching, educational psychology, and even business and scientific communication in an attempt to understand what happened during our collaboration. The literature on narrative inquiry itself came primarily from education and the social sciences.

Collaboration

The library literature on collaboration is massive, but we were interested here in two specific areas: collaborations with writing center personnel and collaborations with writing instructors. Bender was both a writing instructor for English 122 and the director of the Newark Campus Writing Center during our collaboration. Elmborg and Hook presented an entire book about innovative writing center director/librarian collaborations.[4] Both Alvarez and Foutch emphasized working together with the campus writing center to support the writing/research activities of students.[5] Cooke and Bledsoe outlined the common concerns of reference librarians and writing consultants, with some comments on blending the research/writing processes.[6]

Isbell and Broaddus, plus Huerta and McMillan, emphasized librarian–writing instructor collaboration with writing and research as a single process.[7] Building a shared instruction model through conversation between librarians and composition instructors was the concern of McMillen and Hill.[8] Jeffrey discussed the building of shared vocabulary as the product of a crossdisciplinary collaboration among "researchers with different educational backgrounds."[9] Carter suggested that talk is an important part of the midcareer professional development of women in business.[10] One message from many of these sources is the accomplishment of common aims through the building of shared instruction models and shared vocabularies. Conversation is not just a social exchange; it is also a medium for sharing and

developing ideas and for developing professionally as well.

Pedagogy

One of the most useful streams of pedagogical literature to explain what we were doing came out of adult education: Mezirow's theory of transformative learning,[11] especially as used and interpreted by some of his adherents. Lange talked about the role of disruption as a beginning point for transformative and restorative adult learning.[12] Dominice discussed the uses of autobiographical writing and small-group discussion with college students.[13]

Another pedagogical cornerstone was Zimmerman's self-regulated learning (SRL), emphasizing the development of self-reliance and self-monitoring behavior in the student as well as the use of modeling in the teaching of skills.[14] Bandura wrote about social learning and self-efficacy, while Ren discussed the role of library instruction in the self-efficacy of students learning how to use electronic library resources.[15] Vygotskii concerned himself with bringing the student further in her learning than she could go by herself (zone of proximal development).[16]

Kuhlthau's Information Search Process (ISP) emphasized the affective as well as the cognitive side of acquiring new knowledge,[17] while the updated Guided Inquiry method clarified the concept of research in the educational context.[18] The frame of Guided Inquiry is K–12 teaching, but the ideas apply much more broadly. Kuhlthau's zones of intervention for librarians helping students echoed Vygotskii's zone of proximal development.[19] Both Mezirow and Kuhlthau emphasized making meaning as part of the educational process.[20]

Two authors helped to frame some of the issues that are particular to working with underprepared students from many cultures. Freire, who is famous for teaching basic literacy to farmers in Latin America, reminded us that prior knowledge and the preservation of culture are important to the adult student and that students and teachers must discover knowledge together through dialogue if that knowledge is to be useful and transformative to both students and teachers.[21] Rose identified the lack of self-awareness that sometimes marks an underprepared college student: the individual is not doing well, but does not realize it until confronted with a failed test or other uncomfortable academic situation.[22] These sources on underprepared students underscore some of the same themes as Mezirow and his followers, including disruption as a stimulus for learning and respect for prior learning and the culture of the individual.[23]

Narrative Inquiry

Narrative inquiry is a research technique for analyzing stories. Statistics deal with trends and averages, but narrative inquiry deals with the experiences of individuals in a certain place at a certain time. As Susan E. Chase puts it in her chapter on narrative inquiry in the classic *SAGE Handbook of Qualitative Research*:

> Contemporary narrative inquiry can be characterized as an amalgam of interdisciplinary analytic lenses, diverse disciplinary approaches, and both traditional and innovative methods—all revolving around an interest in biographical particulars as narrated by the one who lives them.[24]

As is true with most qualitative methodologies, one of the most startling aspects of narrative inquiry is that it welcomes rather than limits subjectivity as useful data. As Clandinin and Connelly explained:

> When narrative inquirers are in the field, they are never there as disembodied recorders of someone else's experience. They too are having an experience, the experience of the inquiry that entails the experience they set out to explore. . . . The narrative researcher's experience is always a dual one, always the inquirer experiencing the experience and also being a part of the experience itself.[25]

The value of narrative inquiry lies, not in forming a hypothesis beforehand as is often done in other methods of research, but in looking at messy realities, pondering meanings, exploring the literature of a field or fields for theoretical frameworks, and

arriving at a considered analysis rooted in genuine experience. It is an alternative way, sometimes a supplemental or exploratory way, of conducting valid and useful research. Both Flick and Merriam are among the authors who retain a very strict position that narrative inquiry is a narrow subset of qualitative research.[26] By contrast, some of the writers in education, among them Clandinin and Connelly, and Lyons and LaBoskey broaden the definition to include a wider variety of sources and techniques.[27]

We actually began our inquiry under Schon's banner of reflective practice.[28] We also identified our activities as action research.[29] The approach we use in this chapter conforms, however, to the explanation of narrative inquiry in teaching given by Lyons and LaBoskey:

> Narrative practices are intentional, reflective human actions, socially and contextually situated, in which teachers with their students, other colleagues, or researchers, interrogate their teaching practices to construct the meaning and interpretation of some compelling or puzzling aspect of teaching and learning.[30]

If one replaced *teacher* with *librarian* and *teaching* with *librarianship*, this method could be useful in any librarian's reflective practice or action research. Although narrative inquiry is often used in education (for one example in librarianship education, see Farmer[31]), it is apparently not as common among practicing librarians. A search of *LISA* (search: "narrative inquiry," yield: four articles; search: "naturalistic inquiry," yield: seven articles) and *Library Literature and Information Science* (search: "narrative inquiry," yield: five articles; search: "naturalistic inquiry," yield: two articles, Constance Mellon's 1990 book,[32] and eight reviews of that book) proved disappointing. We can conclude from this dearth of articles that narrative inquiry is still a fertile field, perfect for working librarians looking at stories or sequences of events and deriving meaning from them.

Methodology

The stories, interviews, notes, conversations, letters, and other pertinent documents gathered during the research experience are called *field texts*.[33] There are many ways to originate or gather field texts for narrative inquiry, including interviews with subjects or observations of subjects.[34] Audio or video recordings can be field texts as well, although transcriptions, summaries, and written analyses are somewhat easier to work with as intermediate products of the field experience. (We used a lightly edited transcription of our dialogue.)

Clandinin and Connelly described the search for methodology in narrative inquiry thus: "There were a number of what seemed to be similar theoretical approaches; *phenomenology, ethnography, ethnomethodology,* and *grounded theory*."[35] In the end, we followed the same approach as educators Clandinin and Connelly, who chose their own method of classification.[36] While veering close to both grounded theory and ethnographic analysis without actually conforming to either,[37] we extracted themes from our narrative as outlined below. To the qualitative study of the language we added a quantitative component: counting frequencies of the most common words as well as terms we had identified as significant through theme extraction. Each of our complementary approaches revealed a different aspect of the narrative that was ultimately useful for answering our three research questions. Flick describes the use of multiple methods on the same data as one type of "triangulation."[38]

In order to extract themes, Tipton went through the narrative document line by line, making a list of every significant idea and quotation, plus her own reactions to the reading; she then looked at repeti-

TABLE 4.1
Representative Sample of Major Themes

Voice/voices! The need to be heard; the need to know why your voice is important (What is scholarship?)

Emotion. This is not just "academic". How much "writer's block" is an intellectual decision—why open yourself up again? . . .

Add it all up: community of a new kind was founded.

TABLE 4.2
Tipton Reacts to Bender's Notes

(Bender) Metacognition
(Tipton) Sometimes we used the term "aware" or "awareness." We mean self-awareness in special contexts. Do we also mean self-regulation in some ways? Is metacognition the way to independence and self-reliance? I also wonder about the relationship of context (another repeated word) to metacognition. Are they second cousins?

tions and groupings of ideas. Bender reread the document and wrote her own list about the major points in the whole document as she perceived them. Table 4.1 is a representative portion of her list:

In the next round, we wrote reactions to each other's lists. Table 4.2 is an entry in which Tipton reacts to one of Bender's entries:

So we independently extracted themes from the dialogue, reacted to each other's themes, and then discussed possible hierarchies of ideas based upon the text. Our negotiated thematic analysis then became part of our shared vocabulary and the basis for future work.

Our two methods of analysis together preserved the subjective, complex flavor of the narrative, which could be seen as either a strength or a weakness. While it can certainly be said that our methods failed to fit exactly an established mold, they also defended us against prematurely jumping on a theory bandwagon that would distort our experience and, perhaps, fail to answer our research questions in a meaningful way. As a result of this strategic delay, we discovered some better theories (e.g., Mezirow's transformative learning[39]) to explain what we were seeing in reality.

Findings
Themes

Following is a discussion of the primary themes which we ground in our narrative.

Metacognition. Metacognition can be described as "the awareness of and knowledge about one's own thinking."[40] Although we didn't use the word until well into our collaboration, we were practicing and fostering—and sometimes resisting—metacognition every step of our journey. When we started our work together, we used the words *aware* or *awareness* (see the Word Frequencies section below). We meant self-awareness in special contexts. We defined our work very personally and encouraged our students to do the same.

Context. Both of us felt that building context for the students and ourselves was a primary activity in our respective fields. The reference librarian helps the user build context so that both the search process and the material discovered make sense. The writing teacher helps students build context for their writing practice so that it has meaning for them. Building context and practicing metacognition are paths to intellectual self-reliance and self-regulated learning on the part of students who might doubt their own scholarly talents. As Bender explained in the narrative:

> [Writing expert Peter] Elbow emphasizes this[41] and returns to this idea that context is the most important thing. If you're writing for yourself, that's one context. If you're writing for a class, that's a very different context. If you're writing in business, that's a context. So this idea of context frees students up to recognize that in some contexts, they're already doing very well.

Inclusion. In our context at Rutgers–Newark, inclusion means writing classrooms filled with students with a variety of writing expertise, confidence, and desire. (These composition courses are required.) We are also fortunate to work with a large number of students for whom English is not a first language and who come from socially diverse and often economically disadvantaged backgrounds. This means, by virtue of the students' expertise, that we were pointed in new directions in terms of our teaching research and practice.

Whenever possible, we exploited opportunities to look through a variety of lenses as we focused on how to succeed as teachers and learners in this specialized arena of academic writing. Our approach had to be organic, flexible (course corrections were both anticipated and welcomed), and interdisciplinary. Building community involves accepting different approaches plus developing common vocabulary. We built common vocabulary in three ways: by actually introducing basic concepts such as metacognition in class, by using class readings from writing teachers who reflect on the writing process, and by using the Kuhlthau ISP framework.[42] We, and the students, read Ann Lamott (*Bird by Bird*);[43] Pat Schneider (*Writing Alone and with Others*);[44] and Peter Elbow (*Writing with Power*).[45] Tipton introduced Kuhlthau's Information Search Process (ISP) as a way of thinking about research.[46] As teachers, we are also students. Our approaches involve both theory and practice from multiple fields: writing, research, and pedagogy. Everything is "both and." As Bender said in the narrative:

> It's about confidence. It's about belief. It's about self-esteem. It's about all these things, which I suggest is more than enough for one teacher. But with the two of us together, somehow we've made the class big enough to truly address these things, and I mean in a real way.

Affect. In a writing/research course, it is imperative to define scholarship as voice plus research, but the idea of *voice* is dismissed by many students and academics alike because of its aura of subjectivity. Yet there is a human need to be heard: the need to know why your voice is important and how others will consider your perspective. Determined to acknowledge that our students came into our classrooms with something to say and ways to say it, we set out to find ways to bolster their research skills so that they could act, in ever-growing ways, as scholars who questioned the world around them and honed their techniques for investigating that world. Kuhlthau's ISP[47] helped with this approach because the affect and the cognition are equally parts of each research phase. Scholarship involves emotion plus technique. Learning involves emotion and cognition; learning is both individual and social. Writing/research involves messiness, paradox, and complexity.

While neither of us claimed academic expertise in psychology or sociology, we recognized that how students felt about writing and education played a significant role in their performance as writers and learners. Support for some of our practice can be found in educational and psychological literature (for example, Bandura's self-efficacy,[48] Vygotskii's zone of proximal development,[49] and Zimmerman's self-regulated learning [SRL][50]), but our richest resource came from our willingness to honor students' language lives—and encourage them to do the same, gathering strength from the social, heritage, and religious languages that they already had in place and building on these foundations to strengthen their mastery of academic language.

Mentoring. Throughout our collaboration, we acknowledged the mentoring that we received from each other. Our own mentors—Schneider, Lamott, Elbow, and Kuhlthau, through their work—were part of our conversations in the classroom as well. When students researched writers of their choosing, their own awareness—their metacognitive processes—pushed them to find text and advice that mattered to them.

Over time we built capacity for our collaboration by talking about the class at frequent intervals and by sharing discoveries in our respective literatures. Bender read Kuhlthau; Tipton read Lamott, Elbow, and Schneider. We both studied personal coaching. We also mentored each other through the taping and study of our dialogue. After all, our reflections and resulting course corrections came from our personal—and distinct—reading, writing, and research lives. As Bender said in the narrative:

> [O]ne of the most important things is that students see you and me talking about writing, and we do approach it from very different perspectives. And when we mapped our research processes . . . our maps really were very, very different. But we ended up in the same place, and that is creating something that could be presented and that did meet standards. But we did arrive at it very, very differently. And I think when students see that there is no one way, and that we had to learn it, too, they respond. In other words, we weren't born knowing how to do this.

Standards. Even though we encountered some skepticism from colleagues about all this use of *autobiography* with students at a research univer-

sity, another significant theme that emerged as we reflected on our work through our interview is our insistence on standards. Could standards also be thought of as part of context? One role of research in this process is to provide evidence that can be viewed as scholarly.

Word Frequencies

The language of our dialogue was informal, with many sentence fragments and slang expressions as well as sentences that just went on and on. Some frequently used words as well as words that we judged to be significant to the meaning of the narrative are included in table 4.3.

The word frequencies indicate concerns with students, their affects, and their metacognitive processes, which reflected the reality of our concerns about students in the class (occurrences: *students,* 156; *free* or *freeing,* 19; *emotional* or *affect,* 7; *fear* or *fears* or *fearful* or *terrified,* 15; *aware* or *awareness,* 24). We

---

TABLE 4.3
Frequencies of Significant Words in the Narrative

students (156 occurrences)
writing (105)
writer or writers (39)
research (61)
together (17)
common or collaborative (7)
autobiography or autobiographies or autobiographical (6)
free or freeing (19)
aware or awareness (24)
context or contexts (21)
gap or gaps (5)
intellectual (7)
room or space (12)
emotional or affect (7)
fear or fears or fearful or terrified (15)
complicated or messy (13)
paradox (8)
process or processes (19)
structure (7)
standards (5)

saw a group of students who began in fear and some-times even distrust and anger because they had been forced, by failing a test, to take yet another com-position course; we worked with them through ini-tially disruptive structures and processes that could be complicated, messy, and filled with paradox in order to free them to be the writers and scholars they could be. Our collaboration followed a similar arc, from initial concept to optimism, through a steep learning curve, disruption, and doubt to a satisfy-ing conclusion. We set out to do a kind of collabo-ration neither of us ever tried before, and it appeared to work for the students and for ourselves.

Rather than yielding a single answer or a list of techniques, our analysis revealed a group of approaches that, taken together, led to successful classes and a successful collaboration. While valuing the intellect, we did not forget the emotional side of learning for our students. We began with autobiographical reflec-tions on learning, writing, and research that honored and included the previous experiences of the stu-dents, fostered metacognition and the recognition of context for academic work, and worked toward standards for presentation. Research/writing or writ-ing/research was presented as a single process, one that we were still learning along with the students. Coaching and mentoring were modeled along with the content in both class presentations and small-group discussions.

Discussion

As narrative inquiry preserved subjectivity, so did it preserve complexity as well. Our apparently straightforward questions had complex, tentative answers. No single theory or technique accounted for every success or failure we experienced, but our eclectic approach reflected a number of accepted theories and techniques.

Why Did Some of Our Students Do Better Than Before? What Did the Librarian Add to the Class?

Ramping up. Instead of *dumbing down* for under-prepared students, we *ramped up* instruction to treat students more like adult learners—individuals with their own learning histories. Even at its best, this was a difficult class that required a lot of effort on the part of the student. The use of targeted autobiographi-cal writing ("What is your best memory of writing? Your worst?" "Describe the last time you researched something for yourself."), small-group discussion, and the final assignment—a synthesis of the student's writing life with the writing life of an author impor-tant to that student—meant that the students were writing constantly both in and out of class. (By the way, plagiarism is unlikely with personal writing like this.) The autobiographical component is consistent with Dominice's methods,[51] and the selection and use of an author personally important to the student echoes the Guided Inquiry method.[52]

Librarian influence. Zimmerman talks about the use of modeling (as well as self-monitoring and reflection) to improve student skills.[53] The librarian met with the class multiple times, and not always in *bibliographic instruction* mode, but also as a self-reflective writer and researcher. Tipton visited as an expert in research but also as a participant in the writing/research process. The talk she gave about her own research notebook as a part of her working life was one that the students frequently discussed later in class and in their writing. In addition to providing research support throughout the class, she attended as an informed audience member when the students gave their oral research proposals. The librarian provided a second person who was interested in the students' learning lives and in their academic suc-cess, just as the library electronic classroom provided a second place for learning. Tipton and Bender also discussed research/writing issues in front of the class, modeling the uncertainties and sometimes disagree-ments we had about the process. The message: "We are still learning, too, just like you."

Why Did the Collaboration Work?

Common interests. The common interests between writing instructors, writing center directors, and ref-erence/instruction librarians are well documented.[54] Both of us had worked in classrooms and one-on-one with students for years. Each of us came to the project with a history of collaborative work in our respective fields. Furthermore, we had worked together previously on a series of graduate writing workshops. Both of us believed sincerely that writing/research or research/writing is a single, iterative, intertwined, creative process and that separating the parts just confuses students.

Conversation and common vocabulary. Carter shed light on midcareer women's learning through conversation,[55] and our collaboration certainly fit that model. We were each trying something new in midcareer, and the support we gave one another in our learning was invaluable. In addition, academic discourse as a conversation is one of Bender's favorite metaphors,[56] so we included ourselves as well as the students in that conversation. We talked often about the course and what *we* were learning. We read each other's literature and were constantly sending articles and e-mails back and forth. We read educational psychology literature together and even studied personal coaching with coaching expert Thomas Leonard as another way of framing our work.[57] Bender also deliberately built a class lexicon with her students, so it was not much of a stretch for us to build common vocabulary for ourselves as well, echoing Jeffrey's observations about common vocabulary as a product of successful cross-disciplinary collaboration.[58]

Transferring and Scaling Up the Lessons Learned

Although our collaboration on the course came to an end in 2007 when English 122 was retired under a change in New Jersey law regarding the transfer of credits from public two-year schools, Tipton had been thinking about library staffing, information transfer, and scalability issues as our style of collaborative teaching was labor-intensive.[59] The good news is that the learning gained during the collaboration continues to inform our work. Both Bender and Tipton have gone on to other successful cross-disciplinary collaborations with other individuals. Tipton has collaborated with other teaching faculty, in some cases embedding library content in their Blackboard class shells. Tipton has also continued the Dana Library tradition of building online library guides with an instruction component,[60] experimenting with a teaching wiki and LibGuides in 2010.

Conclusion

Narrative inquiry allowed us to examine our own professional experience in a systematic manner and to put that experience into context. Although the research method is founded upon using text and attempting to avoid preconceived notions, we wish we had known more about some theoretical and methodological considerations at the beginning of our journey to this chapter. It is not possible that the next foray into qualitative research will be as free-flowing, for now we have been contaminated with Theory! On the other hand, we might have documented our field texts differently if we had known we would need such things as memos along the way in order to do real grounded theory. Our frequent e-mails and discussions actually filled this function, but we had no idea how we should be using them at the time. Our message to both instructors and librarians is: "Go ahead. Jump in with both feet." You will learn a lot about theories and methods that support your daily work. If you are a librarian working in the academy, your daily contact with teaching faculty and graduate students will be more lively and informed as well, because you will better understand the challenges they face as researchers.

Acknowledgments

Our thanks to editors Lesley Farmer and Doug Cook for their assistance; to Patricia Libutti for proposing this project; to Minglu Wang, Ed Berger, and Chris Singh at the John Cotton Dana Library for all their help; and to our students, who taught us so much.

Notes

1. *2009–2010 Fact Book,* Rutgers Office of Institutional Research and Academic Planning, http://oirap.rutgers.edu/instchar/factbook.html (accessed Dec. 2, 2010).

2. Steven J. Diner, "Chancellor Diner's 2009 Address to the Campus, November 10, 2009," http://www.newark.rutgers.edu/provost/index.php?sId=09address.

3. Patricia Bender and Roberta Tipton, taped dialogue, Newark, NJ, Jan. 4, 2004.

4. James K. Elmborg and Sheril Hook, *Centers for Learning: Writing Centers and Libraries in Collaboration,* ACRL Publications in Librarianship 58 (Chicago: Association of College and Research Libraries, 2005).

5. Barbara Alvarez, "A New Perspective on Reference: Crossing the Line between Research and Writing" (paper presented at Shifting Points of Reference and New Directions in Higher Education, "5th Reference in the 21st-century" Symposium at Columbia University, March 9, 2007), https://www1-columbia-edu.proxy.libraries.rutgers.edu/sec/cu/libraries/bts/img/assets/9337/Columbia paper.pdf; Leslie J. Foutch, "Joining Forces to Enlighten the Research Process," *College & Research Libraries News* 71, no. 7 (2010): 370.

6. Rachel Cooke and Carol Bledsoe, "Writing Centers and Libraries: One-stop Shopping for Better Term Papers," *The Reference Librarian* 49, no. 2 (2008): 119–27.

7. Dennis Isbell and Dorothy Broaddus, "Teaching Writing and Research as Inseparable: A Faculty-librarian Teaching Team," *Reference Services Review* 23 (1995): 51–62; Deborah Huerta and Victoria E. McMillan, "Collaborative Instruction by Writing and Library Faculty: A Two-tiered Approach to the Teaching of Scientific Writing," *Issues in Science and Technology Librarianship* 28 (2000), http://webdoc.sub.gwdg.de/edoc/aw/ucsb/istl/00-fall/article1.html; D. Huerta and V. McMillan, "Reflections on Collaborative Teaching of Science Information Literacy and Science Writing," *Resource Sharing & Information Networks* 17, no. 1 (2005): 19–28.

8. Paula S. McMillen and Eric Hill, "Metaconversations: Ongoing Discussions about Teaching Research Writing," *Research Strategies* 20, no. 3 (2005): 122–34; Paula S. McMillen and Eric Hill, "Why Teach Research as a Conversation in Freshman Composition Courses? A Metaphor to Help Librarians and Composition Instructors Develop a Shared Model," *Research Strategies* 20, no. 1/2 (2004): 3–22.

9. Paul Jeffrey, "Smoothing the Waters: Observations on the Process of Cross-disciplinary Research Collaboration." *Social Studies of Science* 33, no. 4 (2003): 539.

10. Teresa J. Carter, "The Importance of Talk to Midcareer Women's Development: A Collaborative Inquiry," *Journal of Business Communication* 39, no. 1 (2002): 55.

11. Jack Mezirow, ed., *Transformative Dimensions of Adult Learning* (San Francisco: Jossey-Bass, 1991).

12. Elizabeth A. Lange, "Transformative and Restorative Learning: A Vital Dialectic for Sustainable Societies," *Adult Education Quarterly* 54, no. 2 (2004): 121.

13. Pierre F. Dominice, "Composing Education Biographies: Group Reflection through Life Histories," in *Fostering Critical Reflection in Adulthood: A Guide to Transformative and Emancipatory Learning,* ed. Jack Mezirow (San Francisco: Jossey-Bass, 1990), 194–212.

14. Barry J. Zimmerman, "Becoming a Self-regulated Learner: An Overview," *Theory into Practice* 41, no. 2 (Spring 2002): 64–72.

15. Albert Bandura, *Self-efficacy: The Exercise of Control* (New York: W. H. Freeman, 1997); Wen-Hua Ren, "Library Instruction and College Student Self-efficacy in Electronic Information Searching," *Journal of Academic Librarianship* 26, no. 5 (2000): 323–28.

16. L. S. Vygotskii and Michael Cole, *Mind in Society: The Development of Higher Psychological Processes* (Cambridge, MA: Harvard University Press, 1978).

17. Carol Collier Kuhlthau, *Seeking Meaning: A Process Approach to Library and Information Services,* 2nd ed. (Westport, CT: Libraries Unlimited, 2004).

18. Carol Collier Kuhlthau, Ann K. Caspari, and Leslie K. Maniotes, *Guided Inquiry: Learning in the 21st Century* (Westport, CT: Libraries Unlimited, 2007).

19. Ibid., 23.

20. See, for example, Jack Mezirow, "Making Meaning," in *Transformative Dimensions of Adult Learning,* ed. Jack Mezirow (San Francisco: Jossey-Bass, 1991), 1–36; Kuhlthau, *Seeking Meaning.*

21. Paulo Freire, *Pedagogy of the Oppressed*, new rev. 20th anniversary ed. (New York: Continuum, 1993).

22. Mike Rose, *Lives on the Boundary: The Struggles and Achievements of America's Underprepared* (New York: Collier Macmillan, 1989), 173.

23. Mezirow, *Transformative Dimensions of Adult Learning*; Jack Mezirow, ed., *Fostering Critical Reflection in Adulthood: A Guide to Transformative and Emancipatory Learning* (San Francisco: Jossey-Bass, 1990); Lange, "Transformative and Restorative Learning."

24. Susan E. Chase, "Narrative Inquiry: Multiple Lenses, Approaches, Voices," in *The SAGE Handbook of Qualitative Research*, 3rd ed., ed. Norman K. Denzin and Yvonna S. Lincoln, (Thousand Oaks, CA: Sage, 2005), 651.

25. D. Jean Clandinin and F. Michael Connelly, *Narrative Inquiry: Experience and Story in Qualitative Research* (San Francisco: Jossey-Bass, 2000), 81.

26. Uwe Flick, *An Introduction to Qualitative Research*, 4th ed. (Los Angeles: Sage, 2009), 176–93; Sharan B. Merriam, *Qualitative Research in Practice: Examples for Discussion and Analysis* (San Francisco: Jossey-Bass, 2002), 286–326.

27. Clandinin and Connelly, *Narrative Inquiry*; Nona Lyons and Vicki Kubler LaBoskey, *Narrative Inquiry in Practice: Advancing the Knowledge of Teaching* (New York: Teachers College Press, 2002).

28. Donald A. Schon, *The Reflective Practitioner: How Professionals Think in Action* (New York: Basic Books, 1983); Donald A. Schon, *Educating the Reflective Practitioner: Toward a New Design for Teaching and Learning in the Professions* (San Francisco: Jossey-Bass, 1987).

29. Rebecca Watson-Boone, "Academic Librarians as Practitioner-researchers," *The Journal of Academic Librarianship* 26, no. 2 (March 2000): 85–93.

30. Lyons and LaBoskey, *Narrative Inquiry in Practice*, 21.

31. Lesley S. J. Farmer, "Narrative Inquiry as Assessment Tool: A Course Case Study," *Journal of Education for Library and Information Science* 45, no. 4 (Fall 2004): 340–51.

32. Constance A. Mellon, *Naturalistic Inquiry for Library Science: Methods and Applications for Research, Evaluation, and Teaching* (New York: Greenwood Press, 1990).

33. Clandinin and Connelly, *Narrative Inquiry*, 80–118.

34. Chase, "Narrative Inquiry," 651–79; Clandinin and Connelly, *Narrative Inquiry*, 92–118.

35. Clandinin and Connelly, *Narrative Inquiry*, 127.

36. Ibid., 127–29.

37. Mellon, *Naturalistic Inquiry for Library Science*, 69–95; Clandinin and Connelly, *Narrative Inquiry*, 127–29.

38. Flick, *Introduction to Qualitative Research*, 449–53.

39. Mezirow, *Transformative Dimensions of Adult Learning*.

40. Zimmerman, "Becoming a Self-regulated Learner," 65.

41. Peter Elbow, *Writing with Power: Techniques for Mastering the Writing Process*, 2nd ed. (New York: Oxford University Press, 1998).

42. Kuhlthau, *Seeking Meaning*.

43. Anne Lamott, *Bird by Bird: Some Instructions on Writing and Life* (New York: Anchor Books, 1995).

44. Pat Schneider, *Writing Alone and with Others*. (Oxford: Oxford University Press, 2003).

45. Elbow, *Writing with Power*.

46. Kuhlthau, *Seeking Meaning*.

47. Ibid.

48. Albert Bandura, *Self-efficacy: The Exercise of Control* (New York: W. H. Freeman, 1997).

49. Vygotskii and Cole, *Mind in Society*.

50. Zimmerman, "Becoming a Self-regulated Learner."

51. Dominice, "Composing Education Biographies."

52. Kuhlthau, Caspari, and Maniotes, *Guided Inquiry*.

53. Zimmerman, "Becoming a Self-regulated Learner."

54. Huerta and McMillan, "Reflections on Collaborative Teaching"; Huerta and McMillan, "Collaborative Instruction by Writing and Library Faculty"; Isbell and Broaddus, "Teaching Writing and Research as Inseparable."

55. Carter, "The Importance of Talk."

56. McMillen and Hill, "Metaconversations"; McMillen and Hill, "Why Teach Research as a Conversation?"

57. The late Thomas Leonard was one of the leaders of the modern personal and business coaching movement. He was a founder of Coach University, one of the first training schools for coaches; the International Coach Federation, a primary accrediting body for coaches; and Coachville, a global, online community and training center for coaches (http://www.coachville.com). A biography can be found at http://www.thomasleonard.com/bio.html.

58. Jeffrey, "Smoothing the Waters."

59. Roberta L. Tipton, and Patricia Bender, "From Failure to Success: Working with Under-prepared Transfer Students," *Reference Services Review* 34, no. 3 (2006): 401.

60. Ka-Neng Au and Roberta Tipton, "'All for One and One for All': A Collaborative Approach to Developing and Maintaining Research Guides," in *The Development of Subject Librarianship and Personal Librarianship*, ed. Yue Hu (Beijing, China: Capital Normal University Press, 2008), 337–45; Ka-Neng Au and Roberta Tipton, "Webpages as Courseware: Bibliographic Instruction on the Internet," *Proceedings of the 18th National Online Meeting*, ed. Martha E. Williams (Medford Lakes, NJ: Information Today, 1997), 21–26.

5

Understanding Social Networking: The Benefit of Discourse Analysis

Mariaelena Bartesaghi and Ardis Hanson

Abstract. By adopting a discursive approach to social network analysis, the authors of this chapter pursue three main goals. They first perform an analysis of naturally occurring online interaction to demonstrate the usefulness of discourse analysis as an empirical window onto the features of library users' talk. Second, they connect talk within institutional praxis—situating concepts of information and information literacy. Finally, they reflect on how a discursive approach and the tools of discourse analysis may allow librarians to examine their roles in online communities in a more explicit way and bring meaningful learning opportunities to service users.

Introduction

The example shown here is an exchange between a female librarian (L) and Ed, a middle school student (S).

In her discourse analysis of this exchange,[1] Chelton focuses on the interactional work the librarian requires of Ed to remedy the social breach of the overdue books.[2] By asking Ed to produce a version of events with which she is already familiar (see lines 2–3 and 5), including his own name (line 17; line 1 is evidence that she knows it), and by using the computer as a virtual witness to bolster her own institutional version (lines 11–12 and 14–15), the librarian leads Ed through a ritual of social humiliation and eventual redress. From the very first summons on line 1 (which begs for an alternative "Can I help you?"), the librarian's contributions reveal that the question-

answer dynamic is a far cry from the expectations of a service encounter.

Although several authors advocate for discourse analysis (DA),[3] Chelton's study is a unique example of what we will describe as DA in our own discussion: the connection between talk as social interaction and social order.

As a communication scholar (Mariaelena) and a research librarian (Ardis), we begin our contribution where Chelton left off.[4] Our first step is to shift the focus of the exchange between librarian (L) and student (S) to one about information and information literacy. The librarian's questions (lines 2–3, 5, 7, 13, and 17) are possible because they make interactional sense within a dynamic of an information asymmetry. That the librarian asks the first question, thereby constraining Ed's next option in the

Example[a]

1	L:	Ed?
2		Ed, did you return your two books you had
3		out?
4	S:	Yeah. ((Walks up with two books.))
5	L:	They're in the book drop?
6	S:	Well, I returned them Monday.
7	L:	((Glances at computer.)) Monday? ((Nods and leans over as if to look at the computer with her. Turns toward computer.))
8		You have two books here
9		that (inaudible) says are overdue.
10	S:	(inaudible) I returned it Monday.
11	L:	((Looks at computer.)) Two different ones- Take Me to
12		the Air and All About Basketball.
13	S:	They're still out?
14	L:	((Looks at computer.)) One was out October, from
15		October. ((Student straightens up abruptly.)) The
16		other was from November. ((Turns and looks at him.))
17		You're Ed, right?

a. Mary K. Chelton, "The 'Overdue Kid': A Face-to-face Library Service Encounter as Ritual Interaction," *Library and Information Science Research 19* (1997): pp. 391-392.

exchange by requesting an answer,[5] and that Ed does indeed offer the answer setting up the questioning dynamic shows that the asymmetry is in her favor. Notice that, although grammatically formulated as interrogatives, her questions violate the notion of a question.[6] If the librarian were actually looking for information, she would be satisfied with even one of the student's answers. But her responding to his affirmative (line 4) with a challenge, for one, indicates that she is not asking for information, but that she has instead initiated a dynamic of elicitation and challenge that she intends to win.

L's questioning is situated within an institutional construction of the library as archival temple[7] and of information in library and information sciences (LIS) discourse that Frohmann critiques in his work.

He writes:

the discourses of LIS are thoroughly intertwined with specific institutional forms through which power over information, its users, and its uses is, has been, and will continue to be exercised. These discourses include specialized talk about information, its organization, who uses it and does not, what its uses are …and even identities of its keepers.[8]

The librarian's access to the computer, from which Ed is precluded because he is not an institutional member, further bolsters her access to privileged institutional information, tipping the scales of information literacy in her favor. On lines 7–9, the librarian uses the computer to impugn both the student's responses (lines 4 and 6) about the overdue books. Although Ed's account, as a first-person version of events of how he returned the overdue books, is also *information*, it is the librarian's institutional identity that allows her to position Ed as information *illiterate*, both literally and figuratively; he is precluded from access to the computer, which acts as a source of independent institutional information *about* Ed but which Ed cannot contest. In lines 11–12 and finally in lines 14–16, the librarian's construction of information as privileged resource, accessible only to her by means of a portal which only she can access (as if computers were independent of human activity), allows her a degree of information literacy that is very much in line with Frohmann's notion of "power over information."[9]

At the start of a new millennium, it is difficult to imagine Ed being so helpless. How might today's Ed respond to the librarian? Like Budd and Raber, we take "the meaning of the word information" to be

relative in that it does not denote a single, unitary, agreed-upon substance or idea. Since there is potential variability of interpretation, an interpretive method of study seems to make sense as a means of examining what information is, or at least how writers and speakers use the word. Discourse analysis is such a method.[10]

The push for a situated,[11] ethnographically engendered[12] understanding of literacy, coupled with the critique of the cognitive paradigm in library studies' construction of information as a pre-existing and objective entity,[13] invite a qualitative, thick description of participants' construction of information and information literacy. The growth of online tools and resources requires new strategies and conceptualizations of information as a situated resource, further problematizing the construction of information and information literacy in LIS discourse.

As the use of social networked tools dematerialize libraries' institutional spaces and transform them into virtual *cybraries* of information as social interaction,[14] librarians/cybrarians need to broaden how they work with users to reconstitute a notion of information literacy. In short, I, as the user, might know I need information and have identified the library as the place where I can get to information. And yet: How do I evaluate it? What sort of information do I need? As the librarian, how do I understand users' needs and my responses in terms of communication, and our communication about information as a dynamic in which we participate? How can I mine the data in social network tools to assist my users?

Many researchers in library and information science use social network analysis, essentially quantifying numbers of users, frequency of interaction, and the number of times the same words appear. In this chapter, we offer an alternative way of mining data in social network tools to better understand our users and to provide more relevant services.

As Chelton suggests,[15] discourse analysis can illuminate service users' online interactions (such as chats, Skype, social network sites, or instant messaging, to name a few) within a constitutive model of communication: as a selective, purposeful, and conscious act.[16] Discourse analysts look for communication strategies, sequences, and dynamics, where notions of information and information literacy are resources for performing interactional functions at the same time as topics of the interaction. As discourse analysts, we find our definition of *information* and *information literacy* as they are constituted as topics by speakers. Although we do present the American Library Association definition of these terms (see below), our purpose in this chapter is to show how a discursive approach offers an alterna-

tive way to explore the notion of definitions from the inside out: as they are negotiated by the users for whom these definitions are made. From their exchanges, sequences, and accounts, LIS scholars may reconstruct *information behavior models*[17] and *information-seeking models*[18] by considering how they are accomplishments of social interaction. This is true whether these models are needed to addresses intentional or unintentional *information behaviors* or specific *seeking strategies* to resolve a gap in the user's knowledge of a topic.

Our chapter proceeds in three parts, as follows. In the first part, we provide a brief critical account of social network analysis. The second part of the chapter describes and illustrates a discursive approach. By analyzing extracts of online interaction, we show how discourse analysis (DA) can illuminate important features of users' talk and connect talk to a larger discursive framework in librarianship—situating concepts of information and information literacy. We conclude the chapter with a reflection on information literacy and how DA may allow librarians to examine their roles in online communities in a more explicit way, allowing them to bring meaningful learning opportunities to those they help.

Social Networking: A Brief Reconstruction

In May 2009, the New York Times reported that for the first time people in the United States spent more time on social networking sites (SNS) than on e-mail.[19] Yet social networking is not news; computer-mediated communities have existed since the early days of the Internet. In 1978, Ward Christensen and Randy Suess[20] created the Computerized Bulletin Board System (CBBS) in Chicago. It was similar to its physical analog in the way it worked: public users could post messages, files, images, and so on to the BBS for general online consumption. With the advent of Web 2.0 technologies, early Internet communities, with their online and archived chats, news services, and games, morphed into the current form of SNS. The STM Social Media Survey reported that social media "will be the future of scientific information dissemination,"[21] and libraries will be in the thick of it as we prepare students for professional life.

SNS come in many forms, utilizing Web 2.0 technologies to share message archives, photo albums, files, calendars, and links, and to participate in open and private chat sessions. General networking sites include Internet message boards and sites, such as Yahoo Groups. Social bookmarking sites, such as Digg, Delicious, and CiteULike, let users store, organize, search, manage, and share bookmarks of Web pages, using social tags or folksonomies. Friend-of-a-friend (FOAF) SNS, such as MySpace, Facebook, or LinkedIn, have descriptions of its members, their activities, and their relations to other people or objects. FOAF sites introduce individuals to each other or find people through mutual contacts. A mobile social networking site, such as Twitter, allows individuals to connect and converse with each other over mobile phone technology. Geosocial networking uses geotagging and geocoding to enable social interactions using location-based services. In this last case, social networking encourages face-to-face interaction.

Social Network Analysis

The study of social networks predates their appearance online. In the early 1900s, sociologists[22] examined the effect of network size on interactions and the likelihood of interaction in loosely knit networks. Social network theory emerged in 1930 with the work of Moreno,[23] who used a network of diagrams to describe the interconnectedness of individuals, mapping mathematical graph theory onto social life. Hence, SNA required analysts to be conversant with statistics, algebra, sociometry, and graph theory.[24] Until the 1950s, the study of social networks was embedded in several methodological approaches, including small-group analysis, or sociometry.[25] Mid-century work in anthropology became the foundation of social network analysis as we know it today.[26] Currently, software tools provide both a visual and a mathematical analysis of human relationships and collaboration patterns.[27]

Since SNA is the study of social relations among a set of actors,[28] SNA researchers map and measure two things. The first is the type and form of rela-

tionships; the second is the flow of information between people, groups, and organizations. Dyadic constructions of social relations are very important in SNA. These include kinship (sister of X; mother of Y), social roles (friend of X; employer of Y), co-occurrence (goes to the same school as X; the same club as Y), and actions (talks to X; goes to movies with Y). It also examines affective and cognitive components (likes X; knows Y).

As figure 5.1 shows, the nodes in the network are the people and groups, while the links show relationships or flows between the nodes. We can see from the diagram that Mary is a central person in this network. However, she is connected directly only to persons within her immediate network. To get to the network of Sue, John, and Mike, she must go through Jim.

SNA researchers study the *substantive effects* and *determinants* of social network variables and the *network determinants* of network variables. Studies focusing on the *effects* of social network variables often examine the attributes of the respondents' networks, such as access to resources, influences, and how something is diffused through the network or individuals' positions within the network, often with a focus on risks, opportunities, and outcomes. Network determinants often examine the relationship between density of a network and centrality of the individuals in the network, as in our example above; homophily (similar values strengthen informal relationships); and strategic networking (power and positioning).

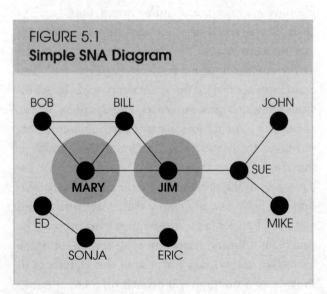

FIGURE 5.1
Simple SNA Diagram

Social Networking Analysis Models

Over the past few decades, social network analysts have developed increasingly sophisticated models and metrics to examine the activities on networks. Many of these models have been built upon a structural conception of social networks, that is, examining who is tied to whom and the frequency of interactions.[29] In an oft-cited essay dedicated to social networks, boyd and Ellison describe social networking as

> web-based services that allow individuals to (1) construct a public or semi-public profile within a bounded system, (2) articulate a list of other users with whom they share a connection, and (3) view and traverse their list of connections and those made by others within the system.[30]

Note how boyd and Ellison's definition constructs *connection* in terms of whom network members know. Thus, they ignore the *conversational* qualities that SNS users consider salient to their connections. We believe there is more to discover in users' talk and interaction than just a "focus on patterns of relationships."[31] Beer suggests moving away from social network analysis of users and toward qualitative methodologies, such as ethnography and in-depth interviewing.[32] We offer two more suggestions. The first is to operationalize social networking as *computer-mediated social interaction* to highlight the interactional nature of participant exchanges. Our second suggestion, following Beer, is to develop an interactional epistemology of social networking, which focuses on a *discursive* understanding of users' communication.

Discursive approaches are not new to social networking research, or, for that matter, to library and information science. In his critique of social network analysis, Mohr suggested that scholars shift their focus from issues of individuals' connections to each other, and instead interrogate how particular social identities are discursively constructed.[33] Diamond examined status and power in verbal interaction among online communities.[34] Mische and White considered episodes of talk online as intersections between multiple networks and sociocultural domains.[35] Advocates of discursive approaches in library and information science, where DA is considered part of the multidisciplinary research methods perspective, emphasize its advantages in analyzing both spoken and written communication.[36]

Consider, for example, the many possible meanings and consequences of the word *information* in its myriad contingent contexts of its invocation—social, political, and technical—across disciplines, across users. Like the "po-tay-toe" vs. "po-tah-toe" dilemma raised by the song, how we say something and in what context raise practical implications for the relational universe that our speech reflexively calls into question. It follows that behaviors and actions are created in the discursive practices of users, who make strategic decisions at every turn, and in coordinated interaction with each other. In this sense, agency (choice) is no longer a cognitive phenomenon of the individual, but a social phenomenon visible in interactional choices.[37]

Talja, for example, used interview data to reveal regular interpretive practices[38] through which participants construct versions of actions, cognitive processes, and other phenomena.[39] Studies of interpretive practices reveal the situated and occasioned nature of the very construct of "information," illuminating how the barriers individuals find when searching for "information" reflexively affect their self-construction as successful or unsuccessful information seekers.

A discursive approach may also provide a researcher with the ability to reframe a question from the theoretical to the real-world, i.e., from research to practice. Bates urged researchers to take a person-centered approach when researching human information behavior.[40] She argued that qualitative techniques provide a particularly useful methodological framework for studies of everyday-life information-seeking behavior among people.

Our own proposal for the study of information-seeking behavior is more radical than Bates's and McKenzie's;[41] it reconstitutes the very notions of information seeking *and* behavior by siting them as situated dynamics of interaction. Further, we claim that discourse analysis can illuminate four important principles of (online) interaction: (1) meaning making is cooperative, (2) turn taking is a key organizing feature of interaction, (3) meaning making is strategic, and (4) social identities are always at stake. These four principles are shown in the following section. This discussion is by no means an exhaustive review of how DA works. For that, we suggest further review of the references included in the chapter. It provides a very basic understanding of what DA does, what it looks like, and what it can provide as a qualitative research framework in librarianship.

Social Networking as Interaction: Users' Talk and Discourse Analysis

Tracy suggested that DA is interpretive metatheory,[42] which allows the analyst to make claims about social meanings by reflexively situating them in interactional data—and interaction is meaningful only in relation to a context.[43] As qualitative researchers, we make sense of both those features of the interaction that are unique and patterned, and we connect these to larger social patterns and meanings. We look for patterns in how sequences of talk are organized and predictable in particular ways. Budd and Raber's example of a reference exchange[44] as an organized series of discourse units or utterances identified by Austin as speech acts[45] (or actions in talk, such as asking, promising, committing, inviting, rejecting, excusing, accepting, and so on) is an excellent one:

> The patron (asks) a question of a reference librarian. The librarian might reply with another . . . request for clarification or further information about the nature of the initial question, or . . . with a statement designed to respond to the initial (question).[46]

At the same time, we look for richness in uniqueness and violations to expected patterns (such as the challenges on the librarian's part to Ed's statements that he had returned the books) to make sense of what the violations reveal about the relationship and identities between the participants within the social order, as they orient to it in the ongoing interaction.

As DA practitioners, we begin with a research question aimed at a theoretical position. One researcher might be interested in identity, i.e., how a user identifies him- or herself as information literate. Another researcher might be more interested in power rela-tionships, such as the larger dynamics of institutional authority.[47] One example may be a user's willingness to cede authority to a librarian as the expert in information strategies and resources. Budd and Raber noted how discourse analysis examines both form and function of language and communication,[48] that is, both its content and its contextual or interactional meaning, or what language says and what it does. We agree. Unlike Frohmann, whose brand of discourse analysis was grounded in the work of Foucault, and therefore focused on discourse (texts) as structural,[49] a communication approach situates institutions in everyday performances (talk and texts), such as the opening conversation between the librarian and Ed.

The discourse analyst's research question is not so much a scientific hypothesis, but rather more of an understanding of how language is used to see "how people present themselves, manage their relationships, assign responsibility and blame, create organizations, enact culture."[50] Nevertheless, DA can be colored by the research question, which frames the analysis.

An analysis begins with a transcription of the data. Transcription of talk data involves a conventional system of symbols including parentheses, ellipses, and equal (=) sign, square brackets, dashes, and question marks, to name a few (see table 5.1).[51] Each of these symbols denotes certain actions that happen in talk.

In addition, each line in the transcript is numbered (see table 5.2). This provides the reader and the analyst with a common reference when illustrating specific details or sequences in the transcript. Identified speakers are noted by name or function (e.g., librarian), or simply a single letter. Unidentified speakers are also noted as speakers. In table 5.2, note the use of the equal sign to indicate latched speech, as well as the indication that there is a pause of one and a half seconds.

Because online exchanges that do not have an audio component can be downloaded as screen captions (e.g., Ask-a-Librarian, IM, Twitter, or Skype), the analyst is lucky enough to be presented with ready-made transcripts with ordered turns of talk, pauses, and paralinguistic markers such as ellipses, parentheses, or emoticons.[52]

TABLE 5.1
Transcription Symbols Used in Discourse Analysis

Symbol	Meaning	Example	
(.)	(.1) Pause in increments of a fraction of a second	Mike:	I think that (.3) it's possible
…	Interruption	Bill: Cindy:	No, I haven't um … Finished that report?
=	Latched speech (immediately contiguous utterance, whether within a turn or between turns)	PATRICIA LIB:	I don't have a suggestion for what that is, but= =and that's fine
(	Words/phrases spoken at the same time	Caller: Radio host:	It makes me want to (swear (Thank you caller
(---)	Inaudible speech	Marge:	As I was saying (---)
(?)	Uncertainty of the preceding word	Emelda:	Where's Annaliese (Annaliese?)
GOOGLE	All capitals indicate raised volume in a word or part of a word.	Jini:	I spent ALL day on GOOGLE for nothing
(())	Double parentheses indicate transcriber's comment.		((Several people talking at once))

Working from a transcript, the researcher can identify themes, strategies, and claims in the exchange by tracking how participants orient to these in the course of the interaction. This notion of participant orientation is an important one, for it marks a split with cognitive approaches. Positing that social interaction is essentially visible, sociologist Harvey Sacks urged his students to not worry about what conversational participants are thinking;[53] motivations, cognitions, intentions, and all that cannot be located in the empirical notion of what interaction does.[54] The freedom from guessing what is hidden in people's minds is the freedom to focus on what is going on in the dynamic of their communication.

The following examples, which illustrate themes, strategies, and claims, are from a transcript of a Skype conversation among five working professionals who are also graduate students. At issue here is what is known—or to be taken as information—about psychotropic drugs.

TABLE 5.2
Transcription Format

1	Librarian:	Memorable, inspirational, right.
2	Patricia:	So I would have to advocate for something in between
3	Librarian:	okay okay
4	Patricia:	I don't have a suggestion for what that is, but=
5	Librarian:	=and that's fine (.5)
6		I'm not suggesting that in the next 45 minutes that we have to
7		wordsmith this to death
8		but what I would like is maybe some suggestions about what aspects
9		you'd like to focus on (1.5)
10		((Several people talking at once))

That meaning making is cooperative means it is not to be found in the contributions of single participants. Interactional meaning, or rather meanings,[55] are emergent and shifting, shaped by the way each participant orients to the others' contributions as they build the interaction together.[56] Another way of saying this is that with each contribution, what the interaction means is contingent on what came before and will affect what is to come. At the same time, each participant approaches an exchange from a particular position, context, or meaning. An analyst can identify the theme(s) of an interaction by the categories of meanings that participants orient to. Information is the topic of the interaction we will examine below. But the themes require that the analyst connect interaction to a category of meaning; that is, they require that the analyst make an interpretive claim, as we illustrate in our analysis below.

The examples that follow are excerpted from an extended Skype exchange among graduate students Bill, Harry, Anna, Jean, and Molly. (See appendix for complete transcript.) All five students are taking a class on behavioral health care and are working professionals in the fields of social work, psychology, and rehabilitation and mental health counseling. One of the students, Bill, also occasionally teaches as an undergraduate adjunct instructor. These students take part in an after-class Skype session one of the authors runs[57] on topics that emerge from the weekly discussion board where they post comments on the class readings. This particular session turned into a larger, off-class discussion on defining information, particularly when we talk about using information on the Internet for patient treatment. Although we use Skype as our preferred medium (students' choice), DA translates as easily to more traditional chats, ask-a-librarian sessions, or IM sessions.[58] Since the purpose of the Skype session is to encourage talk among the participants, we did not stress correct grammar and punctuation over content, which explains why the transcript's excerpts appear to be poorly constructed.

In example 1, we see how the participants co-construct the importance of the right information after Bill describes his desire for both sides of a story when it comes to finding information on psychotropic drugs.

Example 1		
17	Anna:	well the Google stuff both with some of the childhood disorders and
18		especially with the drugs you have to be so careful about where the
19		Web site comes from
20	Harry:	absolutely
21	Bill:	I teach an undergraduate class and every semester I get people citing
22		sources that I'll go look at and find out they are actually drug company
23		Web sites and they'll - they'll present information as fact
24	Jean:	right
25	Harry:	right
26	Bill:	that is pretty much opinion or you know certainly subject to discussion
27		but students look at it they cite the Web site obviously they are citing it
28		appropriately because I can find it but you know you just have to do a
29		little searching to see who sponsors it or go down to the bottom and it'll
30		say you know Pfizer and company uh obviously it's not an impartial
31		scientific data reliable data.
32		(5.0)
33		And I think that's a big problem no it's a huge problem.

In this excerpt, two themes emerge. First, there is the definition of information, as in "information as fact." However, there is a second theme of biased information. This is seen in Anna's comment on how careful the user needs to be when looking at a Web site, confirmed by Harry's response of "absolutely" and Bill's evaluation of the site as "not an impartial scientific data reliable data." There is a more detailed discussion of the theme of information as a dilemmatic resource based upon how information is constructed by the graduate students throughout the entire section.

Discourse strategies involve the choice of language, which may be conscious and strategic, or unconscious, habituated patterns. For a discourse analyst, the given starting point is that "communicative action is strategic and goal-oriented."[59] When Mariaelena approaches a transcript,[60] her focus is on how participants formulate their contributions to accomplish diverse tasks in talk-in-interaction, as they work cooperatively to make meaning. We always have choices in how we formulate our contributions to an exchange (how we ask that something be done, how we answer in monosyllable, or with a bit of detail, and so on). Furthermore, each choice is tied to expectations and consequences of others' responses. Therefore, discourse strategies can be described as how goals are linked to the ways participants make choices in the way they contribute in the course of the interaction and are always a great place from which to appreciate the dynamics of meaning making. There is no better place to understand the interactional stakes that the participants are involved in.

Turn taking has been a central topic of study for interaction scholars since Sacks, Schegloff, and Jefferson's ground-breaking article.[61] One of the central tenets of conversation is that turn taking is sequential (one participant speaks, followed by the other) and that only one participant speaks (or holds the floor) at one time. As we talk, what we say and how we say it provide an opportunity for other speakers to reply with verbal and nonverbal responses and pauses. Sometimes, we permit individuals to complete their sentences before we jump in. Other times, we engage in talk that overlaps and latches with that of another speaker.

Overlapped speech occurs as one speaker's turn is constructed in such a way as to begin before the previous speaker's turn has completed his or her own conversational turn. Latched talk occurs as one individual pauses in his or her turn and another individual picks up the conversational thread. These speech behaviors may indicate many things—from enthusiasm, to dominance, to nervousness, to reflection or uncertainty—depending upon the context in which the utterance occurs. These actions may be significant as to where the conversation goes and who drives the conversation.

In addition to identifying *who* talks, discourse markers denote strategies, the *how* of talk. They provide coherence, showing relationships between the different units of talk (e.g., ideas, actions, and turns). Interpersonal markers such as "right" and "you know," *often appearing as tag questions,* appeal to shared social knowledge between speaker and hearer and build bridges between them to strengthen the speaker's claims.[62] In example 2, you see Jean and Harry agreeing with Bill about the ubiquity of pharmaceutical sites offering information seen as fact (with the markers "absolutely" and "right"), as well as acknowledging a shared understanding of the problem of using biased information.

And again, in example 3, lines 39 and 40 where "right" is asking for the listener to confirm her statement as reasonable in her conversational turn, Bill confirms this, with emphasis, by using "right" twice and then responds with a question to the others.

Example 2

20	Harry:	absolutely
21	Bill:	I teach an undergraduate class and every semester I get people citing
22		sources that I'll go look at and find out they are actually drug company
23		Web sites and they'll - they'll present information as fact
24	Jean:	right
25	Harry:	right

Example 3 (Molly speaking)

38		It would be really useful to have some short descriptions of how
39		legislative information is organized, right?
40	Bill:	Right, right but tell me why I can't GOOGLE it

Strategies also include types of responses. Preferred responses are often declarative, delivered promptly, are brief, and indicate agreement ("absolutely" in line 20 and "Right, right" in line 40). Dispreferred responses may involve hesitation, rudeness, ambiguity (explanations that go nowhere), or put-downs. How we choose to respond may be tied to how we view ourselves and our social world. Therefore, in a discursive approach, identity is an interactional accomplishment.[63] Unlike the fixed psychological construct of personality, discursive identity is dynamic and shifting; it is claimed, maintained, and affirmed both strategically and in cooperation with others in interaction, where others' contributions may question and threaten it. In the examples in this chapter, Jean and Anna describe one information paradox.

As librarians, we place a lot of emphasis on authority of a source. This is echoed in the American Library Association's (ALA) evaluative component in its definition of information literacy. However, how does one know that one knows enough to be information literate? In example 4, Jean's formulation (lines 15–16)—which may be understood as the paradox of knowing too much but not enough—is embedded in the terms generated by the others to describe information as a thing of tension. For example, both Anna's (lines 18–19) and Bill's (line 39) terms are reactions to the anxiety of the knowledge paradox presented by Jean: but if Anna's approach is to be extra careful, Bill's take is to be enticed by the lure of Google. Jean's dilemma (lines 15–16) may, therefore, have much to say about why so many resort to Google in the first place. Google is a way out of the information paradox: a safe place to go for those who don't feel that they know enough to know more, to know different.

Claims are positions put forward in talk. Tracy and Buttny suggest that claims should be coherent

(i.e., seen within and across the talk) and plausible (i.e., make sense in relation to other knowledge).[64] They also insist that claims should reframe issues, create new relationships, and raise new questions. To this, Potter and Wetherell add that claims should also be fruitful and provide novel explanations.[65] We will show how claims are made and substantiated in the analysis in the next section.

Reconstructing Information Literacy: Discourse Analysis and Social Networking

The American Library Association defines information literacy as information seekers' ability to do four things: recognize when information is needed, locate the needed information, evaluate the suitability of retrieved information, and effectively and appropriately use the needed information.[66] The presumption in this definition is that information itself is a transparent, objective entity, decontextualized from users' linguistic, cultural, ethical, and situated meanings.[67] By arguing that DA highlights meaning making as the situated accomplishment of online users' strategies, our broader goal supports previous and ongoing research that shows how an appreciation of communication as reflexive and constitutive shakes the edifice of social network analysis at its core. It is with the same spirit that we propose a shift in the current formulation of information literacy—a shift from the mechanistic, top-down model where the notion of information does not take into account users' *in situ* definitions and applications, towards a discursive notion where the very meaning of information emerges in the context of users' interaction.

Analysis of a Social Exchange: The Construction of Information

Let us rejoin the discussion among Bill, Harry, Anna, Jean, and Molly. That the students co-construct information as a complex, contradictory presence in their everyday sense making on both virtual and library resources is an important piece of the puzzle for librarians. To our Skypers, "information" is

Example 4		
15	Jean:	Sometimes you need enough information to know how to ask what it
16		is that you're trying to ask, you know

simultaneously both easy to recognize and hard to pin down.

Let's start first with the notion of an information search as it is discussed in examples 5 and 6. An information search is fraught with pitfalls. In this respect, notice how Jean's and Harry's overlapping contribution on lines 24–25 cooperatively underscores their agreement with Bill's information-fact dilemma on line 23, how Harry's semantically strong "absolutely" (line 20) underscores the importance of the drug company press release masking as information, which is a focal topic of discussion in lines 17–33, and how Bill begins his rejoinder on line 40 with "right, right," mirroring Molly's tag "right" on line 39.

Bill's reasoned pause (line 32) is also worthy of note. The fact that it prefaces his evaluative statement about the drug company theme on line 33 adds to his substitution of "huge" for "big" as descriptor terms, both in terms of the dimensions of the problem he is addressing and of the force of his utterance.

How do these students define information? Notice that, in thirty-nine turns, Bill, Molly, Jean, Anna, and Harry refer to "information" as such only three

Example 5		
20	Harry:	absolutely
21	Bill:	I teach an undergraduate class and every semester I get people citing
22		sources that I'll go look at and find out they are actually drug company
23		Web sites and they'll - they'll present information as fact
24	Jean:	right
25	Harry:	right

Example 6	
30	say you know Pfizer and company uh obviously it's not an impartial
31	scientific data reliable data.
32	(5.0)
33	And I think that's a big problem no it's a huge problem.

Example 7		
15	Jean:	Sometimes you need enough information to know how to ask what it
16		is that you're trying to ask, you know
		(...)
23		Web sites and they'll - they'll present information as fact

Example 8	
38	It would be really useful to have some short descriptions of how
39	legislative information is organized, right?

times, on lines 15, 23, and 39. Each time, it means something quite different.

In lines 15–16 of example 7, we see that information is defined by Jean in terms of a tension between what she already knows and what she still does not know. And in line 23, Bill actually posits a surprising distinction between information and fact, stipulating that the former may masquerade for the latter.

Finally, Molly's account (lines 38–39) in example 8 of how users should have information and the organization of information is in line with the "information dilemma" introduced by Jean, with the additional dimension of how those consulting a catalogue may go about sorting through what they already know.

Other terms used by the students to communicate to each other about information are "sources" (lines 2 and 22), "something factual, dispassionate" (line 5), "the whole picture" (line 7), (more) "background" (line 10), "the Google stuff" (line 17), "fact" (line 23), "opinion" (line 26), "data" (line 31), "single one place" (to go to) (line 11), "the stuff I need" (line 13), and what is found (as in "I'm not finding much on it" [line 35]).

This discussion reveals two important things. The first is that a quantitative assessment, such as a frequency or keyword count of the term *information* such as that produced by a content analysis or a survey asking users about their information-seeking behaviors, would have potentially provided the researcher with an invalid measure of the importance occupied by "information" in their lives. This is because frequency counts and surveys would run the risk of constructing information as an analytically transparent construct, that is, according to the parameters set by the ALA's definition.

The second thing that the situated definitions of our social networkers reveal is that not all information is obviously created (or evaluated) equally, and that how this is done relies on implicature,[67] that is, a tacit stock of cultural knowledge about information which participants invoke in the course of interaction. Jean's formulation (lines 15–16)—which may be understood as the paradox of knowing too much but not enough—is embedded in the terms generated by the others to describe information as a thing of tension. Her paradox, echoed by Anna (in lines 17–19) and Bill (line 40), also requires strategies. Jean needs some kind of information *now*. Jean's dilemma (lines 15–16) may, therefore, have much to say about why so many resort to Google in the first place. Google is a way out of the information paradox: a safe place to go for those who don't feel that they know enough to know more, to know differently.

Also apropos are questions of library service users' identities as information seekers, as these are tied to their co-construction of information as a dilemmatic resource. For instance, the way that the students see Google as a double-edged sword in their information dilemma is very much connected to how they self-identify as researchers and teachers. Are they "so careful" (line 18) to identify problems with data (line 28–31), or do they risk being sloppy? Are they good teachers to their students, or drug company dupes (lines 21–23)? Molly's frank admission as a student who works full-time of her desire to "be done with" the proverbial "it" (line 13) is an important piece of the puzzle for research librarians endeavoring to put together a picture of the well-meaning yet overwhelmed researcher. What would it mean for Molly, Bill, Anna, Jean, and Harry to be information literate? And according to whose definition might they be considered such?

Implications for Librarians and Researchers

With the multiplicity of online systems and interfaces, librarians must go one step beyond the ALA's definition of information literacy. We must consider three things. First, is the student able to gather data about an environment? Second, is he or she able to understand cause-and-effect relationships? Finally, does he or she have the ability to do deductive reasoning within an academic or learning environment?

There is an astounding expectation by many students that their peers, and even librarians, should be on *at least* one of the networked sites they use.[69] Further, students prefer to make contact and be contacted through informal venues rather than by formal university e-mail or course sites, proving just how much these sites are part of the daily fabric of service users' lives. Librarians and researchers must become familiar with the study behavior of the Net Gens, Millennials, and Nexters if we are to stay close to understanding the new ways of doing, interacting, and being of those with whom we co-construct the meaning of information and information literacy every day.[70]

Since the advent of the Web, library services have evolved from traditional face-to-face reference and instructional interactions with patrons, singly or in small groups, to an increasingly electronically mediated format. The electronic formats have also changed significantly. From e-mail as the primary method of communication to IM to Skype, how we interact with patrons has layers of technology, requiring different modalities and communication skills.[71] The steady progression to distance learning classes also requires librarians to move to online instructional venues. We go where the students go. We use the technologies the students use. Blogs, wikis, Facebook, MySpace, and podcasts are opportunities to engage students in instructional activities. Whatever, whenever, wherever, and however the students are, librarians are there as well. The rules of engagement in online communities require us to change how we listen, how we see the interactions among the students, as well as in the many virtual places they now call home.

To their lists of virtual places, we, as librarians, need to ensure that students are literate in the academic and research worlds of information. How do we shift their paradigms of information-seeking behaviors from the casual to the informed? How do students learn the intricacies of the many social languages of information, from the discipline-based knowledge they hope to acquire in their fields of specialization to the larger world in which their discipline is embedded? How can we ensure knowledge transfer of search constructions and create a coherent framework for future study? Layered onto these questions is our desire to accomplish this in an online environment. For reaching out to students virtually means that librarians/cybrarians will have the new task of determining the differences between those who use social network sites and those who stay away when building instructional media-based, interactive modules. In light of this change, we will consider issues such as how to best frame authoritative sites, reliability of content, scaffolding lessons to build competency beyond the minimal "find this book by title, and find an author." And we will have to confront and dispel new anxieties such as not knowing what our users need from us if we lose the familiarity of the face-to-face service encounter.

These questions are ubiquitous to librarianship. Discourse analysis provides answers by means of a rich, thick description of interaction and voice among the participants. It provides insights into how individuals construct their understanding of instructional interactions with a technology or module as well as the interpersonal talk in interactions with fellow students or librarians regarding learning styles, effective questioning, and responses indicating problems. We claim that DA explores how best to understand the questions and the answers, with the aim of improving library services and librarians' skills.

Services include instructional models that capitalize on student strengths and match content and structure of training events to the student's conceptual structure. DA provides librarians more insight into the information-seeking and resource-discovery process. The development of adaptive, personalized instructional systems, an emerging trend in education, addresses learner styles with personalized training schemes, with a focus on lifelong learning, just-in-time training delivery, and integrated training across campus and virtual settings. Interactivity, an attribute highly valued by generation Xs and Ys, provides active and situated learning through simulations and online collaboration with other learners and instructors. DA can show through the talk how learning happens in user-centric environments. Finally, if research skills require practice, a single traditionally conducted library research class will not significantly improve the ability of the user to perform research. By using a discursive approach, a close reading of texts generated through chats and SNS can show librarians how to better understand and leverage social network sites as a way to increase information literacy among students.

Since "any change in the technologies of discourse is inherently and necessarily a change in the discourse itself,"[72] using DA in a computer-mediated environment extends methods from the fields of linguistics, communication, and rhetoric to create a language-focused form of content analysis sensitive to the technological features of computer and networked technologies.[73] Having considered the issues surrounding information raised by the five graduate students in the exchange above, it is obvious that social networking opens the door to a universe of interaction, inviting librarians to step right in. In this universe, a discursive approach is the key to understanding a wealth of available textual material in transcript form. Users can be found making connections centered on their information dilemmas, that is, their own situated understanding of what is valuable, what is risky, what puts them at a disadvantage and the dichotomy between, as Bill so aptly puts it "information" as "fact" or, with aptly placed emphasis "tell me why I can't GOOGLE it." Bill's provocation, with which instructors who assign research papers to undergraduate (if not graduate!) students are met at least once every semester, before sending them "to the library!" symbolizes librarians' work. We dare say it is even central to the endeavor of a volume such as this one.

If institutionalized discourses set the terms in which *needs* for information are articulated, discourse analysis offers librarians the opportunity to focus on the messages our patrons are trying to tell us, and locate them within historical and social contexts of library services and interactions. Couched in the languages of librarianship and of our users, words establish the hypotheses, questions, issues, data, and methods we use in our daily practice and research. Hence, DA allows us to see the social and political context of information within our respective institutional settings. DA also offers us a broader research toolbox, incorporating additional qualitative frameworks and analyses. Most importantly, discourse analysis allows a close examination of the ways of thinking that underpin text and speech. For each of us, librarians and users, to be effective means we must be credible, to use each other's language and the context in which it is meant, not what we want it to mean. We engage in numerous social interactions, spoken and written. With the increased use of technology (chat, Skype, other social network tools), DA offers librarians an opportunity to examine specific opportunities and barriers in an online exchange.

Our analysis sought to make manifest the interactional practices that situate users within the institutional order, that is, levels of our users as they perceive the task of being information literate and the social Web. Speaking as a librarian, I (Ardis) have found DA an effective tool in tracking the links and schisms between talk and institutional policies, such as how the ALA's statement on information literacy, for example, is then interpreted by students and librarians in our attempts to create a shared understanding of the importance of how the worlds of information are constructed, bounded, searched, discovered, and utilized. Working together as a discourse analyst and a research librarian, our contribution has been to propose that the first step in any critique or social and policy change is to make institutional policy visible; for this task, we have proposed discourse analysis, as a situated analysis of online connections, illuminating how meanings are practically and reflexively constituted in the dynamic of interaction.

Notes

1. Mary K. Chelton, "The Overdue Kid: A Face-to-face Library Service Encounter as Ritual Interaction," *Library and Information Science Research* 19 (1997): 387–99.
2. Erving Goffman, *Relations in Public: Microstudies of the Public Order* (New York: Basic Books, 1971).
3. Ibid.; John H. Budd and Douglas Raber, "Discourse Analysis: Method and Application in the Study of Information," *Information Processing & Management* 32 (1996): 217–26; Bernd Frohmann, "Knowledge and Power in Library and Information Science: Toward a Discourse Analysis of the Cognitive Viewpoint," in *Conceptions of Library and Information Science: Historical, Empirical, and Theoretical Perspectives*, ed. Pertti Vakkari and Blaise Cronin (London: Taylor Graham, 1992), 135–48.
4. Chelton, "The Overdue Kid."
5. See Harvey Sacks, *Lectures on Conversation* (New York, NY: Blackwell, 1992) on question-answer as adjacency pairs.
6. Gunther Kress and Roger Fowler, "Interviews," in *Language and Control*, ed. Roger Fowler, Bob Hodge, and Tony Trew (London: Routledge and Kegan Paul, 1979), 63–80; Mariaelena Bartesaghi, "Conversation and Psychotherapy: How Questioning Reveals Institutional Answers," *Discourse Studies* 11 (2009): 153–78.
7. Cushla Kapitzke, "Information Literacy: The Changing Library," *Journal of Adolescent & Adult Literacy* 44 (2001): 450–56.
8. Bernd Frohmann, "Discourse Analysis as a Research Method in Library and Information Science," *Library and Information Science Research* 16 (1994): 119–38, p. 121.
9. Ibid.
10. Budd and Raber, "Discourse Analysis," 217.
11. J. Paul Gee, *Situated Language and Learning* (London: Routledge, 2004).

12. Elizabeth C. Fine and Jean Haskell Speer, "A New Look at Performance," *Communication Monographs* 44 (1977): 374–89.

13. Chelton, "The Overdue Kid;" Frohmann, "Discourse Analysis."

14. Kapitzke, "Information Literacy."

15. Chelton, "The Overdue Kid."

16. Budd and Raber, "Discourse Analysis."

17. Donald O. Case, "Information Behavior," *Annual Review of Information Science and Technology* 40 (2006): 293–327.

18. Christine S. Bruce, *The Seven Faces of Information Literacy* (Adelaide: Auslib Press, 1997); Carol C. Kuhlthau, *Seeking Meaning: A Process Approach to Library and Information Services*, 2nd ed. (Westport, CT: Libraries Unlimited, 2004).

19. Teddy Wayne, "Social Networks Eclipse E-mail," *New York Times* (May 17, 2009): B3.

20. Ward Christensen and Randy Suess, "Hobbyist Computerized Bulletin Board," *Byte* 3 (1978): 150–57.

21. Barbara Brynko, "Research 2.0: The Age of Collaboration," *Information Today* 25, no. 8 (2008): 34.

22. Georg Simmel, *On Individuality and Social Forms: Selected Writings* (Chicago: University of Chicago Press, 1971).

23. Jacob L. Moreno and Helen H. Jennings, *Who Shall Survive? A New Approach to the Problem of Human Interrelations* (Washington, DC: Nervous and Mental Disease Pub. Co., 1934).

24. Stanley Wasserman and Katherine Faust, *Social Network Analysis: Methods and Applications* (New York: Cambridge University Press, 1994).

25. Jacob L. Moreno, *Sociometry, Experimental Method and the Science of Society: An Approach to a New Political Orientation* (Beacon, NY: Beacon House, 1951).

26. Linton C. Freeman, *The Development of Social Network Analysis: A Study in the Sociology of Science* (Vancouver, British Columbia: Empirical Press, 2006).

27. Peter J. Carrington, John Scott, and Stanley Wasserman, *Models and Methods in Social Network Analysis* (New York: Cambridge University Press, 2005).

28. Jonathon E. Mote, Gretchen Jordan, Jerald Hage, and Yuko Whitestone, "New Directions in the Use of Network Analysis in Research and Product Development Evaluation," *Research Evaluation* 16, no. 3 (2007): 1–13.

29. Wasserman and Faust, *Social Network Analysis*; Carrington, Scott, and Wasserman, *Models and Methods*; Nicolas Marschall, *Methodological Pitfalls in Social Network Analysis: Why Current Methods Produce Questionable Results* (Saarbrücken, Germany: VDM Verlag, 2007).

30. danah m. boyd and Nicole B. Ellison, "Social Network Sites: Definition, History, and Scholarship," *Journal of Computer-mediated Communication* 13, no. 1 (2008): article 11.

31. Caroline Haythornthwaite, "Social Network Analysis: An Approach and Technique for the Study of Information Exchange," *Library and Information Science Research* 18, no.4 (1996): 323–42.

32. David Beer, "Social Network(ing) Sites: Revisiting the Story So Far. A Response to danah boyd," *Journal of Computer-mediated Communication* 13, no. 2 (2008): 516–29.

33. John W. Mohr, "Soldiers, Mothers, Tramps, and Others: Discourse Roles in the 1907 New York Charity Directory," *Poetics* 22, no. 4 (1994): 327–57.

34. Julie Diamond, *Status and Power in Verbal Interaction: A Study of Discourse in a Close-knit Social Network* (Amsterdam, Netherlands: John Benjamins, 1996).

35. Ann Mische and Harrison White, "Between Conversation and Situation: Public Switching Dynamics across Network-domains," *Social Research* 65, no. 3 (1998): 295–324.

36. Raya Fidel, "Qualitative Methods in Information Retrieval Research," *Library and Information Science Research* 15, no. 3 (1993): 219–47; Freeman, *Development of Social Network Analysis*; Budd and Raber, "Discourse Analysis."

37. Sanna Talja, "Analyzing Qualitative Interview Data: The Discourse Analytic Method," *Library & Information Science Research* 21, no. 4 (1999): 459–77.

38. Ibid.

39. Pamela J. McKenzie, "Communication Barriers and Information-seeking Counterstrategies in Accounts of Practitioner-patient Encounters," *Library & Information Science Research* 24, no. 1 (2002): 31–47.

40. Jessica A. Bates, "Use of Narrative Interviewing in Everyday Information Behavior Research," *Library & Information Science Research* 26, no. 1 (2004): 15–28.

41. Ibid.; McKenzie, "Communication Barriers."

42. Karen Tracy, "Discourse Analysis in Communication," in *Handbook of Discourse Analysis,* ed. Deborah Schiffrin, Deborah Tannen, and Heidi E. Hamilton (Oxford, UK: Blackwell, 2001), 725–749.

43. Nancy Ainsworth-Vaughn, *Claiming Power in Doctor-patient Talk* (New York: Oxford University Press, 1998).

44. Budd and Raber, "Discourse Analysis."

45. John L. Austin, *How to Do Things with Words* (Oxford: Oxford University Press, 1962).

46. Budd and Raber, "Discourse Analysis," 220.

47. Bartesaghi, "Conversation and Psychotherapy."

48. Budd and Raber, "Discourse Analysis."

49. Frohmann, "Knowledge and Power."

50. Tracy. "Discourse Analysis," 734.

51. Jonathan Potter and Margaret Wetherell, *Discourse and Social Psychology: Beyond Attitudes and Behaviour* (London: Sage, 1987).

52. Michael Nicholas, Mariaelena Bartesaghi, and Jane Jorgenson, "Between Text and Talk: Managing Interactional Issues in the IM Interview," *Electronic Journal of Communication* 19, no. 1–2 (2009).

53. Sacks, *Lectures on Conversation.*

54. Charles Antaki and Sue Widdicombe, *Identities in Talk* (London: Sage, 1998).

55. Karen Tracy, *Everyday Talk: Building and Reflecting Identities* (New York: Guilford, 1999).

56. Francesca Pridham, *The Language of Conversation* (London: Routledge, 2001).

57. Karen Tracy, *Everyday Talk..*

58. Nicholas, Bartesaghi, and Jorgenson, "Between Text and Talk"; Gihan Osman and Susan C. Herring, "Cross-cultural Chat: Patterns of Facilitation and Interaction," in *Proceedings of World Conference on Educational Multimedia, Hypermedia and Telecommunication* (Chesapeake, VA: AACE, 2008), 3010–13.

59. Karen Tracy, *Understanding Face-to-face Interaction: Issues Linking Goals and Discourse* (Hillsdale, NJ: Routledge, 1991), p. 1.

60. Mariaelena's approach takes meaning as an interactional accomplishment.

61. Harvey Sacks, Emanuel A Schegloff, and Gail Jefferson, "A Simplest Systematics for the Organization of Turn-taking for Conversation," *Language* 50 (1972): 696–735.

62. Deborah Schiffrin, *Discourse Markers* (Cambridge: Cambridge University Press, 1987).

63. Antaki and Widdicombe, *Identities in Talk.*

64. Karen Tracy and Richard Buttny, "Review of Social Accountability in Communication," *Language in Society* 24, no. 2 (1995): 279–82.

65. Potter and Wetherell, *Discourse and Social Psychology.*

66. American Library Association, Association of College and Research Libraries (ACRL) *Information Literacy Competency Standards for Higher Education* (Chicago: ACRL, 2000).

67. Bill Cope and Mary Kalantzis, *Multiliteracies: Literacy Learning and the Design of Social Futures* (New York, NY: Routledge, 2000); Sheila Webber, Stuart Boon, and Bill Johnston, "A Comparison of UK Academics' Conceptions of Information Literacy in Two Disciplines: English and Marketing," *Library and Information Research* 29, no. 93 (2005): 4–15.

68. H. Paul Grice, "Logic and Conversation," in *Syntax and Semantics, Volume 3: Speech Acts,* ed. Peter Cole and Jerry L. Morgan (New York: Academic Press, 1975), 41–58.

69. Amy Tracy Wells and Ardis Hanson, "E-reference," in *Building a Virtual Library,* ed. Ardis Hanson and Bruce Lubotsky Levin (Hershey, PA: Idea Group, 2003), 95–120.

70. Andrew Schrock, "Examining Social Media Usage: Technology Clusters and Social Network Site Membership," *First Monday* 14, no. 1 (2009), http://firstmonday.org/htbin/cgiwrap/bin/ojs/index.php/fm/article/view/2242/2066.

71. Carie Windham, "Getting Past Google: Perspectives on Information Literacy from the Millennial Mind," ELI Paper No. 3007 (Boulder, CO: Educause, 2006).

72. Ardis Hanson, "Reference Services," in *Integrating Geographic Information Systems into Library Services: A Guide for Academic Libraries*, ed. John Abresch, Ardis Hanson, Susan J. Heron, and Pete Reehling (Hershey, PA: Idea Group, 2008), 7.

73. Ron Scollon and Suzanne Wong Scollon, *Nexus Analysis: Discourse and the Emerging Internet* (New York, NY: Routledge, 2004).

APPENDIX
Complete Transcript of Skype Conversation

1	Bill:	And that ties back to what Molly was saying we can spend so much
2		time trying to validate and cross validate sources that we can wind
3		end up spending you know so much time and at the end of the day
4		we're still not 100% sure you know.
5		Just want something factual dispassionate and presented both
6		concerns about side effects and you know positive spins about
7		efficacy you know like whatever to draw the whole picture instead
8		of just half. That's why I think if people could look at the
9		commentaries for the DSM I think it would make a lot of sense
10		that's what we need more background
11	Molly:	now see that's what I like better is the idea of a single one place to go
12		to I don't want to spend the time doing the search I just want to go
13		to that one thing let the stuff I need and be done with it and move on to
14		the next thing.
15	Jean:	Sometimes you need enough information to know how to ask what it
16		is that you're trying to ask, you know
17	Anna:	well the Google stuff both with some of the childhood disorders and
18		especially with the drugs you have to be so careful about where the
19		Web site comes from
20	Harry:	absolutely
21	Bill:	I teach an undergraduate class and every semester I get people citing
22		sources that I'll go look at and find out they are actually drug company
23		Web sites and they'll - they'll present information as fact
24	Jean:	right
25	Harry:	right
26	Bill:	that is pretty much opinion or you know certainly subject to discussion
27		but students look at it they cite the Web site obviously they are citing it
28		appropriately because I can find it but you know you just have to do a
29		little searching to see who sponsors it or go down to the bottom and it'll
30		say you know Pfizer and company uh obviously it's not an impartial
31		scientific data reliable data.
32		(5.0)
33		And I think that's a big problem no it's a huge problem.
34	Anna:	I'm interested in involuntary commitment mostly about Baker Acting
35		and that kind of thing and I'm not finding much on it.
36	Molly:	That would be the actual legislation and for the Administrative Code. And
37		the Baker Act Reports, Are those available through the library catalogue?
38		It would be really useful to have some short descriptions of how
39		legislative information is organized, right?
40	Bill:	Right, right but tell me why I can't GOOGLE it

Remote and Rural Voices: Using Interviews to Understand the Information Literacy Experience of Alaskan Special Educators

Jennifer Diane Ward and Thomas Scott Duke

Abstract. In this chapter, the authors discuss the process and results of a study investigating the role of distance-delivered information literacy instruction in the lives of special education teachers in remote and rural Alaskan villages. The researchers (a librarian and education faculty team) designed a phenomenological study using qualitative semistructured life-world interviews. Among the results, four themes emerged: (1) development as a learner and researcher, thinking about (and interacting with) information in a new way; (2) application of information literacy and research skills; (3) distance-delivered information literacy instruction; and (4) information literacy issues in rural P–12 contexts. The authors discuss how this research informs their work and suggest ways interview research can be used by other librarians.

Introduction
Background

The importance of information literacy instruction in providing preschool–grade 12 (P–12) teachers with competency in critical thinking and research skills has previously been established in the library and information science (LIS) and teacher education literature. This literature highlights the benefits of librarian and faculty collaboration in teaching information literacy and research skills to P–12 teachers[1] and strongly suggests that it is not enough for academic librarians and teacher educators to help pre-service and in-service teachers acquire advanced searching, retrieval, evaluation, and critical thinking skills, but

that teachers must also be taught how to teach these information literacy and research skills to their own P–12 students.[2]

What is less apparent is what happens to teachers who live and work in remote and rural communities—teachers who, by necessity of location, develop information literacy and research skills through their participation in distance-delivered teacher education programs and/or distance-delivered professional development courses. What benefits can teachers who live and work in geographically isolated and sparsely populated communities gain from distance-delivered information literacy instruction? And when these teachers work with students with disabilities, how might this change the story? Can academic librarians and teacher educators listen to the voices of rural P–12 special educators to better understand the unique (and often daunting) challenges these teachers encounter as they strive to offer safe, effective, and culturally responsive instructional services to students with disabilities? By having conversations with rural special education teachers about their information needs and issues and then systematically analyzing their stories, can we come to a greater understanding of the rural special educator's lived experience with information literacy? In other words, can we use qualitative interview-based research to better understand what it means to rural special education teachers—and, by extension, to their P–12 students—to be information literate?

This chapter describes how one academic librarian (the primary investigator for this study) and a special education content instructor (the coauthor of this study) used qualitative interview-based research to gather information to better understand—and following that, respond to—the real-life needs of our graduate students (rural P–12 teachers enrolled in a distance-delivered, graduate-level special education teacher certification program at the University of Alaska Southeast).

Qualitative Interviews and LIS Research

The LIS literature abounds with reports of quantitative research, but qualitative studies are a "relatively recent addition to the library literature."[3] Creswell identified five broad approaches to qualitative inquiry: case study, ethnography, phenomenology, narrative research, and grounded theory.[4] Researchers who utilize these five approaches typically conduct in-depth interviews to gather data from individuals who have direct experience (i.e., lived experience) with the research topic. The qualitative interview is exploratory in nature; in this exploration, researchers can connect themes discovered through the interview process to existing knowledge and make connections with other research.

So, how can using interviews inform our work as academic librarians? In discussing the qualitative

interview as an important means of gathering data, Walter noted "interviewing provides an opportunity to restore the voice of individual librarians to the literature while still coming to conclusions that can inform broader scholarly inquiry and professional practice."[5] Since qualitative interview-based research can restore the voices of individual librarians to the LIS literature, then it stands to reason that the interview process may also be used to represent the voices of library users. Interviews can be an important tool for practicing librarians who want to better understand the unique experiences—and thus, better serve the individual needs—of our students, our faculty, our university staff and administrators, and the public patrons of our institutions. The philosophical approach we take in this study, phenomenology (further defined in the research design section), "points to an interest in understanding social phenomena from the actors' own perspectives and *describing the world as experienced by the subjects, with the assumption that the important reality is what people perceive it to be*"[6] (emphasis added). As librarians, we serve diverse communities of patrons, we organize information resources, and we provide a wide variety of services. In order to be effective, we need to work from the starting point of how our customers perceive the library; we need to understand their predispositions, find out how (or if) they value our services, and discern the role information literacy can have in their lives.

Numerous LIS researchers have used interviews to help shed light on and better understand individuals' experiences; in many cases, these interviews have been used as a part of a mixed-methods research design.[7] How have interviews contributed to our understanding of LIS as a discipline? Let us take a look at the LIS literature to see how some researchers have used qualitative interviews with academics, librarians, and college students to gather data for their research studies.

Academics as participants. In an influential study, the Australian researcher Christine Bruce used a phenomenographic method to identify seven different ways that people in academia experience information literacy. Phenomenographic research involves conducting in-depth, qualitative interviews focused on a few key questions. Bruce interviewed higher educators (i.e., lecturers, counselors, staff developers, and academic librarians) from the Queensland University of Technology and Griffith University in Australia. She had "sixteen participants contribute to the core data, participating in interviews, while a further forty-four participants provided supplementary data in written form."[8] The concepts, or experiences, identified by Bruce included the (a) information technology experience; (b) information sources experience; (c) information process experience; (d) information control experience; (e) knowledge construction experience; (f) knowledge extension experience; and (g) wisdom experience. Other researchers, including Asselin and Doiron, Ford and Mansourian, Jamali and Nicholas, Mansourian and Ford, and Veach have also conducted qualitative interviews with people in academia to gather data for their LIS research on many topics, such as the role of school libraries in teacher preparation, cognitive understandings of the invisible Web, e-print depositing behavior of physicists and astronomers, academics' perceptions while Web searching, and faculty attitudes toward teaching information literacy.[9]

Librarians as participants. A number of LIS researchers have used qualitative interviews with librarians to study conceptions of identity. In one recent study, Walter explored the idea of teacher identity in the professional lives of academic librarians. This study situates the interviews and data collected within a discussion of the education literature of teacher identity and learning to teach. Walter discusses the themes he uncovered by analyzing data generated through face-to-face interviews with six teaching librarians; Walter's themes included (a) the centrality of teaching, (b) the importance of collegial and administrative support, (c) the stress of multiple demands, (d) the problems with professional education, and (e) stereotypes and misperceptions.[10] Julien and Pecoskie used semistructured interviews to investigate the librarian experience of the teaching role and identified themes of identity and power.[11] Other LIS researchers have interviewed instruction librarians at New York City colleges and universities, instruction librarians in Canada, male librarians, African American female librarians, and digital repository managers.[12]

College students as participants. Sadler and Given used ecological psychology as a theoretical framework to explore how graduate students "perceived and used the *library's* various 'opportunities for action' (e.g. books, databases, instructional sessions, librarians, physical space, etc.) and compared these perceptions and behavior with librarians' intentions and expectations."[13] Gross and Latham interviewed undergraduate students to understand their perceptions of information literacy. The researchers used semistructured interviews and then followed with an information literacy test with twenty undergraduates. Among their findings, these authors relate the perception of information seeking focused on "product or outcome," as opposed to the "skills that lie behind the ability to achieve this result" and "evidenced in the assumption that these are skills that everyone has . . . [and] that what you need to know can be self-taught."[14]

Other disciplines. Professional journals devoted to disciplines outside the field of LIS have also published interviews that explore information literacy issues. For example, Caidi and MacDonald conducted an intriguing study published in a Canadian telecommunications and government issues publication examining the information practices of Muslims.[15] Other researchers have conducted qualitative interview-based research in the fields of educational technology, museum management and curatorship, and disability studies. Also appearing outside the LIS literature are studies involving community college instructors and members of a human services information-providing consortium.[16]

In summary, interviews with academics, librarians, and students appear in the literature illuminating the information literacy experiences, habits, and perceptions of each unique set of participants. Researchers from disciplines outside the field of library and information science have also used qualitative interviews to study aspects of information literacy.

Purpose of This Study

Issues of information literacy instruction in distance-delivered teacher education contexts have been discussed in the LIS and teacher education literature, but the voices of teachers who live and work in geographically isolated, sparsely populated communities are barely a whisper in LIS research. Duke and Brown (the authors of this chapter); Duke, Ward, and Burkert; and Manathunga all described the information literacy needs of pre-service and in-service teachers enrolled in distance-delivered teacher education programs, as well as the design and implementation of distance-delivered information literacy instruction, but these authors did not explore the lived experiences of the teachers who received such instruction.[17] Likewise, Brown and Duke (the authors of this chapter) conducted a phenomenological self-study that examined the collaborative efforts of an academic librarian and special education content instructor who provided distance-delivered information literacy instruction to special education teachers, but did not focus on the information literacy experiences of our rural teachers.[18] Two questions remain unanswered by this body of literature:

1. What role does information literacy play in the lives of teachers who live and work in geographically isolated and sparsely populated rural communities?

2. How do special education teachers (and their students) in remote locations benefit from distance-delivered information literacy instruction?

In this investigation, we wanted to take a closer look at the real-life results of our efforts by listening to, recording, and then systematically analyzing the voices of rural special education teachers who were enrolled in a distance-delivered graduate degree program. Each rural special educator who participated in this study had received more than one hundred hours of distance-delivered information literacy instruction (provided by the authors of this chapter) as part of the program of study. The purpose of this phenomenological study was to (a) describe the role that information literacy plays in the lives of special education teachers who live and work in geographically isolated, sparsely populated, and predominately Alaska Native communities in rural

Alaska; and (b) describe how these special education teachers and, by extension, their P–12 students have benefited from distance-delivered information literacy instruction.

Case and Context

In the summer semester of 2007, the Master's of Education (MEd) in Special Education degree program at the University of Alaska Southeast (UAS) admitted its first cohort of thirty special education teacher candidates. Some of these candidates lived and worked in Alaska's urban communities (e.g., Anchorage, Fairbanks, or Juneau); most, however, taught in one of the more than two hundred geographically isolated, sparsely populated, and predominately Alaska Native communities that are scattered across Alaska's vast terrain. The mission of the MEd in Special Education program at UAS is to prepare information literate teachers to provide culturally responsive instructional services to students with disabilities in Alaska's remote, rural, and Alaska Native communities. This special education teacher certification program is designed to accommodate working teachers; courses are, therefore, offered in the afternoons and evenings and in the summer. Courses are delivered via audioconference and augmented with online resources, including Elluminate Live!, an interactive Web conferencing system, and Adobe Acrobat Connect Pro (formerly Macromedia Breeze), a software program used to create informational presentations; this distance-delivered instructional format allows teachers to remain in their home communities while completing their graduate studies.[19]

Library instruction is embedded throughout the MEd in Special Education program at UAS, and special education teachers who graduate from the program receive more than one hundred hours of information literacy instruction from an academic librarian as part of their program of study. Three required research methods courses are cotaught by an academic librarian (the principal investigator for this study) and a special education content instructor (the coauthor of this study). These three courses include ED 626 (Classroom Research), EDSE 692

(Secondary Research Methods), and EDSE 698 (Master's Thesis Project). In all three of these courses, students learn to conduct systematic and reproducible Boolean searches of databases that index articles related to the disciplines of special education and disability studies, including ERIC (EBSCOhost), Education Journals (ProQuest), Education Abstracts (OCLC Firstsearch), the Professional Development Collection (EBSCOhost), Academic Search Premier (EBSCOhost), and PsycINFO (EBSCOhost). These students also learn to search databases related to Alaska Native issues (e.g., the Hubert Wenger Eskimo Database, Alaska Native Knowledge Network, Alaska's Digital Archives, Alaska and Polar Periodical Index).[20] Additionally, students are taught to recognize and distinguish among different publication types (e.g., empirical studies, descriptive works, position papers and opinion pieces, technical guides, annotated bibliographies, reviews of the literature), to classify empirical studies according to research design (e.g., quantitative, qualitative, and mixed-methods research designs), to identify the participants and data sources used in empirical studies, and to summarize and synthesize the findings of such studies.

As previously mentioned, our primary purpose in conducting this investigation was to discover how rural special educators experienced distance-delivered information literacy instruction. Four public school teachers—all women—participated in this phenomenological study. One teacher was Alaska Native; one teacher was Mexican American; and two teachers were of European American ancestry. All four of these teachers were enrolled in the distance-delivered MEd in Special Education degree program at UAS when this study was undertaken; each of these four teachers graduated from the program in May 2009, shortly after they were interviewed for this study.

While they were taking distance-delivered graduate courses at UAS, the four teachers lived and worked in geographically isolated, sparsely populated, and predominately Alaska Native communities in rural Alaska. Two of the teachers taught children and adolescents with a wide range of exceptional learning needs in Yup'ik Eskimo communities in western Alaska; one of the teachers worked with high

school students and young adults with severe cognitive impairments in an Inupiaq Eskimo community in the high Arctic; the other teacher who participated in this study taught elementary school children with and without disabilities in an inclusive classroom setting in a Tlingit Indian community in southeast Alaska. These four communities—like most of the more than two hundred similar communities—lacked both community libraries and on-site professional development opportunities for special education teachers. The four participants, therefore, relied on distance-delivered library services offered through the UAS Egan Library to complete their course assignments (e.g., research papers, case studies, their master's thesis projects), and to obtain professional development resources that could help them provide safe, effective, and culturally responsive instructional services to their students (e.g., research-based instructional strategies, information about specific disabilities, culturally responsive lesson plans based on Alaska Native traditions).

Duke, Ward, and Burkert[21] teach distance-delivered graduate courses to teachers enrolled in the MEd in Special Education program at UAS. These three authors described the unique—and often daunting—challenges encountered by special educators who live and work in rural Alaska as they attempt to provide safe, effective, and culturally responsive instructional services to students with disabilities. They wrote:

> Our graduate students are often the only special educators in their respective villages, and many of our candidates provide instructional services to students with a wide range of exceptional learning needs and developmental levels. One of our candidates—Judy (not her real name)—teaches in a geographically isolated Yup'ik Eskimo community of approximately 300 people. There are no roads leading into or out of her village. For most of the year, the only way to reach Judy's village is by chartered plane; in the winter months, when the river system is frozen solid, the village is also accessible by snow machine. Judy, who is one of only four certified teachers in this village—and the *only* special educator—provides instructional services to 11 [sic] students, including: a pre-school child

with developmental delays; a second grader with a hearing impairment and language delays; a medically fragile fourth grader who uses a wheelchair; a fifth grader with a reading disability; another fifth grader with attention deficit hyperactivity disorder (ADHD); three middle school students with specific learning disabilities; an eighth grader with fetal alcohol spectrum disorder (FASD) and severe behavior problems; a sophomore with autism; a nineteen year old with Down syndrome; and a twenty year old with traumatic brain injury. Judy's situation is not unique—many of the teachers in our program are confronted with equally challenging caseloads.[22]

The authors proceeded to describe the importance of information literacy to the professional development of special education teachers who live and work in rural Alaska. These authors noted:

No single special educator can be expected to possess highly specialized knowledge about such a daunting array of exceptionalities and developmental levels; even a bright, capable, and highly motivated special education teacher—like Judy—is unlikely to become a specialist in early childhood intervention, hearing impairments, communication disorders, orthopedic disabilities, health impairments, specific learning disabilities, ADHD, emotional and behavioral disorders, autism, intellectual impairments, and traumatic brain injury. And no teacher education program can adequately prepare an individual special education teacher to *specialize* in such a vast array of exceptionalities and developmental levels. What we, as a distance-delivered teacher education program, can do, however, is prepare . . . information literate special educators who recognize when they need highly specialized information about particular exceptionalities and developmental levels, and are able to locate, critically evaluate, and effectively use such information to develop culturally responsive instructional services that benefit their students.[23]

The four teachers who participated in the present study had much in common with Judy. All four had challenging caseloads characterized by students with a wide range of exceptional learning conditions and developmental levels; all four lived in similar communities; all four lacked access to community libraries and on-site professional development opportunities; and all four relied on distance-delivered library services (provided by the UAS Egan Library) to both complete university coursework and access professional development resources. This phenomenological study explores the role that information literacy played in the lives of these four special educators who taught students with disabilities.

Research Design

In the social constructivist view that we take in this study, "individuals seek understanding of the world in which they live and work. They develop subjective meanings of their experiences—meanings directed toward certain objects or things."[24] In this study, we used the interview process to explore the meaning of the information literacy skills our graduate students acquired through their participation in a distance-delivered teacher education program, specifically a qualitative semistructured life world interview in a phenomenological study of the meaning of information literacy in the lives of four special education teachers.

Phenomenology

Phenomenological research describes a phenomenon as experienced by one or more individuals. The researcher (or phenomenologist) gathers information (i.e., data) from individuals who have experienced the phenomenon under investigation. Typically, "the process of collecting information involves primarily in-depth interviews . . . with as many as 10 [sic] individuals. The important point is to describe the meaning of the phenomenon for a small number of individuals who have experienced it."[25] The phenomenologist attempts to set aside prejudgments regarding the phenomenon being investigated through a process known as "bracketing." The researcher also relies on intuition, imagination, and systematic methods of analysis—often employing the Stevick-Colaizzi-Keen method of data analysis (which we describe in the Methods section)—to interpret the data. The ultimate goal of the phenomenologist is to develop succinct, vivid, and comprehensive summaries that describe the "essence" of the participants' "lived experience" of the phenomenon under investigation.[26]

The Qualitative Semistructured Life World Interview

The qualitative interview is "focused on the 'qualities' of respondents' experiences . . . whatever the subject matter, it can have diverse qualities or meanings in people's experience."[27] This type of interview is "designed not so much to collect the facts, as it were, as to gather information that meaningfully frames the configuration and salience of those facts in the interviewee's life."[28] Kvale and Brinkmann define the semistructured life world interview as "an interview with the purpose of obtaining descriptions of the life world of the interviewee in order to interpret the meaning of the described phenomena."[29] The purpose of the semistructured life world interview (i.e., to obtain "descriptions of the life world" of individuals who have experienced a particular phenomenon "in order to interpret the meaning of" that phenomenon)[30] is closely aligned to the goal of the phenomenologist (i.e., to describe the "essence" of an individual's "lived experience" of a particular phenomenon),[31] making the semistructured life world interview a highly effective data generation activity to use in the conduct of phenomenological research.[32]

Preparing for the Interviews

As we prepared to conduct qualitative semistructured life world interviews with the four teachers who participated in this study, we consulted several sources for advice. Kvale and Brinkmann offer their readers helpful sample questions, transcriptions of interview questions and answers, detailed discussion of the interview process, and learning tasks to help with question formulation.[33] Also particularly helpful for composing thoughtful questions were texts by Janesick and Creswell.[34] We also consulted other interview studies as we developed the interview protocol for this study (see appendix).[35]

Methods
Purposeful Sampling Strategy

Unlike quantitative researchers, qualitative researchers do not randomly select participants; instead, they intentionally—or purposefully—select participants who can "inform an understanding of the research problem and central phenomenon in the study."[36] Miles and Huberman identified numerous purposeful sampling strategies used by qualitative researchers.[37] Creswell, however, observed a narrower range of purposeful sampling strategies employed by researchers working within the phenomenological tradition of qualitative inquiry. He noted that *criterion sampling*—where all of the participants meet the same selection criteria—is frequently used in phenomenological research and explained that "criterion sampling works well" in a phenomenological study "when all individuals studied represent people who have experienced the phenomenon" under investigation.[38]

We used criterion sampling to select the four teachers who participated in this phenomenological study. All four of our participants met the following criteria:

1. The participants were public school teachers who taught children with disabilities at schools located in geographically isolated, sparsely populated, and predominately Alaska Native communities in rural Alaska.
2. The participants were enrolled in a distance-delivered MEd in Special Education degree program at UAS.
3. The participants had taken three graduate-level research methods courses cotaught by an academic librarian and a special education content instructor (i.e., the coauthors of this study) and had received more than one hundred hours of distance-delivered library instruction as part of their program of study.

We recruited for the study with a few enthusiastic class announcements several weeks in a row and mentioned we would provide a $25 gift card from Amazon.com as a token of appreciation. Five of our graduate students volunteered to participate. At the time that they volunteered, all five were enrolled in EDSE 698 (Master's Thesis Project)—the very last course in their graduate program. It was late in the semester when these students volunteered, and all five had already completed their master's thesis projects, but we had not yet submitted their final grades, and they had not yet received their diplomas. We stressed the voluntary nature of their participation, and made it very clear—both verbally and in writing—that their participation (or their *lack* of participation) would in no way affect their final grade in EDSE 698 or their graduation from the MEd in Special Education program. We e-mailed each participant an informed consent form, and they faxed or mailed back the signed forms before the interview date.

One of our five volunteers was a special education teacher who lived and worked in an urban community in south-central Alaska; she did not meet all of our selection criteria of geographic isolation, so we did not include her in our study. This urban special education teacher did, however, participate in a pilot study that we conducted to test the location, the equipment (e.g., telephone and recording system), and our interview questions. After we conducted the pilot study, we adjusted some of our interview questions, and the main study took place several weeks later.

Bracketing

Creswell described several approaches taken by phenomenological researchers; investigators use a technique called "bracketing" where they "set aside their experiences, as much as possible, to take a fresh perspective toward the phenomenon under examination."[39] Before we began collecting data for *this* study, the authors of this chapter analyzed thirty-nine journal articles and book chapters that examined issues related to the preparation of information literate teachers in the United States, Australia, Canada, New Zealand, Taiwan, and the United Kingdom.[40] Five themes emerged from our metasynthesis of

that body of literature: (a) information literacy skills, education, and democracy; (b) information literacy pedagogy; (c) collaboration; (d) technology and information literacy; and (e) information literacy standards. In order to "bracket out" our beliefs and experiences with the phenomenon of preparing information literate teachers, we engaged in a reflective writing activity, connecting each of these emergent themes to our respective roles as an academic librarian and special education content instructor. In a previously published phenomenological self-study, we explored our beliefs about librarian and faculty collaborative instruction, librarian and faculty collaborative research, and distance-delivered teacher education.[41] We reviewed the themes that emerged from that previously published self-study—*before* embarking on *this* study—to further "bracket out" our beliefs about and experiences with issues related to the delivery of information literacy instruction in a distance-delivered teacher education context.

Data Collection

We conducted semistructured telephone interviews with each of the four participants who met our previously stated selection criteria. The interviews were scheduled near the end of the semester—in the evening—to accommodate the teachers' work schedules. Each participant dialed into an audio-conference system, where the interviewers (i.e., the coauthors of this study) were waiting on the line. We began each interview with warm greetings and informal conversation in an attempt to help the participants feel comfortable and at ease; it should be noted, however, that we had already established good rapport with our four participants, since each participant had taken three graduate courses that we cotaught as part of their degree program; additionally, we both had extensive interaction with our participants throughout their programs of study in our respective roles as academic librarian and special education academic advisor.

Before we began each interview, we verified that the participants had read and understood the informed consent document and that they had returned the signed forms. The interview protocol began with us asking the participants if they had any questions before we began. The academic librarian (i.e., the primary investigator for this study) asked the participants questions from the previously developed interview protocol (see appendix), while the special education content instructor (i.e., the coauthor of this chapter) asked follow-up and clarification questions when appropriate. The tone of the interviews was informal and conversational. Each interview lasted approximately forty-five minutes.

We used the audioconference equipment to record each interview, and we each took independent field notes while conducting the interviews. Immediately after each interview, we discussed our respective notes, compared our initial observations, reflected on the interview—and on each other's observations and interpretations—and then wrote further notes based on our comparisons and reflections; hence, the process of conducting the interviews—and of recording and interpreting the data—was reflective, collaborative, and interdisciplinary (i.e., guided and informed by the shared perspectives of a librarian and a special educator). Independently, we revisited the recorded audioconferences and continued to expand upon our initial notes, writing down (verbatim) statements from the participants and partially (i.e., selectively) transcribing each interview.

Data Analysis

The Stevick-Colaizzi-Keen method is a highly reductive method of data analysis frequently used by researchers working within the phenomenological tradition of qualitative inquiry to systematically distill essential concepts, issues, and themes from text.[42] We used a modified version of the Stevick-Colaizzi-Keen method previously employed by Brown and Duke, Duke and Ward, and McCarthy and Duke[43] to analyze the data gathered through the interview process. We first identified "significant statements" from our respective field notes and transcripts. For the purpose of this study, we defined "significant statements" as those statements that addressed the role that information literacy plays in the lives of our

participants. We then developed a list of nonrepetitive, nonoverlapping (verbatim) significant statements with (nonverbatim) "formulated meanings." These "formulated meanings" represented our interpretation of each participant's (verbatim) significant statements. Finally, we grouped the formulated meanings into "theme clusters" and developed "emergent themes." These "emergent themes" represent the essence of our participants' experience with information literacy and distance-delivered library services (including distance-delivered library instruction).

Results

Four broad themes emerged from our analysis of the interviews that we conducted with the four rural special education teachers who participated in this study. These four emergent themes were (a) development as a learner and researcher, thinking about (and interacting with) information in a new way; (b) application of information literacy skills and concepts; (c) distance-delivered information literacy instruction; and (d) information literacy in rural P–12 contexts.

Theme 1: Development as a Learner and Researcher, Thinking about (and Interacting with) Information in a New Way

Participants discussed what they liked and found "handy" about library services offered at a distance. One of the teachers remarked: "I really like the interlibrary loan—I thought that was great. The library does all the work for you." She continued: "I was thinking of how I would use this [ILL services] after this class." Participants also identified the new searching strategies they learned. One teacher described the importance of strategically choosing search terms and carefully "picking out the keywords [to find] what I'm really looking for." She explained:

> When looking for some of those other articles, adding a word here and there brought up an entirely different list of articles, and some were totally off

track—not even in the ballpark of what I was looking for—so it made me realize that word choice and how you go about searching for what you are looking for is very important.

Another participant concurred: "I still have to work on it, but finding the right phrases—the subject descriptors and keywords—knowing how to do that . . . is important." Still another explained: "Before I learned to refine the searches, my searches were too broad. I would get frustrated and quit." The participants also discussed the importance of developing selection criteria. One teacher explained that "going in without selection criteria, you'd never get anywhere . . . . [that] would get you nowhere. I totally understand why you would want to focus from the beginning because there is a lot out there." Other participants also viewed the development of selection criteria as essential to systematic, strategic database searching, including one teacher who discussed the importance of "knowing what is peer-reviewed." Another skill that the teachers identified was "how to use AND/OR."

The participants discussed their new skill sets with a sophisticated understanding of the search process, and they described their development as learners. One teacher observed: "I had never done anything more than a quick EBSCO search, and it wasn't anything really in depth." Another noted: "I never thought about doing it [i.e., database research] that way, keeping a journal and daily note taking. That is a pretty handy . . . [research] skill to have." This same participant added: "I came a long ways. Prior to these research classes, I wasn't using the library and I wouldn't have been very successful at it." Other participants described their previous experience as undergraduate students using physical libraries. One such teacher noted: "Before, I got frustrated searching through library hard copies. I was not refining it [the search process], and what I wanted got lost in the jumble." Another teacher, who had conducted library research as an undergraduate student, felt that her graduate program had strengthened her information literacy skills and deepened her understanding of research concepts. She explained:

I think I was reacquainted with the whole secondary research business. I had a biology major originally, and . . . I was in the library not really knowing what I was doing . . . this time, I actually felt like I knew what I was doing, having you walk us through it.

Participants also expressed a deeper, more contextual knowledge of their field of study and a more sophisticated appreciation for the information they were tapping into. In the words of one participant: "It was info I had never looked at before," and these sources were "more in depth and research-based than anything I had gotten my hands on up until that point . . . so it was like waving a carrot in front of a rabbit . . . it's like 'Okay, that's how you do this.'" Supporting the idea of deeper understanding, one participant referred to being able to "get beneath the surface" and "get more information." She continued: "[There is] a lot of information to navigate through . . . using Boolean searches help[s] me sift through it to get a handle on all the info. . . . I can find what I need when I limit it." Another teacher concurred: "Boolean searches can do it. Having [advanced search] skills helps." Still another noted: "I hate using the Internet [as opposed to the databases] . . . a real waste of time . . . so many dead ends." These teachers, as a result of the library research embedded into their graduate coursework, began to think about information—and the process of retrieving and evaluating and synthesizing information—in a new (more systematic and strategic) way, and as they interacted with information in a more systematic and strategic manner, they developed greater confidence in themselves and in their teaching and researching abilities. One participant noted: "The [research] skills make you feel confident in what you learn." Another teacher explained: "Having written that paper [a metasynthesis of the literature on a special education topic], I feel very confident, and I feel I'm well backed up in what I've learned."

The participants came to see themselves as researchers—or as teacher-researchers (i.e., teachers whose practice is guided and informed by the research process). One such teacher observed: "I feel empowered to educate myself" and to use the "empirical and theoretical literature" to make instructional and curricular decisions that benefit her students. Another realized that she had "only used textbooks before" to gather information for her teaching, "not scholarly articles." The participants also valued their ability to access "unfiltered" data. One such teacher explained: "I really liked . . . to find data on my own," while another noted:

A lot of information that's available to us is kind of through somebody else's lens, [and] if you really get down and dirty—and do these searches—you are seeing the whole gamut of information out there, and what's worked and not worked, and [with] what populations.

In summary, the participants developed the knowledge and skills needed to retrieve, evaluate, and synthesize information related to their work as rural special educators, and they learned to interact with this information systematically and strategically. They valued and appreciated their new information literacy skills, and they discussed these skills with a sophisticated understanding of the research process. They developed greater confidence in themselves, as teachers and as learners. They came to view themselves as competent researchers who had learned how to learn. They felt empowered.

Theme 2: Application of Information Literacy and Research Skills

The rural special education teachers who participated in this study used the information literacy and research skills that they acquired through their graduate program to strengthen the quality of the instructional services that they offered their P–12 students with disabilities. A special education teacher who worked with a child with fetal alcohol spectrum disorder (FASD) conducted Boolean searches to locate articles that described effective instructional strategies for students with FASD; she then used these strategies in her own classroom to support the learning of

her student. She observed: "It was nice to have that tool, so now—if I have another student [with FASD] coming in, I'll know a more efficient and effective way . . . to find that information." She continued: "Having walked through this process" of searching the databases has "given me the strategies to learn and help my students." She noted: "I am now able to access" needed information and added: "The practicality of it all was huge. I am using these strategies to help students." This same teacher prized her ability to locate, recognize, and evaluate empirical studies and to summarize and synthesize the findings of such studies; she noted that this particular set of information literacy skills has "helped me to implement the IDEA [Individuals with Disabilities Education Improvement Act of 2004] mandate that teachers use research-based" instructional strategies in their work with students with exceptional learning needs. She explained: "Everything has to be research-based. Your curriculums . . . if they are not already district-mandated, you have to prove they are research-based." She noted that administrators in her school district are

really looking closely at what teachers are using in their classrooms. They're clamping down on teachers because they're trying to get accurate data on whether certain programs are working with the populations in our district. It's an ongoing struggle because everyone tries to throw in things they think might work, or they just use programs they're already comfortable with . . . but now, they must prove that what they're doing is research-based.

She added: "I feel comfortable finding research-based" instructional programs and curricular resources "now that I have these skills under my belt, whereas, before [I took these courses], it wouldn't have been a clear process. Now I think I can tackle it more effectively."

Another participant, an Athabascan teacher who worked in a predominately Tlingit community in southeast Alaska, used the information literacy skills that she learned in her graduate program to locate culturally appropriate and historically accurate curricular resources for her Tlingit students. She valued her ability to access educational research conducted by American Indian and Alaska Native scholars and said that locating this particular body of literature was like discovering "a whole new hemisphere" of knowledge. She described this body of research as "credible," and noted: "It's important that you trust the information that you are receiving." This same teacher conducted Boolean searches to locate articles on the learning styles of American Indian and Alaska Native children and evaluated each article to ensure that it accurately represented the values, beliefs, and histories of American Indian and Alaska Native peoples. She used this information to develop a series of culturally responsive lesson plans based on Alaska Native traditions. She then searched a number of databases that index articles related to the field of special education, located information on instructional strategies that have proven to be effective with young children with a wide range of exceptional learning needs, and used this information to make adaptations to each one of her lesson plans so that students with disabilities in her combined second/third grade classroom could actively participate in the lessons in a meaningful way.

One of the participants, who identified herself as a teacher with a disability, taught elementary school students with and without disabilities in a predominately Yup'ik Eskimo village in western Alaska. She, too, used the information literacy skills that she learned in her graduate program to access a body of literature that empowered and inspired her. This teacher reviewed numerous articles that explored the lives and experiences of other teachers with disabilities; she concluded that teachers with disabilities act as valuable and realistic role models for all students and bring unique qualities to the classroom, including a passion for inclusive education and creative methods of instruction. She noted: "Recognizing my own experiences in the [disability studies] literature validates my lived experience" as a special education teacher and an individual with a disability. She paraphrased the disability rights activist Stephen Brown when she noted that this particular body of literature was instrumental in helping her make the "journey from disability shame to disability pride."

She hopes to empower her students with exceptional learning needs to make this same "journey to disability pride" by establishing a "positive disability culture in my classroom"—i.e., a classroom culture informed by the literature, art, life stories, and other contributions of people with disabilities. She added: "I want to encourage my students to seek out research that validates their life experiences."

Another one of the participants, a special education teacher who provides life skills instruction to high school students with cognitive impairments in a small Inupiaq Eskimo village in northern Alaska, valued the reflective nature of the qualitative research methods she learned in her graduate courses. She observed: "I was amazed by the results of what I could gather from being reflective. I stop and think, 'Whoa, you sure can get a lot out of that.'" This same teacher taught her own high school students with cognitive impairments to use search engines to locate electronic information resources on traditional Inupiaq subsistence activities (e.g., hunting, fishing, the gathering of medicinal plants) and to collect primary data on these same subsistence activities by conducting interviews with members of their community. She noted: "Being able to do a little research on your own . . . is effective in whatever we do . . . we can all be little scientists I guess."

In summary, the rural special education teachers used the information literacy and research skills that they acquired through their graduate program to strengthen the instructional services that they offered their own P–12 students with disabilities. They conducted Boolean searches to locate articles on the characteristics of students with particular disabilities, effective instructional and behavioral programs, culturally responsive curricular materials, the learning styles of American Indian and Alaska Native students, and Alaska Native cultural traditions—and they used these information resources to guide and inform their instructional practice. The participants felt better prepared to meet IDEA 2004 requirements that special educators use research-based instructional strategies in their work with students with disabilities because they now had the skills to locate, critically evaluate, and effectively use educational research. Several participants incorporated information literacy concepts and research skills into their own classroom teaching by developing inquiry-based learning activities based on real-world information resources—e.g., they taught their P–12 students to use search engines to locate electronic information relevant to their communities and to gather primary data by conducting interviews with community members.

Theme 3: Distance-delivered Information Literacy Instruction

The four special education teachers who participated in this study lived and worked in geographically isolated Alaska. Campus-based learning was, therefore, unavailable to them, and on-site professional development opportunities were extremely limited. Distance-delivered higher education has its advantages and disadvantages, but—in the words of one participant—for teachers in rural Alaska, "it's the only game in town." Two of the four participants described some of the disadvantages of "meeting over the telephone" and "learning online." One of these teachers "missed the friendship and interpersonal connectedness of campus-based learning." She stated: "You don't really form close friendships" in a distance-delivered learning environment. Another teacher noted that her "inability to see my instructors and classmates, and the lack of nonverbal communication cues, was a challenge." However, the other two participants preferred the distance-delivered instructional format to the "face-to-face learning that usually takes place in a traditional college classroom." One of these teachers noted that "distance-delivered courses are more convenient and fit into my schedule better" than campus-based courses, while the other teacher explained: "I am an independently motivated, self-directed learner, so distance-delivered instruction adequately met my learning needs."

Attempting to master complex information literacy skills and research strategies via a distance-delivered instructional format can be quite challenging, but interactive Web-based technologies—and patient, responsive instructors—can make this task much less intimidating for students. In EDSE 692 (Secondary Research Methods) and EDSE 698 (Master's Thesis

Project), the authors of this study used Elluminate Live! an interactive Web conferencing system to teach our graduate students to conduct Boolean database searches. We offered each participant a series of fifteen-minute individualized instructional sessions and used Elluminate Live! to help them construct search strategies; each participant received one individualized tutorial session per database. All four of the teachers felt that using interactive Web conferencing technology in an individualized tutorial format was a highly effective way to learn to conduct systematic and reproducible advanced searches of the various databases. One participant observed:

> being able to walk us through—and then 'Click here'—and then I can see where you are clicking. And being able to explain why you are narrowing the search that way—that was the ideal way to learn. I can't imagine having to struggle through that [without using Elluminate Live!]. I know I wouldn't have been as effective without that technology.

Another teacher noted that the Web conferencing technology was "intimidating at first, but a lot easier than I thought it would be." This same teacher "liked the fifteen minute hands-on sessions . . . [using] Elluminate Live!"

In summary, the four special education teachers who participated in this study had no access to campus-based higher education. The distance-delivered instructional format of the courses allowed the participants to remain in their home communities while they pursued their graduate degrees. It can be quite challenging to learn complex information literacy skills and research strategies in a distance-delivered format, but interactive Web-based technologies and individualized tutorial sessions with the academic librarian and special education professor helped the participants develop strong library research skills.

Theme 4: Information Literacy Issues in Rural P–12 Contexts

Many special education teachers who live and work in rural Alaska experience isolation, burnout, high turnover rates, limited access to other professionals, and limited on-site professional development opportunities. One such responding teacher observed: "Teachers in remote and rural communities need to be able to access electronic information" to counteract isolation, to feel connected to other special educators, and to continue to develop professionally. Another participant noted: "As a teacher in a remote place, I need the Internet, e-mail, and interlibrary loan" services. This same rural teacher likes "electronic access to things" because it is "convenient."

When discussing how important information literacy skills are to rural teachers, one participant said she felt like "a pro." She added: "[Now], I feel empowered to educate myself," and "continuing to educate myself keeps me connected to the international [disability studies] literature" and "makes me excited to teach." She continued: "Being connected to something bigger than myself—like an international body of literature, or a community of scholars and learners—keeps me motivated to stay current in my practice." This same teacher explained: "Turnover is a huge problem in rural communities. I think teachers would be less likely to get burnt out and leave if they felt connected to something larger than themselves." Another rural participant observed that it is "easy to get bogged down by the village issues—by village politics. It's easy to burnout in the Bush [i.e., rural Alaska]." However, being information literate

> keeps me more informed. I'm able to stay informed without leaving the village. We are like an island, we are remote. I feel like I lose a vocabulary word every day out here [laughter]. But, I can be informed if I put in the effort [because] we all have computers.

One of the teachers said that her ability to conduct sophisticated Boolean searches in the education and social sciences databases "opened up a world of educational discourse on disability that I wouldn't otherwise be able to access in a remote, rural community." Another teacher noted the lack of on-site professional development opportunities available to her as a "teacher in Bush Alaska." She said the information literacy skills that she learned in her

graduate program helped her both "keep up with current research in [P–12] education," and "follow the [IDEA 2004] mandate" that "special education teachers use research-based [instructional] methods." She added: "Before, when I was using Google searches," instead of systematically searching specialized databases, "research-based [information] was unavailable to me." Still another participant used her newly acquired information literacy skills to locate research-based information resources about her students' particular exceptional learning conditions "on an as-needed basis"—a crucial skill for a woman who was the only special educator in her village. She said that her graduate program "made me more interested in learning about specific kids' learning disabilities," and gave her the skills—and the confidence—"to get . . . [information] I need when I need it." Other teachers located—and used—research-based information resources on educational issues in impoverished communities, research-based information resources on positive behavior supports for students with severe emotional and behavioral disorders, and research-based information resources on Alaska Native cultural traditions. One special educator, who teaches Yup'ik Eskimo children in western Alaska, noted that many P–12 textbooks exclude—or misrepresent—the contributions of American Indian and Alaska Native peoples. She wants to teach her Yup'ik students to critically evaluate their textbooks and other curricular materials. She stated: "I'm inspired now to teach [my] students to be their own filters of information rather than [allow] others to filter it for them."

Several participants noted that their school libraries had "very limited"—and often outdated—collections. One such teacher noted: "The library hasn't purchased any new materials in a long while." This same teacher intends to use her information literacy skills to obtain curricular materials that are presently unavailable in her school's "very limited" library collection.

In summary, on-site professional development opportunities are very limited for special educators in rural Alaska, and libraries in Alaska's geographically isolated communities have limited—and often outdated—resources; however, all schools have Internet access. Special educators who teach in rural Alaska must be able to access and critically evaluate a variety of electronic resources to keep up with current issues, trends, and research in the field of special education. The four special educators who participated in this study felt empowered to be lifelong learners; they now have the knowledge and skills to find, evaluate, and use electronic information on an "as needed" basis.

Discussion and Reflection

The authors have cotaught ED 626 (Classroom Research) every semester for the past five years and have offered information literacy instruction to hundreds of rural Alaskan teachers enrolled in this—and other—distance-delivered, graduate-level courses. However, we didn't begin to truly understand our rural teachers' lived experience with information literacy until we conducted in-depth, qualitative interviews with the rural special educators who participated in this study. After long hours of preparing the interview questions, conducting the interviews, and analyzing the data (i.e., the voices of four women who teach P–12 students with disabilities in rural Alaska communities), we began to have a greater understanding of our rural teachers' lived experience with information literacy.

Four major themes emerged from these interviews. The four rural special education teachers who participated in this study described their development as information literate teacher-researchers who learned to think about—and interact with—a wide variety of information resources in a new (and more systematic and strategic) way; they explained how they used the information literacy and research skills that they learned in EDSE 626 (Classroom Research), EDSE 692 (Secondary Research Methods), and EDSE 698 (Master's Thesis Project) to strengthen the instructional services that they offer to their own P–12 students with disabilities; they discussed the pros and cons of receiving information literacy instruction in a distance-delivered format; and they described a number of information literacy issues that profoundly

impact the lives of teachers who work in rural Alaska.

Our dialogue with our participants led us to consider what might be next for these four special educators and their P–12 students. Will these teachers continue to seek out and use the empirical and theoretical literature to develop culturally responsive, research-based instructional strategies for their students with exceptional learning needs? Will they continue to conduct primary and secondary research that both guides and informs their work as special educators and improves the lives of their students? Will they continue to teach information literacy and research skills to their own P–12 students? Three of the participants indicated that this was likely for them, but a fourth expressed some insecurity about her own information literacy and research skills—despite her excellent work in our courses.

The process also led the authors to consider some of the information literacy challenges unique to teachers who live and work in geographically isolated, rural communities with very limited library services—or, in some cases, no library service at all. Libraries in rural Alaskan villages are usually part of the local P–12 school; their library collections are often limited to school materials (e.g., trade books and series for classroom teaching), and some of these libraries haven't purchased new materials "in a long while." Very few of these rural communities have a professional librarian, and some villages lack libraries altogether. Three of our four participants lived in communities with very limited library services (which were offered through their schools), and one participant lived in a village without a library. As graduate students at the University of Alaska Southeast, all four of these teachers had access to the full array of distance-delivered library services offered through the William A. Egan Library (e.g., access to some forty-eight thousand electronic book titles; access to interlibrary loan services; access to one hundred electronic databases with approximately thirty-two thousand online journals and newspapers; and access to national and international information resources through databases such as WorldCat). But what happens to these teachers once they graduate? How will they continue to meet their professional development needs? How will they stay current with the latest research in the rapidly changing field of special education? How will they continue to access information resources that benefit their P–12 students?

We discussed several options with our four participants. All teachers in Alaska have access to SLED—the Statewide Library Education Doorway Digital Pipeline Databases.[44] The Digital Pipeline is a way for any Alaskan resident with an Internet connection to conduct database/journal research. Much of the content is available in full text—e.g., the ERIC and Professional Development Collection databases are offered through the EBSCOhost interface. But how will these teachers gather articles cited in these databases or in the references of a study they read if these items are not available in full text? We explained to our participants that one possibility would be for them to join the University of Alaska Southeast Alumni Association upon graduation; membership in the alumni association would allow them to continue receiving interlibrary loan services through the Egan Library (free of charge). Another option would be for them to continue using the Egan Library's reference services, which are offered via telephone, e-mail, and chat and are available to the general public. Still another option would be 800# ILL School Services, which is funded by a grant from the Alaska State Library and offers a toll-free interlibrary loan service by mail to small schools in rural communities; however, teachers in rural school districts do not always have the library services infrastructure necessary to access this service (e.g., loan requests must be made through a school librarian or school district media coordinator, and not all school districts employ such personnel).

In response to the needs and experiences we uncovered through this interview study, the authors have begun to enhance the classes we teach together in order to offer all future students enrolled in ED 626 (Classroom Research), EDSE 692 (Secondary Research Methods), and EDSE 698 (Master's Thesis Project) information on "what comes next" for their library research options after they have completed the MEd in Special Education program and graduated from the University of Alaska Southeast. The

academic librarian is currently in the process of contacting other librarians across the state of Alaska to gather information for rural teachers; it is her intention to make all library services available to teachers in rural Alaska known and understood in a more consistent fashion.

Limitations and Ethical Considerations

The ethical considerations for interviewing have been discussed in the literature,[45] and Kvale and Brinkmann note that "interviewers ought to reflect on the role of power in the production of interview knowledge."[46] In this study, did having two interviewers with one participant create a power asymmetry? In this case, we think the presence of both interviewers made for a more relaxed dynamic with the participants; both researchers had previously established relationships with the participants (e.g., we cotaught three graduate courses to the four participants, and we both served on each participant's master's thesis committee).

We both made every effort to put the participants at ease before—and during—the interviews. We stated numerous times that the participants were doing us a favor and that their participation in the study—or their lack of participation—would in no way impact their graduation from the MEd in Special Education program. The interviews were conducted *after* the participants had already submitted their approved master's thesis projects. We believe our participants liked us and trusted us; they appreciated our efforts on their behalf (as their course instructors, academic advisors, and master's thesis committee members), and they valued the information literacy and research skills that we taught them. We believe that they generously gave their time to us (by participating in the interviews) because we had generously given our time to them.

Another ethical question that often arises in qualitative interview-based research is how much the participants can (and should) participate in the verification and analysis of the data they provide. Many qualitative researchers conduct follow-up interviews with their participants—or submit transcribed interviews and drafts of the research manuscripts to the participants—so that the participants can verify the accuracy of the data. We did not share our field notes, transcripts, or draft versions of this manuscript with our participants (mainly due to time constraints), and both researchers consider the lack of participant verification to be a major limitation of this particular research study.

Brainstorming about Interviewing—Tips and Tools for Librarians

This chapter described a study of a unique population of students (i.e., special education teachers who live and work in rural Alaska) and their experiences with information literacy. As the outreach services librarian for our university, the principal investigator's aim was to improve distance education services for this particular group of students. Discussing the perspectives of our end users and then looking at the common themes of their experiences helped us to understand them better and to find ways of making systemic changes in the way we teach information literacy and provide library services. Other librarians with different focuses can also benefit from this process. Instruction librarians could interview students taught in their face-to-face courses in order to elicit more in-depth student attitudes about learning activities. Though more of a time commitment than open-ended surveys, interviews can draw forth more detailed, nuanced ideas that surveys cannot provide—because you can follow up when a participant says something intriguing—and the "here and now" discussion adds to the dynamics of exploring the topic. We referenced studies in the literature review that were mixed methods—some researchers use surveys to begin collecting their data and then follow up by conducting qualitative interviews with some or all of the respondents. Public services librarians could interview students (and other constituent groups) in order to get to the heart of what programming and workshops are desired or to determine people's perceptions of the library—the study could be an exploration of the perceptions of a particular user group. Liaison librarians could use the interview process to explore faculty member attitudes and ideas about large-scale program development. This could be implemented at a school where perhaps there are competing ideas about the best way to implement critical thinking and information literacy instruction throughout a program.

One way to think through the methods and design your study will use is to peruse other interview studies in the library literature as well as from other disciplines. Give yourself plenty of time to do it right—at least one year from the time you start to the time you complete the final version of your manuscript (if you plan to publish). The authors of this chapter found the process of getting our university's Institutional Review Board (IRB) committee to "bless" our study took far too long (this committee is made up of other very busy faculty), and this could have been problematic for us if they had found problems with our proposal. The study this chapter describes qualified for "expedited" review under our university's IRB rules.

It is widely advised to do a pilot test run of the interview questions (to make sure they sound right when you say them out loud—and also to make sure that the participant gives an answer that really does address your question). Sometimes, just one jargon-laden question can trip up the entire interview process. Also, pilot test the location and equipment you will be using, making sure your recording equipment works properly—it would be very disappointing to lose that data.[47] We tested our audioconference system and recording capability before the main interviews. After the interviews, we revisited the recordings again and again to get to the exact quotes our participants used. It would have been quite impossible to write up the themes without having that data to return to in the weeks after we actually conducted the interviews.

Be prepared to ask those clarifying questions that may not make it to your script, and be prepared for times when participants answer several questions with one answer. A carefully constructed interview protocol, as well as a pilot testing of your instrument, may mitigate unforeseen problems; nevertheless, we found ourselves saying: "You may have already partly addressed this, but 'How did these skills help you?'"

In conclusion, we found the interview to be an effective tool to have a discussion with our participants about the library instruction services that we provided. Why not ask interview questions in a semi-structured, deep way through a back-and-forth discussion? The meaning of our services from our users' perspective is intriguing and necessary for us to hear in order to stay relevant to those we claim to serve.

Notes

1. American Library Association Presidential Committee on Information Literacy, *Final Report* (Chicago: American Library Association, 1989), http://www.ala.org/ala/mgrps/divs/acrl/publications/whitepapers/presidential.cfm; Association of College and Research Libraries, *A Progress Report on Information Literacy: An Update on the American Library Association Presidential Committee on Information Literacy: Final Report* (Chicago: ACRL, 1998), http://www.ala.org/ala/mgrps/divs/acrl/publications/whitepapers/progressreport.cfm; Thomas Duke and Jennifer Ward, "Preparing Information Literate Teachers: A Metasynthesis," *Library & Information Science Research* 31, no. 4 (Dec. 2009): 247–56; Corey M. Johnson and Lorena O'English, "Information Literacy in Pre-service Teacher Education: An Annotated Bibliography," *Behavioral & Social Sciences Librarian* 22, no. 1 (2003): 129–39; National Council for Accreditation of Teacher Education, *Professional Standards for the Accreditation of Schools, Colleges, and Departments of Education* (Washington, DC: NCATE, 2002); Nancy O'Hanlon, "Up the Down Staircase: Establishing Library Instruction Programs for Teachers," *RQ* 27, no. 4 (1988): 528–34.

2. Marlene Asselin and Ray Doiron, "Whither They Go: An Analysis of the Inclusion of School Library Programs and Services in the Preparation of Pre-service Teachers in Canadian Universities," *Behavioral & Social Sciences Librarian* 22, no. 1 (2003): 19–32; Jennifer L. Branch, "Teaching, Learning and Information Literacy: Developing an Understanding of Pre-service Teachers' Knowledge," *Behavioral & Social Sciences Librarian* 22, no. 1 (2003): 33–46; Duke and Ward, "Preparing Information Literate Teachers"; Karen Dutt-Doner, Susan M. Allen, and Daniel Corcoran, "Transforming Student Learning by Preparing the Next Generation of Teachers for Type II Technology Integration," *Computers in the Schools* 22, no. 3 (2005), 63–75.

3. Scott Walter, "Librarians as Teachers: A Qualitative Inquiry into Professional Identity," *College & Research Libraries* 69, no. 1, (2008): 54.

4. John W. Creswell, *Qualitative Inquiry & Research Design: Choosing among Five Approaches.* (Thousand Oaks, CA: Sage, 2007).

5. Walter, "Librarians as Teachers," 65.

6. Kvale and Brinkmann, *Interviews:* 26.

7. Marlene Asselin, Angel Kymes, and Virginia Lam, "A Critical Examination of Information Literacy Instruction during a Grade 9 Research Project," *Simile* 7, no. 4 (Nov. 2007): 1–18; Kai Wah Samuel Chu, "Inquiry Project-based Learning with a Partnership of Three Types of Teachers and the School Librarian," *Journal of the American Society for Information Science and Technology* 60, no. 8 (2009): 1671–86; Samuel Kai-Wah Chu and Nancy Law, "The Development of Information Search Expertise of Research Students," *Journal of Librarianship and Information Science* 40, no. 3 (Jan. 1, 2008): 165–77; Ann Craig and Sheila Corrall, "Making a Difference? Measuring the Impact of an Information Literacy Programme for Pre-registration Nursing Students in the UK," *Health Information & Libraries Journal* 24, no. 2 (June 2007): 118–27; Mark Hepworth and Marian Smith, "Workplace Information Literacy for Administrative Staff in Higher Education," *Australian Library Journal* 57, no. 3 (Aug. 2008): 212–36; Michelle Honey, Nicola North, and Cathy Gunn, "Improving Library Services for Graduate Nurse Students in New Zealand," *Health Information & Libraries Journal* 23, no. 2 (June 2006): 102–9; Heidi Julien and Stuart Boon, "Assessing Instructional Outcomes in Canadian Academic Libraries," *Library & Information Science Research* 26, no. 2 (2004): 121–39; Heidi Julien and Cameron Hoffman, "Information Literacy Training in Canada's Public Libraries," *The Library Quarterly* 78, no. 1 (Jan. 2008): 19–41; Marianne McTavish, "'I Get My Facts from the Internet': A Case Study of the Teaching and Learning of Information Literacy in In-school and Out-of-school Contexts," *Journal of Early Childhood Literacy* 9, no. 1 (April 2009):

3–28; Dorothy Williams and Louisa Coles, "Evidence-based Practice in Teaching: An Information Perspective," *Journal of Documentation* 63, no. 6 (Dec. 2007): 812–35; Dorothy Williams and Louisa Coles, "Teachers' Approaches to Finding and Using Research Evidence: An Information Literacy Perspective," *Educational Research* 49, no. 2 (June 2007): 185–206.

8. Christine Bruce, *The Seven Faces of Information Literacy* (Adelaide, SA, Australia: Auslib Press, 1997): 94.

9. Asselin and Doiron, "Whither They Go"; Nigel Ford and Yazdan Mansourian, "The Invisible Web: An Empirical Study of 'Cognitive Invisibility'" *Journal of Documentation* 62, no. 5 (Oct. 2006): 584–96; Hamid R. Jamali and David Nicholas, "E-print Depositing Behavior of Physicists and Astronomers: An Intradisciplinary Study," *Journal of Academic Librarianship* 35, no. 2 (March 2009): 117–25. Yazdan Mansourian and Nigel Ford, "Search Persistence and Failure on the Web: A 'Bounded Rationality' and 'Satisficing' Analysis," *Journal of Documentation* 63, no. 5 (Oct. 2007): 681; Grace L. Veach, "Teaching Information Literacy to Faculty: An Experiment," *College & Undergraduate Libraries* 16, no. 1 (Jan. 2009): 58–70.

10. Walter, "Librarians as Teachers."

11. Heidi Julien and Jen Pecoskie, "Librarians' Experiences of the Teaching Role: Grounded in Campus Relationships," *Library & Information Science Research* 31, no. 3 (Sept. 2009): 149–54.

12. Rebecca Adler, "The Librarian in the Trench: The Workaday Impact of Information Literacy," *portal: Libraries & the Academy* 3, no. 3 (July 2003): 447–58; Barry W Cull, "Voices in the Wilderness: A Report on Academic Information Literacy Instruction in Atlantic Canada," *Canadian Journal of Information & Library Sciences* 29, no. 1 (March 2005): 1–26; Andrew Hickey, "Cataloguing Men: Charting the Male Librarian's Experience through the Perceptions and Positions of Men in Libraries," *Journal of Academic Librarianship* 32, no. 3 (May 1, 2006): 286–95; Sharon K. Epps, "African American Women Leaders in Academic Research Libraries," *portal: Libraries and the Academy* 8, no. 3 (July 1, 2008): 255–72; Alesia Zuccala, Charles Oppenheim, and Rajveen Dhiensa, "Managing and Evaluating Digital Repositories," *Information Research: An International Electronic Journal* 13, no. 1 (March 1, 2008), http://informationr.net/ir/13-1/paper333.html.

13. Elizabeth Sadler and Lisa M. Given, "Affordance Theory: A Framework for Graduate Students' Information Behavior," abstract, *Journal of Documentation* 63, no. 1 (Jan. 2007): 115.

14. Melissa Gross and Don Latham, "Undergraduate Perceptions of Information Literacy: Defining, Attaining, and Self-Assessing Skills," *College & Research Libraries* 70, no. 4 (2009), 346.

15. Nadia Caidi and Susan MacDonald, "Information Practices of Canadian Muslims Post 9/11," *Government Information Quarterly* 25, no. 3 (July 2008): 348–78.

16. Liz McDowell, "Electronic Information Resources in Undergraduate Education: An Exploratory Study of Opportunities for Student Learning and Independence," *British Journal of Educational Technology* 33, no. 3 (June 2002): 258; Paul F. Marty, "Finding the Skills for Tomorrow: Information Literacy and Museum Information Professionals," *Museum Management and Curatorship* 21, no. 4 (Dec. 2006): 317–35; Janet Murray, "The Implications of Inclusive Schooling for School Libraries," *International Journal of Disability, Development & Education* 49, no. 3 (Sept. 2002): 301–22; Don Quick and Timothy Gray Davies, "Community College Faculty Development: Bringing Technology into Instruction," *Community College Journal of Research & Practice* 23, no. 7 (Oct. 1999): 641–53; Adrian Kok, "Enhancing Information Literacy in an Interdisciplinary Collaboration," *Journal of Technology in Human Services* 24, no. 2 (2006): 83–103.

17. Thomas Duke and Jennifer Brown, "Teacher as Researcher: Librarian and Faculty Collaboration in Teaching the Literature Review in a Distance-delivered Teacher Education Program," in *Teaching Information Literacy Skills to Social Sciences Students and Practitioners: A Casebook of Applications*, ed. D. Cook and N. Cooper (Chicago: Association of College and Research Libraries, 2006), 131–45; Thomas Duke, Jennifer Ward, and Jill Burkert, "Preparing Critically Conscious, Information Literate Special Educators for Alaska's Schools," in *Critical Library Instruction: Theories and Methods,* ed. M. Accardi, E., Drabinski, and A. Kumbier (Duluth, MN: Library Juice Press, 2010), 115-131; Catherine Manathunga, "Designing Online Learning Modules: An Australian Example in Teacher Education." *International Journal of Instructional Media* 29, no. 2 (2002): 185–95.

18. Jennifer D. Brown and Thomas S. Duke, "Librarian and Faculty Collaborative Instruction: A Phenomenological Self-study," *Research Strategies* 20, no. 3 (2005): 171–90.

19. University of Alaska Southeast Catalog, http://www.uas.alaska.edu/catalog/documents/09-10/catalog.pdf.

20. University of Alaska Fairbanks, Hubert Wenger Eskimo Database, http://www.wengereskimodb.uaf.edu; University of Alaska Fairbanks, Alaska Native Knowledge Network, http://www.ankn.uaf.edu; Alaska's Digital Archives, http://vilda.alaska.edu; University of Alaska Fairbanks Rasmuson and Biosciences Libraries, Alaska and Polar Periodical Index, http://goldmine.uaf.edu/aprindex.

21. Duke, Ward, and Burkert, "Preparing Critically Conscious Special Educators."

22. Ibid., 118.

23. Ibid., 118–119.

24. Creswell, *Qualitative Inquiry & Research Design*, 20.

25. Ibid., 131.

26. Clark E. Moustakas, *Phenomenological Research Methods* (Thousand Oaks, CA: Sage, 1994).

27. Jabber F. Gubrium and James A. Holstein, ed. *Handbook of Interview Research: Context & Method* (Thousand Oaks, CA: Sage, 2001), 57.

28. Ibid.

29. Kvale and Brinkmann, *Interviews*, 3.

30. Ibid.

31. Ibid.

32. Readers interested in learning about other forms of interviews beyond the scope of this chapter are encouraged to read *Handbook of Interview Research*, an edited collection by Gubrium and Holstein (see note 27), which includes chapters on in-depth interviewing, the life story interview, survey interviewing, focus group interviewing, postmodern trends in interviewing, and journalistic interviewing, as well as many other forms of interviews.

33. Kvale and Brinkmann (*Interviews*, 134–36) outlined and defined different types of interview questions, including (a) introductory questions, (b) follow-up questions, (c) probing questions, (d) specifying questions, (e) direct questions, (f) indirect questions, (g) structuring questions, (h) silence, and (i) interpreting questions and recommend that "the interviewer's questions . . . be brief and simple."

34. Valerie J. Janesick (*"Stretching" Exercises for Qualitative Researchers*, 2nd ed. [Thousand Oaks, CA: Sage, 2004], 72–73) outlined different types of interview questions and provided examples of each; she described (a) basic descriptive questions, (b) follow-up questions, (c) experience/example questions, (d) simple clarification questions, (e) structural/paradigmatic questions, and (f) comparison/contrast questions; Creswell (*Qualitative Inquiry & Research Design*, 132–34) provides advice on the development of the interview protocol and practical guidance in the conduct of the interview.

35. Other sources of inspiration instrumental to the development of our interview questions—and to the broader design and implementation of this phenomenological study—included Walter's ("Librarians as Teachers") inquiry into the professional identity of instructional librarians; Caidi and MacDonald's ("Information Practices of Canadian Muslims") study of Canadian Muslims' information practices; and Patricia Ann Lather and Chris Smithies's (*Troubling the Angels: Women Living with HIV/AIDS* [Boulder, CO: Westview Press, 1997]) beautiful, powerful, and haunting study of women living with HIV/AIDS.

36. Creswell, *Qualitative Inquiry & Research Design*, 125.

37. Matthew B. Miles and A. Michael Huberman, *Qualitative Data Analysis: A Sourcebook of New Methods*, 2nd ed. (Thousand Oaks, CA, Sage, 1994), 28.

38. Creswell, *Qualitative Inquiry & Research Design*, 128.

39. Creswell, *Qualitative Inquiry & Research Design*, 59-60.

40. Duke and Ward, "Preparing Information Literate Teachers."

41. Brown and Duke, "Librarian and Faculty Collaborative Instruction."

42. Creswell, *Qualitative Inquiry and Research Design*.

43. Brown and Duke, "Librarian and Faculty Collaborative Instruction"; Duke and Ward, "Preparing Information Literate Teachers"; Kathrin McCarthy and Thomas Duke, "The Observation, Documentation, and Shared Reflection Process: Preparing Early Childhood Educators to Teach in Alaska Native Communities," *Journal of Early Childhood Teacher Education* 28, no. 2 (2007): 97–113.

44. Alaska Library Network, SLED Digital Pipeline Databases, http://sled.alaska.edu/databases.

45. Gubrium and Holstein, *Handbook of Interview Research*.

46. Kvale and Brinkmann, *Interviews*, 34.

47. This happened to the special education content instructor when he was conducting an interview for another study. His recording equipment wasn't working properly, and he lost several hours' worth of data. Fortunately, his participant agreed to redo the interview several weeks later.

APPENDIX
Interview Protocol

Hello, _____ good evening. How are you? Thanks for joining us. We have one pre-question, and about 10 questions to ask you tonight.

Pre-Question 1: Do you have any questions about the study, your role, or anything at all before we get started? (Discuss informed consent).

Q: What are some of the skills you learned in our class?

Q: (follow up) What do these skills mean? (what are their meanings to you)?

Q: How did these skills help you to navigate the vast amount of information and resources out there?

Q: What was it like for you learning these skills in a distance delivered format?

Q: (follow up) How did having the class delivered via audioconference and Elluminate impact your learning?

Q: Do you find you are using any of these skills currently?

   In your teaching?

   In your personal life?

Q: (If appropriate) Can you elaborate (provide a specific example?)

Q: Are there skills that you are currently passing on to your students? (How about to your own children?)

Q: What is your opinion about the importance of these skills to you as a teacher in a remote place?

Q: What is your opinion about the importance of these skills to your students living in a remote place?

Q: Are there any questions we have not asked that you would like to elaborate on?

Thank you so much for your time and your valued perspective!

Observing Relationship Building in the Library Instruction Classroom: Peer Observation and Consultation

Carolyn L. Cook and Karla M. Schmit

"The world has changed for librarians and students alike. Few service situations allow for the development of an interpersonal relationship. . . ."[1]

Abstract. Librarians hope that students will internalize information-seeking strategies that will serve them throughout their career as students and their experiences as lifelong learners. This study examines the notion that becoming a part of students' community is as important to their information literacy as is teaching them facts and skills. This study's goal was to discover strategies that use instructional time both to teach and to establish a connection with students. The researchers (a librarian and an education faculty colleague) used data from observation field notes, reflective journal entries, and e-mail communications between students and the librarian as a basis for coding and analysis. This peer observation study resulted in clarifying for the librarian that her teaching practices were indeed assisting her to build community with her students.

Introduction

A graduate student once told Karla that at the beginning of her doctoral work she was so overwhelmed by her academic coursework, department expectations, and the rigor of conducting research that she was almost ready to drop out of her program. Her confidence in her abilities was very fragile. She told Karla that an academic librarian had turned those despondent feelings around for her. The librarian helped her understand the library's resources and how to find them, assisted her in understanding the research process, and made her feel that no question

was unintelligent and that she was not selfishly taking up the librarian's valuable time. The graduate student said that a librarian provided the bridge of support she needed to help her become independent in her research pursuits and to see that she could indeed complete a graduate degree. Karla has always wanted to be that kind of librarian—one who makes those connections, and as a result, makes a difference in the academic lives of students.

According to Foster, academic librarians have the opportunity to influence significantly the information-seeking behavior of university students by providing support as well as subject expertise as students deal with professors, course assignments, information resources, and the management and understanding of new knowledge.[2] Many times, library instruction, while often face-to-face, is a one-shot session with students. Riehle and Witt state that the one-shot library sessions often focus on helping students find the resources they need for a specific assignment.[3] At other times, students need library basics, such as the location of resources and information about library services. Hopefully, students leave the instruction session with a greater understanding of the resources as well as enough information to start and complete a course assignment. Librarians also hope that students will internalize information-seeking strategies that will serve them throughout their career as students and their experiences as lifelong learners. Can that actually happen as the result of a one-time library instruction session? It is very difficult to impart essential information literacy skills that are evaluative, informative, and ethical in a one-time meeting.[4] Students often leave feeling overwhelmed and confused by the services offered by the library. Or they leave with little understanding of how the library and librarians can provide information, instruction, and support for their long-term academic pursuits.

As an academic librarian, Karla is always searching for ways to make lasting connections with the students whom she encounters. She wants to convey to them that the library can offer considerable support as they pursue their degrees. Riehle and Witt state that librarians need to actively seek out students to offer research assistance.[5] The role of the librarian must be transformed from one of passivity to one of active engagement with students.

As a new librarian at Penn State, Karla observed her mentor conduct a library instruction session. The one statement in particular that her mentor made had a significant impact on Karla: she wanted the students to think of her as their *personal librarian*[6] during their studies. Librarians need not only to reach out to a variety of groups (e.g., freshmen, international students, campus organizations, etc.) but also to develop welcoming, collaborative environments and to use engaging instructional pedagogies. One of Karla's goals as a library instructor is to use instruc-

tional time to both teach and establish a connection with the students. Asking education majors to think of her as their personal education librarian during their academic career humanizes the role of the librarian as a person of support. By doing so, her hope is that students will feel comfortable contacting her later when they have questions about an assignment, information resources, or library services. In this view, the librarian has an opportunity to take on a long-term role rather than being just the one-shot library instructor.

In considering Karla's mission to connect with undergraduate and graduate students in significant personal ways, she decided to have her library teaching behaviors observed. Searching for ways to improve interpersonal relationships with students could occur only if Karla had a clear idea of which of her teaching practices supported building personal connections with students. She wanted to know specifically what teaching patterns she had that either invited students to seek librarian support or caused them to turn away from the library as a supportive entity. Karla asked her colleague and friend, Carolyn, to join her in a collaborative research assessment of Karla's library instruction behavior through peer observation.

Peer observation provides information about classroom events, teaching strategies, language patterns, and even mannerisms that the instructor may not even be aware of. By asking a peer to observe her interactions during teaching, Karla created an opportunity to build on a relationship with a colleague. In turn, this relationship allowed the opportunity to identify areas that need improvement while affirming those strategies that Karla used that connect with students. In short, classroom observation provides the opportunity to gain new perspectives and to generate ideas for better teaching.

Karla and Carolyn were uniquely situated for using peer observation to improve professional teaching and learning relationships. They had both taught previously in the same university laboratory school, where university students, primarily pre-service teachers, observed them teaching on a daily basis. Weekly, they each had over fifty college students observe them teach and interact with their elementary school students. Karla and Carolyn also observed pre-service teachers and provided advice and feedback for the betterment of their interns' instruction. In a setting such as a laboratory school, one quickly becomes accustomed to observation and actually forgets that there are additional people observing the learning situation. They had developed a trusting relationship through their professional and personal endeavors; because of these experiences, they have honest reflective discussions about their teaching. Carolyn is currently an assistant professor at another university and observes pre-service teachers as a part of her faculty load.

This chapter provides an overview of the peer observation process and explains the methodology and steps taken to conduct peer observation. To illustrate the process, samples of the data collected from Carolyn's observation of Karla's instruction, including coding and analyzing, are discussed. We then reflect upon the process from each of our perspectives. The chapter concludes with a summary and implications for how others can use peer observation in library instruction.

Literature Review

There has been a long history of peer observation in academic research studies.[7] However, peer observation has seldom been used in information science research studies. According to Baker, this trend is changing[8] as researchers are trying to find ways to better understand the role of information in people's everyday lives. Observation is a complex, challenging, and creative qualitative research method that often requires the researcher to engage in several roles utilizing various techniques to collect data.[9]

Conducting qualitative inquiry is based on empirical research, which has the ultimate goal of allowing the actions and thoughts of the participants to be told.[10] Detailed analysis of the data results in going beyond the data collected to develop ideas that can be generalized and theorized to a particular situation. Observation is an important method when conducting qualitative research. Through observation, a complex interaction such as a library instruction session can be studied in its natural social setting.[11]

Peer observation requires systematic note taking and recording of events, behaviors, and artifacts in a particular setting. Flick concurs by stating that the most important task during observation is documenting actions and interactions through context protocols, research diaries, or field notes.[12] Understanding the verbal and social interaction between teacher and student is also an important part of observing to see how talk and conversation are used to make meaning in the particular setting.[13] The process and procedures followed through peer observation allow the associations studied to be transformed into text, which is the basis for the actual analysis.

The method of observation is usually one of two types—participant observation or nonparticipant observation—depending on the degree to which the observer becomes involved with the participants.[14] The participant observer becomes engaged with the community members in the action and may have a long association with them. The participant observer becomes an insider to the group so that she can learn to see, feel, think, and even behave as an insider. This type of observation is often used with longer-term ethnographic studies of cultures or subcultures. In contrast, the nonparticipant observer is unobtrusive and does not become involved with the members while observing and recording events and behaviors. Nevertheless, the nonparticipant observer may have some effect on the setting simply by being present.[15]

In either case, the observer records observations via field notes.[16] The analysis then involves making broad descriptive categories from all the details that are observed and written in the field notes.[17] The observer and the participant may exchange information, reflecting on the practices and the field notes.

Coding usually occurs next by researchers deciding what concepts are most appropriate. The researchers need to think about and generate ideas or relationships among data observed, always keeping in mind that analysis of data must remain as true to the actual occurrences as possible. In other words, coding is a link between the data and sets of concepts or ideas.[18] Coffey and Atkinson state, "concepts are identified or constructed from prior material, theoretical frameworks, research questions, or the data themselves."[19] Data are continuously resorted and organized into categories. Coding is essential in providing new contexts for this reorganized data, allowing for conceptualizing, and raising questions and temporary answers about data relationships. This process of coding provides the opportunity for continuous discovery that moves the researcher towards analysis and interpretation.

Baker notes that reliability and validity must be addressed in qualitative research studies.[20] Johnson defines validity as research that is "plausible, credible, trustworthy, and defensible."[21] One threat to validity is researcher bias, which may result in being too selective while observing and recording information or in being too subjective in interpreting situations. To address bias, qualitative researchers can use additional observers or multiple data sets. We decided to also look at Karla's students' follow-up e-mail correspondence and the reflection journal that Karla kept throughout the study. This triangulation of data allowed the researchers to look at various perspectives when describing and explaining the phenomenon being studied and determining how consistent the data were.

Silverman states that when analyzing and interpreting data, the researcher needs to start with a set of general questions that are guided by the research inquiry and the theoretical focus.[22] Concepts and categories that are repeated lead to a construction of themes that are tested using triangulation with other related data sets.[23] The process involves continuous comparing and contrasting of various sets of data with peer debriefing between the observer and the participant. This collaboration allows for a critical examination of emerging patterns. Silverman proposes assumptions in the analysis of data in a qualitative environment.[24] The first assumption is that common sense exists in social practices, making common sense multifaceted and complicated. Second, researchers try to explain phenomena observed through the activities of specific people in specific settings. Finally, phenomena are considered through an interwoven pattern that includes observation, data collection, and hypothesis construction.

Baker writes that qualitative research is often criticized for lacking generalization for other studies, making it less reliable than quantitative research.[25] However, generalization is not typically a goal of qualitative research. Adler and Adler suggest that qualitative researchers can address the reliability of findings by strictly adhering to the prescribed conventions of the methodology.[26] Carolyn observed Karla's teaching for more than one instruction session with a variety of student groups, which provided clues to the teaching patterns that Karla exhibited over time and place. As qualitative researchers of this study, we are not as interested in generalizing the results as we are in providing a flexible framework to other researchers for using peer observation to address a variety of issues in library instruction situations.

Gorman and Clayton suggest that there are advantages and disadvantages to using peer observation.[27] Advantages include flexibility in that a variety of perspectives or degrees of involvement can be used in the situation or activity that is being observed. Observation involves recording what is happening as it occurs in a natural setting and carries with it what these authors call a "reality verifying" character.[28] What that means is that what the person being observed says she is doing compared to what she is actually doing can be confirmed or contradicted. A series of peer observations allow data to be considered in increments over time that create meaning or understanding of the overall range of teaching behaviors.

Disadvantages of peer observation include the fact that people who are aware of being observed sometimes tend to behave in different ways than they would normally. Secondly, spontaneous events are difficult to anticipate, and not all kinds of events lend themselves to observation. Thirdly, observation can be time-consuming for the participant and the observer. Fourthly, the subjectivity of the observer always needs to be considered.[29]

After obtaining a foundation of knowledge about peer observation, that is, the definition of terms as well as advantages and disadvantages, one is ready to move on to the steps of conducting peer observation. The next section provides an overview of how Karla and Carolyn began their peer observation research.

Overview of Research Design

As a reflective academic librarian, Karla regularly thinks about her instruction sessions to attempt to make future ones more productive and successful. In this case, Karla decided that her goal for the semester was to find out through peer observation what teaching patterns, particularly verbal cues and actions, affect her ability to initiate a positive connection with the students. What patterns did she exhibit in her library instruction sessions that fulfilled this goal? Unfortunately, since Karla's instruction sessions are often one-shots, there is little time to establish a relationship with the students. In order to accomplish this goal of using the instructional time to both teach and establish a positive connection, Karla decided to improve student-to-student and student-to-teacher interaction during the instructional session. She made the assumption that if students are actively engaged in an instruction session, they would be more likely to seek similar engagement with the librarian after the session. Karla's belief in the active engagement of students in the learning process comes from social constructivism theory. Students make more sense of a learning situation when they collaborate with others and the teacher. In this way, knowledge is built rather than transmitted. Wells notes by creating caring, collaborative classrooms, students and teachers can make meaning that will inform their immediate and future learning needs.[30]

Each library instruction session includes university students and their professor who make up a learning community or a community of practice. According to Harris, a learning community and a community of practice share many characteristics.[31] Both are comprised of members who have similar goals, a shared common knowledge, and uses of language that are distinct to the group. Karla's instruction sessions are learning communities that are building on the communities of practice of the academy.

Harris writes that the idea of communities as locations for information literacy learning is relatively new among librarians and information professionals.[32] We feel that the library and librarians are a vital component of the community of practice. Karla's hope is that initial library instruction can move beyond the one-shot gathering to include her within the community of practice for further information sharing and assistance as students move forward in their educational pursuits. In this approach, students in various learning communities (e.g., courses, clubs, internships, etc.) within their discipline learn to construct their information literacy practices within the community of practice.

Lave states that it is through the social interaction of communities of practice that students gain expertise, knowledge, and skill[33] rather than through individual learning in *out-of-context* abstract ways. These out-of-context or one-shot library instructions can be contrived. It is through authentic learning situations that students will move from being novices to experts in the information literacy learning process. Simons, Young, and Gibson suggest that creating reciprocal communities of practice can provide opportunities for learning library information in multiple ways[34] (e.g., in-office appointments, e-mails, personal contacts, Web-based contacts, etc.).

Reciprocity exists between the members of a community of practice as ideas are exchanged, new knowledge is shared, and best practices are performed. Contemporary theorist Wenger calls a "community of practice" groups of flexible people interacting with one another by discussing and thinking together to develop relationships.[35] These learning communities of students continually intersect with the library and the librarian. In this way, the librarian is extending the community of practice from the classroom to the library.

After determining that Karla's instructional goal of improving student-to-student and student-to-teacher interaction was grounded in theory, she reviewed her teaching schedule to determine on which classes to focus this qualitative research. Karla teaches many instructional lessons throughout the semester, but chose fourteen sessions to reflect upon and analyze, which included teaching 297 students from freshman to doctoral level. One group with which she worked was the Humphrey Scholars, who were educational professionals, and now graduate students, from around the world working on various research agendas for one year. The doctoral students whom she taught were often new to the university. The undergraduate student groups included freshmen, sophomores, and juniors. Most instruction was to education majors, but one session was to undeclared freshmen.

Carolyn observed two of these instruction sessions, which became a focal point to begin the discussion of what was occurring in Karla's teaching. Karla kept a reflection journal (see table 7.6 for a sample) for each of these fourteen sessions. She filed all e-mails she received from the students and professors from these sessions. Karla also tracked any follow-up office visits made by these students.

A plan needed to be designed to accomplish Karla's goal of making connections during instruction. Qualitative research does not occur by following a set of predetermined steps, but rather by understanding the process because each study is unique to the particular context.[36] Our chosen plan was a model of a research process rather than a checklist of steps. We followed Maxwell's interactive process model: (1) establish a research relationship, (2) decide the method of gathering data, (3) collect data, and (4) analyze data.[37] Following is an overview of the observational process used to help Karla meet her instructional goal.

1. Establishing a research relationship with a colleague is of utmost importance for successful peer observation. Personal and professional association lays the foundation for successful reflective dialogue, which is an essential part of peer observation. The instruction librarian can use peer observation to provide an opportunity to choose someone with whom to develop this working relationship.

2. It is vital to decide how to gather data so that the data describe the phenomenon in relationship to the question. We created a tool for gathering the observation data as well as a post observation discussion form. (See tables 7.1 and 7.2.) We also decided which sessions Carolyn would observe.

3. The next decision centered on the types of observation data Carolyn would collect as she watched Karla teach. It was not Carolyn's job to record everything that occurred, but rather to note the behaviors and dialogue that would demonstrate whether the goal was being met. In addition, Carolyn recorded the layout of the rooms and collected the demographics of the students in the courses.[38]

4. After each observation, the instruction session was discussed. Carolyn shared the data she collected to member check with Karla. Member checking involves soliciting feedback from the participants in the study to confirm and validate the findings of the researcher.[39] The goals and procedures were revisited when necessary. In the end, coded and analyzed data included two observations, fourteen journal entries, eighteen e-mails, blogs from one assignment, and unnumbered office visits by students.

5. Finally, while analyzing the data we looked for patterns and coded for themes. As we discussed the findings, we also checked to see if the various sources of our data confirmed or contradicted our themes.

Thus, the beginning steps in utilizing peer observation involve setting a goal for instruction, choosing the population for observation, and then understanding the interactive process model of observation. The next section provides more details on the methodology of peer observation.

Methodology

After deciding on the classes to include in our assessment and agreeing on the general protocol, we decided to gather observation data consistently by creating an observation form. A qualitative observation form is different from an evaluative form because the form is specific to the objective of the research question and not an overview of all the aspects of teaching the lesson. In this case, we were looking only at student and teacher engagement: what the teacher is doing to increase interaction during the lesson to lay the foundation for further connections with the students. We wanted a form that would allow us

TABLE 7.1 **Observation Form**[a]				
Observer:			**Teacher:**	
Session Title:			**Course:**	
Number of Students:		**Room Number:**	**Date:**	
Instructional Librarian Goal: To improve student to student and student to teacher interaction				
Observation and Field Notes				
Time	**Instructor**	**Students**	**Materials**	**Comments/Questions of the observer**

a. Adapted from Virginia Adult Learning Resource Center, "Notes for Classroom Observation."

to record data about how the teacher and students interacted within the instruction session.

In creating our observation form, we first reviewed forms from various sources. We did not want a form that utilized a Likert scale[40] because we needed to be more descriptive.[41] Most forms that we reviewed encompassed evaluating the complete teaching process, and the criteria closely aligned with the goals of the institution utilizing it.[42] After viewing many forms and discussing our specific needs, we adapted a form from Virginia Adult Learning Resource Center.[43]

The top of the observation form (see table 7.1) included all the general information about the instruction: observer, teacher, session title, course name, number of students, place, and date of instruction. The instruction librarian's goal was stated at the top of the form to assist in focusing the observation and post discussion. Notes were taken in five columns labeled Time, Instructor, Students, Materials, and Comments/Questions. After designing this form, we created a post observation discussion and reflection form (see table 7.2).

Immediately after Carolyn observed one of Karla's instruction sessions, we met to discuss the observation. First, Carolyn shared her field notes, comments, and questions with Karla. Then Karla added her

comments or corrected any misconceptions. The post observation form directed the discussion with the following questions: (1) What do the data say? (2) How do the data match the instruction librarian's goal? (3) What will be the goal of future instruction

TABLE 7.2 **Post Observation Discussion and Reflection**
Date:
1. What do the data say?
2. How do the data match the instruction librarian's goal?
3. What will be the goal of future instruction sessions?
4. What do we need to refine and discuss? (note-taking strategies and other research tools and procedures).

sessions? (Although Karla did not meet with the same group a second time, this goal was related to how she could better connect with students in any future instruction sessions.) (4) What do we need to refine (note-taking strategies and other research tools, procedures)?

Other aspects to consider were what data to collect for this semester-long study. Instruction sessions to be observed were chosen according to our schedules. In addition, Karla collected e-mails that were related to instructional lectures she had taught during the semester. In the end, we collected data from journal entries, e-mails, and some personal interactions at the library, as well as the peer observations.

In summary, before Carolyn observed Karla, we created the observation tools that were specific to the goal of the observation. Then we decided what other data to collect to help triangulate findings. Following are our steps for collecting and discussing data.

Collecting Data

As an education librarian, Karla works primarily with students taking courses in the College of Education. She provides information literacy support, instruction, and research assistance for undergraduate and graduate students. The courses chosen in this study represent some of the variety of education courses within the community of practice that is the College of Education (see table 7.3) and are courses that Karla often teaches each semester. The language and literacy courses include World Languages Education (WLED), Children's Literature, and Adolescent Literature.

The World Language Education students need to find books and teaching materials to create lesson plans to instruct children in a language that is not English. The WLED library session involves providing the students with instruction in finding language resources and assisting in generating ideas for lesson plans. These students return to the library often to get additional materials throughout the semester and to ask advice about books that will fit thematic units. This assignment is authentic because the students teach local children a new language.

The Children's Literature course typically has five to six sections each semester with a total of 150 students. This methods course is comprised of juniors who will be completing their student teaching experiences the following year. During the library session, Karla instructs the students on how to find children's titles, discusses children's literature genres, and describes how to use databases such as the Children's Literature Comprehensive Database. Karla describes this class as the one in which she works the hardest to improve from semester to semester. In many cases, this contact will be a first-time library experience for the students. Karla often sees these same students again in other education methods courses. These students have greater potential to contact the librarian for assistance during their future student teaching experiences. The Adolescent Literature course is one in which Karla guest lectures on trends in young adult and adolescent literature and censorship.

Karla works with many master's and doctoral students. The Humphrey Scholars, Special Education PhD students, and the PhD colloquium classes are represented in our study. The library sessions for these groups often involve giving a tour of the library as the students are returning to academic studies after a period of time. These classes are heavily research-oriented. The library sessions involve discussion and instruction in library services, library resources, databases, search techniques, and research methodologies. The students many times contact Karla for individual information and research assistance as they become more immersed in their particular research topics.

The groups that Karla works with less frequently are the freshmen and sophomores. In our study, they include freshman seminar, undeclared freshmen, and English Education students. Many times, these course types need a general library orientation, but in each of these three classes, the students had a specific assignment. The freshman seminar students look for supporting articles on education hot topic issues for a paper they write. In the undeclared freshman class, Karla shares educational databases with the students, using "technology in education" as the search topic. The students respond with a blog

TABLE 7.3
Summary Information Regarding the Sessions in the Study

Sessions (In chronological order) Total 14	Number and Level of Students Total 297	Data Types Total Observations 2 Reflection 15 E-mails 18 Office Visits 11+	Other Information
Humphrey Scholars *August 15, 2008*	14 international accomplished midcareer professionals	Observation Reflection E-mails Office visits	Karla attended presentations by 6 students.
Special Education PhD students *August 20, 2008*	4 PhD students	Reflection E-mails Office visits	3 follow-up meetings plus individual contacts
World Languages Education *September 9, 2008*	23 undergraduates (sophomores and juniors)	Reflection E-mails Office Visits	Interactive during class
Freshman Seminar *September 9, 2008*	24 freshmen	Reflection	
PhD Colloquium *September 12, 2008*	25 PhD students 6 sessions	Reflection E-mails Office visits	5 students: instruction session, 1 student: video help, Many students: ILL help
Children's Literature *September 16 and September 18, 2008*	150 undergraduates (juniors)	Reflection E-mails Office visits	Talked with every student during session via mini assignment
Undeclared Freshmen *October 1, 2008*	17 freshmen	Observation Reflection Blogs	Karla visited the session with the blog assignment she gave. More student interaction
English Education Students *October 10, 2008*	24 undergraduates (sophomores)	Reflection	A lot of class interaction
Adolescent Literature *October 22, 2008*	16 undergraduates (sophomores and juniors)	Reflection E-mails Office visits	

assignment to write about their experience with technology in elementary, middle, or high school, as well as considering the role of technology in the future. Interestingly, the instructors for this course asked Karla to write the blog assignment. The English Education students have to write an education grant for their assignment. Karla shares her own educa-

tional grant success stories from her experiences as an elementary classroom teacher and as a school librarian. She assists the students in how to find education grant information and discusses ideas with each group informally.

Peer observation of several of Karla's sessions was an important part of the data collection process as it provided a reflective observation of Karla's activity. Post observation discussion was invaluable, as were the student e-mails and Karla's reflection journal. Data collection is not a linear process, although it may seem like it as we describe the procedure.

At the time of the two instruction sessions that Carolyn observed, Carolyn would meet Karla at the assigned room. Karla introduced Carolyn to the faculty members and students when appropriate.

In particular, the Humphrey Scholars were involved in research projects, so they were very interested in what we were doing. Carolyn observed the sessions with the Humphrey Scholars and the undeclared freshmen.

During the instruction session, Carolyn recorded data on the observation form previously discussed. The session with the Humphrey Scholars included a tour of the library and classroom presentation of

---

TABLE 7.4
Coded Observation Form

Underline = student actions/words coded green originally.
Bold italics = teacher words coded yellow originally.
Underline italics = teacher actions coded blue originally.

A Sample from Carolyn's Observation and Field Notes of the Humphrey Scholars on Aug. 22, 2008

Time	Instructor	Students	Materials	Comments/Questions
10:30	Assists all the find a seat Hands out packet, _gives out card and email_ **Email is the best way to get me** Walks through the booklet with overview **Just email me**	Asks about phoning her	Packet, booklets	_Makes eye contact_ _Smiling while talking_ _Gestures to booklet and card_
	Asks faculty member best way to find PSU info	Ask about finding a special book		faculty member makes suggestions about marking PSU homepage as a favorite
	I will find out that as well as the sq. feet	Q: What does CAT mean?		faculty member says Americans are not good at explaining acronyms
	What topic is someone interested in?	A few students answer and topic is chosen by them		_Points to screen while talking_ Looks at leader
	Thanks faculty member for sharing info	Asks questions about access to the library		faculty member answers
	Explains ILL system	Comments about issues' list		
	YES, _nodding_ (reference to student comment)	Question about seeking and saving info Student agrees he does the same thing		

library databases. During the tour, Carolyn kept notes, utilizing a clipboard while following along. Immediately afterwards she typed her notes. During both observation sessions, Carolyn sat in the back of the room with her laptop taking field notes as an unobtrusive observer. Before the session began, she would complete the information noted at the top of the form and sketch the layout of the classroom, including where the students sat as they entered. During the session, she recorded the appropriate descriptions of what the teacher and students were doing and saying. In the last column, she recorded comments, questions, and impressions of the instruction session. (See table 7.4.)

Immediately after both instruction sessions Carolyn observed, we met to discuss the observation in light of the research question. We used the computer to record our information, making it easy to revise the field notes. First, we reviewed the data on the observation form. Karla read the data to confirm or correct any of the field notes. Then we completed the post observation form (see table 7.5) We recorded our comments as we discussed the questions. The following is an excerpt from our discussion of Carolyn's peer observation on August 22, 2008, of the session with the Humphrey Scholars with whom Karla conducted a library tour and shared instruction in library services, resources, and databases.

1. *What do the data say?* Students' engagement was noted through their facial expressions and many questions. The students seemed comfortable asking questions. Karla's enthusiasm was observed as she connected with the students via personal stories. The tour pace was good, but the total session was too long. When we arrived at the instruction room at the completion of the tour, a number of students seemed relieved to be able to sit down for a while. Their body language suggested that they were tired. It did not seem to be the ideal time for an instruction session. Even though they seemed a bit exhausted, they were engaged in the instruction session and actively interacted with their peers, their professor, and Karla.

2. *How do the data match the instruction librarian's goal?* Student-to-student interaction was noted through question clarification and students' choices for topic searches. Carolyn observed student-to-teacher interaction when Karla answered general questions.

3. *What will be the goal of future instruction sessions?* Karla decided to provide an outline or handout, which would structure a more thorough presentation. When it is a small graduate student group, she wanted to allow time for introductions, which provides a more personal foundation for building community. Karla would also like to meet the Humphrey Scholars in two or even three sessions rather than trying to

---

TABLE 7.5
Sample Coded Postobservation Form Regarding the Humphrey Scholars Question 1 from Table 7.2

Underline = student actions/words coded green originally.
Bold italics = teacher words coded yellow originally.
<u>*Underline italics*</u> = teacher actions coded blue originally.

Date: Aug. 22, 2008 Carolyn and Karla

What do the data say?
- Karla made connections with **stories** to students
- The tour pace seemed good because students felt comfortable to stop and ask questions
- Karla gave out her **E-mail** contact and said she would find the answers to questions she did not know
- Karla showed her positive feelings by *smiling* a lot
  ○ Students said they will contact her and return with questions
- The session was too long (tour plus session) because the students seemed tired at the end

TABLE 7.6
Karla's Reflection Journal Regarding Her Session with the Humphrey Scholars Coded

<u>Underline</u> = student actions/words coded green originally.
Bold italics = teacher words coded yellow originally.
<u>*Underline italics*</u> = teacher actions coded blue originally.

Humphrey Scholars Aug. 22, 2008

This session included a tour of the library and an overview of general library information, the electronic card catalog -the CAT, and databases. This is the first time that I was asked to provide library information for this group. The Humphrey Scholars come from all over the world. A number of the scholars mentioned that <u>they were amazed at the size of the library and the number of services that were provided</u>. It was also mentioned by one gentleman that in his country, libraries did not have exhibit areas like Pattee and Paterno do (Waring Museum, Lion Exhibit, Holocaust Exhibit, Olympics Exhibit in Special Collections etc. and so on…).

The tour lasted for an hour and I felt that the <u>scholars were interested and attentive in the information that I shared</u>. By the end of the tour, I felt that a <u>few of them were tired from going up and down stairs and all over the library</u>. We ended the tour in the EBSL instruction room which is fairly small. I gave a **general overview of library procedures** such as checking books out, a brief demonstration of the card catalog and library databases. I didn't go into a great deal of detail. I mentioned to the group **that I would be happy to work with anyone who wanted to get together to review doing library searching** after they were more immersed in their research or I'd be happy to help with any library needs that may arise.

I felt overall positive about the session and that it was successful.

I have since <u>heard from a couple of the Humphrey Scholars via email</u>. One scholar asked me to **help find article/book titles**. Another scholar and I are <u>*planning to meet in a week or two; she would like to talk to me about a book*</u>. I don't know any other details about the purpose—if it is a book that she is writing or a book she is looking for or a book that she would like the library to order. I'll find out when I meet with her.

do everything in a two- to three-hour long session. She will make that suggestion in future meetings.

4. *What do we need to refine and discuss?* It would be helpful to tally data of classroom interactions in order to accumulate quantifiable data. It would be important for Karla to create a journal so that she can write her reflections whether she was observed or not.

By the conclusion of our post observation discussion, we had reviewed the observation data, connected the data with the research question, and refined future goals. In addition, after the discussion, we recorded our impressions and questions regarding the session on the bottom of the post observation form.

Karla's reflection journal, plus e-mails and personal contacts with students constituted the other data collected. After the teaching sessions, Karla wrote about the experience in her reflection journal, often returning to add other insights or examples of connections made with students (see table 7.6.) These journal entries not only captured Karla's impressions and description of the instruction, but also recorded connections and questions for discussion when we met. Karla filed all e-mail correspondence on her computer; later she copied the information into a word processing document to be coded and analyzed. We did not realize until well into the semester how many students would drop by to speak to Karla. In hindsight, we approximated this data number based on Karla's notes in her calendar (see table 7.3).

Data collection is an ongoing process, which only begins with the peer observation. Post-observation discussion about the observation provides more data that help to interpret the field notes and direct the next instruction session. Karla's reflection journal along with e-mails and visits from students supplied data for triangulation purposes. Multiple data sets allow for building a more complete picture of the instruction session and developing a more thorough interpretation to answer the research question.

Coding Data

When coding, it is necessary to reflect upon the research question in order to view the data through that lens. Since this study entailed observing Karla's teaching patterns, Carolyn began by looking at what Karla said and did by highlighting all the talk and actions from her instruction as recorded on the observation form. Carolyn color-coded this talk on the observation form by using yellow for Karla's talk, blue for Karla's actions, and green for student talk and actions. Students' gestures and talk were combined in coding because we were primarily interested in Karla's behavior. Then Carolyn transferred the colored phrases to a list, in which themes became more evident. We discovered five kinds of talk that Karla employed during instruction. We defined *Informal Talk* as conversation that initiates or concludes instruction but is not directly related to the goal of the lesson (e.g., welcome, overview of class). We used *Storytelling* to denote the act of telling a tale that elaborates a topic to be learned as well as entertains the audience (e.g., personal teaching experiences). *Relationship Talk* involved providing information that will encourage future connections (e.g., e-mail, office location, etc.). *Question and Answer Talk* is self-explanatory and occurred before, during, and after instruction. And finally we used the term *Instructional Talk* to represent explaining or modeling the information to be learned. Karla exhibited all of these types of talking patterns.

Since the 1970s, linguists have noted the connection between words and actions in various situations, labeling them to better study talk in context.[44] Cazden classified one type of talk as that used by the teacher to convey meaning and call attention to relationships.[45] The categories chosen to describe Karla's talk fit into these criteria.

Next, Carolyn reviewed the students' talk and actions, looking for ways they interacted with Karla and with each other. The students' data were specific to the instruction. In the session with the Humphrey Scholars, there were many questions from the students for Karla (thirteen questions noted), and there was much interaction among the students (seventeen verbal comments or gestures). On the other hand, in the undeclared freshman library session, there were fewer questions directed to Karla, but the students were engaged via technology because they followed along with their computers as Karla demonstrated education databases. Undeclared freshmen made

comments or gestures or answered Karla's questions a total of seven times. In addition, their follow-up was conducted via a blog assignment.

It is vital to triangulate data from various sources in order to confirm or contradict findings. E-mail correspondence was another set of data we collected. E-mail text was color-coded using yellow for the words describing Karla's comments and green for the students' inquiries. The data were reviewed, looking at what initiated the contact by the student and how Karla responded. The topics were highlighted as previously noted, and then Carolyn wrote an overall comment about the interaction. For example, in an e-mail on September 25, 2008: "Karla answers a specific question by a PhD student with a Web site and a detailed response."

Then Carolyn listed all the comments with their corresponding courses in order to discern any other patterns. There were ten e-mails from graduate students and Humphrey Scholars, six e-mails from undergraduate students, and three e-mails initiated by Karla. Two Humphrey Scholars asked questions of Karla, to which she provided e-mail responses. In addition, one Humphrey Scholar contacted the librarian to whom Karla had referred in her instruction. Karla was copied on the e-mail from the librarian, and then she confirmed the information that the librarian had shared with the student. After an initial instruction session, four doctoral students in Special Education asked Karla to provide them with additional instruction on specific databases. Following this meeting, Karla interacted with them numerous times via e-mail and with personal appointments. On September 25, 2008, Karla e-mailed detailed instructions on how to find materials; and on October 8, 2008, she contacted a student to see how she was progressing with obtaining her needed journal article. The undergraduates queried Karla numerous times on how to find articles or reviews and how to do lesson plans with children's literature. In each instance, Karla provided a detailed response for them to follow as well as an opportunity to meet with her in the future if they still had questions as noted in e-mails from October 7 and 14, 2008. In summary, Karla responded to e-mail queries in a timely manner and with sufficient details to support the students. Through this study, it was confirmed to Karla that she has a great deal of additional contact with students via e-mail. Since doing this study, she automatically puts e-mail correspondence in folders that help her to organize queries from students, cross-reference information from students asking the same information, and keep track of the number of times a student contacts her. By continuing to do this, Karla is able to see even more student contact patterns emerging than were observed in this original study. She has especially begun to note word-of-mouth contact, in which a student will say something such as: "I'm having trouble with 'x, y, or z' and my friend suggested that I contact you for help."

Karla's reflection journal entries were another source of data. After reading the journal entries, Carolyn coded them with the same colors previously noted: yellow for descriptive words denoting Karla's actions and green for the students' queries. Blue was used to highlight Karla's reflective thoughts. When all the data from observations, e-mails, and journal entries were placed together, themes were confirmed or contradicted with the evidence.

Based on the data collected, Karla connected with many students from the instruction sessions that she taught. Many of the 150 students from the Children's Literature class came to Karla in the library for assistance. She supported many of the doctoral students from the Colloquial Seminar with interlibrary loan procedures and helped one student who needed to obtain a video. In addition, five doctoral students arranged for Karla to provide library instruction for the classes they were teaching. Karla extended the learning community by participating with students beyond the initial instruction sessions. She read the blogs from the undeclared freshman library class, and attended class the following week to listen to the students' blog presentations. Karla attended presentations by six Humphrey Scholars. Although these students are on campus for only a year, during the session on August 22, 2008, they remarked very positively about the library and the support provided by the staff.

Analyzing the Data

At the beginning of a qualitative analysis, it is good practice for the researcher to self-disclose or lay out any potential bias that may affect the research.[46] The researcher needs to make her history, values, and assumptions open to scrutiny as a way to make conscious and unconscious baggage visible in the observation and interpretation stages.[47] For these reasons, we would like to describe Karla, the librarian. Karla has a positive attitude toward teaching and working with students. She has been working as an educator for twenty-seven years and has always believed that she makes a difference in the lives of her students. She is a very service-orientated librarian. Her goal for teaching is that information literacy sessions should be relevant, authentic, and meaningful. To that end, it is important to Karla that she help students to become independent in their information literacy needs. She believes that a key way of doing that is by building professional as well as personal connections with students.

During the process of observing, gathering, and coding data, we constantly reflected on what we found, what it meant, and how it related to Karla's teaching goal. Although this procedure is a recursive one, at this point we would like to explain how we analyzed these data. We began by returning to Karla's goal and asking ourselves, "Did Karla's teaching style establish positive connections with students and foster their willingness to return to the library for more assistance?" In order to answer this question, we needed to first analyze the data gathered via peer observation. As mentioned previously, the talk themes discovered were Question and Answer, Storytelling, Relationship Talk, Instructional Talk, and Informal Talk.

Throughout Karla's instruction session, she reached out to the students in many ways. Most teachers utilize questions to engage students, and so did Karla. To the undeclared freshman class on October 1, 2008, she connected by asking about what had been taught previously as well as students' school technology experiences. This group of students responded in a limited fashion. In contrast, on August 22, 2008, the Humphrey Scholars initiated many questions, not only about library use (e.g., "How do I find a particular book?"), but also about library trivia (e.g., "What square meters of space is used for museum displays at the library?"). Teaching by connecting to prior knowledge is good pedagogical practice, but how the students respond cannot be predicted. Karla's goal was to encourage more interactions by asking both personal and academic questions. Asking and answering questions is also a way to build an interactive community. Although the use of questions typically is employed to query students, this strategy was one that Karla used to build relationships.

Most people love a good story, and Karla wove in many tales into her lessons to prepare for learning and building relationships. As observed on October 1, 2008, her students were entertained with stories of her past teaching experiences, thus making the subject matter more authentic. Even while touring the library on August 22, 2008, she regaled the Humphrey Scholars with campus folklore about the school's mascot, the Nittany Lion. Through storytelling, Karla seemed more approachable to the students, and therefore they were more likely to return for assistance. Purdue eloquently writes that stories are transformative because they require active participation on the part of the students hearing them.[48] Stories heard are also stories begging to be retold, which results in further engagement within the learning community of the instruction librarian and her students.

As Karla established a relationship with the students via questions and storytelling, she constantly reminded the students how they could contact her for help, as observed on August 22, 2008, and October 1, 2008. First, she shared her e-mail many times and stated that this is the best way to contact her. Next, she explained where her office was and invited students to visit her personally. Lastly, she shared library information about other colleagues and the information desk. Karla reminded students

that the library is a friendly place and that everyone wants to help them.

During her instructional and informal talk, Karla connected with students via questioning and storytelling as well as encouraging the students to reconnect when needed by e-mail or in person. We wanted to find evidence that Karla successfully established positive connections with students and fostered their willingness to return to the library for more assistance. We looked at the other data that we collected. Did students e-mail her? There were sixteen e-mails from students. Most of them were from graduate students asking for specific research assistance with books, articles, interlibrary loan, or class instruction. Undergraduate students sought help for completing assignments related to creating lessons with children's literature or finding books and journal articles. Even in Karla's e-mails, she reached out to the students in various ways. For example, on October 14, 2008, Karla wrote, "Let me know if I made this confusing or you need further help. . . . I'll try again and if you want to meet with me for assistance just let me know, we can set something up."

Did students contact her personally? Out of the fourteen sessions, Karla worked personally with students from eleven sessions. Students more readily contacted her when there was a specific assignment associated with the presentation. For example, the undergraduate students from Children's Literature had to complete their reading diaries by evaluating children's books. In her reflection journal, Karla wrote on September 9, 2008, about the World Languages Education class. "A few days later, a young woman from this course asked me to help look for fairytale retellings to use in her teaching in this program," as well as "I assisted a number of students from this group when they were in the stacks to find additional language materials." Students from a majority of the instruction sessions contacted Karla personally asking her for assistance with their studies.

Through Carolyn's observation of two sessions, we were able to name the types of talk that Karla used in her instruction. By Karla's keeping a reflection journal and collecting student e-mails, we were able to document her continued interaction with students. By analyzing these data, we learned that Karla's teaching style was conducive to building relationships with students in order to foster further connections with the library. Through this research project, we have labeled Karla's teaching behaviors, and she has become more aware of how her teaching style affects the learning community. This awareness will help her to continue to strengthen her interpersonal connections with students.

Discussion

The data analysis revealed to Karla information about herself as an instruction librarian and how she was doing in her goal of building relationships with students and making connections that invited future contact and support. Karla felt that the peer observation process was valuable to her in determining what teaching behaviors she exhibited regularly—those strategies that were an integral part of her teaching toolkit.

Karla was interested to learn that her inventory of teaching tools included five kinds of talk as identified through coding and analysis of the data. She was not surprised that Informal, Instruction, and Question and Answer Talk were evident. They seemed likely for the type of instruction that is typically conducted in library settings. She was pleased to see that Relationship Talk was in her repertoire, as that seemed to be an important aspect of building bridges of support to the students. She was surprised and delighted to discover that Storytelling was something she did naturally without realizing it. She identifies herself as a storyteller, so to see that what she believed about herself was actually true was reassuring. By emphasizing these behaviors, she can continue to build on them to improve her goal of making connections with students throughout their academic careers. The field notes and other data provided tangible clues as to how she was doing in the process. We both agreed that she had a good beginning in her quest; she could continually work on identifying additional ways to reach out to students. She had evidence of what she did well and

information about what she might do to improve academic relationship building so that the number of students seeking additional support after a one-shot library instruction would hopefully increase.

Karla gained a number of insights about her teaching from this study. The first is that reflection using a written journal is timely and valuable in assessing how sessions went. By returning to these journal reflections repeatedly after contact with students and feedback from professors, ideas were generated for ways in which instruction could be improved to better serve students. Since completing this study, Karla has refined her overall instruction in a number of the courses that were highlighted. The data from student e-mails and personal connections made her realize where students were getting confused. This reflection caused her to add different and specific content instruction. In the Children's Literature class, the students did not have a good definition or understanding of particular genres, so they had difficulties doing their assignment. Therefore, during Karla's instruction sessions, she more clearly defined genres and provided examples so students had a stronger background for completing the assignment.

The second insight from e-mail and journal data was the ripple effect of future connections. Doctoral students who were participants in an instruction session not only contacted Karla to assist with their research but also to provide library instruction for undergraduate courses they taught as teaching assistants. Then, in turn, their undergraduate students later contacted Karla about the assignments they needed to complete. This knowledge confirmed that students made connections from many levels and beyond the initial instruction.

The third realization regarded variables that can influence interaction. For instance, the Special Education PhD students were a small group with focused needs, which resulted in more interaction and personal contact, in contrast to the undeclared freshman class, who initiated no further contact beyond the class blog assignment.

These data provided evidence that resulted in Karla's awareness of her teaching style and how it affected students' interactions with the library. Through this process, we are able to name and label Karla's teaching behaviors so that she could more aptly adjust them to increase student interaction within the learning community of library instruction. She will continue to work to establish positive relationships with students and develop ways to make connections for their academic needs.

Being immersed in this research has made Karla more conscious of the many interactions that she has with students since their initial library instruction. Undergraduate students seek her assistance in finding sources for research papers in other courses. Many students have asked for recommendations of children's books for a variety of reasons. Surprisingly, one student contacted Karla for database help while the student was doing her student teaching overseas. In addition, a number of graduate students have requested individual research consultations concerning their master's thesis or doctoral dissertation topics.

Reflection

Goal-oriented peer observation is a useful type of qualitative assessment for librarians interested in studying specific skills, behavior, or dialogue associated with their job responsibilities. Utilizing peer observation not only encourages collaboration but also adds objectivity to reflective teaching practices. In this section, we reflect on using peer observation, including what we have learned as an observer and a participant, as well as how a qualitative study like this can contribute to a practitioner's ability to observe, reflect, and act.

As an observer, Carolyn learned to hone her observation skills as well as develop her analytical skills while working with data and dialoguing with Karla. The lens of Karla's goal directed Carolyn's note taking during the observation. Discussions with Karla after instruction sessions, as well as throughout the semester, helped Carolyn to explain more clearly what she saw and how it affected Karla's goal. Coding and analyzing the data helped Carolyn to see an overview of Karla's teaching. Again, when we met to talk about the data, we clarified and challenged our ideas as we discussed them. By using peer observation in a qualitative study, Carolyn was able to provide qual-

ity feedback to Karla that specifically addressed her instructional goal.

Karla learned that a long-term peer observation study is not as daunting a task as it might seem. In fact, it proved to be a supportive way in which to assess a teaching goal beyond just a one-time evaluative observation. By completing a set of observations, we were able to look for patterns across sessions and time. Even the data collected were more comprehensive than just taking notes during an observation; they also included instruction librarian talk, student talk, and actions as well as e-mail data and reflection journal entries. These data collections provided valuable information in ascertaining an overall picture of what occurred between Karla and the students during library instruction. Seeing herself through Carolyn's eyes afforded Karla a new look at her teaching. The ability to be able to confer with Carolyn in a frank manner contributed to a sincere and honest assessment of how Karla was faring in reaching her teaching goal.

Our learning during this qualitative study involving peer observation was multifaceted. We learned to be better collaborative colleagues through inquiry, analysis, and dialogue with each other. Karla's reflective teaching practices were confirmed by the data we collected. Her students benefited by having lessons that were adapted and improved based on data gathered from this study.

Through this peer observation study, Karla gained awareness about her teaching and her interpersonal relationships with students. First, she learned exactly what kinds of teaching patterns she used when conducting a library instruction class. Knowing these specifics can help her capitalize on her strengths as an instruction librarian. Second, she learned that in general, she has good rapport with the students that she works with, but she needs to continually explore other ways that she can make connections with them. Future avenues to connect with students might include utilizing Web 2.0 applications. Third, she saw the value of reflection and collaboration for refining her library teaching practice; it is powerful and transformative to engage in a study of one's own practices. Finally, she has continued to save e-mail correspondence from students in succeeding semesters and is noting that students from the semester when the observations took place are contacting her beyond the one course and the one semester. In fact, there seems to be a possibility that data collected from repeated contacts from students will provide more information regarding student connections from semester to semester, across courses, and through a student's academic years, and beyond.

We feel that dialogue has been the most important feature in the process of this peer observation. Pertinent and insightful discussion was evident throughout our data analysis. However, the next time we embark on similar research, we would be cognizant of certain aspects of the project. First, scheduling additional peer observation sessions would provide more data and stronger patterns of themes. Second, we would plan more carefully for the collection of data detailing students' personal contact with Karla. Third, we would interview students and professors to gain their perspective on what was accomplished in the instruction session. Did it meet their expectations or goals? Would the students be likely to contact Karla again after the session? We have learned valuable information from this experience, which will impact our future research.

Implications for Further Research

Librarians of all types can conduct action research using observation with a peer. School librarians can replicate what was done by the instruction librarian in this chapter. Reference librarians could reflect on their one-on-one interactions with students. Public librarians could use action research to analyze their programs and outreach.

Librarians can address a variety of questions to initiate research using peer observation, for example, "How can I improve my reference dialogue with students?" To answer this question, librarians could ask a colleague to observe students as they seek information at the reference desk. A new innovative service like roving reference might be explored by observing librarians as they roam patron and student study spaces. Such a study could pose the question, "Does it make a difference to go where the students are to meet their information needs?"

In utilizing peer observation, there are limitations. The observer needs to describe objectively what is seen and be careful not to be evaluative. Also, the observer might misunderstand what was seen or said during the session. Thus, the post observation dialogue afterwards is very important to member check what occurred in the session. The observer might focus on the wrong factors in the observation especially if the research question is not focused enough. In addition, the one being observed might act differently knowing that the research is being conducted. It is vital that these limitations be acknowledged and examined during the research process.

Summary and Conclusion

We hope that through the example of the study we conducted involving peer observation that readers will be able to replicate aspects that pertain to their own goals as instruction librarians. Peer observation with analysis and interpretation can provide rich, textured data that can inform a variety of librarian questions regarding library instruction and services. The data that we collected could be used to answer a number of other questions if we changed our focus or goals. For example, we could more deeply analyze the "question and answer" talk data to evaluate student and teacher interaction. Types of questions as well as wait time could also be analyzed. Just by changing this study in subtle ways, we would be able to answer additional research questions with this methodology.

The process that we used in this peer observation involves the following:

- Choose a goal.
- Create observation tools.
- Set observation dates.
- Gather data (e.g., field notes, e-mails, reflection journals, etc.).
- Debrief (oral and written).
- Code data.
- Analyze data.
- Interpret data.
- Increase awareness (to create adaptations and/or implement change).

Within these guidelines, we discovered some further helpful techniques to facilitate the process of peer observation.

- Adapt observation forms to meet goals.
- Color-code emerging themes.
- Dialogue frequently.
- Write reflections.

We have provided some guidelines and explicit techniques about the process of conducting peer observation that can be applied to almost any other research goals that involve library instruction and service. We encourage librarians to use peer observation as an opportunity to influence the information-seeking behavior of students by providing a bridge of support from the classroom to the library. Peer observation as part of a qualitative study can contribute to a practitioner's ability to observe, reflect, and act.

Notes

1. Nancy Fried Foster, "The Mommy Model of Service," in *Studying Students: The Undergraduate Research Project at the University of Rochester,* ed. Nancy Fried Foster and Susan Gibbons (Chicago: ACRL, 2007), 75.
2. Ibid.
3. Catherine F. Riehle and Michael Witt, "Librarians in the Hall: Instructional Outreach in Campus Residences," *College & Undergraduate Libraries* 16 (2009): 107–21.
4. Ibid.
5. Ibid.
6. Ellysa Stern Cahoy, Assistant Head, Library Learning Services at Penn State University, coined this phrase.
7. Lynda Baker, "Observation: A Complex Research Method," *Library Trends* 55, no. 1 (2006): 171–89.
8. Ibid.
9. Ibid.
10. Amanda Coffey and Paul Atkinson, *Making Sense of Qualitative Data: Complementary Research Strategies* (Thousand Oaks, CA: Sage, 1996).
11. Catherine Marshall and Gretchen Rossman, *Designing Qualitative Research,* 4th ed. (Thousand Oaks, CA: Sage, 2006).
12. Uwe Flick, *An Introduction to Qualitative Research,* 3rd ed. (London: Sage, 2006).
13. Norman Denzin and Yvonna Lincoln, *Strategies of Qualitative Inquiry,* 2nd ed. (Thousand Oaks, CA: Sage, 2003).
14. Wilhelmina C. Savenye and Rhonda S. Robinson, "Using Qualitative Research Methods in Higher Education," *Journal of Computing in Higher Education* 16, no. 2 (2005): 65–95; Denzin and Lincoln, *Strategies of Qualitative Inquiry.*
15. Stephen Kemmis and Robin McTaggart, "Participatory Action Research: Communicative Action and the Public Sphere," in *Strategies of Qualitative Inquiry,* 3rd ed., ed. Norman Denzin and Yvonna Lincoln, (Thousand Oaks, CA: Sage, 2008), 271–330.
16. In some cases, recording and transcription are used in conjunction with field notes. In this instance, we decided to use field notes alone, as field notes can provide text for immediate analysis.
17. David Silverman, *Interpretive Qualitative Data: Methods for Analyzing Talk, Text, and Interaction* (Thousand Oaks, CA: Sage, 2004).
18. Coffey and Atkinson, *Making Sense of Qualitative Data.*
19. Ibid., 31.
20. Baker, "Observation."
21. R. Burke Johnson, "Examining the Validity Structure of Qualitative Research," *Education* 118, no. 2 (1997): 282.
22. Silverman, *Interpretive Qualitative Data,* 70.
23. Brenda Capobianco and James Lehman, "Integrating Technology to Foster Inquiry in an Elementary Science Methods Course: An Action Research Study of One Teacher Educator's Initiatives in a PT3 Project," *Journal of Computers in Mathematics and Science Teaching* 25, no. 2 (2006): 123–46.

24. Silverman, *Interpretive Qualitative Data*, 70.

25. Baker, "Observation."

26. Patricia A. Adler and Peter Adler, "Observational Techniques," in *Handbook of Qualitative Research,* ed. Norman. K. Denzin and Yvonna S. Lincoln, 377–92 (Thousand Oaks, CA: Sage, 1998).

27. G. E Gorman and Peter Clayton, *Qualitative Research for the Information Professional: A Practical Handbook* (London: Facet, 2005).

28. Ibid., 104.

29. Gorman and Clayton, *Qualitative Research for the Information Professional.*

30. Gordon Wells, *Dialogic Inquiry: Towards a Sociocultural Practice and Theory of Education* (Cambridge: Cambridge University Press, 1999).

31. Benjamin Harris, "Communities as Necessity in Information Literacy Development: Challenging the Standards," *The Journal of Academic Librarianship* 34 (2008): 248–55.

32. Ibid.

33. Jean Lave, *Situated Learning: Legitimate Peripheral Participation* (Cambridge: Cambridge University Press, 1991).

34. Kevin Simons, James Young, and Craig Gibson, "The Learning Library in Context: Community, Integration and Influence," *Research Strategies* 17 (2000): 123–32.

35. Etienne Wenger, *Communities of Practice: Learning, Meaning and Identity* (Cambridge: Cambridge University Press, 1998).

36. Joseph Maxwell, *Qualitative Research Design: An Interpretive Approach* (Thousand Oaks, CA: Sage, 1996).

37. Ibid.

38. Silverman, *Interpretive Qualitative Data.*

39. Thomas A. Schwandt, *Dictionary of Qualitative Inquiry*, 2nd ed. (Thousand Oaks, CA: Sage, 2001), 155-156.

40. Community College Survey of Student Engagement, "Classroom Observation Form," 2006, http://www.ccsse.org/publications/CCSSE%20Classroom%20Observation%20Form.pdf (accessed December 6, 2010).

41. Silverman, *Interpretive Qualitative Data.*

42. Center for Teaching Effectiveness, The University of Texas at Austin, *Preparing for Peer Observation: A Guidebook,* 1999, http://www.tlataskforce.uconn.edu/docs/resources/Texas_Peer_Observation_Guidelines.pdf.

43. Virginia Adult Learning Resource Center, "Notes for Classroom Observation," http://www.aelweb.vcu.edu/projects/observation/directnotes.pdf (accessed August 20, 2008; site now discontinued).

44. Courtney Cazden, "The Situation: A Neglected Source of Social Class Differences in Language Use," *Journal of Social Issues* 26 (1970): 35–60; William Labov and David Fanshel, *Therapeutic Discourse: Psychotherapy as Conversation* (New York: Academic Press, 1977).

45. Courtney Cazden, *Classroom Discourse: The Language of Teaching and Learning* (Portsmouth, NH: Heinemann, 1988).

46. Michelle Ortlipp, "Keeping and Using Reflective Journals in the Qualitative Research Process," *The Qualitative Report 13,* no. 4 (2008): 695–705.

47. James Joseph Scheurich, *Research Method in the Postmodern,* Qualitative Studies Series 3 (Washington, DC: Falmer Press, 1997).

48. Jeff Purdue, "Stories, Not Information: Transforming Information Literacy," *portal: Libraries and the Academy 3,* no. 4 (2003): 653–62.

Content Analysis: Deconstructing Intellectual Packages

Penny M. Beile

Abstract. This chapter describes content analysis as a research approach of particular use to the library field and discusses how systematic review of documents such as course syllabi can be used to inform instructional decisions. The objective of the study was to explore the extent of library instruction integration throughout eleven teacher candidate programs at a large urban university. Syllabi were identified from fifteen courses that were common to all programs or that were required in more than eight of the eleven programs. Using content analysis, data were collected from each of the syllabi. Findings were compared to timing and content of library-provided instruction. Results indicated that students who were given assignments requiring library research skills generally had library instruction scheduled with the class, that the content of offered library instruction sessions was aligned with the types of skills needed to complete the assignment, and that the content of the library instruction sessions generally built upon library research skills introduced earlier. However, the saturation of assignments that required research skills was lower than expected, and the majority of those assignments required only basic level library research skills to complete.

Introduction

Critical thinking and problem-solving skills as they relate to an individual's recognition of their information need and their ability to efficiently and effectively meet that need are fundamental to success in a rapidly changing, technology- and information-intensive environment. Students are expected to learn these skills in school, yet concerns exist as to whether teachers are adequately prepared to teach them. Perhaps this is one reason why the National Council for the Accreditation of Teacher Education,[1] the American Association of School Librarians together with the Association for Educational Communications and Technology,[2] and the International Society for Technology in Education[3] have adopted information literacy as a key outcome for teacher education students. This chapter explores the extent of library instruction integration throughout eleven teacher candidate programs at a large urban university, first by describing the campuswide information fluency initiative as context, then reporting on the results of a content analysis of course syllabi study to investigate exposure to and sequencing of library instruction for teacher education students.

Information fluency was adopted by the University of Central Florida (UCF) in 2006 in response to the request for a Quality Enhancement Plan (QEP) by the Southern Association for Colleges and Schools

(SACS) Commission on Colleges, the institution's regional accrediting body. In its *Handbook for Institutions Seeking Reaffirmation*, the Commission on Colleges states that the QEP both reflects and confirms a commitment to enhancing the quality of higher education and places student learning at the heart of the mission of academia.[4] Upon selection of information fluency as the QEP topic, a week-long professional development institute was held on campus to refine participants' understanding of the concept and to arrive at an implementation plan.

The institute consisted of a series of meetings attended by librarians, program faculty, and administrators. The university relied on the Associated Colleges of the South's definition of information fluency, which states that information fluency uses critical thinking skills and appropriate technologies to collect necessary information, evaluate and analyze it, formulate conclusions, and present them in an appropriate and effective way.[5] Institute attendees worked from this definition to come to a shared understanding of what an information-fluent student would look like, whether information fluency skills varied by program or degree, and how information fluency skills could be integrated throughout general education and program curricula. In following educational best practices, attendees agreed that students should progressively acquire information fluency skills as they advanced through their programs. Research and technology skills introduced in earlier classes would be built upon by continuing to offer increasingly complex information-related skills and assignments.

Four major programs were initially selected to implement information fluency across their curricula. These programs were the College of Nursing, the Burnett Honors College, the Philosophy Department, and Strategies for Success (which is part of the First Year Academic Experience program). The initiative was envisioned as a joint effort between program faculty and librarians, with faculty assuming primary responsibility for the critical thinking and technology components of information fluency and librarians providing support for information literacy training. Participating faculty were expected to define the characteristics of information-fluent students upon the students' exit from the program, and they were primarily responsible for implementing and assessing information fluency concepts across their respective programs. Library subject specialists worked in close collaboration with faculty from the pilot programs to identify student learning outcomes, design instructional activities, and assist in mapping those outcomes and activities throughout the curriculum.

Other academic programs, including the teacher education program, participated to a lesser degree. A number of education faculty quickly adopted the ACRL *Information Literacy Competency Standards for Higher Education*,[6] created assignments that included information literacy components, and scheduled library instruction sessions in response to the adoption of information fluency as the institution's QEP. However, a large portion of the remaining teacher education program faculty either did not recognize the value of information fluency as a core learning outcome or had course schedules that were too compressed to include additional assignments or library instruction sessions. Librarians were concerned that they had been only moderately successful in implementing an information literacy program across the undergraduate teacher education curriculum. This limited success seemed especially possible given earlier successes with a similar doctoral program.

Several years previous, librarians and program coordinators had worked to infuse information literacy concepts and library instruction throughout the doctor of education program. This collaboration resulted in a complete revision of the EdD program, with a substantial part of the new program dedicated to using the scholarly literature to critically analyze and thoroughly understand problems and issues in education. The genesis of the revision was based on assessment results that indicated doctoral candidates did not have a sophisticated understanding of the scholarly publication process and lacked the necessary skills to effectively access and use the academic literature. Drawing from the success of the doctoral program revision, it was decided to examine the state of information literacy and library instruction integration for the undergraduate teacher education program. Results of the study would be shared with program faculty, and further coordination of library instruction or library-related assignments would be suggested, if indicated.

Prior to the current study, librarians and program faculty had targeted three key teacher education courses at the undergraduate level that would include a library instruction component. The courses selected were EDG 2005, Introduction to the Teaching Profession, a prerequisite course that students were expected to take in their freshman year, prior to being admitted to the program; EDG 4603, Analysis and Application of Ethical, Legal, and Safety Issues in Schools, a course generally taken as students matriculated into their upper division courses, at the end of their sophomore year; and EDG 4410, Teaching Strategies and Classroom Management, a course taken just before students started their internships, toward the end of their program. The first two courses were selected based on the rationale that students would receive a traditional library instruction class early in their program of study and again before moving into their specialization areas. The third course, Teaching Strategies, was dedicated to creating lesson plans and conducting *microteaches*, which are twenty-minute presentations delivered to fellow students to demonstrate teaching techniques appropriate to their grade level and subject expertise in preparation for the students' internship experiences. Students enrolled in this course attend an orientation to the curriculum materials library, where they receive instruction on locating materials on effective teaching strategies, lesson plans and state education standards, and PK–12 teaching resources.

Despite the plan to have students attend three library instruction classes spread out over their academic careers, librarians and teaching faculty questioned whether this level of research skills training was sufficient and if the instruction was appropriately sequenced. To address these concerns, information needed to be gathered about the number and types of assignments students were expected to complete, whether the assignments required research skills, and which research skills were associated with each assignment. The goal of this study was to analyze course syllabi from an undergraduate teacher education program for assignments that required research

skills for the purpose of investigating whether current levels of instructional support reflected best practices for curriculum-integrated instruction. Course syllabi were selected as the data source because they already existed, were easily obtainable, and were thought to contain the information needed to address the research questions. Given this decision, content analysis was deemed the research approach best suited to analyze syllabi from identified education courses for assignments that require library research.

The remainder of this chapter provides a brief overview of the history of content analysis and its use in library and syllabus studies, an explanation of content analysis methods and the five-part methodological framework used in this study, and a discussion of the study's findings and conclusions.

Literature Review

At its most fundamental level, content analysis is a research approach that has been widely used to study the content of human communication. Content analysis has been traced as far back as the seventeenth century, when researchers and scribes used it to analyze religious documents; accordingly, it has been credited as one of the earliest forms of systematic analysis.[7] Content analysis continued to be used throughout history to study texts and documents, but re-emerged in the 1940s as an approach for studying propaganda messages.[8] Since that time, it has been increasingly employed in communication and media studies, and content analysis techniques have been widely applied to study aspects of marketing and business, literature, cultural studies, and other areas in the humanities and social sciences.[9] Content analysis has a long history as a methodology that incorporates a variety of analytic techniques. This diversity remains a central characteristic of the approach and allows it to be simultaneously characterized as both a qualitative and a quantitative methodology.[10]

Content Analysis Defined

Definitions of content analysis reflect this diversity and vary according to whether emphasis is placed on analytic technique or research process. Early researchers, who tended to privilege analytic technique over the process, generally describe content analysis as a quantitative methodology.[11] Berelson's definition of content analysis as "a research technique for the objective, systematic, and quantitative description of manifest content and communications"[12] is consistent with many similar definitions from the quantitative school of thought. However, other researchers emphasize the inferential aspects of content analysis and describe it based on process rather than analytic technique. Busch and her colleagues broadly define content analysis as a method that is "used to determine the presence of certain words, themes, [and] concepts within documents and to analyze this presence in an objective and systematic manner."[13] Stemler draws from noted authors in the field, including Berelson, Krippendorf, and Weber, to arrive at a succinct definition of content analysis as a "systematic, replicable technique for compressing many words of text into fewer content categories based on explicit rules of coding."[14]

A content analysis study conducted from a quantitative perspective emphasizes the use of predetermined hypotheses, terms and concepts, and coding rules. The following example, adapted from Kimberly Neuendorf's *Content Analysis Guidebook*,[15] describes steps generally performed when conducting a quantitative content analysis study. First, research questions and hypotheses are defined, and a determination as to what content will be examined is made. Next, the terms or concepts are operationally defined, and the categories they will be assigned are determined. Coding rules and a coding form are then created based on these conceptualizations, and a census of the content is taken and a sampling frame established. Content is then coded, and definitions or categories are refined, if needed. Finally, results are tabulated and reported.

When performing content analysis from a qualitative perspective, a researcher often begins with open-ended research questions that guide data gathering and analysis. The actual process of conducting a content analysis follows steps similar to those outlined above, regardless of approach. However, as with other qualitative methods, qualitative content analysis allows for a design that is often described as emergent and iterative. A qualitative design is emergent in the sense that significant concepts and analytic techniques, such as the sample and coding scheme, unfold during the course of the study rather than being decided upon prior to coding the document. The process is iterative because the researcher continually seeks to identify and refine definitions and categories during the coding process.

Researchers often find they have no choice in deciding whether to use an emergent design as opposed to using predefined terms and concepts. If no theory or research exists to inform coding decisions, then a researcher may be compelled to explore the content to identify pertinent terms and concepts. A researcher who chooses (or is obliged) to conduct a qualitative content analysis study starts with an identified problem or a series of open-ended questions and selects a purposive sample most likely to include complete, accurate answers to the questions. During the process of iteratively reading or reviewing the data, significant concepts and patterns are identified, and the researcher begins to decide how to distinguish among them. A coding scheme that defines rules and categories is ultimately decided upon, and selected documents are coded. Finally, results are analyzed and reported.

Content Analysis in Library and Syllabus Studies

Content analysis is a popular methodology in the library field and has been used with varying goals and objectives. A summary of the diverse types of studies conducted using content analysis as a methodology was presented in a 2006 publication authored by White and Marsh.[16] The purpose, technique, and type of analysis were described for twenty-five content analysis studies conducted in the field of library and information science between 1991 and 2005. Of the twenty-five studies reviewed, fifteen were qualitative, two were quantitative, and eight employed a mixed-methods approach. The study topics ranged from examining the portrayal of librarians in popular culture, to investigating students' perceptions of research and research paper anxiety, to comparing communication patterns of participants on consumer health electronic lists.[17] Data analyzed for these studies were pulled from the following resources, respectively: obituaries in the *New York Times*, student narratives on the research paper experience, and posts from consumer health electronic lists.

More recently, content analysis has been used to analyze open-ended responses to LibQUAL+, which is a survey designed to help librarians understand users' opinions of their services. Dennis and Bower systematically explored the content of narrative responses to the survey by coding them into meaningful categories which were used to more easily interpret survey results.[18] The researchers identified and evaluated issues of greatest concern to their customers to aid decision-making processes and strategic planning. These topics and sources illustrate the diverse application of content analysis as an analytic technique in the field of library and information studies.

Well-written course syllabi can contain a wealth of information, and content analysis methods have been used to pull meaning from them. Course syllabi have been analyzed to identify core content and teaching methods taught across strategic management and social work programs,[19] to determine theories and philosophies underlying course designs in multicultural teacher education,[20] and to investigate course content and how consistent instruction is with identified competencies for spiritual counselors.[21] Content analysis also has been used to analyze courses offered among library schools to arrive at an understanding of the preparation of library professionals for specific work.[22] In another study, course catalog descriptions, syllabi, and course and degree requirements were analyzed to determine the current level of instruction for working with serials or continuing resources,[23] and syllabi of business information courses being taught at library and information science programs were analyzed for similar purposes.[24]

Syllabus analysis studies in library settings also have been used to cull reading lists to develop collections and to inform library instruction decisions. Analysis of assignments from well-written syllabi, tracked over a program, has implications for coordinating and integrating library instruction. VanScoy and Oakleaf analyzed syllabi for research skills required of first-year students in college to provide evidence for the importance of broad-based library instruction.[25] They reported, "97 percent of students were required to find research resources during the first semester of their first year of college"[26] and concluded that the basic tier of instruction should address a wide range of research skills.

Methodology

Content analysis is a research approach that has been widely used to unobtrusively analyze human communication and was the methodology employed for this exploratory study. To conduct a content analysis, a document is coded into categories, which are based on actual words or the sense of the words, phrases, or themes found in the document, and then examined through an identified methodological protocol. Results of the analysis are used to make inferences about the messages within the documents or about the context from which the documents were derived.[27]

Content analysis can be broken into two general types, *conceptual analysis* and *relational analysis*; conceptual analysis generally corresponds to a quantitative approach, while relational analysis is more aligned to a qualitative perspective. Early content analysis studies tended to rely on conceptual analysis as an analytic technique. This type of analysis establishes the existence and rate of occurrence of words or concepts in or among documents, so word counts are generally performed to determine the frequency of the identified words and concepts.[28] In more recent years, researchers have started using content analysis to analyze concepts or models rather than simply words and to examine relationships rather than simply presence. Thus relational analysis expands conceptual analysis one step more, by examining the relationships among concepts in a document or to the context of the document. A researcher performing a relational analysis study relies on inference to establish the existence of relationships, which is a hallmark of the qualitative genre.

Similarly, two types of content can be coded: *manifest content*—that which is clearly evident and therefore easily countable—and *latent content*, which is more abstract in nature. Manifest content is most closely aligned with conceptual analysis, while latent content is associated with relational analysis. An example from a recent article by Spurgin and Wildemuth[29] can be used to illustrate these differences. The article reported on a study that investigated the level of library anxiety in user narratives. If the objective of the study was to interpret the level of library anxiety apparent from the narratives, researchers could have conducted the analysis by counting the frequency of manifest indicators of library anxiety, or the identified words, themes, and phrases that reflect anxiousness related to using libraries. This approach could be described as coding manifest content to conduct a conceptual analysis.

However, if the researchers chose to explore associations between the presence of library anxiety and the context of the event in which it occurred, they would be conducting a relational analysis. In this instance, the researchers would move from identifying the presence or levels of library anxiety in the narratives to examining contextual relationships between anxiety and at what points of the information-seeking process anxiousness is most likely to occur. Relational studies rely on inference, and ensuring that the study is as precise and accurate as possible is of utmost importance. Thus, extreme care must be taken when coding indicators beyond the obvious (latent content) or when seeking to establish connections between a construct like library anxiety and the context in which it occurs. To maintain rigor in the study, these associations should be grounded in psychological theory, expert knowledge, or previous research, when possible.[30]

While reviewing definitions and histories of content analysis and studies that report using various approaches and methods, loose associations begin to emerge. Typically, earlier studies relied on quantitative counts of words or concepts to determine their presence and frequency for conceptual analyses. Relational analysis, which is a more recent analytic technique, often begins with the same counting approach as conceptual analysis, but ultimately aligns with naturalistic traditions when relating the underlying context of the message to theory or relevant research. The current study employs a conceptual analysis approach when counting the frequency of assignments, which are explicitly stated, manifest concepts, and when coding the concepts into distinct categories. However, as little relevant research or existing theory was uncovered, the study, by default, was more inferential and iterative than objective and predetermined, thus placing it firmly in the qualitative tradition.

Following Okumus and Wong,[31] the study was undertaken utilizing the following five steps: (1) developing research aims and a research framework, (2) finding and selecting appropriate cases to study, (3) analyzing documents so that significant concepts are identified, (4) refining the categories, and (5) analyzing and summarizing the findings. The remainder of this section describes how the study progressed through the five stages.

Develop Research Aims and Framework

First, the aims and objectives of the study were decided upon and an initial coding framework was developed. The goal of the study was to identify assignments that require research skills from course syllabi in an undergraduate teacher education program, with the purpose of comparing results to suggested best practices for curriculum-integrated information literacy instruction. The coding framework was developed in order to gather sufficient information to address study aims and included the following fields:

1. Type of class (whether it was a prerequisite or core)
2. Course number and title of the class
3. Assignment outcomes associated with each course
4. A determination as to whether research skills were required to complete each assignment
5. Assignment components, or the types of materials needed to complete each assignment

6. Discrete skill categories, or actual skills required for component parts of the assignment
7. The level or intensity of the assignment as it relates to research skill levels

The first four fields were part of the initial framework and were coded based on information found in the syllabus. The remaining fields were added at a later step and were inferred from information gleaned in the first five fields.

Select Appropriate Cases to Study

One of the disadvantages of content analysis is that it can be extremely time-consuming; therefore, many researchers choose to select a sample from all the documents of interest. Selecting a sample is a critical step when conducting a study, and it is imperative that the sample be of adequate breadth and depth to represent all dimensions of the field to which it will be generalized.[32] For example, if you want to be able to make recommendations that cover the time period from when a student enters into a program until he or she exits, you would not limit your analysis to capstone courses. Determining the number of cases to use is equally important, but guidelines exist that suggest fifteen cases can be sufficient[33] and that only slight differences occur among sample sizes larger than twelve.[34]

For the current study, a total of eleven undergraduate programs in education were identified from the university's undergraduate catalog. The programs consisted of Art Education, Early Childhood Education, Elementary Education, English Language Arts Education, Exceptional Student Education, Foreign Language Education (French and Spanish), Mathematics Education, Science Education (Biology), Social Science Education, Sports and Fitness, and Technical Education and Industry Training. Program descriptions were reviewed in an effort to identify classes that were common to all programs. The survey revealed three education program course prerequisites and five education core requirements courses that students in every program were expected to take,

for a total of eight courses. In an effort to enlarge the sample size, more courses were reviewed for inclusion. Seven additional courses were found that were required in more than eight of the eleven programs and were added to the analysis.

Course instructors are expected to place recent copies of syllabi on a local intranet to comply with internal accreditation procedures, and at least one recent syllabus was located for each course. Quite often multiple sections of a single course will be taught by various tenured, tenure-track, or adjunct instructors, and in these cases it was not unusual to find several syllabi for each course. When this occurred, the syllabi from all instructors were compared and the syllabus with the most detailed assignment description was selected for analysis.

Each of the selected syllabi met the information requirements of the study. In other words, each syllabus contained sufficient information about the areas identified in the research framework. A total of fifteen syllabi were selected for review, thus meeting Hodson's suggestion that fifteen cases can be sufficient for an exploratory analysis.[35] The decision to limit the analysis to fifteen syllabi was further warranted as the study, by design, focused on prerequisite and core courses required across the undergraduate education curriculum. If warranted, additional analysis could be conducted on a program-by-program basis at a later point.

Analyze Documents and Identify Concepts

In this stage of the study, the content of fifteen syllabi was analyzed following the coding framework that was established earlier. The purpose of the framework is to systematically apply the criteria to all selected documents in order to extract uniform and standardized data.[36] The coding framework was essential for categorizing the information into the fields and for making decisions about how to distinguish among the category entries as they began to emerge. The first two fields (type of class and course number and title) were easily classified into objective categories. Course number and title were taken from the undergraduate catalog, and type of class was

TABLE 8.1
Sample Coding Framework (first four fields of six assignments from five courses)

Type	Course/Title	Assignment Outcomes	Require Research Skills?
Core	EDG4467 Learning Theory	Microteach	Yes
Core	RED3012 Reading Foundations	Reading portfolio	Yes
Core	EDG4410 Teaching Strategies	Write letter home	No
Core	EDG4410 Teaching Strategies	Jr. Achievement training	No
Core	RED4043 Reading K–12	Annotated bibliography	Yes
Core	EDG4603 Ethical, Legal, Safety	Article critique	Yes

coded as core or prerequisite. These determinations would become useful when comparing assignments to availability of library instructional support and sequencing. Next, all assignments associated with the course were entered into the framework. The assignments varied widely, with examples ranging from conducting a fifteen- to twenty-minute microteach activity, to creating a reading portfolio, writing letters to parents of students, attending Junior Achievement training, summarizing the literature for an annotated bibliography, and critiquing an article. Assignments were then coded as to whether they required library research skills to complete them (see table 8.1).

The library-related assignments were further parsed into discrete components of the assignment that included all related outcomes that students would need to complete the assignment. For example, the assignment field included entries such as microteach, reading portfolio, annotated bibliography, and article critique. Components of the microteach assignment consisted of locating lesson plans and state standards, as well as finding teaching resources and information on the topics to be taught (see table 8.2). The reading portfolio assignment component required that students locate, read, and summarize fifty young adult books. Following this step, assignment components were translated into library research skills and assigned skill intensity levels.

Refine Categories

Neuendorf suggests that terms and concepts to be analyzed should be based on existing theory, but in lieu of theory, terms and concepts can be drawn from personal expertise.[37] However they are arrived at, terms and concepts to be examined should be operationally defined, and units of data to be collected should be aligned to defined categories that are exhaustive and mutually exclusive.[38] Several earlier syllabus studies also grouped assignments into various categories, but the groups often were too general or stopped at identifying assignment outcomes instead of classifying them by research skills. For example, assignment groups like "library reviews," "periodical assignments," and "research," which are terms used in other studies, offered little insight into the actual skills needed to complete an assignment. For purposes of mapping library instruction throughout the curriculum, the researcher needed not only to know the assignment outcomes, but also to infer the types and levels of skills required of students to complete them.

Only one syllabus analysis was uncovered that coded assignments by skill instead of outcomes. VanScoy and Oakleaf investigated the breadth and types of assignments given to first-year students to make instructional decisions and arrived at five categories of skills.[39] The categories they identified were find Web sites, find articles, find books, find reference books, and find data and statistics. VanScoy and Oakleaf's groups were used as a starting point for the current study and modified as the study progressed. None of the assignments from the fifteen syllabi required students to locate data and statistics, so this group was deleted and replaced with find *realia* (which are also referred to as *manipulatives* or *teaching resources*). This decision was based on the rationale that education students are often required to locate teaching materials for their assignments and that the materials are distinct enough from other resources in the catalog to warrant their own group. Coding for assignment outcomes and the skills needed to complete the assignment provided the information necessary for the researcher to infer skill intensity level.

Finding books by searching the library catalog was the primary skill needed to complete both the microteach and the reading portfolio assignments. However, the *level* of skills needed to complete the microteach assignment, which required that students locate a number of diverse materials found in various libraries and in a variety of formats, was deemed more difficult than the reading portfolio assignment, which required students to locate only one type of item (although a greater quantity). Similarly, students needed to be able to find articles to complete the annotated bibliography and the article critique assignments, but the expectations for the bibliography required higher level skills than for the article critique and were rated accordingly.

At the end of the fourth stage, entries had been reviewed to the point where they were coded into independent, mutually exclusive, and exhaustive categories. Skill levels (basic, moderate, or intensive) also were assigned, and depended on the complexity and requirements of the assignment. This level of categorization permitted discrete activities related to acquiring and using research skills to be identified, which would in turn allow for the skills needed to perform the assignments to be aligned with library instruction objectives. Following this stage, results of the analysis were ready to be summarized and compared to existing library instructional support.

Summarize Findings

Analysis of syllabi from the fifteen courses yielded 143 assignments. Of the assignments, 110 or 73 percent did not require library skills to complete them. Examples of assignments that did not require library skills included writing reflection papers, letters to parents, and newsletters; taking examinations; using technology applications (such as electronic

TABLE 8.2

Sample Coding for Microteach and Reading Portfolio Assignment (select fields)

Course Title	Assignment Outcomes	Assignment Components	Discrete Skills	Skill Intensity
Learning Theory	Microteach	Lesson plan State standards Topic information Teaching resources	Find books Find books Find books Find realia	Moderate
Reading Foundations	Reading portfolio	50 young adult books	Find books	Basic
Reading K–12	Annotated bibliography	Primary resource articles Monographs Citation guides	Find articles Find books Find books	Intensive
Ethical, Legal, Safety	Article critique	Locate a scholarly article	Find articles	Basic

grading systems or video editing software); and participating in field experiences and service learning. Of the 143 assignments, 33, or 27 percent, did require library research skills to complete them.

Library-related assignments were further coded into skill intensity levels that ranged from basic to intensive. Of the 33 assignments, 21 were coded as basic, 7 were moderate, and 5 were intensive. Examples of assignments that were coded as requiring only basic skill levels included "summarize an article" or "conduct a book talk." Examples of moderate skill level assignments were "write a short paper" or "develop a unit plan," and assignments coded as requiring intensive skill levels were "create an annotated bibliography" or "write a lengthy paper."

Assignments were also tracked by class level. Syllabi from four entry-level 2000 classes were analyzed, revealing a total of 41 assignments. Of those assignments, 5 required library research skills to complete them. The three junior-level 3000 classes had 18 assignments in total, of which 3 required research skills. The eight senior-level 4000 classes had 84 assignments, of which 25 required research skills. Skill levels for the entry-level classes ranged from basic to moderate, while upperclass courses ranged from basic to intensive. Table 8.3 shows the range of skills broken out by class level.

As noted earlier, three education courses had been identified as key points in the program for students to receive library instruction. The first course, EDG 2005, Introduction to the Teaching Profession, is a prerequisite and is generally taken when students enter the program. Of the six assignments given in the class, only one required research skills. Assignment components included finding information on a topic,

using subject-specific encyclopedias and periodicals, and presenting the topic to the class. Library instruction offered in conjunction with the class was tailored to the course assignments and focused on how to access and search a periodical database and the library catalog, how to find background information on a topic, and how to locate materials in print or electronically. The skill level needed to complete the assignment was coded as moderate intensity.

Students often take the second course targeted for library instruction, EDG 4603, Analysis and Application of Ethical, Legal, and Safety Issues in Schools, toward the end of their sophomore year, prior to beginning their specialization courses. This course had eleven assignments, three of which required research skills; research skill levels needed to complete the assignments ranged from basic to intensive. An article critique assignment that was coded as "find article" was designated a basic level research skill. This was followed by a short paper that also required students to access the periodical literature. Requirements for this assignment included using primary source, peer-reviewed articles and was rated a moderate skill level assignment. The final assignment was described as an oral presentation and paper. Students were expected to locate background information on a topic and use a minimum of ten articles and monographs for the bibliography. This assignment was rated intensive due to the need to search periodical databases for scholarly articles and the library catalog for encyclopedias, books, and citation guides. Library instruction provided for this course builds upon skills introduced in EDG 2005; students review basic searching techniques and are taught more advanced search skills and concepts.

The third course targeted for library instruction, EDG 4410, Teaching Strategies and Classroom Management, is generally taken the last semester of coursework, just before students start their internships. As in EDG 4603, eleven assignments were associated with this course, and three of them required library skills to complete. The three assignments included presenting a poster session and conducting two microteaches. The poster and microteach assignments required students to locate lesson

TABLE 8.3
Skill Levels by Class Level

Skill Level	Class Level			Total
	2000	3000	4000	
Basic	3	1	17	21
Moderate	2	1	4	7

plans and state standards, find information on their topic and teaching techniques, and use realia in their presentations. Each of the assignments was rated intensive due to its breadth and complexity; several databases would need to be searched using advanced searching techniques and multiple library collections accessed. This library instruction class is held in the Curriculum Materials Center, and students rotate through three workstations where they receive instruction on advanced searching techniques to locate curriculum support materials, textbooks, and lesson plans and how to use equipment such as a laminator, opaque projector, and Smartboard. This instruction reinforces concepts introduced in earlier library instruction classes, but instruction on the use of certain equipment is specific to this class.

Discussion

The overarching aim of the study was to determine whether library research skills were being systematically and progressively integrated across the teacher education curriculum. To address this aim, a content analysis of course syllabi was conducted to investigate whether library instruction for three identified courses was being offered in conjunction with assignments that required library research skills and whether the instruction was sufficient. The researcher was primarily interested in determining if library instruction followed recommendations for best practices by being offered at appropriate points and whether the content of the instruction session was aligned to the level of skills students needed to complete the assignments. Of related interest were the types of library-related projects assigned by the faculty, the level of research skills needed to complete them, and whether they also were progressively stepped throughout the curriculum.

In general, results of the analysis revealed that the three courses identified to receive library instruction were appropriately sequenced and aligned to increasingly complex assignments and skill intensity levels. Further, the content of the instruction provided by the library was targeted to course and assignment needs. Results of the study supported the decision to select the three courses for library instruction.

Based on this analysis, no changes were recommended regarding the content or timing of the library instruction offered in the three courses.

However, other courses offered assignments that required library research skills to complete them, and results were analyzed by the suggested sequence of the course in the program. This was done to ensure that students had received some form of library instruction prior to being asked to complete an assignment that required library research skills to complete it. Courses coded as having library-related assignments were compared by sequence and skill levels to the classes targeted for library instruction. Thirty-three assignments required some research or library-related skills to complete them. Twenty-one of these were designated as basic skills, seven were moderate, and five were intensive. If students followed the suggested sequence for their programs of study, every course with an intensive skill level–rated assignment was held during the same semester or after students received their second instruction session.

Further, courses that have moderate or intensive level assignments were compared to courses that had requested library instruction. Of the fifteen syllabi that were coded, twelve had library-related assignments. Three of the classes were designated key library instruction classes, and the remaining nine were compared to lists of courses that had requested library instruction. Four of the nine courses had scheduled a library instruction session in the past year. Based on the belief that students would benefit from a session to refresh and reinforce skills covered in one of the three targeted courses, one recommendation from the study is to selectively promote the library instruction program to faculty from courses that offer library-related assignments not already targeted to receive library instruction.

Twenty-seven percent of assignments required library research skills to complete them. No benchmarks were found to indicate whether this figure is high or low. However, of some concern is that of the thirty-three assignments requiring library research skills, twenty-one could be completed using basic level skills, while only twelve called for moderate or intensive skills. This leads to the question of whether faculty are unaware of the library instruction sequence and thus reluctant to ask students to perform at higher levels or if there is another explanation. Either way, this finding will be brought to the attention of faculty on the Undergraduate Curriculum Committee, with the recommendation that some of the basic level assignments found toward the end of the program be revised to require higher level library-related skills to complete them.

Summary and Conclusion

The overall intention of this study was to achieve some degree of understanding of how library instruction is aligned to assignments from the core curriculum of an undergraduate teacher education program. Curriculum-integrated library instruction is an elemental aspect of information fluency; however, surprisingly little research was found that actually reported on the state of instructional integration for a particular programmatic area or that described a methodological approach for investigating it. Results of the content analysis helped to clarify the extent to which library instruction was aligned to course assignments that required some level of library research skills to complete them. As one of the first empirical research studies in this area, this paper adds to the professional literature by reporting on a systematic analysis of syllabi of core courses across an undergraduate teacher education curriculum.

When conducting a syllabus study, it is understood that each institution and each program is unique and that research findings are pertinent only to the curriculum studied. Therefore, the results of the study are not generalizable to other situations. This is one reason why VanScoy and Oakleaf challenged librarians who are planning curriculum-integrated instruction programs to undertake their own syllabus studies.[40] At the local level, syllabus studies can be conducted across various disciplines or programs or across the institution, such as the first-year experience or the general education program. Rather than relying on declarative knowledge or anecdotal information, an ongoing investigation of syllabi may lead to a deeper understanding of the processes in place and the purposes behind them for any given curriculum. Certainly, making recommendations based on

research findings of a systematic analysis adds credibility when discussing instructional support or future directions with the teaching faculty or administration.

The methodology employed by this study offers one lens through which library instruction programs can consider their alignment with the subject area curriculum and also presents a replicable model for similar studies. However, as programs across institutions are as distinct as the reasons for conducting content analyses of syllabi, each analysis will likely involve some modifications to this study's methods. Content analysis studies, by nature, offer flexible methodologies, but core aspects must be adhered to when planning and carrying out a study. For example, when modifying the coding framework or designing a new one, researchers should ensure that the fields and categories are unique, exhaustive, and mutually exclusive. Indeed, any successful and rigorous study is contingent upon careful planning and explicit, consistently applied rules for proper categorization and systematic decision making.[41]

Content analysis as used in this study is an emergent design, and the fundamental concern with these designs (as with all qualitative research) is that conclusions reached by inferential analysis can be challenged. Underlying analytic techniques that rely on inference is the question of whether conclusions follow from the data or whether they are explainable due to some other phenomenon. Threats to validity, or the correspondence of the categories to the conclusions, may occur when trying to attain a higher level of interpretation and draw meaningful inferences about contextual relationships.[42] Stemler states, "When used properly, content analysis is a powerful data reduction technique" and notes the importance of following stringent guidelines by emphasizing that "it is a systematic, replicable technique for compressing many words of text into fewer content categories based on explicit rules of coding."[43]

Citing the usefulness of content analysis studies, Krippendorff affirms that they have potential to provide new insights, increase a researcher's understanding of particular phenomena, or inform practical actions.[44] VanScoy and Oakleaf suggest that in addition to informing local instructional decisions, reporting the results of these types of studies can also contribute to the professional conversation on the topic.[45] Content analysis as a methodological approach proved to be an effective analytic tool to study the content of course syllabi and to adequately address the questions of this study. However, the approach itself must be strengthened and refined through additional inquiry and application to other issues for increased credibility and validity. As more studies are conducted and reported in the literature, methods will become more sophisticated and result in better, more credible research.

Ultimately, syllabi proved to be unobtrusive but powerful indicators of course and program curricula, and they have proven to be useful tools for substantive deliberations about course content and class assignments, the nature of teaching and learning outcomes, and classroom support materials in the form of books and articles. Similarly, content analysis as an investigative approach can be used to mine relevant information from all types of existing documents and communications and has been widely used to investigate a variety of questions in library settings. Due to its versatility and potential for application to an almost endless array of library-related issues, it is anticipated that content analysis will continue to grow in popularity as a research method in the field of library and information studies.

Notes

1. National Council for Accreditation of Teacher Education, *Professional Standards for the Accreditation of Teacher Preparation Institutions* (Washington, DC: NCATE, 2008), 22, http://www.ncate.org/Portals/0/documents/Standards/NCATE%20Standards%202008.pdf (accessed Dec. 7, 2010).

2. American Association of School Librarians and Association for Education Communications and Technology, "Information Literacy Standards for Student Learning: Standards and Indicators," (excerpt from AASL, *Information Power: Building Partnerships for Learning* [Chicago: ALA, 1998]), http://www.ala.org/ala/mgrps/divs/aasl/aaslarchive/pubsarchive/informationpower/InformationLiteracyStandards_final.pdf (accessed Dec. 7, 2010).

3. International Society for Technology in Education, "The ISTE NETS and Performance Indicators for Teachers (NETS•T)," 2008, http://www.iste.org/Libraries/PDFs/NETS_for_Teachers_2008_EN.sflb.ashx (accessed Dec. 7. 2010).

4. Southern Association of Colleges and Schools, Commission on Colleges, *Handbook for Institutions Seeking Reaffirmation* (Decatur, GA: SACSCOC, 2010), 34–35, http://www.sacscoc.org/pdf/081705/Handbook%20 for%20Institutions%20seeking%20reaffirmation.pdf.

5. Associated Colleges of the South, "Information Fluency Working Definition," ACS Technology Center Archives, 2006, http://www.colleges.org/techcenter/if/if_definition.html (accessed Dec. 7, 2010).

6. American Library Association, Association of College and Research Libraries (ACRL) *Information Literacy Competency Standards for Higher Education* (Chicago: ACRL, 2000), http://www.ala.org/ala/mgrps/divs/acrl/standards/informationliteracycompetency.cfm.

7. Klaus Krippendorff, *Content Analysis: An Introduction to Its Methodology* (Thousand Oaks, CA: Sage, 2004).

8. Gordon Marshall, *A Dictionary of Sociology* (New York: Oxford University Press, 1998).

9. Doug Bond, "Content Analysis," in *Encyclopedia of Social Measurement*, ed. Kimberly Kempf-Leonard (London: Elsevier/Academic Press, 2005), 481–85; Carol Busch, Paul S. De Maret, Teresa Flynn, Rachel Kellum, Sheri Le, Brad Meyers, Matt Saunders, Robert White, and Mike Palmquist, "Content Analysis. Writing@CSU."" Colorado State University Department of English, 2005, http://writing.colostate.edu/guides/research/content/ (accessed Dec 21, 2010).

10. Bond, "Content Analysis," 482.

11. Bernard Berelson, *Content Analysis in Communication Research* (Glencoe, IL: Free Press, 1952); Ole R. Holsti, *Content Analysis for the Social Sciences and Humanities* (Reading, MA: Addison-Wesley, 1969); Abraham Kaplan, "Content Analysis and the Theory of Signs," *Philosophy of Science* 10, no. 4 (1943): 230–47.

12. Berelson, *Content Analysis*, 74.

13. Busch et al., "Content Analysis."

14. Steve Stemler, "An Overview of Content Analysis," *Practical Assessment, Research & Evaluation* 7, no. 17, http://PAREonline.net/getvn.asp?v=7&n=17 (accessed March 12, 2010).

15. Kimberly A. Neuendorf, *The Content Analysis Guidebook* (Thousand Oaks, CA: Sage, 2002).

16. Marilyn Domas White and Emily E. Marsh, "Content Analysis: A Flexible Methodology," *Library Trends* 55, no. 1 (2006): 22–45.

17. Ibid., 28–29.

18. Bradford W. Dennis and Tim Bower, "Using Content Analysis Software to Analyze Survey Comments," *portal: Libraries and the Academy* 8, no. 4 (2008): 423–437.

19. Fevzi Okumus and Kevin K. F. Wong, "A Content Analysis of Strategic Management Syllabi in Tourism and Hospitality Schools," *Journal of Teaching in Travel & Tourism* 7, no. 1 (2007): 77–97; Philip Young P. Hong and David R. Hodge, "Understanding Social Justice in Social Work: A Content Analysis of Course Syllabi," *Families in Society: The Journal of Contemporary Social Services* 90, no. 2 (2009): 212–19.

20. Paul C. Gorski, "What We're Teaching Teachers: An Analysis of Multicultural Teacher Education Coursework Syllabi," *Teaching and Teacher Education* 25, no. 2 (2009): 309–18.

21. Craig S. Cashwell and J. Scott Young, "Spirituality in Counselor Training: A Content Analysis of Syllabi from Introductory Spirituality Courses," *Counseling and Values* 48 (Jan. 2004): 96–109.

22. Paul L. Hrycaj, "An Analysis of Online Syllabi for Credit-bearing Library Skills Courses," *College & Research Libraries* 67 (Nov. 2006): 525–35.

23. Sarah W. Sutton, "Formal Education in Work with Continuing Resources: Do Barriers Really Exist?" *Journal of Education for Library and Information Science* 50, no. 3 (2009): 143–51.

24. Gary W. White, "Business Information Courses in LIS Programs: A Content Analysis," *Journal of Business and Finance Librarianship* 10, no. 2 (2004): 3–15.

25. Amy VanScoy and Megan J. Oakleaf, "Evidence vs. Anecdote: Using Syllabi to Plan Curriculum-integrated Information Literacy Instruction," *College & Research Libraries* 69 (Nov. 2008): 566–75.

26. Ibid., 570.

27. Busch et al., "Content Analysis."

28. Ibid.

29. Kristina M. Spurgin and Barbara M. Wildemuth, "Content Analysis," in *Applications of Social Research Methods to Questions in Information and Library Science*, ed. Barbara M. Wildemuth (Westport, CT: Libraries Unlimited, 2009), 298–307.

30. Krippendorff, *Content Analysis*, 173.

31. Okumus and Wong, "A Content Analysis of Strategic Management Syllabi," 82.

32. Roberto Franzosi, "Content Analysis," in *The SAGE Encyclopedia of Social Science Research Methods*, ed. Michael S. Lewis-Beck, Alan Bryman, and Tim Futing Lao (Thousand Oaks, CA: Sage, 2004), 186–89; Spurgin and Wildemuth, "Content Analysis," 300.

33. Randy Hodson, *Analyzing Documentary Accounts* (Thousand Oaks, CA: Sage, 1999).

34. Guido Hermann Stempel, III, "Sample Size for Classifying Subject Matter in Dailies," *Journalism Quarterly* 29 (Summer 1952): 333–34.

35. Hodson, *Analyzing Documentary Accounts*, 18.

36. Franzosi, "Content Analysis," 187.

37. Neuendorf, *The Content Analysis Guidebook*, 117.

38. Ibid., 118.

39. VanScoy and Oakleaf, "Evidence vs. Anecdote," 569.

40. Ibid., 573.

41. Maury M. Breecher, Olan Farnall, Joe Bob Hester, Edward Johnson, Bong-Hyun Kim, and William Self, "The Four-stage Evolution of Content Analysis Methodology: An Annotated Bibliography" (paper presented at the Annual Meeting of the American Journalism Historians Association, Salt Lake City, UT, Oct. 6–9, 1993).

42. Busch, et al, "Content Analysis."

43. Stemler, "An Overview of Content Analysis."

44. Krippendorff, *Content Analysis*, 18.

45. VanScoy and Oakleaf, "Evidence vs. Anecdote," 573.

Using Focus Groups to Understand User Needs and Forge New Directions

Michael Weber and Robert Flatley

Abstract. In this era of rapid technological change and decreasing economic resources, it is a challenge for libraries to respond to the developing needs of their users and ensure that the users are being served with quality services. Focus group studies can provide a valuable fount of authentic information for keeping in touch with the attitudes and outlooks of library clientele and exploring their ever-changing information needs. In this chapter, the authors explain the fundamentals of focus group research, give practical advice for setting up a study, and discuss the ways in which they used the results of a focus group study to respond to student needs. The results of this study provided important information and new strategies to be used in decision making to enhance students' library experience. The authors report that students felt that the library was meeting their basic information needs; the Internet and EBSCO's Academic Search Complete were the students' favorite places to search; these students weren't yet ready for digital books; and some library policies and signage were not always helpful.

Introduction

How can we determine if our library is successfully responding to and meeting the needs and expectations of our student patrons? This was a question the authors had been pondering for quite some time. We wanted to know if our current library services were really useful to our patrons. We also wanted to know and understand the perception our users had of our services. How have our students' needs shifted due to the increasing digitization of our collections? The electronic environment offers new sources of information and novel avenues for delivering those information needs. Also the student paradigm has changed. Assignments are increasingly electronic in nature, and group projects and presentations have become more prevalent. How are our students adapting to these changes? Are they embracing the technology? Are we meeting their needs? Are they able to successfully complete their assignments? Are we overlooking any new information literacy opportunities? What changes or improvements would they like us to make? These questions were foremost in our minds, and we wanted answers so we could respond to those realities.

To accomplish our task, at first we considered using a survey questionnaire to answer these questions. But after a few brief discussions, we realized that we were interested in student opinions, behaviors, and attitudes and that this type of information was hard to obtain in a questionnaire format.

We also realized that we were concerned about a broad array of topics and student backgrounds. We wanted to know about students attitudes concerning those services that impacted them and their success. Responses could vary greatly. The student's major, class (freshman, sophomore, etc.), location (on or off campus), and other factors could come into play.

Ultimately we decided to use a focus group format. It turned out to be the perfect methodology for the type of answers we were seeking: student feelings, perceptions, and thoughts on whether the library was meeting their needs. We needed to explore the subject in depth and wanted to be free from the rigid constraints of quantitative research methods. We also hoped to benefit from the unsolicited responses that focus groups often generate: frequently these data can be the most valuable of all.

We organized and conducted a series of focus group meetings in the spring semester of 2007. After we found the answers to our questions, we decided to present the findings to our faculty and dean in order to start a discussion on how to respond to changing students' needs to improve the library. From the discussion with our colleagues, we hoped to develop a common understanding of our students' needs and then implement specific strategies to meet those broader and more specific requests that were uncovered.

This chapter will discuss focus groups as one of the most useful research methodologies for understanding the opinions, feelings, and thoughts of a particular population base. We will discuss how and when to conduct a focus group, along with best practices from the literature and the authors' experience.

Literature Review

The focus group's origin dates back to the early part of the previous century. In the 1930s, researchers began experimenting with nondirect interview techniques. They had found direct interviewing techniques to be too limited in their response expectations; the nondirect method employing open-ended questions elicited a richer response. In the 1940s, these methods were used in a group setting. Many of the procedures that have come to be accepted as common practice in focus group interviews were set forth in the classic work by Robert K. Merton, Marjorie Fiske, and Patricia L. Kendall, *The Focused Interview*.[1] Market researchers have been employing focus group techniques since the 1950s. Academicians rediscovered the method in the 1980s. At the present time, four unique focus group approaches have been noted: (1) market research, (2) academic and scientific, (3) nonprofit and public, and (4) participatory research.[2]

Focus groups are particularly useful for determining the information needs of a specific population. As such, focus groups have a long and diverse history of use in libraries. Often libraries have used focus groups in much the same way as other organizations, for example, using them to determine user satisfaction with services and resources.[3] Becher and Flug reported on how focus groups can be used with LibQUAL+ and other such surveys to aid in strategic planning and assessment.[4] Focus groups helped clarify the quantitative information received in such surveys. Glitz, Hamasu, and Sandstrom's study documented how focus groups can be effectively used to identify needs and focus program planning; the study concluded that the focus group technique is a successful communication and data gathering tool.[5]

Other sources touched on some of the ancillary effects of conducting focus group research. Higa-Moore and her colleagues discussed the benefits that focus groups have on the participants.[6] Through the focus group experience, participants saw the library as a customer-centered organization; they understood that the library staff cared about the patron's opinion. Holding focus groups is good public relations. These researchers also mentioned uncovering some unexpected issues. In particular, the author was previously unaware of the importance patrons attributed to the library's physical space.

Ho and Crowley's focus group study on access services[7] most closely mirrors the study we wanted to carry out. Participants identified a wide variety of issues that could help to improve library services, including circulation and interlibrary loan services, signage, shelving and material arrangement, and the online catalog. The authors concluded that their study was an effective way of identifying areas for improvement. Massey-Burzio, in her study on reference services, concludes that working on the reference desk, reading complaints, and conducting surveys do not reveal user needs, habits, and preferences.[8] Focus group studies are necessary to discover these nuances.

These studies made it clear that the focus group was the methodology that would best allow us to accomplish our goal of determining user perceptions of our library's services and resources. The group interaction would help us to delve deeply into the wants and needs of our students. Not only would we be able to identify potential areas of change, but also we would be able to get at possible solutions for proposed improvement. We would be able to hear the individual stories and circumstances behind the attitude, the need, and the desire for change. This conversation with students would give us a fuller understanding of the need and equip us with a clearer picture of the problem so that we could implement a focused solution.

Methodology

In this section, we will discuss the multiple steps needed to facilitate a successful focus group. Focus group studies are moderated, face-to-face group interviews of usually six to eight people representing a target audience and centered on a single topic, issue, or situation. "The method is useful for explaining reasons behind interviewees' attitudes, feelings, and behaviors."[9] A focus group is about listening to your constituency.[10]

Focus group interviews are conducted using a series of questions that gradually focus in on a more critical question. This ultimate question directly queries the issue that the researchers are interested in resolving or understanding more fully. The answers to this ultimate question may be broad and varied, and depend on the experience of the participants. For this reason, the other transition questions, which support the principal question, are used to elicit information from participants about their experi-

ences with the situation being studied and also to generate insight into related issues.

The results provide a range of responses about the service or issue. Consensus or extent of agreement is not the goal of the study; rather, "the process generates information that increases the library's understanding of a complex issue from multiple perspectives."[11]

The strength of the technique lies in the energy generated by the group process, resulting in greater diversity and depth of responses. New avenues of conversation are initiated and enlivened by the group members. Individuals reflect and refine their ideas and opinions through input supplied by others.[12] The combined group effort results in a richer response than would the collective replies of individual interviews.

The focus group approach often is contrasted to the questionnaire as a data-gathering technique. The focus group is a more interactive technique and is done in a group setting. The group interview process tends to elicit more complete answers because the interviewer can probe for further explanation or clarify misunderstood questions. The technique can also be useful for working with those who prefer not to answer written questionnaires.[13] It is important to differentiate the focus group process from simply interviewing one person as a subject. In the focus group environment, the group dynamic aids and generates discussion. Questions are purposely open-ended and constructed in such a way as to facilitate discussion and personal exploration.

Focus groups are particularly useful for library research given the practical nature of our field. Libraries are service centers dedicated to meeting the needs of our users. What better way to connect with our base than engaging them directly in a structured manner that allows flexibility and in-depth sharing. Focus groups can be used to explore and understand a wide variety of topics including services and resources, marketing, strategic planning, employee concerns, and policy making. Focus group studies are a functional way to look for new directions in library services. Two of our focus group studies concentrated on this very topic. These groups were particularly fruitful. Through this study, we solicited feedback on our current library services and then focused the discussion on improvements to our existing services and ideas for new services.

A focus group study should be used when one is interested in a multifaceted question or in searching for new directions. As opposed to a survey, which can be employed to rate or evaluate clearly defined items such as hours, databases used, services used, etc., focus groups facilitate the exploration of complex issues such as how patrons are using library databases and services, what they like or do not like about the library, or how they feel about services and resources. And, most importantly, in a focus group the librarian has the opportunity to ask patrons why they feel the way they do. The group interaction is a vital part of the process, as participants often bring up different points of view, challenge statements, or corroborate opinions and observations. Hence it is absolutely essential that participants feel comfortable and empowered during the process. The goal is for them to respond sincerely, creatively, and in an uninhibited manner.

Of course, there are pitfalls to using focus group studies. We have all participated in meetings and group exercises that have been a huge waste of time; a focus group is no different. In order to ensure that the group experience is fruitful, it is absolutely essential that the group leaders understand the purpose and the process of the exercise and that they have the required skills to make it work.[14] In addition to having the requisite skills, group leaders must be willing to devote the necessary time. Focus groups are far more time-intensive than surveys. They require a similar amount of time to prepare but a great deal more when completed. After the focus group is done, the real work of decoding and interpreting the data begins. Another pitfall includes relying on just one focus group session to answer the research question. The purpose of your study will determine how many groups you should conduct. Vaughn, Schumm and Sinagub note that focus groups should continue to be conducted until the moderator can begin to predict the responses because they have become redundant, this usually takes a minimum of two to four focus groups.[15] Lastly, researchers need to be clear

about the objectives of their study and not use a focus group just because it is familiar or convenient when a survey or individual interview would work better. The strength of focus groups is determining *why* participants think or feel the way they do; other research methodologies may be more useful for determining *what* participants think or feel.[16]

The construction of a focus group study starts by identifying the goal of the study and the attributes of the participants. From the goal, specific questions are assembled and an evaluation method is determined. Then the event is planned—a setting is prepared, recording methods are determined, a moderator is chosen, and participants are invited. After the event, the data must be processed, evaluated, and presented to stakeholders. Last, and perhaps most importantly, decisions need to be made on how to implement positive change in your library based on the findings from the study.

Determining the Purpose and Deciding to Use a Focus Group

Before beginning a study, the researcher must clearly define the purpose of the study and determine that the focus group method is the best research method to employ. To do this, it is important to understand the problem at hand, the purpose of the study, the type of information you want to obtain, and actions that are planned in response.[17]

In our student focus group study, we were clearly interested in ways to improve our current services and most keenly interested in identifying new ideas for products and services. For this reason we opted to use a focus group study over the questionnaire method. And we were interested in discerning this information for the benefit of the current students, many of whom have high expectations concerning digital delivery of products and services and also have an advanced facility with online products. We were interested in the behaviors and attitudes of technology-savvy students (see table 9.1).

We were not interested in influencing the students. Focus groups are not educational forums for your constituency, nor are they mechanisms for product promotion or team building. Rather the focus

TABLE 9.1
A Checklist of Situations in Which Focus Groups Are Useful[a]

If you can answer "yes" to the following questions a focus group study is probably a good fit for the question you need to explore:

- Are you looking for a range of ideas or feelings that people have about something?
- Are you interested in trying to understand differences in perspectives between groups or types of people?
- Are you trying to uncover factors that influence behaviors or motivation?
- Are you looking for new ideas?
- Are you looking for background information for a larger study?
- Are you looking for qualitative data?

a. Richard A. Krueger and Mary Anne Casey, *Focus Groups: A Practical Guide for Applied Research* (Thousand Oaks, CA: Sage, 2000), 24.

TABLE 9.2
A Checklist of Situations in Which Focus Groups are NOT Useful[a]

You do NOT want to use a focus group in the following circumstances.

- You want a consensus.
- You want to educate your participants.
- You are disinterested in the responses; you only want your participants to feel included.
- Your question is of such a sensitive nature that participants will feel impeded from answering in a group setting.
- The environment is emotionally charged; the topic is polarizing.
- You can't assure confidentiality.

a. Richard A. Krueger and Mary Anne Casey, *Focus Groups: A Practical Guide for Applied Research* (Thousand Oaks, CA: Sage, 2000), 25.

group is a data-gathering technique. And, in order to accomplish this task, the comfort of the participants is of the highest importance. We could guarantee confidentiality, a comfortable setting, and an overall pleasant experience. The issues were not emotionally charged, and the constituency was not contentious. We had a great environment for conducting our study (see table 9.2).

The Questions

Perhaps the most difficult process of developing the study is developing the questions to pose. You should construct six to eight questions for a forty-five-minute session. You would have more questions for longer sessions. Hernon and Altman recommend that sessions be no longer than ninety minutes in length for library focus groups.[18] Questions should be a series of open-ended queries that eventually focus on one last question. According to Krueger and Casey, the questions should have the following qualities:[19]

- should be open-ended
- should sound conversational
- should use language that participants would use
- should be short, clear, and easy to say

The progression of the questions should go from general to more specific and from objective/neutral to more subjective/controversial. The questions should flow from one to the next. The first question should be the easiest question, and it should encourage the participants to get involved in the conversation. Typically the opening question isn't analyzed; it is only used to get people to start talking.[20] Successive transition questions invite the participants to give more and more thoughtful responses to the topic at hand. Key questions are those questions that directly solicit the particular information you want. In a forty-five-minute study, there may be one to three key questions; in a two-hour study, there may be two to five key questions.[21] Often the last question gives the participants a chance to summarize their opinion. (See table 9.3 for questions we created for our focus group study.)

Setting Up Focus Groups

Choose your target group carefully. Make sure the participants you contact can give you the kind of

TABLE 9.3
Focus Group Questions

- Where do you go to meet your information needs?
- Is the library useful to you? Why or why not?
- How can/does the library help you with your classroom work?
- Do you use library resources for your own research and interests? Please explain how and what.
- What do you think is the single most important service for the library to provide?
- In the age of the Internet, what do you see as the role of the academic library on campus?
- In your opinion, how can the library be improved?

feedback you need. Participants should be chosen based on the goals of your study. For example, if you want to learn how graduate students feel about your new interlibrary loan service you would naturally want to talk to graduate students.

It is not easy to determine the number of focus groups that might be needed. You will know when you have reached a saturation point: the point where you hear no new answers to your questions. Often after three or four sessions, you will find that you have heard most of the responses. However, in our study, it took eight sessions until we were sure that we had heard 90 percent of the possible responses for a given participant type. By the time we reached our tenth to twelfth session, we found that we had heard most of the information before. The saturation point will vary depending on your participants, the nature of your topic (including the complexity and breadth), and how well you have defined the topic and managed the process.

We have found that the most challenging piece to successful focus group research is arranging the actual details. Faculty and students have very busy schedules, so incentives are a must. Money is always a great enticement, but it can quickly become an unmanageable expense. Many studies in the contemporary literature employ $25 to $50 for each participant. For even the smallest studies, you will be having at least four groups of six participants

(twenty-four members). So you may wish to find an organization to subsidize your study if you use money as an incentive. Our focus group research was conducted with a very limited budget. We had successfully encouraged participation by using creative alternative incentives including offering coupons from food services or coffee houses, working with Greek organizations needing volunteer hours, using student workers, engaging classes, and offering a free meal. We will review these methods below. Personal face-to-face or telephone invitations work best. The personal touch makes the individual feel valued. We found that our campus dining service was happy to issue coupons for various discounts on food items. In fact, we learned that other university offices regularly offer such gifts and incentives to students for their participation in various activities.

Another successful way we found to recruit students was to engage the Greek organizations on campus. We learned that members of Greek organizations have to commit to doing service on campus and in the community. In our case, the student coordinator of the Greek volunteer program worked in the library. She was able to facilitate contact with Greek organizations that resulted in a steady stream of student focus group participants. We recommend contacting your local Greek council and offering the focus group as a volunteer opportunity. Also, library student assistants are always a good source of focus group participants. They have a different but valuable perspective of the library as both employees and students.

Another strategy we successfully employed was engaging classes. Having students participate in a focus group can be a win-win situation for the researchers and the students, especially if the class is a research methods class. What better way to have students learn about conducting research than to participate in an actual research study? We were successful in engaging a faculty member who teaches an introduction to research class. He viewed the experience as a learning opportunity for the class and was happy to allow us to work with his classes. We divided the class into smaller groups and used multiple rooms.

Like students, faculty have very busy schedules and can be difficult to recruit for focus groups. We have found that one successful strategy is to engage heavy library users. Often these faculty members are happy to spend an hour of their time telling you what they like and do not like about the library. The challenge is in recruiting faculty members who do not use the library frequently. We have found that personally contacting the faculty member by phone and providing lunch works effectively.

The Place

The focus group setting is very important for the success of the study. The location should be accommodating, pleasant, and comfortable. Preferably the session should be conducted outside the library in a windowless, quiet room that can be closed to limit distractions. A spot that is conveniently located and easily accessible is also a plus—especially for special needs participants. Be sure to allow enough time to conduct the session without interruption.

The Moderator

Choosing a moderator takes care and planning, whether you moderate or choose someone from inside or outside of your institution. You need to choose a moderator who is both skilled in group leadership and acceptable to the participants. For this reason it is extremely important to choose a moderator who is empathetic, caring, and nonjudgmental. A good moderator must be an excellent interviewer, adept at managing group dynamics, and quick to understand the research at hand.[22] The moderator needs to be friendly and able to develop a quick rapport with others. The moderator needs to be a good listener and have an excellent memory and strong powers of concentration. Excellent communication skills, organizational skills, and the ability to remain objective are important.[23] Ideally the moderator should understand group process and know how to get people talking and how to get people to stop talking in a courteous manner when the group needs to move on. The moderator should know when an individual should elaborate and when an individual needs to be brief. You may consider a moderator that is in the same age group as those being interviewed, or who has other compatibility aspects—same sex, ethnicity, etc. Ultimately the comfort of the participants is

what is most important.[24] Moderators should also be chameleons when it comes to relating to people of different socioeconomic groups. They should be able to adapt their words and body language to accommodate all participants in the room.[25] They should be able to enliven the inattentive or bored, defuse disagreements and tensions, and curb the overly aggressive.[26]

The session should be started with a welcoming statement, a brief description of the study, and a short synopsis of the ground rules. After the session is underway, it is important for the moderator to encourage the participants to speak openly and freely. The moderator must make sure that everyone gets a chance to speak. The opportunity to get a breadth of opinions and hear everyone's voice is the purpose behind conducting a focus group. However, in any group certain personalities will dominate while others will remain quiet. It is vital that the moderator encourage everyone to participate. One way we accomplished this was by asking quiet participants, "How do you feel about what you just heard?" or "Do you share that opinion?" or "Before we finish this question, we want to know what your thoughts are on it." Another essential is to use the participant's name. This will make that person feel valued.

It is also necessary to use good communication techniques. Make sure that the participants understand the question and that you understand the response. Be ready to rephrase the question, summarize the participant's response, and ask nonjudgmental follow-up questions. The moderator may wish to use phrases such as, "Tell us more; why do you feel that way?" "Is there anything else?" and "Please give me an example."

A related issue is the need to keep the group on task. It is very easy to get sidetracked by library/university gossip, unrelated business, or a dominating personality who wants to focus on his or her issue only. The moderator must also be nonjudgmental at all times by ensuring that all comments and body language show neither approval nor disapproval. The comfort of the participants must be assured.

It is important to avoid arguments among participants. When differences of opinions are presented, it is important to validate all views. Consider comments like the following: "Both opinions are valid," "We need to capture everyone's thoughts," "We are here to gather information, not resolve anything," or "I suggest we move on."[27]

A major role of the moderator is to confirm the information. From time to time, the moderator should summarize the conversation and get consent about the review from the group. A head nod may be an assent to hearing the information but not necessarily agreeing with what has been said, so a clear vocal response should be solicited. When a moderator summarizes what is heard, the group gets a chance to agree, disagree, or possibly open up another avenue for exploration.

In the case of our student focus group study, the authors both served as moderators. Most of the time we worked together with the same group, which made it easier to take notes and digest information. We took turns posing questions. On a few occasions we were presented with larger groups (between twenty-five to thirty students), so we split them into two and each of us moderated one.

The Participants

The nature and purpose of the study will determine the composition of the group. You may choose participants of a certain age, major, expertise, gender, occupation, or other characteristic. In our study we were interested in the student's point of view, so we talked only to students. Participants should represent the diversity of the group under study. Make sure that a group with a variety of characteristics, such as race, nationality, gender, etc., is invited. In our student study we made sure to include undergraduate, graduate, commuters, and distant education students.

For most library research, the ideal focus group size is six to eight members. For marketing applications and more focused studies, ten to twelve people is recommended.[28] A group comprised of more than twelve participants is unwieldy because voices get lost.[29] The size can also be determined by the expertise of the individuals. A group of engaged and avid users will function well with fewer members, but a novice group will work better if it is a little larger. Larger groups also work well for pilot studies.[30]

Make sure the participants understand that only they are to attend. Participants should not bring their friends, children, or other family members with them. If this is unavoidable, consider methods to accommodate others.

What to Do Before the Sessions

Depending on the subject, participants may need preparation beforehand by having literature to read, a Web site to look over, a service or databases to try, or other homework. It is critical to set the room up in advance. Make sure that there is sufficient seating and that the configuration is appropriate for group interaction. Have forms, name tags, flip charts and other items ready. If you are recording the session, pay attention to the microphone placement and do a sound check in advance. The following is a list of items that you may want or need to use in a focus group study: tape recorder, microphone, extension cord, flip chart, focus group script, a watch or clock, blank tapes, name tags, markers, pens, paper, refreshments, handouts and consent forms, and cash receipt forms.[31]

What to Do During the Sessions

Although a focus group is more of an art than a science, there are certain guidelines that should be followed to ensure a successful session. These include starting and finishing on time, encouraging participant response, and keeping the session on task.

People have busy lives, and they are giving you an hour of their time. We feel it is vital to respect that by starting and finishing the sessions on time. Do not delay your start time for latecomers. Instead, integrate them as seamlessly as you can into the session when they show up. Likewise, end the session on time despite how wonderful the conversation appears to be. If someone would like to continue to share, allow them to do so after the meeting or encourage them to write you an e-mail or give you a call. We recommend starting with a brief introduction, thanking the participants for coming, introducing everyone, and providing a brief overview of the study and its purpose. Then explain the mechanics of how the session will be conducted. It is important to tell participants that you want to hear about their experiences and that there are no right or wrong answers. Emphasize that you want as many perspectives as possible. Try to make them feel comfortable saying what they feel and what they have experienced. In every story there is a learning opportunity. The questions should then flow from general to specific. "The classic interview design for both qualitative and quantitative research is the inverted pyramid, going from very broad to more specific."[32]

Recording the Responses

The purpose of conducting a focus group is to learn new information about your library. Hence it is important that responses be accurately recorded. Since focus groups are a research methodology, we recommend collecting basic demographic data as would be done in a survey. In our studies we began by passing out two forms: an informed consent form (required by our university) and a form that asked the following demographic questions: year of student, race, college major, and sex.

After the session is underway, accurately recording the responses is a must. We did this in two ways: note taking and audio recording. Taking notes provides a quick way to compare what has been said and to keep the session on target. It also provides the base for transcribing recorded responses. If your participants are comfortable with a recording device, we highly recommend it. It is the only way to get a truly accurate picture of the responses. We recorded all our sessions and used the recordings to verify and supplement our note taking.

Flip charts or whiteboards can also be a useful tool for recording responses. In this way participants can get a global view of what has been said and elaborate on past comments. We recommend using a flip chart only if a second person (not participating) can help in the session. The moderator should be focused on eliciting responses and taking notes.

Interpreting and Presenting Your Data

Perhaps the most daunting task in focus group work is interpreting and presenting the data. The focus group is free-flowing, and discussion can change direction or open up new ideas and concepts. It is important to get a grasp of the major concepts being presented at each session and, as early as possible, begin to develop a grid of the most important ideas that are discussed.

You can analyze the data in many ways depending on the time and thoroughness you want to put into the study. The most rigorous approach is to analyze the data from the recordings and produce a transcription of them. For this type of analysis, it essential to have good quality recordings of all participants. This type of analysis is very labor-intensive.

We have found the most expedient way is to analyze from our notes, supplemented by our memory. We then use the recordings to clear up questions and reinforce our findings. In this type of analysis we are careful not to introduce our prejudices into the data. Also it is best to act immediately after the sessions are finished to assure that the experience is fresh in your mind.

Qualitative data are not easy to codify. Of course, you will be able to count how many participants used a particular service or resource. However, this is not the purpose of focus group research. The goal is to get a sense of the whole picture with regard to a complex or multifaceted issue by looking at feelings, trends, surprises, and quotations. Feelings are a general sense about how participants like or dislike something. Trends are themes or ideas that occur over and over in many of the sessions. Surprises are unexpected comments or questions that really give you a new insight into the issue and help you see it in a new light. Often a particular position or a quintessential facet of the conversation will be eloquently articulated in a quotation. These gems are well worth sharing and discussing in your follow-up activities. We recommend compiling all results into categories that can be explored during the final part of the process.

Acting on Your Results

Once the results have been obtained, it is critical to learn from them and to begin to implement positive change in your library. Schedule a meeting with appropriate personnel to review the results. Be able to put the focus group information into context. The purpose of a focus group is to help librarians understand the perceptions and feelings of a small population of users. Although the data gathered are very useful, the researcher should be careful not to generalize the findings to the entire population, as they may not be representative.[33] Look for themes that are represented in your data. Decide on the main issues to be acted upon. Discuss and record ways to address these concerns. Prioritize the agenda and assign specific responsibility. Incorporate your findings into your library's strategic planning process, workflow planning, budgeting, assessment, etc.

Results

What we learned from the students was that we were meeting their information needs. In general we were fulfilling their requirements and desires concerning classroom assignments and other research responsibilities. Many students had comments such as this one: "[The library] is useful; I am usually able to find what I am looking for." In addition to this positive finding, several other important issues were brought to light—issues we would not have known about had we conducted a conventional quantitative study such as a survey.

The second item of interest we uncovered was the fact that, next to the Internet, the most popular research tool for students was EBSCO's Academic Search. When we asked our first question, "Where do you go to meet your information needs?" Google and EBSCO and the Internet were among the top responses. Typical comments included the following. "[I go to] the Internet, the library in general, [and] Google." "The major thing is to use the electronic resources." "I first go online, the library website, Google, LexisNexis." "I usually do the same thing. I usually use books as a last resort. I use Google, EBSCOhost and LexisNexis." Furthermore it became evident that the Internet and the brand names EBSCO and Google had become the most identifiable words associated with scholarly information retrieval for our students. The Rohrbach Library was near the bottom of the list of places to go for information, and it was rarely the first response. In

many cases "the Rohrbach Library" came as almost an afterthought as if the person realized, "Oh, yeah we are in a library focus group." It would have been interesting to see how Rohrbach Library would have ranked had the moderators not been librarians and the sessions held outside of the library. The library probably would have ranked much lower.

The third thing we learned was that students still loved books and were not as keen on an "all electronic" library as we would have thought. One student said: "I think the most important service the library can offer is books." Another said: "I like the wide variety of books, and I like the pleasure reading section." They saw the library still serving the role as a warehouse of books, but they relied on electronic access to journals for their research. Several students commented on the ease of use of print materials and the desire to preserve the print format for leisure and cover-to-cover reading. The portability and durability of the book was acknowledged. On the other hand, a few students were happy to dispense with the whole print collection and move entirely over to electronic. One participant said: "One thing [that] would be nice is to do away with the entire print collection [and] have electronic books. It would save space." All students agreed on one thing: for the completion of classroom assignments, research, and all work requiring snippets from larger works, the electronic format was preferred.

The fourth issue we found was that students loved our physical space but found library policy and signage inconsistent and somewhat confusing. In one discussion we started by talking about quiet space and common space. The students wanted more common space, but they also wanted quiet areas that were better monitored. Here is a portion of one conversation.

> [Female Student] To me [the library is] very useful because it is a very nice place. I like to study here. This is where I come to study when I have a break in classes. It has a very nice environment. This is the best study environment on campus. I tried the Student Union. . . . [The library] is very comfortable. What you offer in the way of study areas is very comfortable. The furnishings are good. The design is really good. It's not always quiet. People

are on the cell phone and talking at the tables. But there are lots of rooms that people can use.

[Male Student] [The library] gives me a quiet location to sit and catch up on my readings between classes. I might have a break—an hour here, an hour there—I just come in and sit down for 40 minutes and just get some good reading done. Otherwise I wouldn't, probably not be able, to [do this] because I have trouble reading at my house.

We learned just how important enforced quiet study areas were for our patrons. Many students complained about improper cell phone usage and noise in quiet areas. They were also unsure of our policy. They felt uncomfortable approaching a student about loud conversations without knowing the policy. They also weren't sure how to report the problem. Following is a portion of this conversation.

[First Student] I don't come here to study anymore, because I can't. There are people who sit and are so loud on their cell phones. I don't want to tell them to stop, because it might start something. I would prefer there be designated quiet places that are enforced. And if someone talks there should be someone to tell them to stop. Now we have designed quiet zones, but they are not enforced by a staff member.

[Moderator] So you wouldn't approach someone? [First Student] No, I have seen people go up to people and they say "I really need to talk to this person" or "I was here first."

[Second student] I know of people who talk on their cell phone in their normal loud speaking voice, or go to a computer and play music for everyone to hear. I get so angry, and I go up to them and say "keep it down" or "turn it off," because people deserve a quiet space in the library. Can someone do a general walk through the main collection? Another thing in the library is a sign when you come in that says "turn off your cell phones."

Another discussion centered on computer usage. Students were open to restricting library computer use to activities geared toward classroom assignments. In particular, they did not want students taking

up computer terminals to read e-mail or Facebook pages if a waiting student had research to do for a class.

Signage was also part of the discussion of a fifth very important issue. This particular concern was brought to light by a visually impaired student participant. The inclusion of this student in our focus group study was most fortuitous for us. We learned so much from her about the obstacles she had to overcome to find information. At Kutztown University we do have an active Assistive Technology Center, and our staff has been trained in the use of the equipment through several sessions. But these sessions were nothing like the eye-opening argument presented to us by the student who participated in our focus group. The student went through, in excruciating detail, telling us how difficult it was for her to find print material. Her story went as follows. From the Assistive Technology Center she would print out a call number. Then she had to use our physical signs to find out what floor to go to. Once she arrived at the correct floor she had look up at our overhead signage on the shelving unit to try to find the call number. Then she had read the tiny call numbers on the books. What if the book were on the top row? (By this point in the interview the authors were squirming in their seats.) Then she had to take the book back upstairs to the Assistive Technology Center to read it using the JAWS software, which is designed for visually impaired students. Needless to say this student was an advocate for the electronic library. With electronic books and periodicals, of course, this problem is nonexistent. All research could be done through the computer, and the student wouldn't even have to come to the library—she could find needed information on her computer from home.

In our group discussions we identified these common concerns and attitudes by summarizing what we heard in the session and then reviewing the taped session to find additional items. We also noted a few anecdotal responses. The most telltale and biting response was: "Your Web site is boring like a library Web site should be." As in this case, such a response provides insight into students' perceptions, but does not necessarily point toward an easy solution. Although the design of our Web site was not a general theme of these focus groups, our "boring" Web site needs consideration as well.

Action

Armed with our results, the first thing we did was present the information to library personnel. Our new dean made quite a few changes in the library in the succeeding years. Some of those changes were bolstered by the focus group results.

The formation of a Public Relations Committee, made up of librarians and paraprofessionals, was a major step toward meeting the many needs which came to light in our focus groups. As we mentioned above, the Rohrbach Library was not the first response to the question, "Where do go to meet your information needs?" Google, the Internet, and EBSCO were the top responses. The effects of the branding and marketing of the Google and EBSCOhost search products certainly had its effects on our students. These responses prompted us to think about spending more time promoting the Rohrbach Library.

Some signage and quiet area problems were addressed immediately. In response to the cell phone issue, we made signs that clearly explained our cell phone policy and posted them in appropriate locations. We also created new quiet study areas and designated the entire second floor as the Quiet Floor. In addition we posted more and clearer signs throughout the building.

The problems encountered by our vision-impaired student were also of great concern. To some extent, signage could be changed to facilitate access, but that solution would be rather incomplete. After all there is a limit to what we can do with spine labels, and library space concerns make it impossible to even consider not using the upper shelves on a range of shelving. To alleviate these difficulties, the library is moving more aggressively into the area of electronic access by embracing the e-book and online book formats. These formats have become the preferred format for most book ordering. Electronic formats not only help the vision-impaired student, they facilitate access for the distance learner as well.

The library's Web page layout is also under consideration. We now have a prototype for a Web page based on our information commons service model. This page is more robust and contains more graphic elements and boxes to search popular resources right on the main page.

We also experienced several ancillary effects of the focus group study. First, we felt the positive PR effect of conducting focus groups, as was noted in the study conducted by Higa-Moore and her colleagues.[34] Many students felt happy to be able to be part of the process and more connected with the library. Even the students who were recruited from a professor's class seemed to appreciate having a voice. We also were happy to be providing a learning experience to our students. For most students this was the first time they had ever participated in a research study, and many found the process educational. As an aside, we overlooked a PR opportunity; we did not supply the students with a report of the findings at the end of the process.

Our library now conducts ongoing focus groups. Each month a group of students who have agreed to serve on the library's Student Focus Group Committee are introduced to a new service or resource. The sessions last about one hour; half of the time is spent on a presentation and half on feedback and discussion. These groups have yielded valuable information on such things as federated searching, e-books, and LibGuides software that have directly impacted purchase decisions. Focus groups have also been important in our strategic planning process and our participation with the LibQUAL+ survey. We have used our focus group data to justify elements of our strategic plan and to compare and contrast our focus group results to LibQUAL+ findings.

Conclusion

Focus groups allow librarians to understand the mindset of their patrons at a deeper level than is possible with quantitative surveys. They allow librarians to gain new ideas, uncover feelings and perceptions, and probe deeper into what people think and mean. We feel that by following some simple focus group procedures and techniques libraries can gather a wealth of useful information about their services, resources, and patrons. This information can be used, in turn, to effect positive change in the operation of the library—making the library an even better and more useful resource for the patron.

Notes

1. Robert K. Merton, Marjorie Fiske, and Patricia Kendall, *The Focused Interview: A Manual of Problems and Procedures* (Glencoe, IL: Free Press, 1956).

2. Richard A. Krueger and Mary Anne Casey, *Focus Groups: A Practical Guide for Applied Research* (Thousand Oaks, CA: Sage, 2000), 6–7.

3. Nancy Allmang and Mylene Ouimette, "Case Study: The NIST Research Library's Experience Using Focus Groups in Strategic Planning," *Library Administration & Management* 21, no. 2 (Spring 2007): 77–94; Michael A. Weber and Robert K. Flatley, "What Do Students Want? A Focus Group Study of Students at a Mid-sized Public University," *Library Philosophy & Practice* 10, no. 1 (Spring 2008): 1–11; Makiko Ueoka, "User Study at Keio University Library," *Journal of Information Science & Technology Association* 58, no. 6 (2008): 278–84; Roxanne Missingham, "What the Politicians Think of the Australian Parliamentary Library," *Australian Library Journal* 57, no. 2 (2008): 147–68; Merrill Stein et al., "Using Continuous Quality Improvement Methods to Evaluate Library Service Points," *Reference & User Services Quarterly* 48, no. 1 (Fall 2008): 78–85; Charles Forrest and Amy J. Williamson, "From Inputs to Outcomes: Measuring Library Service Effectiveness through User Surveys," *Georgia Library Quarterly* 40, no. 2 (Summer 2003): 12.

4. Melissa L. Becher and Jance L. Flug, "Using Student Focus Groups to Inform Library Planning and Marketing," *College & Undergraduate Libraries* 12, no.1/2, (2005): 9.

5. Beryl Glitz, Claire Hamasu, and Heidi Sandstrom, "The Focus Group: A Tool for Programme Planning, Assessment and Decision-making—An American View," *Health Information and Libraries Journal* 18 (2001): 30–37.

6. Mori Lou Higa-Moore, et al., "Use of Focus Groups in Library's Strategic Planning Process," *Journal of the Medical Library Association* 90, no. 1 (Jan. 2002): 89.

7. Jeannette Ho and Gwyneth H. Crowley, "User Perceptions of the 'Reliability' of Library Services at Texas A&M University: A Focus Group Study," *Journal of Academic Librarianship* 29, no. 2 (March 2003): 82–87.

8. Virginia Massey-Burzio, "From the Other Side of the Reference Desk: A Focus Group Study," *Journal of Academic Librarianship* (May 1998): 215.

9. Debra Wilcox Johnson, "Focus Groups," in *The Tell It! Manual*, ed. Douglas Zweizig (Chicago: American Library Association, 1996), 176.

10. Krueger and Casey, *Focus Groups,* xi.

11. Johnson, "Focus Groups," 176.

12. Peter Hernon and Ellen Altman, *Assessing Service Quality: Satisfying the Expectations of Library Customers* (Chicago: American Library Association, 1998), 138.

13. Johnson, "Focus Groups," 177.

14. Krueger and Casey, *Focus Groups,* 3.

15. Vaughn, Sharon, Jeanne Shay Schumm, and Jane M. Sinagub. *Focus Group Interviews in Education and Psychology.* (Thousand Oaks, CA: Sage Publications, 1996), 48-49.

16. Rosaline S. Barbour, "Making Sense of Focus Groups," *Medical Education* 39, no. 7 (July 2005): 746.

17. Krueger and Casey, *Focus Groups,* 22.

18. Hernon and Altman, *Assessing Service Quality,* 145.

19. Krueger and Casey, *Focus Groups,* 40–43.

20. Ibid., 44.

21. Ibid., 45.

22. Judith Langer, *The Mirrored Window: Focus Groups from a Moderator's Point of View* (Ithaca, NY: Paramount Market, 2001), 117.

23. Thomas L. Greenbaum, *Moderating Focus Groups* (Thousand Oaks, CA: Sage, 2000), 32–40.

24. Langer, *The Mirrored Window,* 29.

25. Ibid., 31.

26. Greenbaum, *Moderating Focus Groups,* 151–52.

27. Judith Sharken Simon, *The Wilder Nonprofit Field Guide to Conducting Successful Focus Groups* (Saint Paul, MN: Wilder Foundation, 1999), 29.

28. Krueger and Casey, *Focus Groups,* 73.

29. Simon, *The Wilder Nonprofit Field Guide*, 14.

30. Krueger and Casey, *Focus Groups*, 74.

31. Ibid., 121; Simon, *The Wilder Nonprofit Field Guide*, 27.

32. Langer, *The Mirrored Window*, 95.

33. Ronald R. Powell and Lynn Silipigni Connaway, *Basic Research Methods for Librarians* (Westport, CT: Libraries Unlimited, 2004), 153.

34. Higa-Moore et al., "Use of Focus Groups in Library's Strategic Planning Process," 89.

10

Performance-based Self-assessment of a Library Liaison Program Using a Rubric

Aaron Dobbs and Doug Cook

Abstract. In reaction to current higher education trends to create mission statements and performance goals specific to the unit, Shippensburg University librarians were asked to assess their performance as liaison librarians. This chapter describes their creation and use of a self-designed rubric as the basis of a qualitative description of their program. The authors describe their use of short autobiographical narratives and checklists of ideal liaison services in academic libraries to create the rubric. This assessment tool then helped them to determine the common liaison tasks they felt were valuable and to determine the departments' actual performance on these tasks. The result of the study revealed that the librarians' treatment of their academic liaison departments was uneven, at best. This analysis provided information that will become the basis of further discussion and clarification of the liaison role with other library stakeholders.

Introduction

Librarians have traditionally been asked to count things in order to assess how well we are serving our clientele. We've counted the size of our collections, the number of items circulated, the number of questions we have answered, the number of instruction sessions we have delivered, the number of personnel employed, and even the number of paper clips we have handed out at the reference desk. And, in the Great American Way, more has always been better. Recently, however, librarians have been asked to rethink how we have been assessing our services. Accrediting associations have asked us to dig deeper—not to look only at the amount of work we do but also at the quality of the work we do.

This change has occurred because higher education, following the lead of public institutions,[1] has moved to an evaluative paradigm that is primarily goal-based. Institutions and related departments have been asked to formulate mission statements and corresponding goals that can be evaluated by gathering data regarding the actual performance of our stated goals. Historically, goal assessment has been a "widely used criteria of effectiveness."[2] In fact, authors agree[3] that it is impossible now to describe assessment in the field of education without a vision and "meaningful and measurable objectives."[4]

Assessing performance in a qualitative fashion is complex in that many scenarios may prove to have more than one correct way of dealing with the same issue.[5] These situations can be thorny when dealing with the performance of one individual, but can become extremely complicated when dealing with a program with a number of individuals working toward the same objective. As a solution to this intricacy, it has become common practice in education for such multifaceted performances to be qualitatively assessed with a rubric. Hafner and Hafner define a rubric as an "assessment tool that describes levels of performance . . . and is used to assess outcomes in a variety of performance-based contexts."[6] Most librarians are familiar with performance indicators because of the *Information Literacy Competency Standards* published by the Association of College and Research Libraries (ACRL) in 2000.[7] Numerous instances of rubrics for assessing these indicators can be found in journals or on the Web.[8]

Although much of the library scholarship dealing with rubrics focuses on student learning, Oakleaf suggests that "In libraries, rubrics can be employed to examine and evaluate a multitude of library products and services."[9] One such service that librarians often include as part of their collaborative repertoire is the liaison program. In fact, liaison programs are practically ubiquitous in academic libraries. Librarians have written about liaison programs at length, but few attempts at actually assessing their effectiveness have been reported.[10]

This chapter will explain and demonstrate the use of rubrics to qualitatively assess a liaison program. Examples will originate from our liaison librarians' experience creating and applying an assessment rubric at Shippensburg University of Pennsylvania (Ship). We ground this narrative in the literature of qualitative assessment, relating our process of decision making during this review. We then discuss preliminary findings and conclude with suggestions as to how our assessment will be continued with other stakeholders in the process.

Background on Rubrics

Before regaling you with our story, we will explain the concept of creating rubrics to assess performance objectives. A rubric can be defined simply as a "scor-ing tool that lays out . . . specific expectations," divides a task (or a group of tasks) "into its component parts," and provides a "detailed description of what constitutes acceptable or unacceptable levels of performance for each of those parts."[11] Used regularly in the broader field of education, a rubric is created to describe and evaluate more complex types of student work, such as research papers, presentations, portfolios, etc. Rubrics, in fact, provide objectivity and accountability to evaluative tasks that are often very complex.

Rubrics can also be used to evaluate programs as a whole, as well as specific aspects such as courses, faculty, and delivery systems. According to Chance and Williams, "Developing and/or using a rubric for assessment allows one to define and evaluate a comprehensive range of issues that work together to shape overall efficacy of a proposed plan. Rubrics provide a way to achieve a comprehensive, holistic assessment of quality. They graphically illustrate relationships between performance criteria and quality standards."[12]

Rubrics have many benefits when used as part of an assessment program. First and foremost, the creation of a rubric allows the stakeholders involved to put words and definitions to expectations that are often a part of the unspoken culture.[13] Rubrics offer a second benefit in that they result in easily understandable data that can be used for assessment.[14] According to Chance and Williams, rubrics offer a third valuable benefit, as well: "Rubrics also help to inform decision-making, articulate performance measures, and specify quality expectations. Used as such, rubrics can provide means for enhancing self-awareness *and* for simultaneously addressing increased demands for accountability."[15]

The authors first became familiar with rubrics as an evaluative mechanism when discussing their use by national accrediting bodies to evaluate university programs. A colleague at another university was completing the process of applying for accreditation by the International Reading Association (IRA) for a master's level literacy program. Much of the initial application consisted of creating rubrics, individualized to the specific program, which clarified the performance standards set down by IRA.[16]

Such rubrics very clearly specify the performance expectations set for a particular university program desiring to align itself with an accrediting agency such as IRA. Such rubrics also allow for the uniqueness of each program being evaluated. Rubrics are particularly useful when the goals to be evaluated can be expressed in terms of performances. The current emphasis in higher education on setting goals and corresponding objectives lends itself well to the use of rubrics as evaluative tools.

Parts of a Rubric

At its most basic,[17] a rubric consists of four parts:

1. A description of the overall task (or tasks) to be evaluated
2. A list of dimensions that lay out the particular parts of the overall task that must be performed in order to complete the task
3. Descriptions of the dimensions
4. A scale that will be used to describe how well or how poorly the task has been performed

These components are typically displayed in a graphic format in a table. "[The] vertical axis contains performance criteria that describe the characteristics of product or performance. [The] horizontal axis contains headings indicating the increasing levels of performance towards . . . mastery."[18] Using the rubric we created, which will be explained later in more detail, as an example (see appendix, table 10.1), the vertical axis displays the three broad components of our liaison program that we wanted to describe: collection development, instruction, and outreach; and the horizontal axis displays our prescribed levels of service: Basic, Medium, and High, along with group behaviors representative of each level.

Rubrics, as qualitative assessment tools, are instruments that allow the researcher to observe, in an organized and focused fashion, the behaviors of the individual or group under study. Much like survey instruments, rubrics take careful preparation as they are being created in order to result in data that inform the problem under study. The rubric that we eventu-ally created was indeed the result of much discussion regarding the behaviors that we wanted to assess.

Case and Context

Ship has been moving toward more quality-of-performance-based assessment for the last several years. Motivated by circumstances, Ship has repositioned itself toward building a unique vision and mission, and related performance objectives. The library has engaged in these same discussions. One of our major objectives as a library department is to collaborate with and to support our academic departments in order to sustain the university's larger goals for student learning. Recently librarians at Ship were tasked with verbalizing what we were currently doing with our liaison program, with redefining our liaison roles using a more collaborative model, and with determining a methodology to assess the program in a meaningful fashion.

All librarians at Ship are involved as liaisons, whether collaborating in collection development or being involved with instruction with one or several of the thirty-three academic departments and programs on campus.[19] As had many libraries, Ship had historically made it a practice to rely on counting to measure success. Before we transformed our practices into a *Liaison Program*, we initially focused upon managing collection development relationships, specifically the collaboration of the librarian liaisons with their assigned departments' representatives. After we had seriously begun to provide library instruction in the late 1980s, we also counted those instruction sessions, the number of students served, and later also tracked this by department. In the last decade, we began to track reference desk transactions by determining the department from which the students' assignment questions originated. Not until two events aligned—Ship's most recent Middle States Accreditation ten-year re-evaluation visit and the assignment of the library to a new dean—were we encouraged to become a part of goal-oriented qualitative assessment.

Following proper academic library etiquette, we formed a committee to work on this task. Failing to find much evaluative direction in the library literature, we began to answer the question, "What would a liaison program look like if we had unlimited financial resources and personnel?" We found that several other libraries had created very extensive lists of potential activities that liaison librarians might perform to support and collaborate with academic departments.[20]

As qualitative research projects typically proceed, we found ourselves at the very beginning just trying to put a name to what we actually wanted to assess. We found that we, as librarians, did not have an agreement among ourselves regarding the nature of our duties. We decided to begin a multiyear project by looking at ourselves. We felt that before we could begin to assess the contribution we were making to the larger university, it was necessary for us to clearly define our roles. So, in essence, the creation and application of this rubric was a serious attempt at self-assessment. We wanted to put into words our major collaborative contributions to the university and then come to a conclusion among ourselves as to how well we thought we were doing our job.

Qualitative assessment is the process of focusing on one specific area of the job environment that needs more study. Typically the data derived from this type of research are the impressions of the stakeholders under study.[21] In our particular case, we decided to start with ourselves. Looking at the other stakeholders in the liaison program, we listed department faculty to whom these services are typically directed, students who are direct beneficiaries of our collaboration, and finally administrators at our university who have a say in our performance as well, since they supply funding and personnel for us to do our jobs.

One of the hallmarks of rubrics[22] is that they allow broad mission and goal statements to be reworked into plain enough language that it is possible to describe what behaviors or actions will actually be displayed by the meeting of these goals. We felt that being able to actually put our own expectations into measurable objectives was a worthwhile start for year one of this process. So we used this rubric as a self-assessment tool. We fully expect, later, to compare our measurement of ourselves against what other stakeholders believe to be true.

In order to begin the discussion of particular activities that would make up our ideal liaison program, we created a categorized spreadsheet including numerous suggested liaison tasks. The committee organized them loosely and then asked all librarians to consider the value of the tasks included for our situation. We then asked the librarians to rank the tasks in each category according to their importance to the ultimate success of our liaison program and, secondly, according to the amount of time and effort that they would take to complete. Ultimately, we came up with a tailored checklist of performances, which we would eventually use as the basis of a self-assessment tool as we compared our efforts among the academic departments with which we collaborate (see appendix, table 10.1).

Librarians were next tasked with creating a simple, leveled autobiographical narrative based on the checklist, delineating how well we were communicating and collaborating with the departments to which we had been assigned. (See appendix, table 10.2, for an example of the narrative representing seven academic departments in the arts and humanities.) As we wanted to create a baseline, each librarian reported what we all had done for each of our thirty-three departments for the previous few years.

We realized the importance of this process as a means to discuss how well we were doing in providing service to each department as compared to our service to other departments. This list eventually helped us to refine our final assessment rubric.

Broadly speaking, we created a self-assessment narrative of the collaborative efforts we were making and then measured those ratings against our ranked list of ideal and desired performances. Our final chart, appendix, table 10.3, allowed us to name and discuss our collaborative liaison services, to quickly compare our self-assessment of our services among departments, and to identify departments with which we spent the most time and those that we were neglecting.

Looking at our situation in a qualitative fashion worked well for us. It is difficult to find any type of quantitative benchmark with which to compare our liaison program against those of other universities with similar demographics. Because of the uniqueness and the complexity of liaison programs, qualitative assessment with a rubric seemed to fit our situation.

Steps in Creating and Applying the Self-assessment Rubric at Ship

Our process for creating our rubric was quite recursive. What we are describing here as clean and specific actually took many hours of reflection and discussion. As often happens during final reflection, the more difficult and muddled parts of discussion and negotiation fade into the background in light of the final product.[23] Following is a retrospective view of our process.

1. Creating a Description of the Overall Task to Be Evaluated

As previously mentioned, we had initially defined our liaison role very narrowly as the sustainability of a relationship between a particular academic department and an individual librarian. Each librarian at Ship was assigned a set of departments. The librarian served as a communication conduit, primarily regarding budgetary issues related to the development of the library collection.

As budgets shrank, resources went digital, and prepackaged databases made up much of our collection purchases, we, as did many other academic libraries, turned outward to redefine our roles. At a medium-sized library such as ours, collection development took less and less time. Such library literature of the day as *The Collaborative Imperative*[24] inspired us to realize that focusing on users, faculty in particular, provided us with a new opportunity to upgrade our standing as valuable members of the academic community. We felt that it had become necessary to enact a more collegial relationship with faculty regarding scholarship in their discipline as well as to provide specific discipline-related instruction to the department's students.

The enactment of this rubric helped us to put into words this mission to expand our role as liaison librarians. We finally were able to settle on how we wanted to define ourselves as liaison librarians (and what we wanted to assess) with the following liaison-related mission and goals statement:

Mission: The library liaison program will support the educational goals of each instructional department or program at Shippensburg University.

Performance Goals: The liaison program will manage the resources provided to the library by the university to support each department's curriculum; provide each department's faculty and students with the knowledge and skills needed to access and make the best use of librarian expertise and library resources; and collaborate with each department to further the broader instructional goals of the institution.

As often happens in the real world, this mission statement was actually written after we had decided which activities we would include in our liaison program. Unfortunately, describing things in this linear fashion makes it seem as if we were organized enough to come up with a mission without regard to context. Our first step, then, in the creation of our self-assessment rubric was to put into words exactly what we wanted to measure.

2. Creating a List of Dimensions That Lay Out the Particular Parts of the Overall Task That Must Be Performed in Order to Complete the Task

We determined that we would evaluate ourselves in three areas, stated in our Performance Goals:

a. Collection Development. The liaison program will manage the resources provided by the university to support each department's curriculum.

b. Instruction. The liaison program will provide each department's faculty and students with the knowledge and skills needed to access and make the best use of librarian expertise and library resources.

c. Outreach. The liaison program will collaborate with each department to further the broader instructional goals of the institution.

These three dimensions correspond historically with tasks most academic libraries undertake. As mentioned previously, we came up with these categories and with their resulting performance objectives by reflecting on what we were doing, speculating about what we wanted to do, and looking at what other academic libraries were doing.

Our library has defined basic collection development tasks rather well for our needs. We also have done, we think, a good job at defining instructional goals. On the other hand, we have not focused as much attention as we should on outreach goals. For us, this third category of activity was the most difficult to verbalize.

3. Creating Descriptions of the Dimensions

In order to define and exemplify each of these three dimensions, we researched and brainstormed a list of actual behaviors that might be performed by a librarian enacting these dimensions in an ideal library. We supported our data gathering at this point by creating a spreadsheet in which we input any of the brainstormed performances we thought of in each category. We also perused the literature and mined the Web sites of other academic libraries that had gone through this task before in some fashion. We then refined the list according to our own expectations and with the realities of our institution. The final activities we chose (see appendix, table 10.1) will look familiar to seasoned academic librarians. Most are goals with which the profession in general has challenged itself in the face of rapid changes in our milieu.

4. Creating a Scale That Will Be Used to Describe How Well or How Poorly the Task Has Been Performed

Associating these performances with a scale was initially rather difficult. We tried various combinations of scores—grades (A, B, C, D), descriptive words (Excellent, Competent, Needs Work), etc. We finally decided to begin simply, by using a three-point scale

of Basic, Medium, and High. We thought of these in terms of our expectations for ourselves as follows:

a. Basic—All departments in the university should be able to call upon us for basic services. (The word *Low* was deemed too pejorative.)

b. Medium—Services at this level were those that we would like to offer to all departments. This middle level of performances would provide us with realistic services we could provide if we had an opportunity to ramp up our activity to support a particular department.

c. High—If we had all the resources, money, and personnel that we might have in an ideal world, we would be meeting our liaison goals as well as possible by providing these services. We did not expect that we would be able to achieve this level of service to many departments due to our limited personnel and resources; however, we also felt that we needed to describe the ideal so that we could create goals.

5. Using the Rubric as a Basis to Create a Self-assessment Narrative Listing Our Activities for Each Department

The rubric became a document defining the activities that went into the narratives we created for each department (see tables 10.1 and 10.2). As we were assessing our own behaviors, it was necessary to gather autobiographical data in some fashion that represented our job activities performed in support of each department. Providing the initial narrative was difficult in that it was a new task. Once several librarians had begun the process, others were encouraged to engage in the description. Reviewing the results as a group allowed for including forgotten services.

As we worked through this process, we found that the very act of reflecting on our past services and our idealized services allowed us to put our thinking into a simple verbal format that we could use to discuss among ourselves and with the larger community. Creating and applying a rubric assisted us in verbalizing our larger goal for the liaison program, breaking our goal down into categories, and then objectifying it with specific performances that were assessable.

These narratives provided by each librarian regarding his or her activities during the past year, became the data that we used to assess our performance levels. These data were scrutinized by all librarians to make sure that all activities performed were actually recorded. At the end of this part of the process, these logs reflected a record of our liaison relationship to each of our departments. These narratives became the basis for the next self-assessment step, actually using the rubric to evaluate our own performance.

6. Applying the Rubric to Our Departmental Narratives to Achieve a Final Score

In order to facilitate our self-assessment, one of the authors used the rubric (appendix, table 10.1) to assign a performance rating (Basic, Medium, or High) to each of the narratives representing our performance. This process involved comparing the ideal performances in the three dimensions of the rubric—collection development, instruction, outreach—to the actual narratives and gauging if the narrative in each dimension deserved a Basic, Medium, or High score. Each narrative received a score on each dimension.

As first coder, this librarian read through each narrative and determined a ranking. In order to ensure a higher level of reliability, we then met as a group and made a final determination for the ranking given to the amount of activity we had recorded in each narrative. The group served as a panel of coders, to agree with or adjust the scoring of the original coder. The rankings reflected in appendix, table 10.3, are the results of this discussion.

As a final step, we assigned numbers to each ranking (1 = Basic, etc.) and gave each department a numerical score that represented how well we felt that we had provided services to our liaison departments. We realized at this point that we had provided no service in some dimensions for several departments, so in the end we used zero to stand for complete absence of activity (0 = No Services).

A benefit of using such a scale is that we could collapse narrative into numerical ratings so that our overall assessments could be compared among departments or among colleges. Although such scales as these do not lend themselves to complex statistical analysis, they do seem to make sense when used in a descriptive fashion (see appendix, table 10.3).

Results: Initial Analysis of our Baseline Liaison Activities

After the discussion of our goals, objectives, and related performances, and after using the resulting rubric to create a baseline rating for each department with which we collaborate, we began to analyze the results as they were displayed across departments. In order to help us to visualize our liaison activity levels, we took the ratings for each of the three activity areas—outreach, instruction, and collection development—for each academic department and charted this activity using tables.[25] We also sorted our department and program numerical ratings from High to Basic (see appendix, table 10.3). Before we began, we felt that our collection development activities were organized and efficient in comparison to other liaison activity types. Instruction, as well, we felt fairly good about. The area in which we felt that we were most lacking was the quality of our outreach activities to departments. We constantly had to remind ourselves that no librarian has liaison responsibilities as his or her sole duty, nor are all librarians able to take part in the types of outreach activities that we felt ranked highest.

Outreach to Departments

We found that we had provided no outreach service to four departments; Basic outreach service to fourteen departments; Medium outreach service to eight departments; and High outreach service to seven departments. Looking at our self-assessment across all academic departments and programs, we found that our initial feelings were correct in that we scored ourselves at the Basic level (or below) in outreach activities for about half of our thirty-three departments and programs.

We rated ourselves as having provided a High level of outreach to seven departments. In each case, a librarian had a special interest (advanced degree, personal experiences, etc.) in the discipline. In several of these highly rated departments, we felt that our level of outreach activity was related to a collaborative instructional effort with the department. For example, the librarian liaison to Art has an MFA, has taught art courses in the past, and worked closely with the Art department to write a grant to procure a specialized art database.

Instruction for Departments

We found that we had provided no instruction service to eight departments; Basic instruction service to one department; Medium instruction service to seventeen departments; and High instruction service to seven departments. During the past several years, we have made an effort to provide library instruction for as many departments as possible. As in the outreach category, many departments were given no instruction or a small amount of instruction. In our case, Computer Science and Physics fell into this category.

We felt good about the fact that we had provided at least one instruction session to twenty-five of our thirty-three liaison areas. The departments that we had provided a High level of instruction service to were, again, those with which we had established a collaborative relationship. For example, our Instruction Coordinator collaborated with the Biology department to create an online tutorial for the Introduction to Biology class. This effort resulted in a number of other opportunities for us to provide instruction services for Biology faculty.

Collection Development for Departments

We found that we had provided no collection development service to one program; Basic collection development service to twenty-six departments; Medium collection development service to two departments; and High collection development service to four departments. Collection development is our most egalitarian liaison area, in that the limited amount of money that is provided to the library has been spread fairly evenly across all departments and programs. All areas but one have been allocated a basic budget.[26]

We rated six departments as having been provided with Medium or High collection development service. Each of these departments represents an area that had been provided extra monies from grants, had been singled out for an official five-year review by the provost, etc. One example of a liaison department that we feel is provided High collection development service is the Teacher Education department. We have a K–5 elementary school on campus. The school library is directed by one of our librarians, who maintains an excellent children's literature collection used by both elementary students and by college students. Having recently been a public school teacher and librarian, she is very knowledgeable regarding the needs of pre-service teachers as well as of the young children in the school.

Overall Average of Liaison Rankings for Departments

As a way to assess our service as a whole to departments, we averaged the outreach rating, the instruction rating, and the collection development rating. This overall average ranking gives us a self-assessment snapshot of our total liaison program (see appendix, table 10.3).

We found that we had rated six departments as having been provided very little overall service (rankings < 1). We provided Basic services to seventeen departments (rankings of 1 to 1.99), Medium service to eight departments (rankings of 2 to 2.99), and High service to only two departments (rankings of 3). There were six departments and programs that averaged below 1 (Basic): two small programs, an interdisciplinary master's program, and three academic departments.

Departments receiving the highest average scores were Teacher Education and Biology. These liaison exemplars have been mentioned previously as departments with which a librarian had forged a collaborative relationship with a departmental faculty member.

Overall, these self-rankings numerically objectified for us our levels of service provided in various dimensions of our liaison program. In fact, we set a baseline of activity that we had provided up until this initial exercise. These data will assist us in selecting departments and dimensions we would like to improve in the future.

Discussion

In summary, we think that a rubric was a good qualitative tool to help us to plan our liaison activities for the future. Following are several initial summative reflections that may lead to increased or redefined service at Ship:

1. It seems that departments with which a librarian has established a collaborative relationship were rated more highly. We are a small group of nine librarians with responsibility to thirty-three departments programs. It is not realistic for us to believe that we could establish such a close relationship with each department. However, such relationships could be encouraged by reshuffling overall responsibilities so that a librarian had only one liaison department assignment in order to spend more time focusing on that one. Alternatively, if a librarian had strong skills in a particular dimension of service, such as instruction, duties could possibly be reshuffled so that the librarian could spend more time instructing students in many departments and less or no time with outreach or collection development responsibilities.

   This reassessment and reassignment has already started to occur, as we are in the process of rewriting job descriptions. When budgets were large, we needed librarians to carefully select resources to support curriculum. Now with much of

our collection budget pledged to database aggregators and periodical subscriptions, very little money is left to develop legacy collections. Furthermore, because of our increased reliance on digital access and standardized cataloging, such tasks, which were once deemed as only able to be done by librarians, have been reassigned to our staff colleagues. Most of our nine librarians spend much of their time working with patrons and far less time than previously working behind the scenes. We are taking an overall look at each librarian's assignment to ensure that more time can be given to dealing with patrons directly.

2. Collection development operates efficiently because a librarian coordinates the liaison contacts in this area. Although our instruction efforts are less evenly spread across all departments, we have a number of success stories due to the fact that we have, for a number of years, had a librarian who coordinates instruction and aggressively advertises our instructional capabilities. Our outreach function is the least efficient of the three areas on which we have concentrated. One suggestion, which came from our discussion of our findings, was that to ensure that our outreach services are offered to all departments and programs, it would be good to have one librarian coordinate these efforts. This model has worked well for collection development and for instruction. We are discussing the possibility of implementing this strategy in the near future.

3. This seems obvious, but we felt that we should reflect upon our liaison program at regular intervals. The mere act of reflecting and objectifying such complex activities and relationships provides information that can be used to discuss services within the library and to communicate our ideals to the rest of the campus. All administrative units and educational departments at Ship undergo a Provost Review every five

years. The data and findings from the use of our rubric will feed into that review of the library, which was also deemed an appropriate time to re-examine our overall mission and goals.

4. These data have become extremely valuable as we have attempted to explain to our campus managers and decision makers what it is that we do as library faculty. Generally, the roles of classroom faculty are understood at the administrative level. As librarians' roles have changed from protectors and interpreters of huge bastions of books in our buildings to clarifiers and instructors regarding resources that are housed somewhere in cyberspace, administrators with hands on the budget strings wonder if librarians are still necessary. Such rubrics as the one we have described can become the basis for a discussion with administrators regarding the continuing added-value services librarians can provide, which in the end can justify our newly reshaped job descriptions. In fact, redefining our roles in relationship to direct service to our patrons has already provided positive comments from managers.

A Comment about Perspective

One of the difficulties with self-reflection and with self-assessment is that one may end up engaging in a vigorous round of navel gazing. Particularly since this was the first time we tried to assess our liaison program in such a specific fashion, our dean encouraged us to share our assessment with other campus constituencies. Are we, in fact, providing to faculty the services that they want? Are we being too harsh or too easy on ourselves when we say that we are providing overall ideal service to only two departments?

We began by sharing our overall self-assessment with the campus University Library Committee, which consists of the college deans, plus administrative and faculty representatives. This group is very aware of the need for self-assessment as they are engaged in

this process constantly. We found that the departments they represented were also struggling to objectify and assess the same types of complex performances as we were. We also found that other units on campus were adopting rubrics as assessment tools.

Our college deans, in particular, felt that such assessment allows the library a basis for discussion of our services. Although, outreach, instruction, and collection development have traditionally defined what we felt were our responsibilities, some of their initial comments show that each category has a different importance and a different meaning to each department and discipline. The following reflections resulted from this discussion:

1. Differing disciplines have differing views regarding how they define scholarship and have differing levels of need for library support. An obvious example of this is that collection needs for the humanities differ broadly from those in the sciences. When comparing our activities in the future, we cannot assume that all disciplines want the same types of services when describing resources.

2. As Ship is a liberal arts university, several of our departments are called upon to provide general instruction to the entire campus.[27] These departments providing core courses in General Education have a larger need for instructional services than do other programs. In fact, it makes sense that instruction for General Education courses should be considered in a more complex fashion than by merely looking at it by department.

3. As we offer a number of master's level programs, it is again evident that these departments need different attention than those departments that do not offer graduate programs. Possibly paying attention to these departments as a group would be more fruitful than splitting them out as individual departments, particularly in regard to instruction. As an additional complication, we offer numerous interdis-

ciplinary programs, which cannot easily be categorized.

4. Off-campus and distance programs, such as our MBA program and our program in Educational Leadership, also need special consideration. Our Web-accessible resources begin to lay a foundation for service; however, library instruction for these groups takes on a different meaning than for on-campus programs.

5. The college deans also suggested that we should tailor this information and share the pertinent data with specific departments and colleges. As of this writing, we are planning to survey faculty using a form of our rubric to determine which of our liaison services each department feels that it needs most. We assume that comparing our expectation of ourselves with that of departmental faculty may bring about more changes in our services. Overall, this group felt that the exercise was worthwhile and was certainly in keeping with the type of assessment and reporting activity that academic departments were currently performing.

Next Steps

Numerous actions come to mind when we think about using this rubric as an assessment tool over the next years. Currently we can express our immediate intentions as follows:

1. We will continue to track performance with this paradigm for the next few years and determine ways to gather evaluative data from all of our stakeholders.

2. We will increase the amount of dialog that occurs between the library and the academic departments regarding their satisfaction with how well we as librarians meet their needs. We plan to do this with a series of meetings with colleges and departments. Our rubric will provide us with a means to express the types of ser-

vices we are able to, and feel that we do, provide.

3. We will reflect on how we define ourselves as librarians. If instruction, collection development, and outreach are truly the most important things we do in providing service to faculty, are we currently performing duties that can be passed on to others or completely dropped?

4. We will specifically track and match any changes we make to our activities as a result of assessing our efforts to meet goal requirements. This first self-assessment comprises a baseline. Future assessments will be compared to this baseline.

5. We will explore any other data that we collect (such as LibQUAL+ survey data) that will help us to triangulate the veracity of our subjective assessment.

6. We will attempt to validate the authenticity of our rubric by discussing our initial findings with departments and colleges.

Limitations

Goal-oriented assessments, such as rubrics, have the same limitations as do other types of qualitative assessments: particularly that the results are not meant to be generalized to the broader library community. For this reason, we decided not to initially compare our activities to other universities, in that each university has different goals and objectives.

We also decided not to use this exercise as an assessment of each individual librarian's job performance, but instead as a snapshot of how well we judged we were performing as a library department. However, removing personalities from our liaison program assessment actually was quite difficult. As is the case in all libraries, some of our group had more polished skills in particular categories and therefore spent more time performing those activities than in others. Librarians at Ship also have faculty status, and our individual progress is assessed annually before tenure and every five years after tenure; thus, our academic culture requires that we reflect upon our individual prowess as librarians. In order to overcome this emphasis on individual evaluation for this exercise, we decided to emphasize our efforts as a group. We verbalized this emphasis to each other numerous times over the year we spent refining our baseline assessment.

All librarians at Ship are involved in the liaison program. It is important to take this fact into account when attempting to compare our data to other academic libraries. Libraries with more librarians or a different structure may find these reflections less useful than libraries similar to ours. Instead, look at this research as our story as we struggled with assessment.

Suggestions for Application of Our Liaison Rubric to Other Libraries

Rubrics have become a valuable tool in the broad assessment of organizational mission statements that have been operationalized as group performance goals. Although extremely time-consuming to create, as they are specific to each institution and to each department, they do provide a way to verbalize complex group behaviors and allow them to be aired for discussion and evaluation by all stakeholders. Following are several initial suggestions as to how our experience with a rubric could help to streamline the initiation of such practices in other libraries.

1. Creating a rubric is an amazingly amorphous process, akin to nailing Jell-O to the wall. Processes and procedures that have been in place for years have often never been verbalized. As we found, different librarians had different definitions and self-expectations of what each of our dimensions actually meant. So expect ambiguity and encourage discussion. Look at this process as an opportunity to come to consensus on some very important issues. Expect the same ambiguity when you share your rubric with other stakeholders.

2. Rubrics are by their very nature extremely pragmatic. They should be based on real-world performance. Thus we suggest that it is very important to start with what you are actually doing. Using brief auto-

biographical narratives by each librarian allows for each voice to be heard. And when discussed as a group, these short narratives become the basis of common definitions of shared procedures.

3. Oftentimes academicians are handed goals or expectations that have never been operationalized or adapted to the specific unit. Although these lofty goals should be addressed in the creation of a rubric, they ought not to drive the process. As suggested in the previous paragraph, begin with what you are doing and work toward where you would like to be.

4. This process assumes that librarians know what they should be doing and how they should be doing it. This consensus-building process takes a long time. Although a committee was initially appointed to assess our liaison program, one of the authors directed the effort and kept the process moving. Upon occasion he acted as first coder in order to facilitate discussion in the larger group. Whatever procedure you choose to use to create a rubric, do not expect this process to happen quickly. This report represents the work of a full academic year.

Summary and Conclusion

This chapter has addressed the story of our task of creating and applying a rubric to qualitatively self-assess the liaison program at Ship. We grounded this narrative in the literature of qualitative assessment. We also related our process of decision making. We passed on some preliminary findings. And we concluded with suggestions as to how this assessment tool can be applied to other library contexts.

In conclusion, we felt that this self-assessment via rubric provided us with reporting data that will become a basis for dialogue with the rest of the campus. In addition, it provided us with an easy-to-understand, goal-based methodology we can rely on for decision making to refine our services as liaisons to academic departments. We feel that using a rubric to assess our own performance was a worthwhile activity.

Notes

1. Sean Nicholson-Crotty, Nick A. Theobald, and Jill Nicholson-Crotty, "Disparate Measures: Public Managers and Performance-measurement Strategies," *Public Administration Review* 66, no. 1 (2006): 101.

2. Kim Cameron, "Measuring Organizational Effectiveness in Institutions of Higher Education," *Administrative Science Quarterly* 23, no. 4 (1978): 605.

3. Shannon Chance and Brenda T. Williams, "Assessing University Strategic Plans: A Tool for Consideration," *Educational Planning* 18, no. 1 (2009): 38.

4. Cameron, "Measuring Organizational Effectiveness," 609.

5. Sandra Myers, "Performance-based Assessment," *Research Starters—Education* 1, no. 1 (2008): 2.

6. John C. Hafner and Patti M. Hafner, "Quantitative Analysis of the Rubric as an Assessment Tool: An Empirical Study of Student Peer-group Rating," *International Journal of Science Education* 25, no. 12 (2003): 1509.

7. Association of College and Research Libraries, *Information Literacy Standards for Higher Education* (Chicago: Association of College and Research Libraries, 2000).

8. See for example, Megan Oakleaf, "Using Rubrics to Assess Information Literacy: An Examination of Methodology and Interrater Reliability," *Journal of the American Society for Information Science and Technology* 60, no. 5 (2009): 969–83; or rubrics listed at "Information Literacy Rubrics," Lorain County Community College, http://www.lorainccc.edu/Library/Library+Services/Services+for+Faculty/IL+Rubrics.htm (accessed Dec. 8, 2010).

9. Megan Oakleaf, "Using Rubrics to Collect Evidence for Decision-making: What Do Librarians Need to Learn?" *Evidence Based Library & Information Practice* 2, no. 3 (2007): 28. We attempted to gather examples of current real-world library uses of rubrics by posting a query on numerous e-mail discussion lists to determine if other librarians are making use of this assessment tool in areas other than instruction. Although many librarians responded that they were using rubrics to assess instruction in some way, only a few responded with service- or performance-related rubrics. Megan Oakleaf, who is a faculty member at the School of Information Studies at Syracuse University (and also the author of an article on rubrics), has her students develop and use rubrics to assess various library services. Karen Nicholson, Teaching and Learning Librarian at McMaster University, e-mailed that they "use rubrics in a training program we developed to prepare paraprofessionals to work on a blended services desk." Their rubric is available on the Web. Kay Young, a librarian at the University of Wisconsin–Platteville e-mailed that "the search committee for a library director at UW–Platteville has devised rubrics for reviewing applications and for assessing the answers to interview questions." Beth Stahr, head of Reference and Instruction at Southeastern Louisiana University, wrote, "I use rubrics when I observe the instruction librarians teaching the credit-bearing information literacy course in the face-to-face traditional classes and the single-session bibliographic instruction sessions. I also have used the Quality Matters rubric to assess the Internet-delivered credit-bearing information literacy class that is taught here." Alfred Mowdood, head of Research and Information Services at the University of Utah, is using a rubric for staff training and performance assessment.

10. In one of the few examples available, Yang used a survey methodology to gauge faculty awareness of and satisfaction with the library liaison program: Zheng Y. Yang, "University Faculty's Perception of a Library Liaison Program: A Case Study," *Journal of Academic Librarianship* 26, no. 2 (2000): 124–28.

11. Dannelle D. Stevens and Antonia Levi, *Introduction to Rubrics: An Assessment Tool to Save Grading Time, Convey Effective Feedback, and Promote Student Learning* (Sterling, VA: Stylus Publishing, 2005), 3.

12. Chance and Williams, "Assessing University Strategic Plans," 45.

13. Oakleaf, "Using Rubrics to Collect Evidence for Decision-making," 29

14. Ibid.

15. Chance and Williams, "Assessing University Strategic Plans," 45.

16. "Assessments and Reporting Assessment Data," International Reading Association, http://www.reading.org/Resources/ProfessionalDevelopment/Accreditation/Assessments.aspx (accessed Dec. 8, 2010).

17. See chapter 1 of Stevens and Levi, *Introduction to Rubrics*.

18. Adnan Kan, "An Alternative Method in the New Educational Program from the Point of Performance-based Assessment: Rubric Scoring Scales," *Educational Sciences: Theory & Practice* 7, no. 1 (2007): 145–46.

19. Ship is a medium-sized university with three colleges, eight thousand students, and nine library faculty involved in the liaison program.

20. See, for example, "Library Liaison Program Liaison Potential Activities," Emporia State University Library, http://www.emporia.edu/libsv/collectiondev/colldev_liaisonactivities.htm (accessed Dec. 8, 2010); "Library Liaison @ Mac," McMaster University Libraries, http://library.mcmaster.ca/liaison (accessed Dec. 8, 2010); and "Checklist of Potential Liaison Activities," University of Connecticut Libraries, http://www.lib.uconn.edu/services/liaison/liaisonactiv.html (accessed Dec. 8, 2010).

21. Sharan B. Merriam, ed., *Qualitative Research in Practice: Examples for Discussion and Analysis* (San Francisco: Jossey-Bass, 2002).

22. Oakleaf, "Using Rubrics to Collect Evidence for Decision-making."

23. Several authors describe this messy, but fruitful, procedure. See in particular, Judith A. Arter and Jay McTighe, *Scoring Rubrics in the Classroom: Using Performance Criteria for Assessing and Improving Student Performance* (Thousand Oaks, CA: Corwin Press, 2001); Kan, "An Alternative Method in the New Educational Program"; and Stevens and Levi, *Introduction to Rubrics*.

24. Richard Raspa and Dane Ward, *The Collaborative Imperative: Librarians and Faculty Working Together in the Information Universe* (Chicago: Association of College and Research Libraries, 2000).

25. We also tried to display this information with charts, which are easily produced with Excel; however, they quickly became so complex that we found that, although less colorful, tables were also less complex. Table 10.2 represents our primary findings, which we then broke down into tables comparing all departments in a college, all departments with no services, all departments with High services, etc., which we have summarized in table 10.3.

26. We decided several years ago to include Distance Education as a program with which we needed to liaison. Since our distance education courses are representative of our other departments, we did not allocate them any monies for collection development.

27. For example, although our English department does have a number of student majors, much of the faculty time is spent in teaching Writing Intensive First Year Seminar (WIFYS), a General Education curricular requirement that all freshmen must take. Thus they offer thirty-plus sections of WIFYS each semester.

APPENDIX: TABLE 10.1
Final Rubric

Task Description/Mission Statement: The Library liaison program will support the educational goals of each instructional department or program at Shippensburg University.

Performance Goals: The Library liaison program will manage the resources provided by the University to support each department's curriculum; provide the department's faculty and students with the knowledge and skills needed to access and make the best use of librarian's expertise and library resources; and collaborate with each department to further the broader instructional goals of the institution.

	Assessment Scale		
Dimensions/Goals	1. Basic Services to be provided to all departments	2. Medium level services	3. High (Ideal) level services
A) Collection Development	Establish or update new books distribution list (potential) Know the existing strengths of the collection Learn collection development profiling software On an annual basis, communicate methods for adding materials to the collection Order reference materials in discipline	Monitor use of serial titles Promote new and unique library resources Schedule demonstrations of relevant electronic products	Coordinate collection evaluation project Produce information guides on new services, collections, and research tools Write grant for funds to improve collections
B) Instruction	Create a course guide/handout for each course taught Create brochure, etc., advertising instructional services (using a common template) Discuss potential instruction sessions with department members Monitor Reference questions to inform high use curriculum areas Update/Create subject guides on library website	Deliver information literacy classes, sessions, workshops, curriculum—in your Liaison areas Provide research consultations for graduate students, faculty Create tip sheets for specific assignments (Citing Legal documents) Discuss problematic assignments with appropriate faculty Have resources by subject page linked from department, program or Regional Campus web site Provide specific reference services based upon individual assignments	Develop or help develop tutorials/interactive learning modules Establish a teaching partnership with a member of the Liaison departments or programs Schedule regular on site visits, e.g. office or computer lab hours Teach a course or a course component in the Liaison departments or programs Work with dept, program, or campus administrators to insure info literacy is fully incorporated into program curriculum

APPENDIX: TABLE 10.1, *CONT.*
Final Rubric

	Assessment Scale		
Dimensions/Goals	**1. Basic Services to be provided to all departments**	**2. Medium level services**	**3. High (Ideal) level services**
C) Outreach	Create or update electronic distribution list of Liaison clientele Have name added to departmental mail and e-mail distribution lists Learn about the curriculum Learn about the department & its needs—read website, newsletter, meeting minutes, etc. Maintain a current distribution list of departmental faculty email Meet with library representative Meet with new faculty Monitor the library literature with regard to potential Liaison activities for this area Read course descriptions and syllabi Send information packets to new faculty including adjuncts Survey and document faculty research interests	Attend departmental meetings or other faculty inclusive gatherings Become aware of recent changes in research reporting of the discipline resulting from digitization Immerse in the discipline—join listservs, attend classes or workshops, read guides to the literature Meet with department chair Participate in a conference or workshop related to one's subject area Provide information for departmental accreditation/review reports Set up available Alert services—EBSCO, etc.	Assist with department, program, or campus self-study/re-accreditation/grant Prepare and distribute library information news updates (electronic or paper) targeted to the Liaison department Prepare library exhibit(s) relating to Liaison area Read key journals in the discipline Serve on a departmental, program, or campus committee Write a feature or column for departmental newsletter

APPENDIX: TABLE 10.2
Sample Narrative Data for Arts & Humanities Departments, Plus Our Self-assessment Rating Scores for Our Provision of Service to Each Department[a]

Department	Dimension	Sample Baseline Narrative	Baseline Rating	Average Rating
Art	Outreach	Met each semester with department. Met with department members individually. Participated in department functions. Assisted with 5-Year program Review.	3 (High)	2.67
	Instruction	Taught art education classes.	2 (Medium)	
	Collection Development	Monitored allocation. Worked with department for a grant to purchase ARTstor.	3 (High)	
Communication/ Journalism	Outreach	Created department distribution list. Met with department	1 (Basic)	1.33
	Instruction	Taught several classes.	2 (Medium)	
	Collection Development	Monitored allocation.	1 (Basic)	
English	Outreach	Met with WIFYS faculty to plan instructional strategies.	3 (High)	2.33
	Instruction	Provided a basic online tutorial. Taught most of the WIFYS sections.	3 (High)	
	Collection Development	Monitored allocation.	1 (Basic)	
Human Communication Studies	Outreach	Met to discuss instructional strategies for the Intro classes.	2 (Medium)	2.00
	Instruction	Taught numerous Intro classes. Taught Asian American Communication.	3 (High)	
	Collection Development	Monitored allocation.	1 (Basic)	

APPENDIX: TABLE 10.2, *CONT.*

Sample Narrative Data for Arts & Humanities Departments, Plus Our Self-assessment Rating Scores for Our Provision of Service to Each Department[a]

Department	Dimension	Sample Baseline Narrative	Baseline Rating	Average Rating
History/ Philosophy	Outreach	Met with department regarding collection evaluation project. Met personally with numerous faculty. Worked with department on History Day	2 (Medium)	2.33
	Instruction	Taught numerous specialized history classes. Taught graduate archival history classes.	3 (High)	
	Collection Development	Monitored allocation. Collection Evaluation project.	2 (Medium)	
Modern Languages	Outreach	Participated in multi-language poetry reading.	2 (Medium)	1
	Instruction		0 (None)	
	Collection Development	Monitored allocation.	1 (Basic)	
Music/ Theater Arts	Outreach	Met with department. Met with new faculty member. Served on a department search committee.	3 (High)	1.33
	Instruction		0 (None)	
	Collection Development	Monitored allocation. Collection Evaluation project.	2 (Medium)	

a. Table 10.2 actually represents two different parts of our process. We began by providing the narrative portions seen on the table. This was primarily an individual effort, with librarians reporting what they had done recently for and with their department. Other librarians then added activities they had performed. After the narrative was complete, we attempted to assign a score of Basic (equals 1), Medium (equals 2), or High (equals 3) based on the rubric represented in table 10.1. We met as a group to finalize these numerical rankings. We then averaged the three scores for each department to give ourselves an overall comparative ranking.

APPENDIX: TABLE 10.3
Ranked Listing of Departments and Programs by Overall Average Scores[a]

Department	College	Outreach Rating	Instruction Rating	Collection Development Rating	Average Rating
Biology	Sciences	3 (High)	3 (High)	3 (High)	3.00 (High)
Teacher Education	Education & Human Services	3 (High)	3 (High)	3 (High)	3.00 (High)
Art	Arts & Humanities	3 (High)	2 (Medium)	3 (High)	2.67 (Medium)
English	Arts & Humanities	3 (High)	3 (High)	1 (Basic)	2.33 (Medium)
History	Arts & Humanities	2 (Medium)	3 (High)	2 (Medium)	2.33 (Medium)
Chemistry	Sciences	2 (Medium)	2 (Medium)	3 (High)	2.33 (Medium)
Ethnic Studies Minor	Interdisciplinary Program	3 (High)	3 (High)	1 (Basic)	2.33 (Medium)
Human Communication	Arts & Humanities	2 (Medium)	3 (High)	1 (Basic)	2.00 (Medium)
Political Science	Sciences	2 (Medium)	3 (High)	1 (Basic)	2.00 (Medium)
Social Work	Education & Human Services	3 (High)	2 (Medium)	1 (Basic)	2.00 (Medium)
Psychology	Sciences	2 (Medium)	2 (Medium)	1 (Basic)	1.67 (Basic)
Management	Business	1 (Basic)	2 (Medium)	2 (Medium)	1.67 (Basic)
Criminal Justice	Education & Human Services	2 (Medium)	2 (Medium)	1 (Basic)	1.67 (Basic)
Communications	Arts & Humanities	1 (Basic)	2 (Medium)	1 (Basic)	1.33 (Basic)
Music	Arts & Humanities	3 (High)	0 (None)	1 (Basic)	1.33 (Basic)
Economics	Sciences	2 (Medium)	1 (Basic)	1 (Basic)	1.33 (Basic)
Geo-Environmental	Sciences	1 (Basic)	2 (Medium)	1 (Basic)	1.33 (Basic)
Mathematics	Sciences	1 (Basic)	2 (Medium)	1 (Basic)	1.33 (Basic)
Finance	Business	1 (Basic)	2 (Medium)	1 (Basic)	1.33 (Basic)
Counseling	Education & Human Services	1 (Basic)	2 (Medium)	1 (Basic)	1.33 (Basic)

APPENDIX: TABLE 10.3, *CONT.*

Ranked Listing of Departments and Programs by Overall Average Scores[a]

Department	College	Outreach Rating	Instruction Rating	Collection Development Rating	Average Rating
Educational Leadership and Special Education	Education & Human Services	1 (Basic)	2 (Medium)	1 (Basic)	1.33 (Basic)
Exercise Science	Education & Human Services	1 (Basic)	2 (Medium)	1 (Basic)	1.33 (Basic)
Honors (Program)	Interdisciplinary (Program)	1 (Basic)	2 (Medium)	1 (Basic)	1.33 (Basic)
Modern Languages	Arts & Humanities	2 (Medium)	0 (None)	1 (Basic)	1.00 (Basic)
Sociology	Sciences	0 (None)	2 (Medium)	1 (Basic)	1.00 (Basic)
Distance Education (Program)	Interdisciplinary (Program)	1 (Basic)	2 (Medium)	0 (None)	1.00 (Basic)
Women's Studies Minor	Interdisciplinary (Program)	0 (None)	2 (Medium)	1 (Basic)	1.00 (Basic)
Computer Sciences	Sciences	1 (Basic)	0 (None)	1 (Basic)	0.67 (Low)
Organizational Development and Leadership (Program)	Interdisciplinary (Program)	1 (Basic)	0 (None)	1 (Basic)	0.67 (Low)
Physics	Sciences	1 (Basic)	0 (None)	1 (Basic)	0.67 (Low)
Accounting	Business	1 (Basic)	0 (None)	1 (Basic)	0.67 (Low)
International Studies Minor	Interdisciplinary (Program)	0 (None)	0 (None)	1 (Basic)	0.33 (Low)
Professional Studies (Program)	Interdisciplinary (Program)	0 (None)	0 (None)	1 (Basic)	0.33 (Low)

a. The numbers in the columns labeled Outreach, Instruction, and Collection Development are the scores from table 10.2, depicting our numerical assessment of the quality of our service to each department. 1 equals Basic service, 2 equals Medium service, and 3 equals High service. We interpreted average scores in the same fashion; however, we added one more category—Low service. An average of less than 1 equals Low service, an average of 1 to 1.99 equals Basic service, an average of 2 to 2.99 equals Medium service, and an average of 3 equals High overall service to the department or program.

PART 3
Issues Addressed through Qualitative Research

Analyzing LibQUAL+ Comments to Inform Library Decision Making

David A. Nolfi and Laverna M. Saunders

Abstract. Quality decision making and strategic planning require reliable information and thorough understanding of user needs. Many libraries have used LibQUAL+ as a survey research tool to collect both quantitative and qualitative data useful for planning and decision making. A body of case literature provides examples and models of how libraries have worked with qualitative research methodologies and theories such as textual analysis of LibQUAL+ open comments, grounded theory, computer-assisted methods, and follow-up focus groups and summits. This case study demonstrates how Duquesne University used these qualitative research methods to analyze 697 user comments from its 2009 LibQUAL+ survey and shares choices made and resultant discoveries of the experience.

Introduction

How do librarians make decisions? How do librarians discover their users' needs? What information is useful for planning purposes? Picture Gumberg Library, an academic library ready to begin strategic planning at Duquesne University where serving students is *the* primary mission, and you can begin to understand why the librarians needed an instrument to discover what students think about and want in their library. In addition, librarians wanted to learn faculty and staff expectations. This context set the stage for Gumberg Library's selection of LibQUAL+ as a tool to measure user perception and collect specific comments to be used in planning and decision making.

Decision-making Framework

Librarians in all types of libraries make decisions daily. One framework for looking at library decision making includes three types of decisions: operational, critical, and strategic.[1] Most decisions can be categorized as operational because they pertain to general work functions and services. For example, a reference librarian determines which database best meets a user's information need. An instruction librarian decides how to define learning outcomes and organize a class presentation. A cataloger identifies the most appropriate classification number for a new book. The library director decides salary increases for each employee based on performance evaluations. In each of these cases professional training and experience play a role in how the decision is made, but the consequences of a poor decision are not disastrous. One can correct errors, clarify an option, change numbers, or modify a presentation.

Critical decisions are those that are particularly challenging due to risk factors. The consequences of a bad decision could affect the budget, job security, or professional or institutional reputation and might result in legal actions. Examples include difficult personnel matters, outsourcing services, reorganization, downsizing, major collection cancellations, or closing branches. Often there are time constraints and an emotional impact on the decision maker and stakeholders because the choices are so difficult. However, one must consider the available information and options and then exercise professional judgment.

Between the operational and the critical is a third category called strategic decision making. Strategic decisions move the library forward toward realizing an articulated vision. Strategy involves positioning the library within a campus or system context. In order to make strategic decisions, library leaders should be knowledgeable about their institutions and users as well as about trends in libraries, publishing, scholarly communication, and technology. It is also important to understand higher education in general, accreditation and program review standards and expectations, and the political environment governing funding.

Strategic planning is a formal process that helps library leaders develop mission and vision statements and high-level goals within a three- to five-year time frame. Other elements of strategic planning include analyzing the strengths, weaknesses, opportunities, and threats for the organization; articulating core values; creating goals and objectives; and developing implementation and strategic plans.

One of the early steps of the planning process is identifying library stakeholders and constituents—those individuals and groups served by the library. Spohn and Hirshon recommend using surveys, focus groups, or interviews to understand the needs, expectations, and interests of users as well as those who fund and oversee the library.[2] By communicating at the beginning and at subsequent phases during implementation, library planners are more likely to

obtain the buy-in and support of stakeholders as they demonstrate outcomes and improvements. The priorities and expectations of external stakeholders, such as city councils, university administration, and accreditors, also influence library priorities. Each library must determine the most appropriate way to conduct this needs assessment, taking into consideration factors such as resources available (e.g., staff/volunteers, time, money), political environment, and options to ensure the validity of the process. Nelson's recent strategic planning handbook provides detailed procedures for public library planners.[3] Many academic librarians have looked to the Association of Research Libraries for planning models and consulting assistance. Prior to launching strategic planning, many academic libraries use the LibQUAL+ survey[4] as a tool to obtain user perceptions of library performance and to gather comments and suggestions.

Strategic Planning and LibQUAL+

Many academic libraries use LibQUAL+ for the purpose of obtaining information about user expectations and their perceptions of library performance.[5] LibQUAL+, maintained by the Association of Research Libraries, is an online survey that can be made available to campus users and stakeholders. It provides a structure for the library to open communication in an efficient manner. LibQUAL+ supports both structured and open responses. This instrument helps libraries define perceived strengths and weaknesses as well as possible opportunities for new services. Responses, then, help the library understand the needs, expectations, and interests of each category of user. The survey includes

1. Twenty-two core questions asking respondents to rank their minimum, desired, and perceived levels of library service using nine-point Likert scales. These questions fall into three categories: Affect of Service, Information Control, and Library as Place (see table 11.1).
2. As many as five optional locally generated questions (again using nine-point scales for minimum, desired, and perceived levels of service).

3. Three general satisfaction questions using nine-point Likert scales.

4. Five information literacy outcomes items using nine-point Likert scales to indicate level of agreement.

5. Three questions asking respondents to indicate how frequently they use the library building, library Web site, and non-library search engines.

6. An open-ended comment box provided at the survey's end.

Since all libraries administering LibQUAL+ use the core questions (as well as all the quantitative questions), these scores help libraries benchmark performance with designated peers. They also help libraries to measure longitudinal change and improvement when they administer the survey repeatedly. The questions regarding general satisfaction, information literacy, and patron search habits also provide additional information about users. Only the core questions, however, have been nationally normed and can be used for comparison to other institutions having given LibQUAL+.

After patrons have completed the survey, libraries may download an Excel file that includes all responses, plus the comments and user demographic data. As qualitative data, the comments are important and exceptionally valuable for identifying issues the library should address as possible action items in strategic plan implementation. When analyzed objectively, comments can also inform strategic thinking and decision making.

Context

As the Duquesne University administration began work on a second-generation strategic plan in 2008, the Gumberg Library management team selected the LibQUAL+ survey as its preferred research tool prior to starting library strategic planning. Although the library seeks student and faculty feedback in many ways, such as comment cards, brief online surveys, and focus groups, the management team viewed LibQUAL+ as an opportunity to obtain feedback from a large number of users across the whole university.

TABLE 11.1
LibQUAL+ Core Questions

Affect of Service
1. Employees who instill confidence in users
2. Employees who give users individual attention
3. Employees who are consistently courteous
4. Employees' readiness to respond to users' questions
5. Employees who have the knowledge to answer user questions
6. Employees who deal with users in a caring fashion
7. Employees who understand the needs of their users
8. Employees' willingness to help users
9. Employees' dependability in handling users' service problems

Information Control
1. Making electronic resources accessible from my home or office
2. A library Web site enabling me to locate information on my own
3. The printed library materials I need for my work
4. The electronic information resources I need
5. Modern equipment that lets me easily access needed information
6. Easy-to-use access tools that allow me to find things on my own
7. Making information easily accessible for independent use
8. Print and/or electronic journal collections I require for my work

Library as Place
1. Library space that inspires study and learning
2. Quiet space for individual activities
3. A comfortable and inviting location
4. A getaway for study, learning, or research
5. Community space for group learning and group study

Having administered LibQUAL+ in 2006 to establish a baseline for comparing the results of future surveys (as well as to collect valuable information), the management team charged the library's Assessment Committee to coordinate the administration of the survey in 2009. This chapter's case study describes the committee's procedural options and decisions made as a result of analyzing LibQUAL+ data and comments.

Problem Statement

Although the LibQUAL+ quantitative data provided numbers that allowed the library to compare respondents' needs, desires, and perceptions, the Assessment Committee sought to gain further localized insight into the meaning behind the numbers. Using qualitative methodologies, we aimed to gain a more complete understanding, enabling respondents to speak to us using their own words. We believed that analyzing the comments would help us to learn more about the respondents including

- how respondents believed the library affected their abilities to successfully achieve academic goals
- how respondents viewed and felt about their interactions with the library
- any additional concerns not adequately covered by the quantitative portion of LibQUAL+

Finally, the Assessment Committee believed that the respondents' own words might offer the best insight into their perceptions of the library as well as their needs.

The ultimate problem we faced as we began to analyze LibQUAL+ comments was how to translate nearly 30,000 words comprising 697 comments into meaningful data to inform the strategic planning process. In order to approach that daunting task, the Assessment Committee first had to determine how to analyze the comments systematically. Since qualitative methods offer techniques for identifying themes in textual data, the approach seemed obvious. We decided to use content analysis in order to categorize the data and identify patterns and themes in the comments.[6] A related challenge was that as members of the library staff, the Assessment Committee needed to take steps to limit potential bias in the analysis process.

Literature Review

Using LibQUAL+ as a critical information-gathering process prior to formal strategic planning seemed logical. We needed to review the professional literature, however, to find information and best practices on the following issues: What processes and information are needed for quality decision making? How have academic libraries used LibQUAL+ with strategic planning, and what were the results for decision making? How can qualitative research methods be used effectively to analyze user comments in LibQUAL+?

What Processes and Information Are Needed For Quality Decision Making?

Several definitions of decision making from business authors and from the library literature indicate the complexities of the process. In his classic text, *Functions of the Executive*, Chester Barnard noted that a major decision may involve numerous subsidiary decisions or judgments. "The ideal process of decision is to discriminate the strategic factors and to redefine or change purpose on the basis of the estimate of future results of action in the existing situation, in the light of history, experience, knowledge of the past."[7] Barnard's definition of a strategic factor was "one whose control, in the right form, at the right place and time, will establish a new system or set of conditions which meets the purpose."[8]

Herbert Simon, another historic writer on business organizations, treated decision making as "synonymous with managing" and refers not just to the final act of choosing between alternatives but rather to the whole process of decision. In his framework, decision making comprised three principal phases in sequence: (1) intelligence activity, which includes finding occasions for making a decision; (2) design activity, which involves inventing, developing, and analyzing possible courses of action; and (3) choice activity, which means selecting a particular course of action from those available.[9] Simon acknowledged that each phase in making a particular decision is itself a complex decision-making process.

According to Hernon and McClure, library decision making within the context of organizational change and improvement is closely related to planning and the research process.[10] "If one defines decision making as that process whereby information is converted into action, decision making is largely concerned with the process of acquiring, analyzing, and reporting information to accomplish an objective."[11]

In their recent library leadership text, Evans and Ward distinguished between structured (working with known rules) and unstructured (no set rules) decisions.[12] Their theoretical model for unstructured decisions included six steps: (1) define the problem and analyze the constituent parts, (2) clarify and prioritize the goal, (3) consider all the possible ways to achieve the goal, (4) evaluate all the options, considering what would happen if . . . , (5) compare the consequences of each option with the goal, and (6) select the option with the outcomes that most closely match the goal.[13] The authors acknowledged that in reality, practice does not necessarily follow this model. They noted that additional factors such as crises, time, risk tolerance, reliable information, and organizational politics all affect how a leader makes a decision.

Common themes in the foregoing definitions pertain to identifying possible problems or courses of action, obtaining information about possible needs or actions, and then moving toward a choice that sets a direction for action. Given the expectation of developing strategic plans and integrating assessment measures and outcomes into the implementation of plans, most twenty-first century academic libraries need assistance. Clearly these processes take time, expertise, and other resources that challenge most organizations. Quantitative and qualitative results from LibQUAL+ provide rich data which must be analyzed for themes, issues, and opportunities for decisions and actions.

LibQUAL+, Strategic Planning, and Decision Making

Since LibQUAL+ was developed and promulgated by research libraries, the early adopters among the

ARL membership have documented their experiences with case studies.[14] Some of these articles offer insight into the potential use of LibQUAL+ results for strategic planning. Bowling Green University administered LibQUAL+ in 2002, expecting to use the results in developing strategic goals.[15] After analyzing the quantitative data, librarians identified specific areas for follow-up focus group interviews. Shorb and Driscoll shared how the University of Florida administered LibQUAL+ with the intent of incorporating results into departmental and individual plans.[16] They also expected to measure the outcomes of SMART (Specific, Measurable, Attainable, Realistic, Time bound)[17] goals with LibQUAL+ data. The University of Chicago used the LibQUAL+ survey in 2004 prior to developing the library's new strategic plan.[18] Analysis of the comments using qualitative methods led to additional assessment activities and informed setting of organizational goals. Clemson University developed library summits to discuss LibQUAL+ outcomes with stakeholders in the university community and library staff. The themes that emerged from these quantitative and qualitative approaches were used as the basis for the Clemson Libraries' strategic and business plans for 2001–2003.[19] Clemson's system of convening Library Summits has been adopted by other universities.[20]

Not all the literature is positive about the use of LibQUAL+. In a 2007 article, Saunders pointed out the fallacy of using LibQUAL+ results to construct a strategic plan.[21] The planning team at Purdue University Libraries discovered that LibQUAL+ could not help set the goals of their strategic plan because "the shortfalls in library service as revealed by LibQUAL+ were focusing attention on the sins of the past and not on the possibilities of the future."[22] Saunders went on to affirm, however, that LibQUAL+ measures were used as metrics for the goals of the strategic plan. In a subsequent article, Saunders described Purdue's strategic planning experience and the relationship of LibQUAL+ results to the goals of the final plan. Saunders concluded by noting that "the assessment data from the LibQUAL+ survey had a very important influence in the creation of the Purdue Libraries' strategic plan," specifically making librarians aware of particular service issues at the college level, providing facts to inform decision making, and identifying operational needs that must be addressed while working toward a more daring future.[23]

The idea of using LibQUAL+ as a standard component of strategic planning is not documented in current strategic planning guides. For example, *The Library Strategic Planning Toolkit* by Spohn and Hirshon did not mention LibQUAL+.[24] What it did present, however, was the rationale and groundwork for using a tool such as LibQUAL+ to learn and assess what users think about the library. Other qualitative methods such as focus groups would also work. Using this step-by-step guide to strategic planning, a library team could make the necessary connections between the elements of the plan and results from LibQUAL+ even though there is no specific direction in the book. Other recent and influential books on outcomes assessment[25] and assessing service quality[26] discuss methodologies other than LibQUAL+. In addition, *Scorecards for Results: A Guide for Developing a Library Balanced Scorecard* by Joseph R. Matthews did not mention LibQUAL+.[27]

It is important to note that numerous organizations and libraries create strategic plans without using LibQUAL+. Small and even mid-sized academic libraries with limited staff and expertise might be challenged to use LibQUAL+, and cost could also be a deterrent.

Regardless of whether libraries actually build their strategic plans around the LibQUAL+ domains, the literature indicates that many libraries have used the results of LibQUAL+ to make both operational and strategic decisions. Quantitative and qualitative data have driven building designs,[28] organizational restructuring,[29] service improvements,[30] marketing and public relations plans,[31] and assessment plans.[32] These themes appear repeatedly in LibQUAL+ Share Fair[33] abstracts from poster presentations at American Library Association annual conferences.

Qualitative Analysis of LibQUAL+ Comments

At the end of the survey, LibQUAL+ includes an open-ended comment box with the instruction to the patron, "Please enter any comments about library services in the box below." This item gives users their only opportunity to provide feedback in an unstructured manner. Thus, respondents have the freedom to address any aspect of library services currently on their minds. Additionally, an unstructured approach enables respondents to use their own words, allowing them to communicate their thoughts in their own language. Alternatively, the library's challenge is to analyze this large body of textual data in order to inform decision making.

Content analysis is a method used to identify themes in textual data. It usually involves two processes that can involve many steps: coding and analyzing. Coding captures the meaning expressed in the text by standing for a larger passage that pertains to a particular theme. Coding reduces the original text to a more manageable word or phrase that can be compared across all comments made by patrons. Although there are many approaches to devising codes, they typically fit into two different types: (1) codes devised by the researcher based on his or her reading of the text, and (2) codes derived from an existing model or scheme. The researcher first reads the comments and assigns codes to portions of the text. After coding all the text, the researcher begins the analysis by looking for patterns, themes, and relationships between the codes.

Returning to the literature to explore how libraries code and analyze user comments in LibQUAL+ efficiently and effectively, we discovered case studies on a variety of software products used for this purpose. Dennis and Bower, for example, stated, "Many libraries have found these comments helpful since they complement the quantitative findings and provide a level of insight not captured by the twenty seven closed-ended questions."[34] Software used to code LibQUAL+ comments included NVivo/N6/NUD*IST, ATLAS.ti, and Microsoft Access.[35] It is worth noting that libraries may also use various simpler methods as well (for example, highlighting words and phrases and then reviewing the highlights to glean themes).

According to Durkin, computer programs for qualitative data analysis have both benefits and limitations.[36] On the positive side they improve the integrity of research by increasing reliability and validity by "reminding us of data and their contexts at all stages of research."[37] They make it easier to construct, refine, and relate analytical categories as well as code and retrieve data. They help identify patterns and establish data relationships and hierarchies. However, they do not eliminate the need for thinking critically, creating theories, or developing codes.

Emphasizing the importance of analyzing LibQUAL+ comments, Dennis and Bower reported on the experience of Western Michigan University Libraries using ATLAS.ti 5.0 to organize, classify, and consolidate LibQUAL+ comments.[38] Guidry also described the use of ATLAS.ti to analyze unsolicited e-mail messages from libraries participating in a 2001 pilot test of LibQUAL+.[39] Other libraries using ATLAS.ti for comment analysis include the University of Chicago[40] and the University of North Carolina at Greensboro.[41]

Begay and her colleagues detailed how the University of Arizona Library coded LibQUAL+ comments using a grounded theory approach and the N6 version of NUD*IST from QSR.[42] The N6 software supported a systematic, objective analysis of the comments after the coded comments were entered.

Brown University used NVivo to code 819 user comments.[43] Librarians developed a taxonomy or master list of common themes or nodes based on keywords identified throughout user comments. Next they imported comments into NVivo and assigned nodes to each comment based on keywords and finally exported the comments into a database to develop a user interface for viewing by the assessment group. Their final taxonomy included twenty-nine nodes that were used to describe distinct themes in user comments. Oklahoma State University also used NVivo.[44] In 2008 Towson University used NVivo software to track patterns and distill information from LibQUAL+ open comments.[45] Finally, Bowling Green State University used Microsoft Access to analyze comments, breaking them into eight categories.[46]

From the literature we deduced that gathering and analyzing LibQUAL+ results fit appropriately with the intelligence or information-gathering phase of decision-making models. Many academic libraries have contributed to a body of case studies and presentation abstracts published in the past decade showing evidence of using the quantitative and qualitative data from LibQUAL+ for strategic planning and decision making. Qualitative analysis of comments particularly helped with the process of defining library problems and possible action items for operational and strategic decisions. Libraries have successfully used a variety of software products to assist in the process of analyzing qualitative data by constructing categories and identifying patterns, data relationships, and hierarchies. Finally, the process of looking at LibQUAL+ data critically and thoughtfully is a human process that requires knowledge of qualitative research principles and local context.

Duquesne University Case Study

Duquesne University is an urban, Catholic university located in downtown Pittsburgh with over ten thousand students enrolled in nearly two hundred academic programs including undergraduate, master's, and doctoral. Gumberg Library is the university's main library; a separate library serves primarily the School of Law. Gumberg's fifteen full-time librarians and twenty-two staff members serve all ten schools of the university.

In February 2009, Gumberg Library administered the LibQUAL+ survey to all Duquesne University students, faculty, general university staff, and library staff. Using e-mail, posters, Web site announcements, and personal contact, Gumberg Library invited all Duquesne University students, faculty, and staff to participate. Following common practice when administering LibQUAL+ in an academic library, students were offered the chance to enter a drawing for twenty-six different prizes, including iPod Touches, gift baskets, and Starbucks gift cards. The library provided access to LibQUAL+ on a Web page placed behind the Gumberg Library proxy server to restrict access to Duquesne users. When planning began for the 2009 LibQUAL+ survey, the chair of the Assessment Committee had expressed a desire to analyze the comments systematically. Through his work with faculty in the School of Nursing and the Sociology Department, he had become increasingly aware of the value of qualitative methodologies when trying to understand textual data. Of the 1,441 respondents (12 percent of all students, faculty, and staff), 697 (48 percent) wrote comments varying in length from one word to several hundred words.

Developing a Coding Scheme

The Health Sciences Librarian, whose roles are primarily instruction and reference, chairs the Assessment Committee and also serves on the University Academic Learning Outcomes Assessment Committee. Other members of the committee included the Head of Collection Development and the University Archivist.

Although some libraries choose to analyze the comments using the LibQUAL+ dimensions or core questions,[47] we decided to use an approach similar to grounded theory. In grounded theory methodology:

> When coding data, the researcher breaks field notes or interview transcripts into meaningful chunks or clusters. Each cluster is assigned a code, which is a word or phrase that encapsulates the meaning of the cluster.[48]

Our belief was that allowing the coding scheme to arise from the comments would provide a more complete picture of the respondents' perceptions.

In order to begin developing the coding scheme, the Health Sciences Librarian and Head of Collection Management (representing public and technical services) separately read all the comments several times.[49] Each wrote several pages of notes and attempted to identify categories of comments. After reflection, they independently developed categories and then met to discuss their initial thoughts. This approach is similar to the initial step in a grounded theory approach, in which the researcher begins analyzing the data by sorting it into categories.[50] Another approach to coding the data would have been to individually code each comment and then iteratively refine the codes, thereby eventually developing themes. Given that the Health Sciences Librarian and Head of Collection Management both wear many hats in the library organization, they rejected this approach as being too time-consuming. Additionally, recognizing that it would be difficult to work with the large numbers of categories they had initially devel-

TABLE 11.2
Major Categories Mapped to LibQUAL+ Dimensions

Duquesne Category	LibQUAL+ Dimension
1. Service	Affect of Service
2. Building	Library as Place
3. Collection	Information Control
4. Systems	Information Control
5. Hours	Library as Place, Affect of Service

oped, they agreed to move forward by dividing the comments into five major categories (see table 11.2) each had identified in their reading of the comments:

Although we strove to allow the categories to arise from the comments, categories one through four mapped directly to LibQUAL+ dimensions. The fifth category, "Hours," could possibly be mapped to two LibQUAL+ dimensions. We created a separate Hours category because of the large number of comments as well as the strength with which they were expressed.

Coding the Comments

We chose to use Microsoft Access to code the comments because two staff members had experience with the software. We had also considered using NVivo, produced by QSR International, or the University of Pittsburgh's Qualitative Data Analysis Program's free online Coding Analysis Toolkit[51] but chose not to since library staff members had little experience with those software packages. Using Microsoft Access enabled us to match respondents' comments with corresponding demographic data including:

- school or major
- status (e.g., undergraduate, graduate, faculty, university staff, or library staff)
- age group
- gender

After importing the comments into Microsoft Access, we coded each comment with at least one of the five major categories (in grounded theory terms, this step was open coding).[52] Since many of the comments expressed several ideas, it was not unusual to assign more than one major category per comment.

Our next step was to develop the coding scheme further and begin coding the comments. We recruited two additional librarians, one each from public and technical services to form a coding task force. After an initial review, the task force met to discuss ideas on subdividing each category. As a next step, individual task force members developed narrower codes for each major category (akin to axial coding, which in grounded theory is the process of looking for ways to more narrowly code clusters of data).[53] They also defined each code as well as rules explaining how to apply the codes in given situations. Again, our assumption was that multiple codes could be applied to each comment.

The task force met several times in order to allow each member to present his or her codes, definitions, and rules. Members of the task force asked questions and made suggestions in order to help the individual members further refine their codes. Once the codes were developed to the satisfaction of the whole task force, two members added them to the Microsoft Access database and created a data entry screen that enabled members to code the comments by clicking check boxes.

The next step was to break up into teams of two to code comments within the Building, Collection, Hours, Service, and Systems categories. Each coding team included a public service and technical service librarian, who worked together to review each comment simultaneously. Each team discussed how to code each comment and did not move to the next comment until they reached agreement. This process was time-consuming, but we believed that having a public service and technical service librarian jointly code each comment improved intercoder reliability.[54]

During the coding process, the team members sometimes engaged in spirited discussions when trying to interpret and code the comments. We learned that team members sometimes initially interpreted the comments very differently, but after discussion they were able to reach agreement on each comment. Since there were no restrictions on the length of respondents' comments, they could cover almost any subject. Some of the comments were ambivalent and could not be coded easily, but most were relatively clear. Since many of the comments fit into more than one of the five categories, they were often coded by more than one of the teams. However, each team coded only those aspects of the comment related to its category. For example, for a comment addressing both services and collections, the Service team would read and apply only Service codes. Later, the Collection team would read the same comment and then apply only Collection codes.

Limitations

Although the comments were open-ended, we recognized that the respondents were likely influenced by having just completed the quantitative portions of LibQUAL+. One could argue that the respondents were influenced by the questions raised in LibQUAL+. While we acknowledged this possibility, we believed that we needed to analyze the comments as written. We recognized that the respondents had chosen to express themselves by taking the time to type them after completing the survey. Thus, if the respondents believed that these matters were important enough to report, we felt that each comment had value worthy of analysis.

Another key limitation was that as library staff, we were in a sense both the researchers and the research subjects. For example, individual members of the task force occasionally found comments to be frustrating (and even irritating). We attempted to address any bias by using two coders and by following coding rules. Additionally, during the coding we emphasized that we needed to focus on the *words on the screen* rather than our reactions to them. Looking back, we believe that we were successful in limiting our personal bias, but ultimately it is impossible to state conclusively that we were completely successful. On the other hand, as participatory researchers, we had more insight on how to code and interpret the data.

An alternative we considered was an offer from a faculty member to allow a graduate student to analyze the comments. We felt that this approach would not have been as beneficial to the library because we believed that a nonlibrarian would not understand the context of the comments as well as library staff members. We also believed that reading and analyzing the comments multiple times enabled task force members to understand the comments and their themes in greater depth and detail.

Findings

Once the coding process was complete, Microsoft Access enabled the task force to run queries and produce reports showing the numbers of comments within each code and to cross tabulate the codes both with other codes and with demographic data (see table 11.3). Throughout the coding process, members of the coding teams began to develop impressions of

TABLE 11.3
Major Codes for Undergraduates, Graduate Students, and Faculty

Undergraduates		Graduate Students		Faculty	
Category	*N (%)*[a]	*Category*	*N (%)*[a]	*Category*	*N (%)*[a]
Hours Complaints	129 (31%)	Electronic Collection Insufficient	67 (31%)	Staff Praise	25 (48%)
Staff Praise	83 (20%)	Staff Praise	44 (21%)	Electronic Collection Insufficient	18 (35%)
Building Too Noisy	65 (16%)	Print Collection Sufficient	37 (17%)	Web Site Criticism	14 (27%)
Building Too Small	63 (15%)	Service Praise	33 (15%)	Collection is Sufficient[b]	10 (19%)
Service Praise	44 (11%)	Hours Complaints	32 (15%)	Reference Department Praise	10 (19%)
Building Criticism	43 (10%)	Collection is Insufficient[b]	28 (13%)	Collection is Insufficient[b]	9 (17%)
Collection is Sufficient[b]	41 (10%)	Building Too Noisy	24 (11%)	Service Praise	8 (15%)
Printers are Insufficient	39 (9%)	Print Collection Insufficient	23 (11%	Print Collection Insufficient	8 (15%)
Building Praise	37 (9%)	Service Criticism	23 (11%)	Service Criticism	6 (12%)
Building is Outdated	34 (8%)	Web Site Criticism	22 (10%)	ILL Department Praise	6 (12%)
Collection is Insufficient[b]	318%)	ILL Department Praise	19 (9%)	Hours Complaints	1 (2%)

a. Percentages indicate total comments within each respondent user group (412 undergraduates, 213 graduate students, and 52 faculty).

b. "Collection is Insufficient" and "Collection is Sufficient" include comments stating the collection is insufficient but specifying print, electronic, or any other format.

what they believed the comments said as a whole. In some cases, these impressions proved to be correct but in others, team members were surprised to learn that their impressions were off-base.

The major themes we found dealt with dissatisfaction regarding the library's hours, electronic collections, quality of library building, and suitability of study spaces. The overall theme for service was that respondents were generally pleased but undergraduates expressed some dissatisfaction.

One of the early surprises of the analysis occurred when we broke down comments about the hours. At the beginning of the process, we believed that most students wanted the library to remain open later at night. However, after coding and tabulating the comments we learned that an equal number of students wanted the library to open earlier. One respondent summed up many students' feelings on this issue by stating, "It is frustrating that the library is not open before 8:00 am classes."

The quantitative results showed respondents' dissatisfaction with the Library as Place, but analysis of the comments showed that respondents specifically found fault with the building atmosphere, décor, arrangement, and size. One student wrote, "The dim interior and stark architecture makes one feel like they're entering a factory, not a place to learn or study." The comments helped us to understand our users' experiences better. The depth of feeling is evident from comments such as, "I hate walking into it [the library] and feeling as though I'm entombed by concrete" and "It [the library] doesn't show the pride of Duquesne as many of the other buildings do on campus." We believe these quotes will be helpful in convincing university administrators and external agencies of the need for additional funding to support library building improvements.

On the whole, analysis of the comments supported the quantitative results. Yet, they also helped us to understand better the more complex nature of respondents' feelings. For example, our quantitative results showed that Affect of Service scores had improved substantially since our 2006 LibQUAL+ survey. Analysis of the comments showed that respondents were mostly happy with service ("The staff is very courteous and helpful"). However, a theme that emerged was that undergraduates reported being treated poorly by library staff members, "The library staff is not as helpful as they could be." Another stated a library staff member "raised his voice at me for asking if my group could use one of the media rooms."

One of the most surprising findings was a theme faulting the library for not enforcing its noise policies, "I see library staff walking around the floors and nothing is ever said to students who are being loud, disruptive, and distracted." The coders joked that perhaps we were too successful in changing the librarian's professional image because now our students were asking us to "Shush" them! In discussing the matter with staff, we discovered inconsistent understanding of the library's group and quiet study zones. Thus, we began a campaign to distinguish group and quiet study areas more definitively with bold graphics and images.

Communicating LibQUAL+ Findings

After completing our analysis of the comments, as well as the quantitative portions of LibQUAL+, we followed up by communicating results with appropriate campus stakeholders, including the library's Operations Committee, University Library Committee, Student Government Association, University Administration, and the Graduate Council. The University Librarian and Health Sciences Librarian provided brief presentations summarizing the results and discussing the themes culled from the comment analysis.

We were happy to share with stakeholders that the quantitative data showed improvements compared to our 2006 results. In some cases, the stakeholders provided additional comments about the library and we were able to use this data for future planning. However, we believed that the most important aspect of the communication process was showing our willingness to use student and faculty feedback to improve the library.

Using Comment Analysis in Decision Making

The comment analysis provided guidance in the library's operational and strategic decision-making processes but did not factor into critical decision making. Before finishing the comment analysis, the coding teams discovered a few comments that suggested the need for operational decisions:

- One comment noted seeing an offensive drawing and an epithet on a study carrel whiteboard. The task force contacted Circulation staff members who then increased the frequency of inspecting and cleaning study carrels and whiteboards.
- A coding team learned that events held in the library borrowed chairs from study areas. The team contacted the appropriate persons and notified them of correct event setup procedures as well as the availability of supplemental stacking chairs.
- When the coding team gave a preliminary report about requests to open the library earlier, the head of public services noted that staff members were already in the building prior to opening. Since there was no budget impact, we decided to open the building earlier on weekdays.
- We also learned that the library was not open prior to the start of classes on Saturdays—something that the staff deciding the library's hours had not realized. Since changing these hours would have a significant budget impact, this expressed need has been added to the strategic planning process.

After completing analysis of the comments, we believed that the themes that emerged gave us important data for strategic planning and decision making. In some cases, it is not surprising that we feel the need to study these themes further with the intention of learning underlying factors. We used these themes to guide the library's strategic plan, which we were beginning to formulate as the comment analysis neared completion.

Comparing our 2006 and 2009 quantitative scores for service showed strong improvements in ratings across students, faculty, and university staff. As noted above, one theme showed that undergraduates were not satisfied with their treatment by staff. The library management team wrote strategic plan goals aimed at enhancing service to all user groups,

providing services to meet changing needs and expectations, and assessing users' experiences intentionally. Consequently, we are expanding our customer service training and improvement efforts. We are also creating opportunities for feedback throughout the year and doing a better job of communicating changes made as a result of user feedback.

In regard to collections, we noted some interesting phenomena. For example, we had purchased significant electronic and print resources for one of our new academic programs. Based on measures of library inputs and outputs, we believed that this program was among the best supported for library resources. However, the theme emerging from the comments showed that student respondents believed their department had virtually no library support. Faced with the analysis and the individual comments, the librarian liaison made an operational decision and approached the head of the program and was able to get the opportunity to address students and faculty about resources (an opportunity the liaison had previously not been given). Additionally, he received a pledge from the department chair that the faculty would inform students of the availability of the resources.

This case was not unique. We observed other cases in which the students were highly critical of parts of the collection that we considered strong. Consequently, we recognized the need for further study and began to examine what factors contributed to these perceptions. For example, we hypothesized that possible reasons were our Web site, the catalog, user education, marketing, or perhaps other factors. We have discussed using other qualitative methods such as focus groups, comment cards, and targeted brief surveys to study this issue. Analysis of the LibQUAL+ comments also provided useful data for analyzing adequacy of library support to share in the self-study process for graduate program reviews and disciplinary accreditations. On a strategic level, the library's management team wrote goals to encourage use of information resources, improve resource discovery and access, and collaborate with campus partners to advance information literacy.

In regard to comments about the library building, the themes emerging provided confirmation of what we already knew: the vast majority of students, faculty, and staff are dissatisfied with our building. Although the library had already been working on long-term plans to improve the building, the comments helped us learn how students believe the state of the library building negatively affects the quality of their education. Consequently, we have used student comments to justify capital budget requests and provide evidence when requesting higher levels of service from stretched university departments such as housekeeping and facilities management.

On the whole, our analysis of the LibQUAL+ comments is continuing to help the library identify projects and is guiding our decision making by helping us to understand respondents' experiences of interacting with the library's collections, services, and building. In retrospect, it would be virtually impossible to understand student and faculty perceptions and needs without objectively and systematically analyzing the comments. Additionally, we have used analysis of the LibQUAL+ comments as the impetus to encourage the Student Government Association to form a Library Committee. Starting this academic year, members of the library staff have met with the committee and have used the comment themes as the foundation for dialogue.

Reflection

Although we are still working to use our analysis as part of strategic planning and decision making, we have already begun to reflect upon the considerable investment of time required to analyze the comments. In the end, the four staff members comprising the task force worked many hours to complete the analysis. Although we did not record the total number of hours, given that it was our first experience with this approach, it was indeed very time-consuming. We noted that the process accelerated as we gained experience with coding and analyzing the data. Thus, we believe that we will be able to employ this approach more quickly in the future.

One problem we faced during the analysis was that members of the library's management team became impatient with the time it took to analyze the comments systematically. In the spirit of openness,

the Assessment Committee made all the comments available to members of the management team who requested them prior to completion of the analysis. Since the comments comprised nearly 30,000 words divided across multiple academic departments, user groups, and age groups, it was virtually impossible to understand them without systematic analysis. Thus, we were concerned that persons who reviewed the comments without a systematic approach might have reached poor or erroneous conclusions. Given that the task force took steps to reduce bias and to ensure that codes were applied systematically, we believe that our approach helped us to gain the clearest understanding of the comments that we could obtain. In retrospect, we would follow the same process but perhaps restrict access to the raw data until the analysis was complete.

Conclusion

Quality decision making requires reliable information and warrants the identification and thoughtful consideration of options prior to making a judgment. Given the value and importance of making strategic decisions, librarians are well-advised to dedicate the necessary time and resources to collecting and analyzing information that identifies user needs and concerns. Since its launch in 2000, LibQUAL+ has matured as a recognized survey research tool for libraries to collect both quantitative and qualitative data useful for planning and decision making. The body of case literature has grown correspondingly as libraries have worked with qualitative research methodologies and theories such as textual analysis of LibQUAL+ open comments, grounded theory, computer-assisted methods, and follow-up focus groups and summits. The qualitative research side of LibQUAL+ not only complements the quantitative component of the instrument but actually yields substantial value in identifying specific action items and improving the strategic position of the library through active communication with users and stakeholders.

Our case study regarding how Duquesne University employed these qualitative research methods to analyze 697 comments contributed by users responding to our 2009 LibQUAL+ survey demonstrates some of the choices and discoveries of our experience. This is a work still in progress as we continue discussions as part of our strategic planning. We make frequent operational decisions as we take action on items identified in survey data and as we listen to our users speak to us through the comment box, groups such as Student Government Association and University Library Committee, and focused inquiry meetings. Although using a more thoughtful and extensive qualitative approach has taken significant time, it has also produced organizational change appropriate to the values of our institution. Our Assessment Committee has developed new research skills and shared their expertise with others. We have increased our communication with stakeholders, initially reporting out on LibQUAL+ results but increasingly having dialogue around specific topics identified in the comment analysis. Finally, we are moving toward making strategic decisions that will better position the library within the university and the region.

Notes

1. The framework of library decisions being operational, critical, or strategic is based on the authors' extensive professional experience and assimilation of the literature.
2. Steven Spohn and Arnold Hirshon, *Library Strategic Planning Toolkit* (Atlanta, GA: Lyrasis, 2009).
3. Sandra Nelson, *Strategic Planning for Results* (Chicago: American Library Association, 2008).
4. LibQUAL+ Web site, Association of Research Libraries, www.libqual.org.
5. On April 30, 2010, the authors searched Library, Information Science & Technology Abstracts with Full Text and found that since LibQUAL's introduction in 2000, the database included (a) 134 articles that mentioned LibQUAL (not counting articles that mentioned only DigiQUAL and StatsQUAL); (b) 394 articles indexed as "Library Surveys," "Library-Use Studies" (exploded), or "Library Surveys" that specifically mention academic, college*, or universit*. Thus, articles mentioning LibQUAL comprised 34% of the articles about academic library surveys.
6. Heidi Julien, "Content Analysis," in *The SAGE Encyclopedia of Qualitative Research Methods,* ed. Lisa M. Given (Thousand Oaks, CA: Sage, 2008), 2:120–22.
7. Chester I. Barnard, *The Functions of the Executive* (Cambridge, MA: Harvard University Press, 1950), 209.
8. Ibid., 203.
9. Herbert A. Simon, *The New Science of Management Decision* (New York: Harper & Row, 1960), 1–3.
10. Peter Hernon and Charles R. McClure, *Evaluation and Library Decision Making* (Norwood, NJ: Ablex Publishing, 1990), 225.
11. Ibid., 226.
12. G. Edward Evans and Patricia Layzell Ward, *Leadership Basics for Librarians and Information Professionals* (Lanham, MD: Scarecrow Press, 2007), 130–31.
13. Ibid., 130.
14. A substantial body of literature exists on the development of the LibQUAL+ protocol and on the improvements to the protocol based on qualitative interviews of users. In addition, many librarians at participating institutions have contributed articles about their methodologies and experiences using LibQUAL+. Several significant compilations of these articles include Martha Kyrillidou and Fred M. Heath, ed., "Measuring Service Quality," special issue, *Library Trends* 49, no. 4 (2001); Fred M. Heath, Martha Kyrillidou, Consuella A. Askew, eds., "Libraries Act on Their LibQUAL+ Findings: From Data to Action," special issue, *Journal of Library Administration* 40, nos. 3–4 (2004); Martha Kyrillidou, ed., "LibQUAL+ and Beyond: Library Assessment with a Focus on Library Improvement," special issue, *Performance Measurement and Metrics* 9, no. 3 (2008); Colleen Cook, ed., "The Maturation of Assessment in Academic Libraries: The Role of LibQUAL+," special issue, *Performance Measurement and Metrics* 3, no. 2 (2002).
15. Lorraine J. Haricombe and Bonna J. Boettcher, "Using LibQUAL+ Data in Strategic Planning: Bowling Green State University," *Journal of Library Administration* 40, no. 3/4 (2004): 181–95.

16. Stephen R. Shorb and Lori Driscoll, "LibQUAL+ Meets Strategic Planning at the University of Florida," in *Libraries Act on their LibQUAL+ Findings: From Data to Action*, ed. Fred M. Heath, Martha Kyrillidou, and Consuella A. Askew (New York: Haworth, 2004), 173–80.

17. Gary P. Latham, "Goal Setting: A Five-step Approach to Behavior Change," *Organizational Dynamics* 32, no. 3 (2003): 311.

18. Andrea Twiss-Brooks, [Untitled] (presentation at the LibQUAL+ Share Fair at the annual meeting for the American Library Association, Chicago, IL, June 28, 2005).

19. Jan Comfort, "LibQUAL+ and the Library Summit: A Model for Decision-making" (presentation at the LibQUAL+ Share Fair held at the annual meeting for the American Library Association, New Orleans, LA, June 26, 2006).

20. Damon Jaggars, [Untitled] (presentation at the LibQUAL+ Share Fair held at the annual meeting for the American Library Association, New Orleans, LA, June 26, 2006).

21. E. Stewart Saunders, "The LibQUAL Phenomenon: Who Judges Quality?" *Reference and User Services Quarterly* 47, no. 1 (2007): 21–24.

22. Ibid., 23.

23. E. Stewart Saunders, "Drilling the LibQUAL+ Data for Strategic Planning," *Performance Measurement and Metrics* 9, no. 3 (2008): 168.

24. Spohn and Hirshon, *Library Strategic Planning Toolkit*.

25. Peter Hernon and Robert E. Dugan, *An Action Plan for Outcomes Assessment in Your Library* (Chicago: American Library Association, 2002).

26. Peter Hernon and Ellen Altman, *Assessing Service Quality: Satisfying the Expectations of Library Customers* (Chicago: American Library Association, 1998).

27. Joseph R. Matthews, *Scorecards for Results: A Guide for Developing a Library Balanced Scorecard* (Westport, CT: Libraries Unlimited, 2008).

28. Meg Sharf and Kristine Shrauger, [Untitled] (presentation at the LibQUAL+ Share Fair held at the annual meeting for the American Library Association, New Orleans, LA, June 26, 2006).

29. Amy E. Knapp, "We Asked What They Thought, Now What Do We Do? The Use of LibQUAL+ Data to Redesign Public Services at the University of Pittsburgh," *Journal of Library Administration* 40, no. 3 (2004): 157–71.

30. Jane Duffy and Tina Usmiani, "Through the LibQUAL+ Looking Glass: Dalhousie University Post-LibQUAL+ 2005–2007 Initiatives" (presentation at the LibQUAL+ Share Fair held at the annual meeting for the American Library Association, Washington, DC, June 25, 2007); Patrick Griffis, "Using LibQUAL+ Affect of Service Items as a Framework for Designing Service Staff Core Competencies and Values" (presentation at the LibQUAL+ Share Fair held at the annual meeting for the American Library Association, Washington, DC, June 25, 2007).

31. Lyena Chavez, "Meet Me @ McQuade: Using LibQUAL+ to Develop a Student-centered Marketing Campaign" (presentation at the LibQUAL+ Share Fair held at the annual meeting for the American Library Association, Washington, DC, June 25, 2007).

32. Jeanne Brown, "Ramping Up Assessment at the UNLV Libraries," *Library Hi Tech* 23, no. 3 (2005): 396–413; Bob Fernekes, [Untitled] (presentation at the LibQUAL+ Share Fair held at the annual meeting for the American Library Association, New Orleans, LA, June 26, 2006).

33. The LibQUAL+ Share Fair is held each summer at the annual meeting for the American Library Association. Participants make brief presentations highlighting their quantitative and qualitative analysis of results. The event is documented with a booklet of abstracts. The booklets are available on the LibQUAL+ Web site, under Share Fair (http://www.libqual.org/Publications.aspx).

34. Bradford W. Dennis and Tim Bower, "Using Content Analysis Software to Analyze Survey Comments," *portal: Libraries and the Academy* 8, no. 4 (2008): 423

35. Case studies below discuss application of these software tools.

36. Tom Durkin, "Using Computers in Strategic Qualitative Research," in *Context and Method in Qualitative Research*, ed. Gale Miller and Robert Dingwal (Los Angeles: Sage, 1997), 92–105.

37. Ibid., 92.

38. Dennis and Bower, "Using Content Analysis Software."

39. Julie Anna Guidry, "LibQUAL+ Spring 2001 Comments: A Qualitative Analysis Using ATLAS.ti," *Performance Measurement and Metrics* 3, no. 2 (2002): 100–7.

40. Twiss-Brooks, [Untitled].

41. Kathy Crowe, "Sharing Results with Stakeholders and Marketing" (presentation at the LibQUAL+ Share Fair held at the annual meeting for the American Library Association, Chicago, IL, July 13, 2009).

42. Wendy Begay et al., "Quantifying Qualitative Data: Using LibQUAL+ Comments for Library-wide Planning Activates at the University of Arizona," *Journal of Library Administration* 40, no. 3–4 (2004): 111–19.

43. Brown University, " Methodology for Coding Qualitative Data (User Comments), Brown University LibQUAL + Survey 2005: Summary of Findings and Analysis," http://www.libqual.org/documents/admin/BrownU_2005_LQ_qual_method.pdf.

44. Karen Neurohr, "Coding Open-ended Comments: LibQUAL+ Survey Results" (PowerPoint presentation), Oklahoma State University Library, Jan. 14, 2009, www.libqual.org/documents/admin/Coding_Oklahoma%20State_1_09.ppt.

45. Deborah A. Nolan, "Interpreting Data or Interpretive Dance? Presenting LibQUAL+ Results to Stakeholders" (presentation at the LibQUAL+ Share Fair held at the annual meeting for the American Library Association, Chicago, IL, July 13, 2009).

46. Haricombe and Boettcher, "Using LibQUAL+ Data in Strategic Planning," 183.

47. Neurohr, "Coding Open-ended Comments."

48. Maria K. E. Lahman and Monica R. Geist, "Qualitative Methodologies," in *Encyclopedia of Counseling*, ed. Frederick T. L. Leong (Thousand Oaks, CA: Sage, 2008), 1:360.

49. When using content analysis, researchers sometimes develop codes by assigning codes to each comment and then iteratively refining the codes to develop a final coding structure. In other cases, researchers use existing coding structures (for example, some use the LibQUAL+ core questions). In our case, we worked to allow the categories to bubble up from the comments. We began the initial coding development process by having two librarians individually read the comments several times, take extensive notes, and then refine the notes into the categories. They then compared their individual categories and worked together to develop a single set of categories. Although we did not follow a pure grounded theory approach, we followed grounded theory methodology in creating an initial categorization (or sorting) of the comments as a starting point in the process. After this starting point, we asked the four members of the larger committee to create narrower codes based on their readings of the comments within each major category. Again, we followed the approach of reading the comments, taking extensive notes, and devising codes based on that preparatory work. In order to check the validity of the codes, we met as a group to critique each other's codes and then revised as necessary.

50. H. Russell Bernard and Gery W. Ryan, *Analyzing Qualitative Data: Systematic Approaches* (Thousand Oaks, CA: Sage, 2010).

51. "Qualitative Data Analysis Program (QDAP)," University of Pittsburgh, www.qdap.pitt.edu.

52. Lahman and Geist, "Qualitative Methodologies."

53. Ibid.

54. Will C. van den Hoonaard, "Inter- and Intracoder Reliability," in *The SAGE Encyclopedia of Qualitative Research*, ed. Lisa M. Given (Thousand Oaks, CA: Sage, 2008), 1:445–46; Intercoder reliability typically refers to a process of checking the work of two independent coders to ensure that they are applying codes consistently. In our case, the coders worked together to resolve these questions during the coding process.

Design and Analysis Challenges in a Multicampus Research Study

Robin Brown and Willis C. Walker

Abstract. This chapter examines the difficulties encountered in the design, implementation, and analysis of a research study at Rutgers University that looked at the effectiveness of online literacy instruction. Although the larger study did not progress beyond its initial test phase, the issues encountered in designing the larger study, initially testing structured interview questions, and then studying results raise important questions in the design and follow-through of any test of online literacy projects. The authors reflect that some of these issues are inherent in any such test, while others can be avoided by learning from this test study and others previously done. The chapter summarizes other studies from the literature that attempted complex assessments of the effectiveness of online tutorials. The authors discuss several questions that arose while analyzing the results, including the language used in the study's questions. The authors make several recommendations, together with some observations on the intrinsic difficulties of testing one form of instruction when multiple forms of teaching are being used concurrently.

Introduction

By 2004, the Instructional Services Committee of Rutgers University Libraries (twenty-six libraries and centers on three main campuses, serving over 60,000 students, faculty, and staff) was faced with two institutional mandates: to use technology to reach more students with library instruction and to find some way to assess the ongoing instructional work of the RU Library faculty. (The accreditation cycle was coming up, and it was known that the Middle States Association of Colleges and Schools was becoming very concerned about assessing information literacy.)

This dual mandate led to two very closely connected events. First, in 2005 a general asynchronous Web-based tutorial, called Searchpath, was rolled out. As statistics began to be collected about how it was used, there were extended ongoing discussions within the Instructional Services Committee and throughout the Rutgers libraries about assessment. Secondly, the committee adopted a large multicampus trial assessment study that combined both quantitative and qualitative methods (2005–2006). The study was designed by the Education Librarian, who was also the principal investigator.

The Rutgers Searchpath assessment is a very important illustration of how much data can be generated, regardless of the size of the study population, when combining qualitative and quantitative methods. A mixed-methods study offered the opportunity to achieve a deeper understanding of the measurement of information literacy by gathering data about both the student's self-perceptions and the interviewers' perceptions, separate and distinct from whether or not the student completed the required task correctly. The outcome of this study also demonstrates problems with finding resources to complete qualitative analysis. This chapter describes the study design and makes observations about how difficult it was to get the study data analyzed after the principal investigator retired and was not replaced.

Rutgers's Searchpath Project

As just mentioned, Rutgers University Libraries launched an online tutorial named Searchpath in 2005.[1] This research tutorial was adapted by Rutgers University Libraries (RUL) in 2004 from the tutorial at Western Michigan University and owes its inspiration to the University of Texas TILT tutorial, which was the original open source prototype for Searchpath.[2] The Searchpath tutorial was designed to help students learn how to find information sources and then more effectively select and critically evaluate them. Searchpath is comprised of six tutorial modules, each lasting fifteen to twenty minutes. Each module presents a set of concepts and terms and finishes with a brief test on how well the material was learned. The module topics include getting started, choosing a topic, how to use the IRIS (the RUL catalog), how to find peer-reviewed articles, how to use the Web, and how to cite sources. The test at the end of each module consists of ten questions; the modules give the correct answers with an explanation and also provide the student his or her score at the end.

Searchpath was never intended as a stand-alone instructional tool, nor did the Rutgers University Libraries use it as such. There was no university-wide requirement for students to take, much less complete, the tutorial. However, it was required for one set of classes in the Writing Program, and the students in these classes were targeted as the study's subjects. In addition to having the students complete Searchpath, it was typical in these courses to have librarians teach two or three classes in research processes. These classes focused on doing online research

using the academic databases available through the RUL Web site. All of the librarians who participated in the Searchpath assessment were self-selected from those who taught these information literacy classes and so were familiar both with Searchpath and with the writing course.

The Instructional Services Committee for Rutgers University Libraries is made up of the instructional coordinators from all three campuses and provides oversight for the library instruction program.[3] The Instructional Services Committee initiated a research project that attempted to measure the impact of Searchpath on the information literacy skills of Rutgers University students. This was a wide-ranging project, with student interviews being done on all three campuses by nineteen librarians. The study design included both quantitative and qualitative measures, making it an example of both the challenges and the possibilities of this type of mixed research design.

Literature Review as Assessment Was Being Planned

In the early days of the project, the committee consulted the literature on tutorial assessment looking for clues about how to proceed. The debate was framed by theoretical articles, with the preponderance of these articles being reviews of various assessment projects. In a separate group were progress reports that contributed to the research design. Last to be considered were two specific studies that clearly illustrated the problem of controlling variables mirrored in the Rutgers study.[4]

Theoretical Overviews

Some of the articles reviewed were theoretical. For example, Vander Meer gave a thoughtful, thorough write-up of an environmental scan project. She investigated how libraries were using the Web to teach in 2000. There are many ideas here, but unfortunately this kind of article does not age well because some of the projects are no longer available on the Web or are available but long neglected. The importance of interactivity was stressed. She briefly mentioned a list of evaluation techniques.[5]

Dewald wrote a well-reputed article on the pedagogy of Web-based library instruction.[6] She provided an overview of learning theories and their impact on designing Web-based learning. Dewald reviewed the implications of cognitive psychology and behavioral learning theory (including specific adult learning theories) and used those theories to establish pedagogical guidelines for Web instruction, including "the areas of learner motivation, organization of modules, and levels of interactivity."[7] Each principle was illustrated by specific design examples. Although technology has continued to grow, the concern for interactivity and active learning are still very valid.

Iannuzzi discussed different types of assessment in a short essay that is often cited.[8] She wrote a polemic, advocating the development of information literacy assessment in tandem with other agencies on campus. More specifically, she promoted "a library culture for information literacy strong enough to influence the campus culture."[9] Iannuzzi raised several questions about ways to assess information literacy without really providing any solutions.

Jacobson described ideal assessment as being ongoing and integrated into the instruction program,[10] which highlights two of the issues faced in the Rutgers research project: assessment stood apart from the instruction program, and it was not ongoing. On the other hand, the Rutgers project didn't really fit into her typology, which separated evaluation of face-to-face programs from evaluation of online tools, since we did a face-to-face assessment of an online tool.

The theoretical overview put the challenge of assessing the impact of Searchpath within the context of an ongoing movement. Iannuzzi offered inspiration,[11] and the Jacobson article offered the context[12] within which to view the choices that were being made. The committee reviewed the Jacobson article but made some very different choices. They selected a one-time assessment that was not integrated into the instruction program.

Project Reviews

A second type of article reviewed during the initial phase of the assessment at Rutgers was reviews of individual projects. The oldest project review explored

was Johnson and Sager, who described an early computer-based tutorial project.[13] The librarians at the University of Louisville created a computer-based tutorial that taught their students how to navigate their text-based online catalog. Their article described the design process straight through the testing and the rollout. The comments that they received during the evaluation phase of their project were a useful guide to the typical problems of a tutorial design project (e.g., how long is too long?).

Another example of a tutorial story was shared by Bracke and Dickstein.[14] They wrote a description of an assignment-specific online tutorial that was created, deployed, and evaluated at the University of Arizona. They presented a provocative vision suggesting that tutorials should be much more specific and asserting that tutorials can work if they are integrated into a course, with an introductory session done by the classroom teacher.

A sense of what was possible at the time was offered by Dunn's progress report on a multiphase assessment project at California State University.[15] This report overviewed a large assessment project that was done by the CSU system (twenty-three campuses, 370,000 students). After coming up with their own definition of information literacy, system librarians deployed a telephone survey of a representative sample of students, using a quantitative survey (Phase I). Phase II was comprised of "a full day of assessment activities" conducted at four different locations within the system, with qualitative results. This project was similar to what Rutgers did: a large multicampus study. Although this was a progress report and the conclusions of the study were not reported, Dunn did encourage the growth of services that support increased use of digital sources. The article ended on a cautionary note, questioning whether the current definitions of information literacy were concrete enough to be "cleanly assessed."[16]

Cameron wrote about a very comprehensive information literacy assessment program established at James Madison University.[17] That program evolved into an information literacy exam that became a graduation requirement—with an intervention program in place to help the students who did not pass. The JMU program demonstrated that a continuous information literacy assessment effort could succeed, which was a very different model from the one chosen by the Instructional Services Committee at Rutgers University.

Controlling Variables

One of the questions the committee was concerned with was the complexity of the variables that affect student learning. In an assessment study, is it really possible to control for this complexity? Noe and Bishop, as an example, evaluated the Texas Information Literacy Tutorial (TILT), not the students[18]—primarily a difference in emphasis and language. In testing the usefulness of their tutorial, the librarians unfortunately muddied the issue by having two variables (use of the tutorial and live bibliographic instruction), which made it unclear what they were trying to discover. This commingling of variables persisted when they continued to test in the next semester but withdrew the live instruction. They used pre- and posttests on a broad scale. The results were very mixed. Some questions indicated improvement, and some did not. The librarians did not seem to have considered the question of whether the tests themselves were valid. They did point out in their conclusion that there are problematic issues with a general tutorial that was not directly tied to the students' course of study. They speculate about whether improvements in technology will allow customized tutorials.

Orme also did a research study that focused on TILT.[19] Orme asked an interesting question: how well do students retain library instruction from one semester to the next? He constructed a research project with two variables (library instruction and TILT), examining the experiences of four cohorts (no instruction, use of only the tutorial, access to only classroom instruction, and access to both). Each cohort was comprised of approximately thirty students. This study seemed to validate TILT as a teaching tool, but the differences between content delivery methods were small and complicated by the number of different variables the researcher was juggling. This study illustrated how complex some of these projects can unintentionally become.

Both studies—Noe and Bishop[20] and Orme[21]—ran into problems that would be confronted by the Rutgers study. Testing for the efficacy of a tutorial can be confusing if the issue of live instruction is introduced into the study. Looking at live instruction in tandem with an online tutorial made it very unclear what was being tested. Reading widely in both theory and project reports generated excitement in the Instructional Services Committee (ISC) at Rutgers about the research project, but also forced the committee to condense the project. There was not enough time to incorporate what the ISC was learning into the project at hand.[22]

Rutgers Study Methodology

After a wide-ranging discussion of the available literature, the committee selected a one-time assessment protocol. This decision was apparently based on expediency, and was determined by the team leader. The assessment centered on the core question: Does Searchpath actually help students learn how to better search for needed material?

All librarians who participated in this study had or would complete the Certification for Human Subject Testing as mandated by the National Institutes of Health and the Rutgers Office of Research and Sponsored Programs. Training sessions were held for the interviewers, in which the principal investigator explained the interview script and how the data would be collected. (The chapter authors participated in the study as interviewers.)

Research subjects were recruited from the pool of students who had attended library instruction sessions and were required to pass the Searchpath tutorial as part of their English composition classes. The study was explained to them; they were informed that the assessment would take approximately thirty minutes, and they were promised a $25 payment for their participation. Only students who were at least eighteen years of age were recruited.

The students (a total of twenty) were from all of the main campuses of Rutgers, with the majority (thirteen) from the main New Brunswick/Piscataway campus. None were employed by the university. Their majors ranged from journalism to pharmacy, with the

TABLE 12.1

Characteristics of Students Interviewed on Searchpath from Their Prior Experience Questionnaire

	Average Age	Gender	Writing Program Course	Major	Employed by University	Year
New Brunswick/ Piscataway	19.3	M – 5 F – 8	102 – 0 201 – 13 Other – 0	Biology – 2 Psychology – 2 Pharmacy – 3 Journ/Media – 1 Exercise Sci – 1 Economics/Stats – 2 Criminal Justice – 1 East Asian Lang –1 Pharmacy – 1	Yes – 0 No – 13	'07 – 2 '08 – 3 '09 – 6 '10 – 0 '11 – 2
Camden	18.6	M – 0 F – 5	102 – 5 201 – 0 Other – 0	Nursing – 2 Nursing/Psych – 1 Psychology – 1	Yes – 0 No – 5	'07 – 0 '08 – 0 '09 – 4 '10 – 0 '11 – 1
Newark	36.5	M – 1 F – 1	102 – 0 201 – 0 Other – 2 122 – 1 Writing Program – 1	Women's Studies – 1 Biology – 1	Yes – 0 No – 2	'07 – 1 '08 – 1 '09 – 0 '10 – 0 '11 – 0

majority having their majors in the sciences (twelve). Student ages varied from eighteen to fifty-four with the average being twenty-one. (See table 12.1.)

The actual Searchpath Assessment Interview protocol was divided into four parts: (1) the explanation of the assessment and signing of the informed consent form; (2) the filling out of a prior experience questionnaire; (3) the actual assessment; and (4) a debriefing.

Each interview involved three people: the student, an interviewer, and an observer. In general, other than standard introductory remarks, only the interviewer spoke with the students. The observer sat further away from the student and the interviewer and observed the process. The interviewer explained the assessment to the student, presented the consent form, gave the student the prior assessment, and led the student through the assessment. The observer took notes on the progress of the session.

Students were guaranteed their anonymity (other than with the interviewers and principal investigator); they were told that they could opt out of the assessment at any time and that if they chose to do so, their materials would be destroyed. None chose to opt out.

The prior experience questionnaire collected necessary demographic data: age, gender, class year, college, major, which writing program class the student was in, and experience with both Searchpath and the Rutgers University Libraries instruction classes. Further information was gathered regarding the students' paper topics, how much instruction in library searching they may have received prior to Rutgers, and how they assessed their own abilities as a researcher. The questionnaire then asked fifteen specific questions designed to test the student's ability to search.

After completing the prior experience questionnaire, the students were asked to begin the actual assessment of Searchpath. They were told that there would be five information-searching tasks and that if they needed help, the interviewer speaking with them would be able to help. The student was presented with a screen with only the Web browser available on it.

For the first task, the student was presented with a card with the citation for *Freaks: Myths and Images of the Secret Shelf* by Leslie Fiedler in both APA and MLA styles.[23] They were asked to find it among the library resources, using the most efficient search they knew of; they were further directed to talk the interviewer through the steps they employed. The interviewers were trained to prompt them by asking, "Where do you start?" to get the student speaking. Once the title had been located, the interviewer questioned the student on his or her understanding of the record by asking such questions as "What library is the book in?" "What is the call number?" "Is it available to be checked out?" The interviewer used a stopwatch to record the amount of time it took the student to perform this task.

The second task required the students to determine the location in the Rutgers system of the journal *Critical Studies in Media Communication*, based on the following APA citation:

> Smith., S.L. (2005). From Dr. Dre to dismissed: Assessing violence, sex and substance use on MTV. *Critical Studies in Media Communication.* 22(1), 89-98.

The students were further asked in which library a hard copy of the journal could be found and whether or not the journal was available electronically. Again, the students were asked to talk the interviewer through the search, and were timed.

The third task (see figure 12.1), which called for the students to look for five articles on a controversial topic in Academic Search Premier, was more complex and required deeper, more extensive interpretation of the results. The task given essentially consisted of four steps: (1) finding Academic Search Premier; (2) formulating a search query; (3) finding five scholarly articles on the topic; and (4) sending them to a designated e-mail address. (The e-mail instruction was not included in the written directions, but was part of the verbal instructions.)

FIGURE 12.1
Task 3 Interview Card

Searchpath Assessment Interview Card

Task 3:

Look for an article on a topic in Academic Search Premier

You are researching the controversy surrounding genetically modified foods, and whether eating genetically modified foods can cause allergies. For your assignment, you need to find five scholarly articles. Using the Academic Search Premier database, find at least five scholarly journal article citations.

FIGURE 12.2
Task 5 Interview Card

Searchpath Assessment Interview Card

Task 5:

Now let's assume you have chosen this genetically modified foods topic for your research paper for this class. (Choose number according to campus ---102/201). Your teacher also wants you to use some Internet sources, but they have to be reliable and informative. For this task, I want you to go onto the Internet and find at least one relevant Web site that you could confidently use in an undergraduate research paper. Once you find it you can describe to me how you would use it and why you think it would be useful.

Remember: the Web site must be both relevant and reliable.

Please talk me through your steps

Furthermore, as part of this task, the students were asked to explain to the interviewer *why* they felt these articles were relevant.

The fourth task tested the students' ability to discover the availability of articles by using LinkSource within Academic Search Premier. The card for this task gave not only the article, but also directions regarding how to find the article. The interviewer asked for the student to talk through the procedure.

The final task (see figure 12.2) asked students to use the World Wide Web to find information and to assess and evaluate its credibility. The topic stayed the same for this task—genetically modified foods and allergies. The students were asked to find a relevant Web site, explain their rationale for choosing that site, and explain how and why they might use that Web site for a research paper.

Then each student was asked to fill out a debriefing questionnaire that explored each student's perceptions of library instruction and Searchpath. At the end, they were each asked to rate their *information-finding* skills on a five-point scale.

Findings
Participants

The results of the prior experience questionnaire data (see table 12.2) revealed that most of the students had a decent grasp, at least in theory, of how the RUL site could be searched and how to interpret the results they got. The percentages that the students received ranged from 100 percent correct (on four of the questions) down to only 9.5 percent answering one correctly.

Interview

The first task was a search for a specific item in the library catalog. The interviewer used a stopwatch to record the amount of time it took the student to perform this task. Students were proficient at this, with almost 95 percent finding the title with an average time of about three minutes, which seemed fine considering that the university has a complex catalog and a multilibrary system.

The second task was a search for a particular journal article, in hard copy and in digital format (when available). Students did not perform quite as well as in the first task, but considering the more complex nature of finding a journal in the RUL search engine, the results showed that students did under-

stand how to find a journal and how to view and interpret the details of the holdings. Seventeen of the twenty recognized the electronic access that was provided. This task did take longer to perform, almost five minutes, and did call for some prompting by the interviewers. (Typical prompting would have been asking the students if they knew what the first step in the process was and, if they were still having difficulties, telling them where to begin.)

For the third task, each student was asked to use Academic Search Premier to find five relevant articles on a predetermined topic. The students did quite well on this task, although some needed prompting from the interviewers to complete it. The average time to complete the task was almost seven minutes, and while prompts were needed a total of twenty-one times (spread out over the task, from first knowing to open to the RUL home page, to using relevant search terms and Boolean language, through limiting the search to scholarly articles, and finally to search for appropriateness), the overall success rate, with the prompts, was never less than 90 percent.

The fourth task asked the students to use Link-Source (the RUL link resolver). The students performed well on this, although they did need some prompting. Nineteen out of twenty identified Link-Source as the relevant link for the text of the article, and all were able to use one of the paths to the article. The time varied considerably for this task, with the fastest student taking only a minute, while the maximum time needed was a full twelve minutes. The average was approximately five minutes.

For the fifth task, the students were asked to find reliable and informative Web sources on a predetermined topic. Students did quite well with this task. Their average time was just under three minutes. Presumably, students were using the Web on a fairly constant basis and were familiar with ways to search on it and somewhat familiar with methods of assessing reliability. While some students had difficulties in articulating how they would use the information in their papers, this behavior could be due to their relative inexperience in having to spell out the design of their papers. Unfortunately this was one of the facets of qualitative data that was never released or analyzed.

TABLE 12.2

Breakdown of Results from Information Literacy Questions in the Prior Experience Questionnaire

Question	Number and Percentage Correct
Question 1: What cannot be searched in IRIS?	2 correct out of 21 – 9.5%
Question 2: To look up a journal, magazine, or newspaper in IRIS you would use . . .	17 correct out of 21 – 81%
Question 3: What information can you find in an IRIS book record? (Choose two.)	16 correct out of 21 – 76%
Question 4: This book is located in (looking at a sample record).	21 correct out of 21 – 100%
Question 5: This book is about:	21 correct out of 21 – 100%
Question 6: The year that this book was published is:	21 correct out of 21 – 100%
Question 7: The citation for an article in an index will provide the following information:	21 correct out of 21 – 100%
Question 8: When using an index, online access to the entire article is available.	20 correct out of 21 – 95%
Question 9: You are looking for articles on the impact of the amount of sleep on the health of college students. In the search box of an article index, you should enter (Choose one.)	16 correct out of 21 – 76%
Question 10: You have this citation for an article: . . . What part of the citation would you search in IRIS (the Rutgers University Libraries catalog) to see if the library owned this article? (Choose one.)	3 correct out of 21 – 14%
Question 11: When you click on LinkSource in an article index, you will see options for checking the availability of the article. (Choose one.)	19 correct out of 21 – 91%
Question 12: You want to find material about the pros and cons of gun control. Using a search engine, which of these strategies would be most effective?	4 correct out of 21 – 19%
Question 13: All search engines return the same results. (Choose one.)	20 correct out of 21 – 95%
Question 14: Who publishes information on the Web? (Choose all that apply.)	18 correct out of 21 – 86%
Question 15: You don't need to check information from the Web because the Internet has everything. (Choose one.)	19 correct out of 21 – 91%

Discussion

Because the study sample was so small and the data analysis was never completed, this discussion section will focus on the original research design. The challenges for this project cover three different areas. The amount of data that were generated for such a small study population was overwhelming, leading to problems with analysis. The record reflects that there were questions from the corps of interviewers about several of the interview questions. In addition, there continued to be discussions about whether the study population was recruited in such a way that it was possible to study the original research question.

This project included four different sources of data: (1) the prior experience questionnaire, (2) the Searchpath assessment interview report filled out by the interviewer and the observer, (3) the debriefing questionnaire, and (4) Searchpath quiz results. Qualitative data included the self-report of prior experience, the self-report of search skills, the rubric used by the interviewer and the observer's assignment of a numbered search skill level for each student, the relevance scores for the articles generated by Task 3, and the data from the debriefing questionnaire. The quantitative data included quiz scores, task performance, article selection, and Web selection. Quantitative measures were easy to summarize and release. The qualitative data took much more staff time to code, summarize, and interpret. With the retirement of the principal investigator, the qualitative data has not yet been summarized or released.

The record does not reflect that the questions were pilot tested. Those questions that the students had difficulty with, such as the one on the best wording to use to search for information on a controversial topic, did not show that the students could not have done an effective search, but rather that they may have had difficulty in completely understanding the question as worded. The interviewers were not, by and large, part of the original design team for the project (it bears repeating that the chapter authors were interviewers on this project and not part of the original team). This study being discussed here was actually a test of the feasibility of the project, and the interviewers' experiences, comments, and changes were to be built into the eventual rollout of this test to a larger number of students. Problems and critiques of the interview process thus were to be expected and were welcomed.

The interviewers and observers for this project, having often not been directly involved in the design, were free to voice suggestions for change in the project. This situation led to a documented critique of the wording of various questions. This critique should not be seen as a criticism of the project's design, as these criticisms were an actual part of that design. Rather than seek consensus on the wording of each and every question, for the sake of both expediency and real-life input the project was begun, and criticism and rewording invited by the participants.

While the results these questions elicited, as noted before, showed an overall good grasp by the students of how the RUL site worked, several questions seemed to stump the students. Although this finding could indicate areas of instruction that need improving, it is also valid to discuss the wording of the questions. Several interviewers noted reservations about how the questions were framed, saying that they thought the wording may have been vague or might have even led the students to guess an incorrect answer.

The three questions that the interviewers felt strongly about were numbers one, twelve, and fifteen (see figure 12.3).

Question One

This question seems to be an attempt to rank the student on the ability to give the answer librarians wanted. First of all, journal articles *can* be searched, albeit indirectly, through IRIS. Secondly, this question presumes that the interviewee distinguishes between IRIS and the Search Articles buttons on the RUL home page. Choosing "Musical Scores" as the item that cannot be searched in IRIS is actually the intuitive answer, as it is the choice most unlike the others.

FIGURE 12.3
Questions that were debated

1. **Which item CANNOT be searched in IRIS, the library catalog?**
   - A. journal title
   - B. journal article
   - C. musical score
   - D. video recording

12. **You want to find material about the pros and cons of gun control. Using a search engine, which of these strategies would be most effective? (Choose two.)**
    - A. Enter the search gun control.
    - B. Enter a search with quotes around "gun control".
    - C. Use additional words like against and for in your search.
    - D. Use additional words like controversy, debate, or issue in your search.

15. **You don't need to check information from the Web because the Internet has everything. (Choose one.)**
    - A. True
    - B. False

Question Twelve

A number of students chose "D." While observing, we had the idea that a number of these interviewees were mentally assuming the term "gun control" and choosing "D" as the search to combine with the term. A better way to ask this question might have been to offer four sample searches and ask the interviewee to choose among them.

Question Fifteen

This is a mixed item that seems to ask two different questions. Is "Check Information" referring to credibility or to searching? A better question, depending upon what is actually being asked, might be, "Because the Internet has virtually all of the information necessary for research, it is the only source you need to search." Or "Because the Internet contains current, authoritative information, there is no need to search for corroboration for the data found on it."

While the study did bring out these disagreements over wording, it is worth repeating here that it was exactly these sorts of adjustments to the study that this first test was supposed to bring forth. Of course, these disagreements are matters of semantics, and all the wording of all questions can be argued almost endlessly. The whole project, in retrospect, demonstrates how hard it is to assess student learning, particularly when researchers are dealing with something that is as difficult to pin down as information literacy.

In addition to problems with the design of the testing instruments, committee members were also uncomfortable with the decision to recruit volunteers from the Writing Program classes who had received library instruction. This situation repeated a problem that was documented in Noe and Bishop[24] and in Orme:[25] it is impossible to test for the validity of Searchpath if all the students tested also received in-class library instruction.

Study design is not easy. Although we can in hindsight point out problems, it also seems right to congratulate the committee and the principal investigator for a considerable effort.

Recommendations Based on This Study

There are several recommendations that can be derived from this project. The quantity and the complexity of the data and the introduction of new and challenging analysis methods were well-intentioned, but led to an incomplete report. It is not clear how to prevent such an outcome, since institutional follow-through is hard to predict. However, it is safe to say that the pilot testing done here was less rigorous than it could have been. While launching a much larger trial would have needed far more resources, it would be possible. To achieve more precise and usable results in this test, a matrix of four different test groups would have been desirable. They would have been: a group that did Searchpath only, a group that had in-class instruction only, a group that had both trainings, and finally a group that had neither.

The mixed results experienced here also point to the difficulties inherent in designing test questions that are as unambiguous to the subjects as they are to the testers. Were the uneven scores the result of poor teaching, or simply the outcome of a poorly worded question?

Controlling variables is essential. The Rutgers project was clouded by the contradiction between the original research plan (to test Searchpath) and the selection of students from the library instruction program as subjects. Since this error has also appeared in the literature, it suggests that finding students who have used an online tutorial exclusively is very difficult, particularly at a large research university with a distributed presence on multiple independent campuses.

In conclusion, there is regret. This was an exciting and interesting project, and we are grateful for the opportunity to have participated in it.

We could not have foreseen the results of the retirement of the principal investigator at a time when Rutgers underwent dramatic budget cuts (increasing the workload of those who remained). The analysis, standing on the quantitative measures only, was incomplete. The intent behind the design of a multidimensional project in the first place was to tap into the power of qualitative techniques to provide a stronger analysis. With the retirement of the principal investigator, the institutional will to finish the analysis disappeared. This project was instructive both for what it accomplished and where it stumbled. It was a very important moment in the ongoing process of accessing information literacy at Rutgers University.

Notes

1. Searchpath (see http://searchpath.libraries.rutgers.edu) was derived from Searchpath@WMU (see http://www.wmich.edu/library/searchpath), which had been derived from TILT (no longer available online) originally deployed by University of Texas at Austin.

2. The Rutgers version of Searchpath and the Western Michigan version are both still available as of March 2010. TILT, however, is not.

3. The ISC for Rutgers Libraries was replaced in July 2009 by the Instruction Community of Practice. With thanks to Jeris Cassel for clarifying this point.

4. William A. Orme, "A Study of the Residual Impact of the Texas Information Literacy Tutorial on the Information-seeking Ability of First Year College Students," *College & Research Libraries* 65, no. 3 (2004): 205–15; Nancy W. Noe and Barbara A. Bishop, "Assessing Auburn University Library's Tiger Information Literacy Tutorial (TILT)," *Reference Services Review* 33, no. 2 (2005): 173–87.

5. Patricia Fravel Vander Meer, "Pushing the Limits: Creative Web Use in Libraries Related to Instruction," *Research Strategies* 17, no. 4 (2000): 237–56.

6. Nancy Dewald, "Web-based Library Instruction: What is Good Pedagogy?" *Information Technology and Libraries* 18, no. 1 (1999): 26–31.

7. Ibid., 28.

8. Patricia Iannuzzi, "We Are Teaching, but Are They Learning: Accountability, Productivity, and Assessment," *Journal of Academic Librarianship* 25, (July 1999): 304–5.

9. Ibid., 305.

10. Trudi E. Jacobson, "Assessment of Learning," in *Developing Web-based Instruction: Planning, Designing, Managing, and Evaluating for Results*, ed. Elizabeth A. Dupuis, 147–64 (New York: Neal-Schuman, 2003).

11. Iannuzzi, "We Are Teaching."

12. Jacobson, "Assessment of Learning."

13. Anna Marie Johnson and Phil Sager, "Too Many Students, Too Little Time: Creating and Implementing a Self-paced Interactive Computer Tutorial for the Libraries' Online Catalog," *Research Strategies* 16, no. 4 (1998): 271–84.

14. Paul Bracke and Ruth Dickstein, "Web Tutorials and Scalable Instruction: Testing the Waters," *Reference Services Review* 30, no. 4 (2002): 330.

15. Kristina Dunn, "Assessing Information Literacy in the California State University: A Progress Report," *Journal of Academic Librarianship* 28, no. 1 (2002): 26–35.

16. Ibid., 34.
17. Lyn Cameron. "Assessing Information Literacy," *Integrating Information Literacy into the Higher Education Curriculum*, 1st ed. (San Francisco: Jossey-Bass, 2004), 207–36.
18. Noe and Bishop, "Assessing Auburn."
19. Orme, "Study of the Residual Impact."
20. Noe and Bishop, "Assessing Auburn."
21. Orme, "Study of the Residual Impact."
22. Jeris Cassel, personal communication, Feb. 24, 2010.
23. Leslie A. Fiedler, *Freaks: Myths and Images of the Secret Self*, (New York: Simon and Schuster, 1978).
24. Noe and Bishop, "Assessing Auburn."
25. Orme, "Study of the Residual Impact."

13

Approaching Information Literacy Qualitatively

Janice Krueger

Abstract. Librarians are often presented with opportunities for instruction as they interact daily with patrons. While librarians are well-versed in many subject areas, they may have little or no training as a teacher, and the demand for information literacy instruction creates a chance to develop instructional skills. The goal of this study was to gain an understanding of how well the lesson-planning methodology known as *backward design* would give pre-service librarians the necessary skills for planning instruction in different library settings. Twenty-five MSLS graduate and postgraduate students enrolled in an online semester course on instructional strategies for librarians and information professionals participated in this qualitative investigation. Students incorporated backward design for a final project and were directed to reflect on the entire process and to identify where they succeeded and where they encountered difficulties. Final projects for public, school, and academic libraries demonstrated how students took an instructional opportunity, applied the process, and created a plan that acts as a reflective medium for assessment and improvement. Content analysis of student reflections revealed that while backward design provided pre-service librarians with the tools and skills to develop and implement instruction, parts of the process proved to be difficult. Also, the initial investment of time was found to be an obstacle for some.

Introduction

Librarians are often presented with opportunities for instruction. The opportunities stem from a variety of situations, but are most often created by the need for students to become familiar with the library and its resources due to a particular assignment. While librarians are well-versed in a particular subject area, they may have little or no training as a teacher. A natural tendency for new teachers is to be concerned with covering the content, rather than focusing on the actual needs of students. While students may be busy during class, the relevance of the instruction to goals and objectives may be clouded or nonexistent. As a teacher, one way to remain focused is to reflect on this guiding question: "Where are we trying to get, and is this thing we are doing helping us to get there?"[1]

A more structured approach is for librarians, both veteran and beginning, to familiarize themselves with established instructional methodologies through relevant reading or formal coursework in order to enhance their information literacy instruction skills. For students of library science, this can be accomplished through coursework while pursuing the terminal degree. For the practicing professional, activities such as professional development workshops, coursework, or research may be pursued. This chapter, then, serves two purposes. It suggests a strategy for sharpening information literacy instruction skills in general while also reporting the findings from an investigation of pre-service librarians learning how to approach information literacy instruction for the first time.

Context

In order to be proficient and direct students in learning, anyone in an instructional role must have clear goals for their students and an understanding of the skills necessary for student achievement.[2] It follows, then, that one must understand the concept of information literacy before being able to teach it. An important aspect of information literacy and integral to the development of skills called for in today's information environment is an understanding of the many definitions used for it and their evolving nature. The term, *information literacy*, began in the business world and is attributed to Paul Zurkowski, the 1974 president of the Information Literacy Association. In his proposal to the National Commission on Libraries and Information Science, he called for a link between libraries, traditionally considered as the place for storage and retrieval of information, and information activities of the private business sector. Information literate individuals were viewed as those able to apply information resources to work-related problem solving.[3] This view, then, called for a set of skills beyond locating materials held at the library. During the remainder of the seventies, the definition was broadened to include locating information efficiently and effectively for decision making and carried the weight of responsible citizenship.[4]

The advent of modern technologies, such as OPACs, abstracting and indexing electronic databases, electronic journals, and the Internet, called for a further refinement of this definition. Not only did the rapidly evolving technologies demand additional skills regarding their correct and responsible use, but they also required ways for handling the increased amount of information made available to

anyone. Demo was quick to recognize that information technologies created new concerns with regard to accessing and using information meaningfully and responsibly and, because of their highly computerized operations, saw libraries in a strategic position to address these concerns.[5] By favoring a definition of information literacy that emerged from the library community, he positioned it as a key topic for libraries.[6] This definition, pioneered from efforts at Auraria Library at the University of Colorado, stipulated an integration of research, evaluation, and computer skills for using resources in and beyond the library for accessing and retrieving information.[7] The American Library Association (ALA), having established a Presidential Committee on Information Literacy to review relevant reports and the efforts of the library community, issued a final report stressing the importance of this literacy. According to the ALA, information literate individuals are able "to recognize when information is needed and have the ability to locate, evaluate, and use effectively the needed information."[8] These individuals can achieve lifelong learning since they are able to recognize the need for information and can build upon it for desired outcomes. The ALA's definition ultimately called for engaging learners in an active learning process of

- knowing when they have a need for information
- identifying information needed to address a given problem or issue
- finding needed information and evaluating the information
- organizing the information
- using the information effectively to address the problem or issue at hand[9]

Elements of all preceding definitions culminate in this delineated process. The ideas of applying information to solve work-related problems, using information effectively, acting responsibly, and utilizing both library and nonlibrary resources are embedded in the ALA's succinct definition and all-encompassing process. The acceptance of this definition and final report by many educators establishes key roles for libraries and librarians in further developing standards and measurable outcomes for emerging literacies.

The skills embodied in the definition subsequently lead to the creation of standards to express the specific learning outcomes for students. ALA division organizations compiled and published information literacy competency standards for the K–12 and higher education student communities. The American Association of School Librarians (AASL) recently issued revised standards to reflect perspectives for learners in the twenty-first century, such as incorporating new technologies and building new knowledge.[10] The Association of College and Research Libraries (ACRL) created five standards with specific performance indicators and outcomes to monitor the progress of college and university students. Essentially, these standards reflect the need for students to determine information needs, to choose appropriate resources, to critically evaluate resources, to use them, and to understand the legal and ethical issues surrounding their use.[11] To implement these standards, the ACRL offers training opportunities for academic librarians charged with implementing programs for undergraduates. A highly regarded program is the Institute for Information Literacy Immersion, which offers various tracks for improving teaching skills and programs. Another key activity among members is the shaping of the information literacy standards for different disciplines. Many ACRL sections, such as Anthropology and Sociology, Law and Political Science, Literatures in English, and Science and Technology, have recently elaborated on specific competencies for students involved with these major programs of study.[12]

A consideration that results from embracing standards for information literacy instruction is that of assessment. The need to document for accrediting bodies student achievement and school progress in both the K–12 and higher education communities permeates educational institutions. Since K–12 schools have standardized testing in place, one can readily see connections between school libraries and test scores.[13] Higher education, though, has no *mandated* instrument in place to measure information literacy skill acquisition, so librarians use a variety of assessment activities to achieve this end. Some activities include worksheets, discipline-specific pre- and posttests,[14] annotated bibliography analysis, and portfolios of work completed over time with reflective annotations.[15] Recently, however, efforts towards standardized testing in higher education led to the development of the iSkills test from the Educational Testing Service (ETS) to assess information and communication technology skills[16] and the Project SAILS exam from Kent State to ascertain information competency according to the ACRL standards.[17] While Project SAILS is still available for Web or paper delivery, ETS has partnered with Certiport to retool the iSkills exam into the iCritical Thinking certification exam.[18]

Once the content and goals of instruction with corresponding assessments are identified, one can focus on the instructional activities. Current instructional modes of delivery are a combination of past techniques and those created with new technologies. While face-to-face instruction still occurs, Web 2.0 technologies can transcend temporal boundaries. Blogs, wikis, social bookmarking sites, and document-sharing functions, such as those offered by Google Docs, allow librarians to scaffold instruction at the times most needed by students. Librarians share and enliven delivery through Web-based presentation programs or capture and record demonstrations through various software programs, such as Camtasia and Jing. In addition, podcasting provides the opportunity to replay lectures when needed. The developing technologies give librarians the mechanism to deliver instruction according to student needs and location.

Designing Information Literacy Instruction

One strategy that emerged over the years as beneficial to instructors for aligning content, assessment, and activities while also positively influencing student learning is one called "backward design." This process has worked with varying age groups and grade levels[19] and allowed pre-service teachers to attain higher levels of performance when linking learning activities and resources to specific goals.[20] Its process bears a resemblance to qualitative research in that its cyclical nature builds in opportunities for reflection and revision for continuous improvement in achieving true understanding of essential concepts. Interestingly, the three-stage design process mirrors the key concerns for information literacy instruction since it encourages the recognition of concepts embedded in definitions and standards, the development of authentic assessments, and the implementation of learning activities in different ways.

The main thrust of this approach is to derive critical understanding of essential concepts from educational experiences. The first stage of the backward design model focuses on identifying the desired results of the instructional session, unit, or program. Core ideas, essential concepts, and key understandings are prioritized and addressed by establishing goals and thought-provoking questions to stimulate learning. The knowledge and skills necessary for attaining deep understanding of the core ideas and essential concepts are then brought into focus.[21] In order to identify the desired results of instruction or of a program, one must conduct a content analysis of existing program policies, mission statements, information literacy definitions, and resulting standards. Acknowledging the emerging themes, or essential concepts in these documents and others facilitates outlining the knowledge and skills necessary for developing a critical understanding of these core ideas. Overall, the first stage gives a schematic for content analysis and critical reflection on the essential material for instruction.

The key theme of the second stage is assessment and centers on formulating authentic assessments that show understanding of the knowledge and skills embedded in core ideas. Self-assessment and reflection on one's own performance based on guidelines or rubrics are also important.[22] Observation of the teacher/librarian during demonstration sessions provides the background and knowledge for individuals to attempt key learning activities on their own and receive feedback for improvement. Observation of students during instructional periods by the teacher/librarian can provide feedback on how well concepts are grasped and if skills are acquired. Students working together with the guidance of the teacher/librarian can explore content together and receive immediate feedback to align skill development for desired outcomes. Self-assessment according to established guidelines or rubrics provides additional avenues for authentic assessment or can reveal aspects of the instructional component needing revision.

The final stage directs attention to strategies and activities to actualize the core content and ideas from the first stage. It emphasizes the utilization of various learning activities and communicates the focus and direction of instruction. It also incorporates opportunities for individual exploration with different activities and includes time for rethinking and revising work. This critical evaluation and reflection allows individuals to adjust their actions with regard to achieving desired outcomes.[23] Overall, backward design emphasizes a cyclical process for continuous improvement for both instructor and student.

Focus of the Study

Pondering these key points for instruction, especially for information literacy, one is faced with finding an effective way to incorporate the essential content embedded in the definition and standards with the appropriate assessments and the instructional activities. Therefore, the questions that guided the research were: Does backward design allow librarians to build instruction around the essential concepts embedded in the definition and the standards, select appropriate assessments, and determine relevant activities? How would this methodology encourage them to reflect on the process for continuous improvement?

Methodology

The initial challenge to begin the research was to select an instructional methodology that would give the participants relevant skills within the semester timeframe of fifteen weeks and that would provide a structure adaptable to information literacy instruction. Since the overarching goal of this study was to gain an understanding of how well a particular teaching methodology—backward design—would give librarians the necessary skills for instruction during a one-semester course, a qualitative design was used. Specifically, the case study is a qualitative strategy concerned with deriving an understanding about or with uncovering the implications of a particular place, person, group, or event. It is used in evaluation research to explain, describe, or explore phenomena attributed to particular outcomes.[24] A within-site case study approach was employed to study the effectiveness of a selected methodology to plan and to design instruction at a single occurrence bounded by space and time, that is, the semester-long graduate course delivered online through Blackboard. This study was also considered an instrumental case study since a particular instructional methodology was used to gain an understanding of something else, particularly how best to equip librarians with instructional skills.[25] The study was also nested, or layered, since individual participants were singular cases contributing to the overall classroom site. Finally, this case study approach permitted the use of different data, such as documents, class observations, and discussion forum responses.[26]

Participants

The participants for this study were twenty-five MSLS graduate and postgraduate students enrolled in an online course on instructional strategies for librarians and information professionals. Since its inception, the course has been open to any graduate student in the MSLS program and any postgraduate student seeking professional development opportunities or working on a certificate of advanced study. The course was a response to feedback received from students, alumni, and faculty calling for a course on instruction since librarians in all types of libraries are required to provide instruction to varying service communities. Therefore, the participants came from a variety of backgrounds, with some working as librarians or library assistants in academic, public, school, or corporate libraries. The majority had no formal training in education.

Procedure

After some preliminary assignments and discussions, each of the three stages of the backward instruc-

tional design model was gradually introduced in the online course. The students practiced with each stage during the following weeks by redesigning an existing lesson plan of their choice according to backward design. Additional time was given for stage two so students could practice creating rubrics. Likewise, extra time was set aside to explore different learning activities, especially those using various technology tools, such as blogs, wikis, or social bookmarking. The students were asked to incorporate all three stages for a final project. Afterward, they were asked to reflect on the entire process and to identify where they succeeded and where they had difficulty.

Throughout the course, the instructor gauged the understanding of the design process through observations of student performance in discussions, exercises, and group interactions. The instructor analyzed the final project documents for proper application of the backward design principles and categorized the final student reflections for themes related to the usability of the process with regard to information literacy instruction.

Findings Regarding Lesson Planning

Considering the main backgrounds of the pre-service librarians in the class, one representative example for each library type—public, school, and academic—is presented. Each scenario is briefly explained to establish the context of the example, and pseudonyms are used to shield the identity of the pre-service librarian, since each agreed to participate anonymously. The examples demonstrate how each individual took an instructional opportunity, applied the process, and created a plan that acts as a reflective medium for assessment and improvement.

Case One: Reference Training for Circulation Staff

Mary works in a public library as a library assistant and often finds herself explaining to her peers in circulation how to respond to patron questions. She suggests to the circulation supervisor that some reference interview training could help all public service library assistants respond more appropriately to patron inquiries. Here is her application of backward design.

Stage 1—Addressing desired results. The following goals, key understandings, knowledge, and skill statements were derived through a content analysis of Reference and User Services Association (RUSA) Guidelines:[27]

Established Goals
1. Circulation staff will understand the basics of good reference service: approachability, interest, listening/inquiring, searching, and follow-up.
2. Circulation staff will be able to understand and follow the basic steps of the reference interview: open, negotiate, search, communicate, and close.

Understanding
1. The first step is determining if a reference interview is the proper response.
2. Approachability and interest set the tone for the reference interview.
3. Open-ended questions are more effective than closed questions.
4. A successful interview follows the steps of open, negotiate, search, communicate, and close.

Knowledge: Students will know
• the difference between simple and reference questions (simple question—"Where is the ladies room?")
• when to refer, delay, and answer questions
• how to follow the steps of a reference interview
• the difference between open-ended and closed questions

Skills: Students will be able to
• determine what type of question is being asked (simple, reference)
• determine the proper response to the question (refer, delay, interview)
• determine basic steps of a reference interview

Mary generated these open-ended questions for guiding inquiry.

1. How do I determine if a reference interview is necessary?
2. What does a successful interview look like?
3. When should I refer a question to a co-worker or the central reference desk or ask if I can call back with an answer later?

Stage 2—Selecting assessments. Mary integrated the use of peer group work and feedback, authentic assessment of reference interviews, observation by instructor and peers, and self-assessment opportunities in this performance task.

Performance Tasks
Mock Interviews
Students will work in pairs to do mock reference transactions. The library user will be provided with a script, and the librarian will perform a reference interview and assist the user to find an answer to their question. (They will swap roles so both will work through the interview process.) They will then assess their performance in pairs, followed by a group discussion of performance.

Stage 3—Addressing learning activities. By elaborating on the learning activities in stage 3, Mary demonstrated specific activities related to the goals and objectives of the stage. She showed how observation, demonstration, peer groups, and opportunities for rethinking and revising were worked into the instruction.

1. Conduct four mock interviews, demonstrating unsuccessful techniques. Students will be assigned to small groups to analyze interviews.
    a. Conduct first interview without greeting the user, having no eye contact.
    b. Conduct second interview without asking any negotiating questions.

   c. Conduct third interview without accompanying user on search for resource.

   d. Conduct fourth interview without closing the interview.

After each mock interview, ask small groups to decide what went wrong with interview and determine how to fix it. One group member will record responses. Ask groups to come together to discuss the interviews, sharing their responses to each scenario. Make sure discussion includes approachability and interest if it does not come up naturally. Explain open-ended and closed questions when negotiating the question is discussed.

2. Break students into groups of two, giving each pair two scripted reference questions. One student will take the role of the library user and ask the opening question that is written, which will be quite different from the question that the user actually wants to ask. The student taking the librarian role will conduct a reference interview. After the role-playing is finished, the pair will discuss the success or failure of the interview, and then change roles.

3. Returning to the large group, the pairs will be asked to share their experiences with the class. Discuss what parts of the interview the students found to be easy, and which they found to be more difficult.

4. Ask students to share what skills they need to work on in order to plan future training.

Case Two: Undergraduate Students

Tony works part-time in an academic library and assists with information literacy instruction. When working with students, he finds that they are often confused about journal literature. These difficulties include understanding what it is, recognizing it in electronic form, and determining how to locate specific articles. He has been working with different undergraduate students throughout the year and is finally at the point of developing some instruction on accessing specific articles. Here is his application of backward design.

Stage 1—Addressing desired results. The following goals, key understandings, knowledge, and skill statements were derived from a content analysis of the ACRL standards.

Established Goals

1. ACRL Information Literacy Competency Standard 2: The information literate student accesses needed information effectively and efficiently.

2. Performance Indicator 2.3: The information literate student retrieves information online or in person using a variety of methods.

Understanding: Students will understand that

1. Journal articles can be found in various locations in physical and virtual library locations.

2. The holdings information for a journal title will show you where to access the full-text article.

3. The databases offer full-text access to journal articles for different years.

4. Some databases do not allow full-text access to current issues of some journals.

5. Interlibrary loan is an option for obtaining full-text journal articles that are not available locally.

Knowledge: Students will know

1. how to interpret journal holdings

2. how to find the full-text journal article

3. the physical and virtual library locations of journals

4. when to order an article through interlibrary loan

5. where to go for help finding a journal article

Skills: Students will be able to

1. obtain the full-text journal article in any format or from any location

2. interpret journal holdings information

Stage 2—Selecting assessments. Tony provided an opportunity for a structured self-assessment through the use of authentic assessment. His worksheet served as the performance task that the students were asked to complete and self-correct according to established criteria. The students could then reflect on this feedback and understand their strengths and weaknesses.

Performance Tasks

Journal Holdings Worksheet—Students complete a journal holdings worksheet, interpreting journal holdings, and then access the full-text journal article.

Student Self-Assessment and Reflection

- Self-assess the library holdings worksheet according to established criteria.
- Reflect on ability to obtain the full-text journal article at the end of the unit compared to the beginning of the unit.

Stage 3—Addressing learning activities. By elaborating on the learning activities in stage 3, Tony demonstrated specific activities related to the goals and objectives of stage. He showed how observation, demonstration, peer feedback, and opportunities for rethinking and revising were worked into the instruction.

1. Teacher models how to read and interpret the journal holdings information in the library catalog, pointing out:
   a. Some databases offer full-text access to journal articles for different years.
   b. Some databases do not allow full-text access to current issues of some journals.
   c. Some journals are available in other formats such as print, microform, and optical disc.
   d. The databases will link you to the full-text journal article in another database.
   e. Interlibrary loan is an option for obtaining full-text journal articles that are not available locally.

2. Teacher introduces the physical locations and organization for the various formats and models searching the print, microforms and restricted access locations.
3. Teacher models how to access and register and use the interlibrary loan module known as ILLiad.
4. Students will obtain a journal citation using one of the library databases. They will take turns explaining to the class the process they will go through to obtain the full-text journal article with the teacher observing and coaching the students as they present.
5. Teacher models how to get help when searching for the full-text journal article.

Case Three: Elementary Students

Sue volunteers at the library in the local elementary school. Since she is working towards her school library certification, the librarian has her work with teachers and students on various projects. The sixth graders are completing their first research paper, and the teacher wants them to understand how to use the OPAC effectively to locate library materials on their topics. Here is Sue's application of backward design.

Stage 1—Addressing desired results. The following goals, key understandings, knowledge, and skill statements were derived from a content analysis of the AASL standards.

Established Goals

1. Students will use an understanding of the OPAC to find materials related to desired topic.
2. Students will demonstrate mastery of technology tools for accessing information and pursuing inquiry (AASL 1.1.8).

Understanding: Students will understand that

1. The OPAC can be manipulated by title, author, keyword, and subject to find desired materials.
2. Subject headings gather similar materials together.

3. Narrower topics may not be found, but are indeed cataloged under a broader topic.

Knowledge: Students will know
- Key terms: Subject Heading, Keyword, Call Number, OPAC, Title, Author, and Database

Skills: Students will be able to
- Identify the subject headings, call number, title, and author in a record.
- Locate materials using the OPAC.

Sue created these open-ended questions for guiding inquiry.

1. How do I know what to search?
2. What is a subject heading?
3. What is the difference between a subject heading and a keyword?

Stage 2—Selecting assessments. Sue developed a variety of performance tasks, or assessments, to use with the students. She included self-correcting game-like authentic assessments for the children. The students were also given an opportunity for reflecting on their ability to locate books for their research paper.

Performance Tasks
Students will create a book list of at least three possible titles for their research paper.
Other Evidence
- Students will participate in a matching game using terms and definitions.
- Students will complete an OPAC Scavenger Hunt.
- Students will reflect on how to locate materials using the OPAC by writing a brief paragraph on how they gathered the titles for their book list.

Stage 3—Addressing learning activities. By elaborating on the learning activities in stage 3, Sue demonstrated specific activities related to the goals and objectives of stage. She showed how observation, demonstration, peer groups, and opportunities for rethinking and revising were worked into the instruction.

1. Using the topic of Colonial America, demonstrate an OPAC search using subject, keyword, author, title and call number. During demonstration, engage students in a discussion of the definitions of the preceding terms, including the concept of using broader subject terms.
2. Throughout the demonstration, students will complete the Book List worksheet as a class example.
3. After the class book list is completed, each student will receive either a term or a definition. The students will need to move around the classroom until they find their match. Each group will read aloud their term and definition.
4. After the matching game, students will individually complete the OPAC Scavenger Hunt.
5. Students will complete the Book List worksheet using the topic selected for their research paper. This paper will be reviewed by the classroom teacher as the basis for the student's research paper.
6. When students have finished their book list, they will write one paragraph reflecting on how to locate materials using the OPAC. Students will be given the rubric for this assignment to inform them of required concepts.
7. In closing, the teacher, through discussion format, will review key concepts of using the OPAC including the difference between subject heading and keyword.

These three cases epitomize how all twenty-five students were able to apply the principles of backward design for information literacy instruction sessions in different types of libraries with specific service communities. The students also demonstrated how content analysis aided in the identification of knowledge and skills embedded in standards and goals and how reflection and rethinking provided opportunities for self-assessment and improved action.

Findings Regarding Student Reflection on the Process

An analysis of responses from the last discussion forum provides additional insight into how the pre-service librarians regarded this particular strategy. The comments are grouped according to recurring themes.

What Worked Well

Design structure. Students agreed that the three stages required one to be very organized and specific in planning. Katie commented that "it laid everything out and forced you to . . . think specifically about what students are coming into the lesson with . . . and what I want them to leave with." Barbara found it to be "very logical and organized . . . and even encourages the instructor to design the plan . . . to encourage students [to be] responsible for their own learning." Melinda mentioned that "the format . . . makes sense to me and . . . it is part of best practices." Richard stated that "it did get me to think more in-depth about my lesson and what would fit where." Likewise, Amy discovered that "I kept finding myself thinking up elaborate ideas that didn't end up having a lot of substance to them . . . I learned so much that will be very useful down the road." Robert found that he liked the process because "it helps keep everything organized and easy to read. It also makes it easy to continually make corrections throughout the entire design process and to go back and make modifications after the lesson is taught."

Interrelated parts. Students realized that the individual stages contribute to the creation of a cohesive, integrated instructional product. Sam stressed that "the flow . . . of backward design forced me to think about the individual, but closely related, parts of the lesson . . . when writing the activities and assessments; I needed to identify the differences between the two but also understand their relation." Tony discovered quickly that:

Overall I felt like all 3 stages came together, but I did find myself . . . moving between the different stages and going back and forth from one to another as I designed, rather than treating them as separate sections. I think the process seems to work best . . . if all the smaller elements . . . inform each other to create the whole.

For the learners. Course students saw benefits for those they were instructing. Judy commented, "The parts that worked were the performance activities. The students really like the projects and fully participated in them. They grasped the concepts much better than last year's class when I just used notes and class discussions." Another, Betsy, immediately saw how she could have improved instruction for her learners if she had used backward design for a previous instruction session. She stated:

We started a new service this spring: downloadable audiobooks. It was my responsibility to brief everyone on the new service and provide training. I gave a PowerPoint presentation and then just had all staff watch a webinar. There was no follow-up or checking for understanding. The plan I created for this assignment is what I should have done to present the new service. I think I could probably accomplish this program in 3–4 hours (total) over the course of about 2–3 days. Although it would require more time, I think the level of understanding and confidence among the staff would be much greater than what it is now.

What Didn't Work Well

Time. As Betsy mentioned, time could be a factor when using this process. Jennifer emphasized that time was a factor for her in the development phase when stating, "The amount of time required using this process has been a stumbling block. I believe, though, that as I use it more, I'll become more proficient at it."

Assessments and rubrics. Some students found difficulty in planning assessments and performance tasks, and most experienced difficulty in creating rubrics with specific criteria. Tony explained:

I find it somewhat difficult to translate the activities and desired results into assessment pieces . . . trying to drill down to the concise, task-focused statement needed for Stage 2 is a bit of a challenge . . . trying to frame Stage 2 as evidence, versus tasks or activities, was helpful and allowed me [to] break down the information into more concise pieces.

The wording of rubrics also presented a challenge. The tendency was to use vague terms, such as "somewhat," "almost," or "a few," in establishing the criteria. Sue commented, "Students need to have a clear understanding of exactly how their assignments will be graded. So, I agree those words are not very specific, yet I couldn't determine how to make it more specific." Jeremy stated, "The rubrics are the tricky part, as others have stated, and I feel the more you work through and actually would use them to get a final grade, the better you would get at the specific wording."

Linear versus holistic. Finally, one student experienced difficulty with keeping the big picture in mind during the planning process. John explains, "I think the nonlinear, holistic format . . . is deceiving and complex. Rather, I would prefer to write out the lesson using a more linear, straightforward approach. Such a layout would promote an understanding of the whole lesson."

Discussion

Since the students of this course were able to apply the basic principles of this strategy to instruction for information literacy opportunities, backward design proved to be an effective way to plan and to implement instruction. It gave the students the tools to pinpoint the essential concepts embedded in the definition and standards, decide on evidence of understanding, and plan for relevant learning activities. While students encountered some difficulties in expressing assessment pieces and separating them from learning activities, they acknowledged the value in being able to define measurable performance tasks that indicate understanding of concepts and skill acquisition. They also realized that creating rubrics takes some practice but ultimately allows for better feedback on assignments, projects, and other work products called for by the content of instruction. Course students were quick to point out that backward design made them aware of the value of being

able to reflect, rethink, and revise instruction to better meet student needs. It basically builds in a cycle for continuous improvement of instruction.

The researcher, the course instructor in this case study, found the subject of this study, the backward design process, to be a strong, viable strategy for aspiring librarians faced with information literacy instruction. It gave them the basic tools and skills to confidently plan and implement instruction according to their particular work situation. This process also challenges librarians to approach instruction in a qualitative manner by encouraging them to regard each instructional situation as an opportunity to acquire new meaning and understanding of content and to revitalize learning activities.

One result of this study is the acknowledgment that adding a more traditional lesson plan approach could benefit those students who prefer a more linear structure to instruction. Some students may be more suited to outlining a lesson by listing behavioral objectives, resources, and materials for instruction; specifying step-by-step procedures; and identifying one culminating assessment or assignment for the lesson. If both strategies are presented and compared by students, then they could choose which methodology they prefer. It would be interesting to see how the students react to both and how they compare and contrast the processes. Once their chosen lesson approach is implemented, the student can then note the advantages and disadvantages of both and determine which strategy creates more effective learning opportunities.

Application

The process of backward design is applicable to many library situations. As demonstrated in this investigation, librarians dealing with information literacy instruction, whether in an academic, public, or school library setting, can use the process to effectively plan and implement instruction. Additionally, the three-stage process offers a framework for program planning, delivery, and evaluation. Public libraries could benefit by using backward design due to the high number of programs offered, such as summer reading, young adult gaming, or public access computing, to name just a few. Since the emphasis is on focusing on the larger picture rather than on individual, isolated activities, it compels librarians to identify the essential goals and the specific means for evaluation before planning the individual activities. This approach fosters the development of activities more relevant to the major goals of the program. These activities, in turn, will contribute to more meaningful and successful library programming for patrons.

Other qualitative methods that could foster additional understanding of information literacy instruction and programs are program evaluation and historical research. These specific methodologies encourage an investigation and understanding of specific areas of instructional practices or programs. Complete information literacy programs can be reviewed through the variety of data collected during a program evaluation process. This process can provide insight into how to improve alignment of standards, instructional activities, and assessment practices. Finally, researching the history of information literacy and understanding how it developed over the years can shed light on how certain past practices and ideas worked well and how others were ineffective. This perspective can, in turn, provide direction and guidance in future developments for information literacy instruction.

While this study primarily used a case study approach, various aspects of action research and program evaluation were touched upon through it. The investigation of how the backward design process prepared pre-service librarians for information literacy instruction has overtones of action research since it centered on examining one possible solution to a defined issue. The study also demonstrated how the stages of backward design provide a structured framework against which entire program goals, outcomes, and activities can be evaluated and reviewed for continuous improvement. The perspectives of the overall study were linked through the content analysis of historical accounts of information literacy and student work products, the discourse analysis of student discussions, and the observation of student performance in the classroom. All of these interrelated parts supported a greater qualitative understanding of information literacy.

Summary and Conclusion

Twenty-five MSLS graduate and postgraduate students applied the backward design framework to an instructional opportunity of their choice. They initially found the design structure logical and organized, but quickly realized how it actually forced them to think deeply about creating a cohesive, integrated, and effective lesson. As the students developed each of the three stages, they discovered how the process encourages corrections, revisions, and modifications in an ongoing way. They also learned that using this strategy requires time and that the creation of effective assessments and clear rubrics is a skill developed over time.

Backward design provided pre-service librarians with the tools and skills necessary to implement instruction in different library settings. It gave students a structure to pinpoint essential concepts embedded in various information literacy standards, to decide on authentic evidence of understanding, and to incorporate relevant learning activities. Above all, the three stages worked together to encourage reflection and revision, building a cycle for continuous improvement of instruction, as well as providing a framework for analyzing how pre-service librarians learn how to design instruction.

Notes

1. John Holt, *How Children Fail* (New York: Pitman Publishing, 1964).
2. Amy Childre, Jennifer R. Sands, and Saundra Tanner Pope, "Backward Design: Targeting Depth of Understanding for All Learners," *Teaching Exceptional Children* 41, no. 5 (2009): 6–14; Lynn M. Kelting-Gibson, "Comparison of Curriculum Development Practices," *Education Research Quarterly* 29, no.1 (2005): 26–36.
3. Shirley J. Behrens, "A Conceptual Analysis and Historical Overview of Information Literacy," *College &*

Research Libraries 55, no. 4 (1994): 309–22; William Demo, *The Idea of "Information Literacy" in the Age of High-tech* (Bethesda, MD: ERIC Document Reproduction Service, ED 282 537, 1986), http://www.eric.ed.gov/contentdelivery/servlet/ERICServlet?accno=ED282537; Michael B. Eisenberg, Carrie A. Lowe, and Kathleen L. Spitzer, *Information Literacy: Essential Skills for the Information Age*, 2nd ed. (Westport, CT: Libraries Unlimited, 2004).

4. Behrens, "A Conceptual Analysis"; Eisenberg, Lowe, and Spitzer, *Information Literacy*.

5. Demo, *The Idea of "Information Literacy."*

6. Behrens, "A Conceptual Analysis."

7. Ibid.; Demo, *The Idea of "Information Literacy."*

8. American Library Association, *Presidential Committee on Information Literacy: Final Report* (Chicago: American Library Association, 1989), http://www.ala.org/ala/mgrps/divs/acrl/publications/whitepapers/presidential.cfm.

9. Ibid., 4–5.

10. American Association of School Librarians, *Standards for the 21st-century Learner* (Chicago: American Library Association, 2007), http://www.ala.org/aasl/standards.

11. American Library Association, Association of College and Research Libraries (ACRL) *Information Literacy Competency Standards for Higher Education* (Chicago: ACRL, 2000).

12. Association of College and Research Libraries, "The Institute for Information Literacy Announces the Immersion '09 Program," 2009, American Library Association, http://www.ala.org/ala/mgrps/divs/acrl/issues/infolit/professactivity/iil/immersion/invitation09.cfm (accessed Dec. 13, 2010).

13. Eisenberg, Lowe, and Spitzer, *Information Literacy*.

14. Terrence Mech, "Developing an Information Literacy Assessment Instrument," in *Revisiting Outcomes Assessment in Higher Education*, ed. Peter Hernon, Robert E. Dugan, and Candy Schwartz (Westport, CT: Libraries Unlimited, 2006), 327–50.

15. Eisenberg, Lowe, and Spitzer, *Information Literacy*.

16. Educational Testing Service, "iSkills Overview," 2009, http://www.ets.org/portal/site/ets/menuitem.1488512ecfd5b8849a77b13bc3921509/?vgnextoid=159f0e3c27a85110VgnVCM10000022f95190RCRD&vgnextchannel=e5b2a79898a85110VgnVCM10000022f95190RCRD (accessed March 3, 2010), page now discontinued).

17. Kent State University, "Project SAILS: Standardized Assessment of Information Literacy Skills," 2007, https://www.projectsails.org.

18. William Wynne, personal communication.

19. Childre, Sands, and Pope, "Backward Design."

20. Kelting-Gibson, "Comparison of Curriculum Development Practices."

21. Grant Wiggins and Jay McTighe, *Understanding by Design*, expanded 2nd ed. (Alexandria, VA: Association for Supervision and Curriculum Development, 2005).

22. Ibid.

23. Ibid.

24. Michael Q. Patton, *Qualitative Research & Evaluation Methods*, 3rd ed. (Thousand Oaks, CA: Sage, 2002); Robert K. Yin, *Case Study Research: Design and Methods* (Thousand Oaks, CA: Sage, 2003).

25. Robert E. Stake, *The Art of Case Study Research* (Thousand Oaks, CA: Sage, 1995).

26. Yin, *Case Study Research*; Stake, *The Art of Case Study Research*.

27. American Library Association. Reference and User Services Association, "RUSA Guidelines," 2009, http://www.ala.org/ala/mgrps/divs/rusa/resources/guidelines/index.cfm (accessed Dec. 13, 2010).

14

The Reference Interview in Real Time and in Virtual Time

Isabelle Flemming and Lesley Farmer

Abstract. Reference interviews, which are a key service, need constant evaluation to optimize their effectiveness. Determining the patron's specific request can be even more difficult when the discussion takes place in a virtual environment. The use of formal qualitative evaluation, combined with the application of self-reflection, can be implemented to improve services and to enhance managerial decisions based on a full understanding of the process. Evaluation processes and data collection methods are explained, and an action research example shows how qualitative research can be implemented to improve virtual reference service. Anonymous reference question and answer logs from a virtual reference service were analyzed to determine if the homework-related questions from schoolchildren were being answered satisfactorily. Problems with this type of service meeting the needs of this population are discussed.

Introduction and Overview

The reference interview may be described as "a conversation between a reference staff member and a user, *the goal of which is to ascertain the user's information need* and take appropriate action to satisfy that need through skillful use of available information sources [italics added]."[1] Provision of reference and information literacy services has grown with advances in technology and increasing user expectations. While this rich environment has much to offer its patrons, each point of reference is a place where service might need improvement or could simply fail completely. Since the reference interview is the critical factor necessary to clarify what the patron really wants, it is here that misunderstandings often arise.

Therefore, the interview requires constant evaluation, both formal and informal, to pinpoint problems in completely fulfilling the patron's reference need.

Determining the patron's specific request can be even more difficult when the discussion takes place in a virtual environment. There are no visual cues, such as a frown, a smile, or a look of confusion, to guide the librarian. Reference is never an automatic process. It is dynamic and interactive. Each patron and situation is different. The use of formal qualitative evaluation, combined with the application of self-reflection, can be implemented to improve services or to enhance managerial decisions based on a full understanding of the process. On the other hand, the online reference service may archive the transactions, which can subsequently be analyzed to discern patterns of practice that can be improved.

Providing successful reference service requires good communication skills, knowledge of the practices and behaviors that result in optimal service and user satisfaction, and follow-through. Many studies have revealed the need for awareness and improvement in these areas by librarians. Using an actual research project as an example of content analysis of virtual reference interviews with K–12 students,[2] this chapter will discuss the qualitative research methodology of content analysis as a means of service reflection and improvement. This chapter will also discuss best behaviors for both face-to-face and digital (virtual) reference service in order to point out the behaviors that can lead to problems and the instances where qualitative evaluation may be best used to bring about improvement.

The Evolution of Reference Services

The first person to discuss reference help as a function of libraries was Samuel Swett Green, who published an article in 1876 in which he listed four main necessary practices of the reference librarian, although he himself never actually used the word *reference*.[3] David Tyckoson sums these up:[4]

- Instructs patrons how to use the library
- Answers patron queries
- Aids the patron in selecting resources
- Promotes the library within the community

The first three functions can be directly associated with the reference interview. As the role of the librarian grew more prominent, the importance of evaluating performance was recognized. How well did the librarian answer the questions asked? Various early studies developed to test this performance presented discouraging results. These findings prompted closer study of the reference transaction itself to determine what components of behavior were necessary to improve question answering. Gradually the focus of studies shifted from counting correct answers to analyzing components of behavior practiced

by the librarian as well as canvassing user satisfaction.[5] Unobtrusive studies, such as observation and surveys, were one method of gathering information. Some studies used obtrusive methods, such as audio and video recording of transactions. With the development of a professional organization for librarians came the gradual establishment of suitable practices and behaviors. These were refined over time to incorporate practices specific to various divisions of librarianship as well as to new technologies. Today, the American Library Association (ALA) lists core competencies for all librarians, while ALA Reference and User Services division (RUSA) has continued to update best behaviors and practices for reference librarians.[6]

The reference interview has grown in importance, and its definition has evolved. New technologies introducing varieties of virtual reference have required reconsideration of interview techniques. In 2008, the RUSA Board of Directors approved new definitions of the reference transaction and reference work. In part, the definition of *reference transactions* is "information consultations in which library staff recommend, interpret, evaluate, and/or use information resources to help others to meet particular information needs."[7] This is as true for Readers Advisory as for general reference. A modified definition of the reference transaction is offered by the Reference and Users Services Association (RUSA) and applies especially to academic libraries:

> A reference transaction is an information contact that involves the knowledge, use, recommendations, interpretation, or instruction in the use of one or more information sources by a member of the library staff. The term includes information and referral service.[8]

Teacher librarians and special librarians, such as those in corporate libraries or manuscript archives, have adapted practices to meet the needs of their own particular environments. The fundamental concept remains that of providing the best service to users, whether they are elementary students or research scholars.

Research has demonstrated that the patron is the linchpin around which the entire transaction revolves. Therefore, conducting an effective reference interview is essential to clarifying the patron's query.[9] While librarians cannot know everything, they should take the time to understand the questions.

Today, reference guidelines have been adapted for situations not originally anticipated, particularly during virtual reference assistance. Since working with a patron through chat reference or another similar vehicle robs the librarian of nonverbal cues, it becomes more difficult to interpret the patrons' needs. The makeup of patrons and their expectations may differ in each of the electronic environments. Librarians have found it necessary to adapt to such new expectations, demonstrating their interest and willingness to listen.

RUSA has determined five best practices that must be a part of the process in reference services. These practices are discussed in more detail in the RUSA Reference Guidelines[10] and are briefly summarized here:

1. Approachability. This refers to the environment as well as to the librarian. Remote reference services should be prominently posted along with contact information and links where patrons can easily see them. For in-person assistance, maintaining eye contact, leaning forward, and staying visible to the patron are helpful.
2. Interest. Librarians should show strong interest in the patrons' questions to promote patron satisfaction. Remote contact requires timely replies to e-mails and *word contact* during chat sessions. Clear usage instructions should be posted on the library Web site.
3. Listening/Inquiring. Among the skills shown to be most important to users, personal attention ranks high. (See specific skills and tips listed under the general section of Listening/Inquiring in the Guidelines.)[11]
4. Searching. By listening carefully and being familiar with the library's resources, the librarian can make the search more effective. Find out what the patron has tried already, and determine which resources will best serve the patron's needs. Discuss the search with the patron, and identify sources.[12]
5. Follow-up. The librarian is responsible for making sure that the patron found or received what he really needed. Ask whether the patron's question is completely answered. If referral is necessary, call ahead to make sure the agency or institution to which you refer him has the information needed.

Types of Digital Reference Services

The newest trend in reference interviews is virtually conducted interaction. The earliest form of non–face-to-face reference service took place over the telephone in the first half of the twentieth century. Wasik traced the history of digital reference service, noting that its roots lay in academic library services, as represented by the University of Maryland's Health Services Library since 1984.[13] Virtual reference service (VRS) was developed by government agencies, such as AskERIC starting in 1992, and nonprofit entities, such as Internet Public Library founded in 1995. In 1996, KidsConnect, a question-and-answer help and referral service for K–12 students on the Internet, experienced 1,000% growth from twenty questions a week to 200 questions per week.[14]

Now e-mail, instant messaging (IM), virtual reference services, and virtual worlds such as Second Life make distance communication in real or virtual time possible. Smartphones and texting via phone add still another dimension, as do such services as Skype, which allow those communicating to see and hear each other in real time via the Internet.

Virtual reference is reference service initiated electronically, often in real-time, where patrons employ computers or other Internet technology to communicate with reference staff, without being physically present. Communication channels used frequently in virtual reference include chat, videoconferencing, Voice over IP, co-browsing, e-mail, and instant messaging.[15]

For each of the digital reference formats, there are both barriers to good communication as well as advantages over face-to-face reference at the desk.

E-mail

One of the first Internet-based forms of communication to be adapted to answering reference questions was e-mail. E-mail can be used day or night. It is asynchronous because exchanges do not take place immediately between librarian and patron. However, there may be long delays from question to answer, especially when clarification and further information are requested from either side.[16] Sometimes even the information need itself changes, "reflecting a change in the client's knowledge base."[17] The inability to see physical cues to meaning and intent remains a disadvantage. One advantage to e-mail is that the librarian has more time to search appropriate resources for answers. Qualitative evaluation methods for these transactions could include document review, observation, or anonymous testing.

Instant Messaging (IM)

Another Internet-based communication protocol, instant messaging, is also being used for answering reference questions. Instant messaging (IM) is synchronous text chat so that information can be exchanged fairly rapidly. IM is easy to use and already popular with a large market that libraries can reach out to. It is free, does not require special configuring or downloading, and works with most computers and operating systems.[18] IM works ideally for quick reference questions, is informal and easy to use, and connects with a hard-to-reach population—those who grew up with computers.[19] There are negative aspects. Patrons using IM generally expect quick answers, while librarians may be uncomfortable with the number of questions or with multitasking. The use of acronyms is characteristic of IM chat. Librarians using this medium will need to become familiar with these abbreviations.

Virtual Reference Service (VRS)

Virtual reference service (VRS) differs significantly from other types of telecommunication. Typically, VRS represents a reference cooperative among several libraries and offers special services like co-browsing Web sites and communication in real time between a librarian and the user. VRS is based upon complex software packages used by libraries that are part of the cooperative. The particular services used determine the amount of interaction available and the quality of service. Examples of these services are QuestionPoint and AskAway.[20] Although virtual reference takes place in real time as a synchronous service, slight delays occur due to transmission from one type of computer to another or from one server to another, or from heavy use that slows down the system. Technical problems are major factors in the lower-than-expected usage statistics. Virtual reference software that is incompatible with browsers and operating systems or slow Internet connections that have an impact especially on co-browsing drive potential users away. Pop-up blockers and firewalls can prevent making connections at all. Many patrons find that the necessity of configuring browsers to work with the system is simply too much effort.[21] Providing reference assistance in the collaborative virtual environment requires a great deal of tact and patience.

There are also differences in the interaction depending on whether virtual reference is provided through a public library collaborative or an academic network. Public librarians often find that younger students have expectations of quick service and many answers offered up at once, not unlike entering keywords in a search engine. On the other hand, some adults using the service may become frustrated or confused since they do not have as much experience with this technology. Academic virtual reference services generally work with an audience of undergraduate and graduate students, researchers, and professors. Librarians serving the academic community are expected to provide teaching and guidance with the reference assistance so that users can apply the skills themselves in the future.

Smith sums up the experience of providing virtual reference service:

> These abilities translate into the chat environment as the ability to conduct an effective reference interview in real time without nonverbal or auditory cues; knowledge of the library's or organization's reference infrastructure, including subject guides to the Internet and core proprietary databases; learning how to deliver answers to users online and handle questions demanding answers that are not possible or practical to deliver in chat; and finally, learning to function as a team with other library public service points.[22]

Smith highlights the importance of the ability to multitask in this environment. She sees the great advantage of virtual reference services as the fact that patron and librarian are seeing the same Web site, database, or search engine at the same time. This co-browsing is not possible in instant messaging or on the telephone.

Virtual Worlds

Recently some libraries have begun maintaining a presence in the virtual world of Second Life. Real people create avatars to interact in this virtual world. Second Life is constructed to reflect real-world environments and functions and may be used for simulations and gaming. Those entering Second Life can create locations, visit virtual businesses, buy and sell real estate, and more. Quick to see the potential, companies have begun conducting business here, performing transactions and conferences globally in real time. Scientists and other academics have begun to collaborate in Second Life.[23] The first library system to explore the possibilities for remote reference in Second Life was the Alliance Library System of East Peoria, Illinois, in April 2006. Since then an increasing number of professionals participate voluntarily, generating Second Life libraries and library services.[24] The American Library Association can be found on Second Life at ALA Island.

The Future

Greater collaboration among libraries and other information providers is highly likely.[25] Increasing use of texting, "smartphones and social networks," will help place librarians "in all of the spaces inhabited by our users."[26] Increasing interaction using dynamic content and networking online—now often referred to as Web 2.0—will continue to grow.[27] Nor is Web 2.0 the last word. Some see a still more dynamic information environment in which multiple technological methods are used to complete a single transaction. This will involve more collaboration between librarians and researchers and will offer a customized experience in which information seekers can pick and choose the technologies that will answer their needs from the variety offered by providers of information.[28]

Assessing Online Reference Interviews

RUSA has developed specific guidelines for VRS.[29] One major difference between face-to-face and virtual reference service is the set of conditions that must be in place for VRS to exist: infrastructure, software selection and installation, access and authentication protocols, start-up and maintenance costs, and technical support. RUSA's guidelines for VRS specifically state: "Library staff and administration should facilitate regular assessment of the program's effectiveness and commit to adjustments as needed. Assessment should be comparable to the assessment of other reference services." Focusing just on the reference interaction, the following criteria, in addition to guidelines for generic reference interviews, should be used to assess the service's effectiveness:

- As with other delivery formats, VRS requires good communication and interpersonal skills. Because physical cues are limited, additional training and effort may be needed to provide service that is equitable to face-to-face interactions.
- Staff need to practice effective online communication skills and address common

potential problems such as cues during waiting time and signal drop-offs.

- Staff need to insure that online communication, including stored transcripts or records, are kept private and confidential.

While some methods for assessing physical reference interviews apply to virtual environments, such as self-reporting of transactions and time-cost analysis, others methods are harder to implement, such as unobtrusive observation (although a peer could theoretically "shadow" an online transaction). Some virtual reference services include a postinterview user satisfaction survey, which can be used to assess service. Lorri Mon and Joseph Janes's research of unsolicited follow-up messages from e-mail digital reference users found participants tended to be very satisfied with the service, particularly if answers were lengthy, and were grateful for its timeliness and convenience.[30]

On the other hand, face-to-face reference interviews are seldom recorded, unlike online ones. Thus, the most obvious way to assess virtual reference interviews is content analysis of the interview transcript, usually coding the text according to the RUSA guidelines.[31] Luo's synthesis of VRS evaluation methods found that researchers tended to focus on librarian behaviors, although a few also coded the types of questions asked and evidence of user satisfaction.[32] Affective elements are hard to capture beyond the words themselves and occasional emoticons. Nevertheless, these transcripts can be assessed to test for the generally accepted indicators of good reference interviews: the quality of the answer, interview protocols, the quality of search strategies used and reference sources consulted, use of referrals, and the general attitude of the librarian.[33] Content analysis could also drill down to find possible correlations between certain behaviors (both individual and transaction) and demographic information.

Regardless of the context, content analysis provides an unobtrusive way to examine documents that can substantiate decisions and actions relative to an issue. The steps for analyzing VRS transcripts involve the usual protocol for content analysis:

1. Review the underlying problem to be addressed, the research questions, and the context in which the program resides.
2. Immerse oneself in the textual evidence. Jot down re-occurring phrases and concepts, and prioritize participants' words.
3. Build interpretation and theory from the ground up.
4. Categorize and label the text according to the research questions and their subsets; try to provide exhaustive mutually exclusive categories. Link associated categories into themes. Review the rationale for coding in light of emerging patterns.
5. Link categories to theory. Test findings to theory or established practice (such as RUSA's guidelines), noting similarities and differences. Address any gaps. Rework relationships between categories and themes. The themes should relate directly to the theory but should also emerge from the data.
6. Suggest explanations for the findings, keeping in mind the context of the data.[34]

A Case Study in Evaluating VRS Interviews

As a culminating project of her master's work at California State University Long Beach, teacher-librarian Vida Bahremand developed an action research project that focused on the information-seeking experiences of young people. She chose to do an evaluative inquiry into the use of a virtual reference service (VRS) by K–12 students.[35]

The study was motivated by the reality of K–12 students' use of VRS. Many K–12 students may prefer these services because

1. Sometimes they need to ask questions when libraries are normally closed. The services are offered twenty-four hours and seven days a week (24/7).
2. They do not have to go to the libraries physically; online service is more convenient.

3. They do not have to answer librarians' questions face-to-face. Some students are shy and feel awkward when talking to other persons. Students who are English language learners (ELL) may feel shy because they are not fluent in English.
4. Students who have disabilities may find it hard to get to the library physically, so they prefer to use online services.
5. Many students enjoy engaging with computers.[36]

Having an online presence, though, is not enough. For VRS to successfully serve users, one value is emphasized above all others: knowledge of the community to be served. In order to know students' needs and answer their questions correctly, VRS librarians have to interact with the users. Sometimes the most difficult aspect is asking the right questions in order to provide the best possible answers. Librarians must be careful not to make assumptions about their online users, be it in terms of age, ability, knowledge, or behavior. Because teens can be very sensitive and self-conscious, textual communication can be a delicate negotiation. Furthermore, in this abstract environment, librarians need to go the extra mile to demonstrate their responsiveness to their sometimes restless teens.

Abby Kasowitz, Blythe Bennett, and R. David Lankes identified the following working set of standards to assess quality of individual VRS related to the K–12 community.[37]

1. Accessible. VRS for the K–12 community should be easily reachable.
2. Prompt Turnaround (fast). Questions should be addressed as quickly as possible.
3. Clear Response Policy. Clear communication should occur either before or at the start of every digital reference transaction in order to reduce opportunities for user confusion.
4. Interactive. VRS should provide opportunities for an effective reference interview to clarify vague user questions.

5. Instructive. VRS also guide users in subject knowledge as well as information literacy.
6. Authoritative. Librarians involved in a VRS should have the necessary knowledge and educational background in the services given, plus the subject area in order to qualify as an expert.
7. Trained Experts. Services should train specialists to respond to inquiries using clear and effective language. Training of information specialist is one of the most important aspects of planning and operating a VRS.
8. Private. All communications between users and information specialist should be held in complete privacy.
9. Reviewed. VRS should regularly evaluate their processes and services.
10. Publicize. Services providing information to the K–12 education community are responsible for informing potential users of the value that can be gained from use of the service.
11. Provides Access to Related Information. Besides offering direct response to user questions, VRS librarians should be able to offer follow-up or other related avenues of inquiry to the patron.
12. VRS should offer access to supporting resources and information. Services can reuse results from question answer exchanges in resources such as archives and frequently asked questions.

Nevertheless, in examining the literature about digital reference service, Bahremand found little research focusing on VRS for K–12 students, particularly with regard to the impact of reference interaction on K–12 student questioners. Since student satisfaction often depends on appropriate interaction, and examination of those interactions and students' indication of the degree of their satisfaction could lead to the identification of significant aspects of the dialogue that would affect successful reference service, relevant research questions arose:

- Does 24/7 VRS serve students effectively? If not, what are the reasons?
- Are VRS interviews between librarians and students efficient in terms of the questions asked by librarians to deal with students' queries?

Methodology: Content Analysis

To answer these questions, Bahremand chose to analyze the Metropolitan Cooperative Library System's VRS program "24/7," the main service for southern California, which was a well-established, stable service used by all types of users, including students. In 2004, 24/7 was acquired by OCLC and renamed QuestionPoint. It provides 24-hour services, 7 days a week, 365 days a year through the Internet. 24/7 Reference is a customized set of software tools that lets patrons ask questions and get answers in real time on the Internet from the live reference staff. Institutions providing librarians to staff this service are primarily large public library systems, although special librarians offer subject-specific expertise in fields such as law and art. At the time of the study, 24/7 advertised itself to Southern California public and academic library users, who were the primary clientele.

Patrons are able to connect the services from each library Web page by clicking on the icon that says "ask the librarian." The interview process may be perceived from either the patron or the librarian side. On the patron side, the screen is split in to two sections. One shows the shared content window, and the other part shows the chat window, where conversations between patron and librarian occur in real time. On the librarian side, the screen has three parts:

1. The top portion shows the patron information and shared content that is sent to patron.
2. In the lower portion, the librarian types chat, provides URLs, and the like.
3. An area just for the librarian includes prescripted chat and URLs that the librarian can make use of and push to the patron.

Throughout a session, the librarian and patron can converse using the built-in chat function. Librarians guide patrons around the Web, directing them to quality online resources. They type the URL addresses that they would like patrons to see. Patrons can see the Web page in the content window, and they also can continue the conversation in the chat window. The librarian and patron can work together to complete searches; the patron types in the search words or phrases, and the librarian can assist the patron by modifying the search word or phrase. At the end of the transaction, a transcript with all of the chat and all URLs visited is automatically sent to the patron via e-mail. The service also has protected access to tools that generate reports, transcripts, and a wide variety of usage statistics, which allows maintaining and improving reference services.

As noted above, a literature review of methodologies used for evaluating VRS indicated that content analysis of online reference chat transactions was the accepted standard technique. Bahremand gained permission to analyze 24/7's archived chat transcripts for four months in 2003. These months—January, May, June, and November—were chosen because school districts in southern California tend to give students complex research assignments during these time periods. For the time frame under investigation, a total of 182 transactions were identified as involving K–12 students (based on librarian query or student self-disclosure as recorded in the transcripts).

As the transcripts were in text format with little tagging, Bahremand created a protocol that allowed her to code the following variables for each VRS transaction transcript she reviewed:

- How many students daily contact the 24/7 reference services and ask their questions?
- During what times of the day do students ask questions?
- How long do the students have to wait until a librarian joins them?
- What kind of the questions are asked?
- How long does it take for the librarians to answer the questions?

- Are the interviews between students and librarians effective, when evaluated according to the RUSA guidelines?
- If the interviews are not effective, what are the reasons?
- Are the students satisfied with the answers?

To evaluate the quality of the interaction between the librarian and the student, the researcher checked the transcripts against the following criteria, which were drawn from the literature as indicators of conducting an effective interview:[38]

- using a friendly tone
- using open-ended statements, such as: "Please tell me more about what you are looking for" or "What are some more specific details about what you are looking for?"
- paraphrasing the question
- asking more questions for clarification
- asking about the keywords that the student has already used
- asking follow-up questions
- avoiding jargon
- asking the purpose of the question: research paper, project, homework assignment, just finding information about the subject and writing a simple essay, reading interest, etc.
- asking what type of resources the patron needs: print (books, magazines) or non-print
- asking the student's grade level
- asking if the patron is an English language learner (ELL) or native English speaker

The researcher used the above variables to create the content analysis protocol, creating a spreadsheet grid. Each transcript was read, tallying the occurrence of each variable. The type of questions were noted, and then categorized as theme clusters emerged.

The investigator also asked the trainer of the VRS team several questions about how the service works (i.e., process for getting a librarian, text and view-ing area, *canned* questions section for the librarian, etc.). The trainer explained all the procedure from the first moment the patron connects to the service and asks his or her question until the connection ends. The trainer also explained that that the service uses area reference librarians and library science graduate students, all of whom are given one-time training.

Findings

Every day twenty-five to fifty-seven patrons total contacted the 24/7 reference services. Every day different numbers of patrons used the service, although fewer used the service on weekends. Over time, increasingly more patrons used the service. Of that user population, zero to five K–12 students contacted the service per day.

About 4 percent of student questions were asked during midnight to 6:00 a.m., 16 percent of questions were asked between 6:00 p.m. to midnight, and about 80 percent of the questions were asked between 6:00 a.m. and 6:00 p.m.

About 78 percent of the students had to wait less than one minute until a librarian joined them. About 22 percent of the students had to wait more than one minute until a librarian joined them. Fewer than 2 percent had to wait more than five minutes for a librarian to respond.

About 50 percent of the questions were general questions such as library branches, library hours, parking, missing pages in the books, interlibrary loan, how the collections in the libraries are organized, how to put a hold on a video, how to put a yearbook together, magazines in libraries, locating a book, returning the books to the branches from which they were checked out or to other branches, renewing books online, checking out books online, academic journals, losing library card, etc. About 18 percent of questions focused on books/encyclopedias/articles on a specific subject. About 20 percent of the questions were asked about specific books with the titles and the authors. About 20 percent of the questions were asked about specific magazines and periodicals. The common questions the students asked included

- how and where to find information on a subject in history, social science, science, English, etc.; where to find biographies
- where to find an example for outlining a research paper
- how to put a story into a bibliography
- where to find maps
- how to cite a book for a research paper
- where to find textbooks
- Some asked for some interesting fiction books for teens.

About 30 percent of the students had to wait four minutes and more for the answers. The other 70 percent had to wait three minutes or less for the answers. When the librarians were busy, they always informed the patrons that it would take time and told them the reason. They also asked the students if they would like to wait or would prefer the answer be e-mailed to them. Of the 13 percent of patrons who would need to wait for an answer, about 80 percent of them preferred having the answers e-mailed to them rather than waiting right then for the answer or logging out and returning later. Only about 7 percent disconnected without any notice after being informed that it would take time for them to get the answer.

In about 20 percent of the interviews with K-12 students, the librarians did not ask key questions, such as the purpose of the questions or the student's grade level. The vocabulary and sentence structure that the librarian used did not indicate any special accommodation for younger readers.

The researcher observed that about 80 percent of the interviews between the students and the librarians were conducted according to the five RUSA guidelines. The librarians always asked the students whether the answers they got were helpful or if they needed more information. Always before ending the connection, the librarians reminded the students that if they needed further assistance, they could contact the service again. The librarians also mentioned that all the answers would be sent to the students' e-mail addresses.

During and after the interviews, the patrons were asked to fill out a survey form to measure their sat-

isfaction with the service; staff quality; whether, if they were a first-time user, they would use the service again; whether they found the service easy to use; how they perceived the service; and what comments they would like to add. Only 10 to 20 percent of the patrons filled out the survey forms on any given day; none of them were self-reported to be K–12 students.

Discussion

Based on the literature review, which provided a theoretical grounding on the elements of digital reference service, and on the content analysis of 24/7 digital reference interviews as well as interviews with the director of this service, the following conclusions were derived.

Overall, VRS services for students were satisfactory for about 80 percent of students, based on their response to the librarians' query about the service (although students may have been reluctant to answer negatively). However, some of the following specific practices were observed that did not seem effective. Based on reading the interaction, some librarians seemed not to have enough information about academic content frameworks, curricula, standards, and subjects that are taught in schools. It took them significant time to refer the students to the appropriate answers. It was also observed that when the librarian referred the student to some books, the student himself asked if the books were for adults or also good for children. The general librarian did not have any clue and told them to call the library that had the book and to ask the librarian there. The service's trainer stated that the VRS librarians were not specifically trained in serving students online.

Some librarians were not able to recognize the patron as a student, nor did they bother to ask. They just assumed that the patron was an adult. In some cases, in the middle of the interviews, the patron himor herself said that he or she was a student and wanted the information for a research, project, etc.

It was also observed that some librarians did not seem to have patience with younger patrons, and they appeared to be in a rush to end the conversation and get to another patron.

Some students used these services in order to have the librarians do the work for them. For example, one student logged in and asked about the characters of a book and where to find information about the characters. The librarian took time to look for the information everywhere and did not find it.

Based on the conclusions raised from the transcript content analysis, Bahremand generated some recommendations and interventions to improve the quality of 24/7 VRS for K–12 students. Since it was observed that the number of students who refer to 24/7 reference services was very low, she posited that there is a need to market the services effectively. K–12 classroom teachers and teacher-librarians should be asked by the librarians and director of 24/7 VRS to market and promote these services for students and make school communities aware of such services.

Some librarians involved in 24/7, such as children and young adult librarian specialists, should be trained to become familiar with the framework, curricula, standards, and projects taught in K–12 schools. The librarians in these services should collaborate regularly with K–12 teacher-librarians to update information. Once they can recognize the questions as coming from a young student, the trained VRS librarians can conduct the interviews more effectively and serve the students competently with the updated knowledge and information garnered. At the time of the study, K–12 teacher-librarians did not serve as 24/7 reference librarians; they should be encouraged to participate and be trained in online reference interviewing techniques. Such inclusion would also help market the service.

The librarians who interact with the K–12 students should interact in a way that is perceived to be patient. The librarians should consider the following points when interviewing K–12 students:

- Students may not know what to expect.
- Students may have no prior knowledge of the type of resources that will answer their questions.
- Students may not know the terminology used in the reference interview.
- Students may lack knowledge about the subject and the assignment.

- Student may misinterpret the verbal cues.
- Student may be fearful of the system or frustrated about the questions being raised.
- Communications may become miscommunication when a student is unable to verbalize his or her information need.

These recommendations were given to the 24/7 reference service director. The local teacher-librarian preparation program, California State University Long Beach, subsequently incorporated 24/7 training in its reference course, which the service's trainer conducted. She also discussed school assignments with the pre-service teacher-librarians and came to a better understanding of student research processes and school reference services. The pre-service teacher-librarians were also encouraged to serve as 24/7 reference service librarians, but the service was soon bought out, and the basis for staffing the service changed.

Summary and Conclusion

Pascal Lupien's 2006 analysis of virtual reference service noted the disappointingly low use of VRS, with librarians trying to figure out the reason for its lack of acceptance. Lupien suggested that technological frustration for both librarians and patrons because of equipment, software issues, connectivity, protocols, and security created barriers to use. Additionally, many users were not aware of such services, and the service itself was not embraced by many libraries. Since then, IM applications and widgets have simplified the technology, and increasing mobile technology ubiquity has broadened the user base.[39]

Nevertheless, the quality of VRS needs ongoing assessment to maintain effective service. At the least, periodic sampling of transcripts to be analyzed according to RUSA's guidelines for general and virtual reference service can help staff self-examine their practice and find ways to improve specific aspects of the transactions. Not only should librarian behavior be analyzed, but user behavior and interactions should be examined. Librarians could also focus on the specific resources consulted or suggested to see what patterns emerge and what informational gaps exist. As noted above, more detailed demographic information can help staff do targeted training to deal with specific subgroups having unique needs, such as English language learners or K–12 students.

As technology, including data mining tools, improves, VRS can benefit from close analysis that can pinpoint ways that librarians can become more effective information.

Notes

1. Richard E. Bopp and Linda C. Smith, eds., *Reference and Information Services: An Introduction*, 3rd ed. (Englewood, CO: Libraries Unlimited, 2001), 47.

2. The project used in this chapter as an example of action research in the arena of virtual reference was a research project undertaken by master's of education student, Vida Bahremand, under the direction of Dr. Lesley Farmer at California State University Long Beach. All references to this student research are included with permission by Vida Bahremand.

3. Samuel Swett Green, "Personal Relations between Librarians and Readers," *Library Journal* 1 (Oct. 1876): 74–81.

4. David A. Tyckoson, "What Is the Best Model of Reference Service?" *Library Trends* 50, no. 2 (Fall 2001): 183–98.

5. Ralph Gers and Lillie J. Seward, "Improving Reference Performance: Results of a Statewide Study," *Library Journal* 110 (Nov. 1, 1985): 32–35; Patricia Dewdney and Catherine Sheldrick Ross, "Flying a Light Aircraft: Reference Service Evaluation from a User's Viewpoint," *RQ* 34, no. 2 (Winter 1994): 217–31; Joan C. Durrance, "Reference Success: Does the 55 Percent Rule Tell the Whole Story?" *Library Journal* 114 (April 15, 1989): 31–36.

6. American Library Association, "ALA's Core Competencies of Librarianship," approved and adopted Jan. 27, 2009, http://www.ala.org/ala/educationcareers/careers/corecomp/corecompetences/finalcorecompstat09.pdf; American Library Association: Reference and User Services Association (RUSA), "Guidelines for Behavioral Performance of Reference and Information Service Providers," June 2004 http://www.ala.org/Template.cfm?Section=Home&template=/ContentManagement/ContentDisplay.cfm&ContentID=26937.

7. American Library Association: Reference and User Services Association (RUSA), "Definitions of Reference," http://www.ala.org/ala/mgrps/divs/rusa/resources/guidelines/definitionsreference.cfm (accessed Dec. 14, 2010).

8. Ibid.

9. David A. Tyckoson, "Why Is Germany in Europe? And Other Lessons from a Life in Reference," *Reference & User Services Quarterly* 47, no. 3 (Spring 2008): 207–9. This article provides an example of obvious miscommunication.

10. RUSA, "Guidelines for Behavioral Performance."

11. Ibid.

12. Denise E. Agosto and Holly Anderton, "Whatever Happened to 'Always Cite the Source?' A Study of Source Citing and Other Issues Related to Telephone Reference," *Reference & User Services Quarterly* 47, no. 1 (Fall 2007): 44–54.

13. Joann Wasik, "Asking the Experts: Digital Reference and the Virtual Reference Desk," *D-Lib Magazine* 6, no. 5 (May 2000), http://www.dlib.org/dlib/may00/05inbrief.html#WASIK.

14. R. David Lankes, *Building and Maintaining Internet Information Services: K–12 Digital Reference Services* (Syracuse, NY: ERIC Clearinghouse on Information and Technology, 1998).

15. American Library Association, "Virtual Reference: A Selected Annotated Bibliography," ALA Library Fact Sheet 19—Virtual Reference, http://www.ala.org/ala/professionalresources/libfactsheets/alalibraryfactsheet19.cfm (accessed Dec. 14, 2010). This work is highly recommended as a source of links to information about all facets of virtual reference.

16. Eileen G. Abels, "The E-mail Reference Interview," *RQ* 35, no. 3 (Spring 1996): 345–59. Abels's discussion of a three-step project conducted at the College of Library and Information Services at the University of Maryland provides good coverage of the topic.

17. Ibid., 345.

18. Pascal Lupien, "Virtual Reference: In the Age of Pop-up Blockers, Firewalls, and Service Pack 2," *Online* 30, no. 4 (July–Aug. 2006): 19.

19. Aaron Schmidt and Michael Stephens, "IM ME: Instant Messaging May Be Controversial, but Remember, We Also Debated Telephone Reference," *Library Journal* 130, no. 6 (April 1, 2005): 34–36.

20. QuestionPoint (electronic reference service), *QuestionPoint: Overview,* upd. Feb. 16, 2009, http://www.question-point.org/support/documentation/gettingstarted/questionpoint_overview.pdf ; AskAway (electronic reference service), "Flash Video Demonstrations," http://www.askaway.info/flash_videos.html.

21. Lupien, "Virtual Reference," 19.

22. Jana Smith Ronan, *Chat Reference: A Guide to Live Virtual Reference Services* (Westport: CT, Libraries Unlimited, 2003), 96.

23. Lisa Zyga, "Virtual Worlds May Be the Future Setting of Scientific Collaboration," PhysOrg.com, Aug. 4, 2009, http://www.physorg.com/news168608901.html.

24. Jill Hurst-Wahl, "Librarians and Second Life: It's a Source of Information, a Platform for Networking, an Opportunity to Try Out New Approaches before You Take Them to the Real World," *Information Outlook* 11, no. 6 (June 2007): 44–50.

25. Jeffrey Pomerantz, "Collaboration as the Norm in Reference Work," *Reference & User Services Quarterly* 46, no. 1 (Fall 2006): 45–55.

26. Stephen Abram, "Evolution to Revolution to Chaos? Reference in Transition," *Searcher* 16, no. 8 (Sept. 2008): 43.

27. Mike Eisenberg, "The Parallel Information Universe: What's Out There and What It Means for Libraries," *Library Journal* 133, no. 8 (May 1, 2008): 22-25.

28. Raya Kuzyk and Mirela Roncevic, "Future-present: What's Possible Now and Coming Soon in Reference," *Library Journal* 133, no. 19 (Nov. 15, 2008): S4(2).

29. American Library Association: Reference and Users Services Association (RUSA), "Guidelines for Implementing and Maintaining Virtual Reference Services," June 2004, http://www.ala.org/ala/mgrps/divs/rusa/resources/guidelines/virtrefguidelines.cfm.

30. Lorri Mon and Joseph Janes, "The Thank You Study," *Reference & User Services Quarterly* 46, no. 4 (Summer 2007): 53–59.

31. Sarah Maximiek, Erin Rushton, and Elizabeth Brown, "Coding into the Great Unknown: Analyzing Instant Messaging Session Transcripts to Identify User Behaviors and Measure Quality of Service," *College & Research Libraries* 71, no. 4 (July 2010): 361–73; Wyoma van Duinkerken, Jane Stephens, and Karen MacDonald, "The Chat Reference Interview: Seeking Evidence Based on RUSA's Guidelines," *New Library World* 110, no. 3/4 (2009): 107–21; Nahyun Kwon and Vicki Gregory, "The Effects of Librarians' Behavioral Performance on User Satisfaction in Chat Reference Services," *Reference & User Services Quarterly* 47, no. 2 (Winter 2007): 137–48; Fu Zhuo, Mark Love, Scott Norwood, and Karla Massia, "Applying RUSA Guidelines in the Analysis of Chat Reference Transcripts," *College & Undergraduate Libraries* 13, no. 1 (2006): 75–88; Van Houlson, Kate McCready, and Carla Pfahl, "A Window into Our Patron's Needs: Analyzing Data from Chat Transcripts," *Internet Reference Services Quarterly* 11, no. 4 (2007): 19–39; Bruce Jensen, "The Case for Non-intrusive Research: A Virtual Reference Librarian's Perspective," *Reference Librarian*, no. 85 (2004): 139–49; Mohamed Taher, "Real-time (Synchronous Interactive) Reference Interview: A Select Bibliography," *Internet Reference Services Quarterly* 7, no. 3 (2002): 35–41; Melissa Gross, Charles McClure, and R. David Lankes, "Assessing Quality in Digital Reference Services: Overview of Key Literature on Digital Reference" (Tallahassee, FL: Information Use Management and Policy Institute, Florida State University, Nov. 2001), http://dlis.dos.state.fl.us/bld/Research_Office/VRDphaseII.LitReview.doc; David Carter and Joseph Janes, "Unobtrusive Data Analysis of Digital Reference Questions and Service at the Internet Public Library: An Exploratory Study," *Library Trends* 49, no. 2 (Fall 2000): 251–65.

32. Lili Luo, "Chat Reference Evaluation: A Framework of Perspectives and Measures," *Reference Services Review* 36, no. 1 (2008): 71–85.

33. William Katz, *Introduction to Reference Work: Reference Services and Reference Processes,* 8th ed. (New York: McGraw-Hill, 2002), 202.

34. Louis Cohen, Lawrence Manion, and Keith Morrison, *Research Methods in Education,* 5th ed. (New York: RoutledgeFalmer, 2004).

35. Vida Bahremand, "24/7 Digital Reference Services: Does It Work For Students?" (master's thesis, California State University, Long Beach, 2004).

36. James Rettig, "Does Reference Have a Future?" *Public Libraries* 46, no. 1 (2007): 11–12.

37. Abby Kasowitz, Blythe Bennett, and R. David Lankes, "Quality Standards for Digital Reference Consortia," *Reference & User Services Quarterly* 39, no. 4 (Summer 2000): 355–64.

38. Ibid.; Joseph E. Straw, "A Virtual Understanding: The Reference Interview and Question Negotiation in the Digital Age," *Reference & User Services Quarterly* 39, no. 4 (Summer 2000): 376–79.

39. Lupien, "Virtual Reference, 14–19.

Seeing Is Learning: The Synergy of Visual Literacy

Alessia Zanin-Yost

Abstract. Visual literacy is an important but often overlooked part of information literacy for college students. This chapter defines visual literacy, synthesizes points of view from a variety of disciplines focusing on the visual arts, and demonstrates how qualitative research can be successfully adapted to assessment in this field. Visual literacy is closely connected to information literacy. The *Information Literacy Competency Standards* developed by the Association of Colleges and Research Libraries can be used as a starting point to develop outcomes and standards for assessing visual literacy. This chapter models how librarians can introduce the concept of visual literacy to faculty and assess students' visual learning.

Introduction

The concept of visual literacy is not new in education, for it dates from the 1960s. However, much of the literature focuses on how images affect literacy—that is, the development of reading skills.[1] Research demonstrates that visual materials improve learning;[2] in fact, the "propensity to create vivid images during reading correlates highly with overall comprehension."[3] The advent of the computer, low-cost software, and mobile communication tools has increased exposure to visuals into an everyday affair. Images are a part of our culture. If in the past we asked people to think critically about text, now we need to introduce the concept of thinking critically about visuals.

Like information literacy, visual literacy "requires the researcher to consider where the information is coming from and how it has been presented."[4]

Moreover, with visual literacy, the learner needs to think critically not only about how the author uses a visual, but also about what it means individually. Because the concept of visual literacy is broad for the audience members, individualized for the author, and can be controversial, clear standards with measurable outcomes become a necessity so that students are all assessed fairly. The Association of College and Research Libraries (ACRL) *Information Literacy Competency Standards for Higher Education*, adopted in 2000, provides a foundation. ACRL defines information literacy as the ability of an individual "to recognize when information is needed and have the ability to locate, evaluate, and use effectively the needed information."[5] In higher education, faculty are familiar with information literacy; therefore, it seems natural to use what they already know and apply it to the visual literacy field. In addition, it makes sense to adapt the components of information literacy, which have been defined, promoted, and adopted by the ACRL in the field of librarianship, to assess the level of knowledge about visual information. Because the areas between visual and textual information overlap, it is important that visual and information literacy be taught together.

One of the challenges for faculty and librarians is how to assess students' visual literacy skills. Although visual competencies require a multitude of skills, as just mentioned, these skills are very similar to the ones that have been identified as components of information literacy. In 2006, I began to apply the ACRL *Information Literacy Competency Standards* to visual literacy. With a growing plethora of resources, students struggled with how to critically understand using visuals. It became evident that besides teaching about visuals, it was important to determine how to assess students' knowledge and skills regarding visual literacy. As an imbedded librarian,[6] I have the opportunity to work closely with faculty and students for a semester as the liaison to the visual and performing arts departments. Supporting students and teaching them how to find and use images is as important as teaching them how to find and use textual works. This imbedded approach has allowed me to see how students use visuals. Students are able to find images through Google Images with no problem but do not understand how to use the search tool appropriately. Some of the issues that have surfaced have been the inability of students to use sources other than Google Images, misunderstandings about the use and citation of images, and assumptions about the meaning of images.

With these issues in mind, I began to include visual literacy instruction in information literacy instruction sessions. However, some questions remained: Do students understand how to find and use images? Are they visually literate? Do they consider themselves visually savvy? Through a qualitative analysis of one-on-one interviews, I have been able to gain insight about what students understand about how images should be treated in a research paper.

In this chapter, the terms *visual*, *picture*, and *image* will be used to mean the same thing: a two-dimensional representation in any medium of something or someone that is factual or fictional.

Literature Review

"Among contemporary cultural critics," according to Paul Messaris, "it has become commonplace to argue that the increasing societal shift towards visual media is responsible for large-scale impoverishment of people's cognitive capacities."[7] Messaris's point is evident in today's culture. People want to *see* information rather than read it because they can capture the meaning, or what they think is the meaning, faster. In *Ways of Seeing*, Berger notes, "We never look just at one thing; we are always looking at the relation between things and ourselves."[8] How many times have we been to a bookstore or library and while browsing found a book that caught our attention because the cover had a picture that we could connect with at a personal level? Somehow, we hoped that the perception we had of what we saw on the cover was reflected inside the book because, as Bourdieu states, "Any art perception involves a conscious or unconscious deciphering."[9] Looking at an image is a one-of-a-kind experience that cannot be reproduced. What we see in an image will not prompt the same conscious or unconscious understanding in others because the perceptions people have are affected by societies, beliefs, ages, genders, and personal experiences. Educators need to understand the significance of using visuals when teaching, since the process of understanding and deciphering visuals is different from person to person due to diversified experiences.[10]

The perception of how experiences affect our understanding of visuals is evident through the stages of human development. The interpretation and understanding of visuals is dynamic rather than static because, although images offer a variety of information, it is important to remember that the meaning we absorb from the image comes from our previous knowledge and experiences.[11] Freedman and Hernandez state that "We are now in the sixth wave [of communication], one of expansion to include visual culture, which is grounded in global, socio-cultural concerns and what it means to live in increasingly image-based, technological environments."[12] As we are exposed to different beliefs and experiences, we may change our perceptions. We become visually literate because our thoughts are more sophisticated as our knowledge increases. As educators we need to remember that our students come into the library and the classroom with a variety of visual knowledge and assumptions.

The importance of how visuals are interpreted, understood, and used began to be widely acknowledged during the 1960s, when television became part of our everyday lives as it created a make-believe world. It was during this time that the concept of visual literacy made its appearance because, "just as in the nineteenth century Western societies took a literary turn, our times have seen what sociologists call a visual turn. . . . Image management is the order of the day."[13] Forty years ago, Rudolph Arnheim, distinguished psychologist, philosopher, and art critic, emphasized that the visual process is an essential part of our critical-thinking process because images provide a never-ending source of "rich information about the objects and events of the outer world. Therefore, vision is the primary medium of thought."[14] Many scholars, among them Allan Paivio, Rune Pettersson, and Paul Messaris, affirm that visual information is coded differently in our brain and is a specific form of thinking.[15] Visual literacy is one of the multiliteracies that is needed to succeed not only in school, but also in life.[16]

Visuals are used in a variety of ways in the classroom. Teachers use charts, graphs, slides, and other forms of visuals to provide a rapid message to their students. Yet many educators do not teach students how to read visuals, assuming students have this skill already. We forget that visuals may be different or used differently in other parts of the world. For example, when I first came to the United States, I was not sure what the Change Lanes sign was (see figure 15.1). In the United States and in my native country, the signs both have the same symbol in the center, consisting of a straight vertical black line on the left and a bent vertical black line parallel to it on the right; however, the colors and shape of the sign were different. In my native country, the sign is a triangle with red borders and white background, while here, it is a yellow diamond.

FIGURE 15.1

Change Lanes Signs: Different Images with the Same Meaning. United States (left) and Italy (right)

As Freedman points out, we understand visuals because of our previous experiences and knowledge, and what we know best about them often stems from our ethnic, social, and even gender affiliation.[17] When visuals are presented and discussed in a classroom environment, everyone will add to his or her knowledge base the same new information that the instructor provides. When students come to institutions of higher education, they bring with them a wealth of previous knowledge, and they get tested on this knowledge to make sure they take the appropriate course level. However, what is not often tested is their visual literacy competency.

Students use images all of the time in their works: PowerPoint, trifold boards, and movie clips are just a few examples. Although students are successful in finding the images they need, very few are visually literate. Faculty and librarians assume that students in visually oriented majors, such as art, design, theater, and film, may think they are able to find, select, and use visuals. However, even students who work with images on a daily basis do not necessarily have the skills to understand how to treat visuals. Examples may include not knowing how to use an image to enhance or to accompany textual or oral information, using colors and fonts merely because of personal preferences, and not understanding how to cite images.

Because of increased interest in visuals, the International Visual Literacy Association (IVLA) was founded in 1968 to provide a venue for the discussion and sharing of ideas for scholars interested in the many aspects of visual education.[18] Since then, visual literacy has been discussed and defined in many ways. However, some of the commonalities of these definitions are the ability to understand visual messages, the ability to communicate with others with visuals, and the ability to use past knowledge of visuals to construct or reconstruct information.[19] The definition of visual literacy used by IVLA, which is widely accepted, is the one by Fransecky and Debes:

> Visual literacy refers to a group of vision-competencies a human being can develop by seeing and at the same time having and integrating other sensory experiences. The development of these competencies is fundamental to normal human learning. When developed, they enable a visually literate person to discriminate and interpret the visual actions, objects, and/or symbols, natural or man-made, that he encounters in his environment. Through the creative use of these competencies, he is able to comprehend and enjoy the masterworks of visual communications.[20]

A more current study conducted by Brill, Kim, and Branch defines visual literacy in this way:

> A group of acquired competencies for interpreting and composing visible messages. A visually literate person is able to: (a) discriminate, and make sense of visible objects as part of a visual acuity, (b) create static and dynamic visible objects effectively in a defined space, (c) comprehend and appreciate the visual testaments of others, and (d) conjure objects in the mind's eye.[21]

From the variety of existing definitions, it is evident that visual literacy is in broader use than just the field of visual arts. Communication, history, psychology, and film studies all study visual literacy, but each of these disciplines uses the term with a different meaning.[22] For example, in psychology, visual literacy describes the interpretation of symbolism, while in communication and film studies, it is the understanding of how messages can be interpreted by the medium used. With such divergent uses of terms, it is understandable why the definition of visual literacy remains fluid. Streibel notes that one

of the problems with the different types of literacies (visual, media, computer, information, etc.) is that they have been kept separate from each other, while they should be seen as complementing each other.[23] Visual literacy is a mélange of other literacies, yet at the same time, it will be idiosyncratic to a specific discipline.

Visual Literacy Skills

What should a visually literate person be able to do? What are the skills that characterize a person as visually literate? As in defining the term *visual literacy,* the skills that make one visually literate depends on the researcher, but in general are defined as (1) the ability to interpret, understand, and appreciate the meaning of visual messages; (2) the ability to effectively communicate through applying basic principles and concepts of visual design; (3) the knowledge to produce visual messages using some type of technology; and (4) the ability to translate from visual language to verbal language and vice versa.[24] In my opinion, a visually literate person will have many of the same skills as an orthographically information literate person. Thus, I define visual literacy as the ability to use and combine information and media literacies with aesthetic and critical-thinking skills in order to communicate with others. These literacies and skills are connected to each other (see figure 15.2), and I define them as follows:

- *Information literacy.* I use the ACRL definition of information literacy.[25]
- *Media literacy.* While visual literacy is concerned *with* the message, media literacy is concerned with *how* the message is created.[26] For example, when the same information is reported using different media, the message perceived will be different because the tools used create different impressions.
- *Aesthetic skills.* To understand the messages in an image, a person should understand the relationship of the elements of design. The traditional elements of point, line, plane, shape, tone, texture, and color

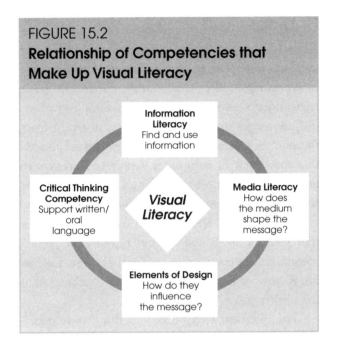

FIGURE 15.2
Relationship of Competencies that Make Up Visual Literacy

can be used to create different types of messages.[27]

- *Critical thinking competency.* I define this competency as the ability to think reflectively and evaluate all information (visual, orthographic, or aural).[28]

Through a combination of skills, competencies and literacies, a visually literate person should be able to (1) understand how to find and access visuals from a variety of sources; (2) incorporate into the original visual a personal perspective that contributes to the exchange of ideas; (3) express visuals in a variety of contexts to support written or verbal language; and (4) recognize legal and ethical issues related to visuals.

Methodology

The literature on visual literacy agrees that students come to the classroom with their own understanding of what is a *good* or *bad* image, assumptions about how to use images, and beliefs about what images mean.[29] Without guidance from the instructor and the librarian, students will continue to make these assumptions. An increased awareness of visual literacy will help students realize that images need to be treated like any other piece of information:

researched, evaluated, properly used, and cited. We can talk to students about these issues, but how can we be certain that students assimilate the visual literacy aspect of the instruction? In order to see if what we are teaching changes a behavior, we need to assess their level of knowledge.

The literature on visual literacy offers examples of ways to integrate a visual literacy component into the curriculum and engage students in lectures by using visuals. Such examples abound in a variety of disciplines and at all levels. The literature also covers how to use a variety of rubrics and other instruments to assess visual literacy skills at the K–12 levels. [30] However, what is missing is an account of what students know about visual literacy skills.

Because the very nature of visual literacy is subject-bound and often differs from discipline to discipline, even from context to context, evaluating the student's skill on visual literacy calls for flexibility in assessment techniques. Qualitative research yields optimal findings in these endeavors, for "designing a study in which multiple cases, multiple informants, or more than one data-gathering method are used can greatly strengthen the study's usefulness for other settings."[31] Qualitative research methodology provides a depth of understanding because it is concerned with the intricacy of human beings. Through the use and analysis of written language, pictures, and objects[32] and by "using tape recorders, video cameras, notes on paper, photographs, personal records of participants, diaries and memos, this type of research proceeds anecdotally to describe what happened at the specific time and place."[33] Qualitative investigation uses several methods: observation, interviewing, content and historical analysis, and focus groups.[34]

In gathering data to assess visual literacy, not all methods need to be used, but only the one that fits with the assessment needs and research questions.[35] Because I wanted to find out, in a short time, if students gained knowledge of visual literacy, my methodology focused on one-on-one interviews. The purpose of the interview is to gather information that is not visible: the researcher wants to find out what the participant is thinking. Interviews can be structured formally with predetermined questions or informally with ad hoc questions. Having a set of criteria and deciding which qualitative method to use helps the librarian to determine what questions to ask and how to use the information in the overall research.[36]

During the 2009–2010 academic year, responses from twenty-five students at Western Carolina University were collected. All of the students, who participated voluntarily, were undergraduates in interior design, art history, art education, art studio, and communication studies courses. All of the students attended an information literacy session in the library where simple notions of visual literacy were integrated. The visual literacy section was included in the information literacy session because the students had to find images to use in their presentations.

During the information/visual literacy sessions, the students were taught how to use the library catalog to search for images (this included an explanation of what keywords to use, a demonstration how to search, and a list of some of the main resources available), how to find images using the databases CAMIO and ARTstor, and how to use the limiters in Google Images. In addition, the students participated in a short discussion about plagiarism. They were shown where to find resources on how to cite images and provided with examples. Time was left at the end of each session for students to apply what they learned and to retrieve at least one image to use in their projects. At the end of the library session, students were randomly selected. The questions were asked one-on-one to avoid interference, and each interaction lasted about two minutes. Because students were able to talk for only a short time, the interviews consisted of only two questions, and the answers were transcribed. The students were not encouraged in any way to answer "yes" or "no." From their answers to these two questions, I expected to have a better understanding of which tools students prefer to use when searching for images and if students perceive citing images as the same as citing textual information. The two questions were:

1. Do you know how to find the same image using another tool (online, paper…)?
2. Do you think it is necessary to cite images when used for a presentation (PowerPoint, poster…)?

Findings

Table 15.1 reports the answers from the survey. For question one, "Do you know how to find the same image using another tool (online, paper…)?" fourteen students responded that they did not know how to find images using a tool that was different from the one they used in class, while eleven responded that they knew how to use a variety of resources to find the same image. From their answers, it was clear that students relied heavily on the Internet to find visuals, although some looked at books on their topics and a few relied on the "flipping the pages" method. It was encouraging to see that some students knew how to find images using the databases that the library provides.

For question two, "Do you think it is necessary to cite images when used for a presentation (PowerPoint, poster…)?" five responded that it was not necessary to cite an image when it is used in a presentation, while fifteen responded "Yes," and five where not sure. It was a nice surprise that the majority of the students answered "Yes," as I was expecting a much lower number. Perhaps the variety of answers is because different instructors make students accountable regarding the resources they use (as student number 14 answered) and teach them how to cite images.[37]

Discussion

The results of this survey led me to think that perhaps students prefer to follow and use what they already know instead of assimilating new knowledge. For some reason, students are assuming that visuals and textual information should be treated differently. Students need to realize that, as Kalantzis, Cope and Harvey state, "The capabilities of literacy involve not only knowledge of grammatical conventions but also effective communication in diverse settings, and using tools of text design which may include word processing, desktop publishing and image manipulation."[38]

Do students understand how to find and use images? From this short survey and the literature, it appears that they do know how to find what they need.[39] They use a variety of tools, such as the Internet, online databases, books, magazines, and

TABLE 15.1
Responses to Survey

Student #	1. Do you know how to find the same image using another tool (online, paper...)?	2. Do you think it is necessary to cite images when used for a presentation (PowerPoint, poster...)?
1	No, I always search online.	No, because you never cite images.
2	No, I always use the Web.	No because it is a presentation, if it was for a paper then yes.
3	Mmm, I have to say no. I always use the Web because it is easier to find stuff.	No . . . Well, I am not sure.
4	No, I always search online.	No if they are online, but if they are from books, then you do.
5	No, I use the Web. I go to Google.	No because the images are up for only few seconds.
6	Yes, I know how to use the image option in Google.	Yes, you also need to write in the bibliography the Web site.
7	No, I use Yahoo.	Yes, because if you do not do it is plagiarism.
8	No, I use the Web.	Yes, just write the artist and title of the piece.
9	Yes, I use the databases for the arts.	Yes, you need to.
10	Yes, I look at the images with the online data-bases for art and usually I can find what I need.	Yes, The images have that information so you just copy and paste it on the paper.
11	I use ARTstor for most of my stuff.	Yes, the information is on the slide. It is easy.
12	No, I always use the same sources, online and clipart.	Yes, you need to.
13	No, I always use online.	Yes, but I am not sure if you do cite graphs or things like that.
14	No, I always use the Internet.	Yes, you need to or you get marked down.
15	Yes, I use books from the library.	Yes, but I tend to cite everything in my papers.
16	Yes, looking at books in the catalog and if there if the little word next to it – the il- I check it out and then look inside.	Yes, all the time.
17	Yes, I look at my textbook and then books.	Yes, but images are cited differently than in the paper. I mean, you cite them but it is like a shorter version.
18	I think there are some databases but usually I use the Web.	Yes, it is part of showing that you did your work.

TABLE 15.1, *CONT.*
Responses to Survey

Student #	1. Do you know how to find the same image using another tool (online, paper…)?	2. Do you think it is necessary to cite images when used for a presentation (PowerPoint, poster…)?
19	No, online is best because it is faster.	Yes.
20	Yes, flipping through magazine or looking at the New York Times.	Yes.
21	No, I usually search in Google Images.	I do not know.
22	Yes, looking for a book on my topic and then look for the images.	I know that for a paper you have to, but I am not sure for a presentation.
23	Yes, I need basic things, so I can use magazines or even newspapers. I just flip through the pages.	I think you have to but I am not sure.
24	Yes, I look at books on the topics for my projects and then I look at the back of the book where there is the list of images.	You do it in a different way, so I guess you need to.
25	No, I usually find what I want online.	Well, it depends from what you are trying to do. Like if you are using clipart you do not need to, but I am not sure if you need to when you use your own stuff.

newspapers, and in the process they also use a use a variety of methods such as "flipping pages" or looking for a description on the library catalog or at the back of the indexes. It also seems that they are able to use, with a degree of success, the images they find. Because they are able to retrieve what they look for, students may consider themselves as visually savvy. However, merely using technology to find images does not mean that a person is visually literate.[40]

Although not all library instruction sessions require the inclusion of visual literacy, students should be made aware of how visual literacy can impact their learning. When the library's mission promotes and supports information literacy, visual literacy can be explained as another form of information-seeking. James Marcum writes that our visual culture has drastically affected our relationship with the world, reducing the use of print media.[41] Therefore, edu-

cators and librarians need to redevelop their teaching methods to facilitate students' understanding of what is going on in our visual culture today. Most of all, students need to understand how images affect the way people communicate. The notion that students today prefer to communicate through visuals is not new because they have "low tolerance to boredom . . . [t]his is mirrored in how MTV throws 100 images each minute at their audiences—it is constantly changing and highly image-driven."[42]

The results of this simple qualitative investigation, conducted with twenty-five students, open the doors to more questions and further investigation. Some areas of research that would be worthwhile to consider are these:

- *What is the students' level of knowledge on the subject?* The answer to this question will help the librarian, especially a librarian who specializes in a subject, to determine if specific terminology should be used and if students will understand references to subject-specific sources. Students in an upper-level course will have a different understanding of the visual resources available than first-year students. In order to ascertain this information, it may be worth surveying students with the questions discussed above before the actual class. Having this information before the instruction session would help the librarian better focus the instruction.

- *What are two concepts that students need to know from the visual and information literacy components?* The limited time a librarian has during a library session, usually fifty minutes, requires focusing on what is really important for the students to learn. The connection between the two literacies needs to be demonstrated and practiced so the experience becomes meaningful to the students. A short instruction session may provide only the opportunity to help students consider the many methods to understand the type of image they are looking for and to actually find it. This situation parallels what often happens in short information literacy instruction sections. Students are assisted in describing their needs via keywords and then in finding online articles that match.

- *How does visual literacy enhance the overall goals of the course?* As mentioned before, not all of the library session needs to focus visual literacy concepts. To be effective, the visual literacy component should have a purpose within the coursework. There is a difference between formulating outcomes to assess learning and using visuals as a source of comparison to illustrate a point or to give background information. Therefore it is important for the librarian to understand the assignment before the class session. Contextualizing the instruction with their assignment not only

provides students with a higher level of motivation, but it also allows the librarian to focus on what students actually need.

- *How can I evaluate learning through visual literacy?* This is perhaps the most difficult task for librarians because the interaction between librarians and students is usually limited to one library session. Therefore, how is it possible to know how the visual literacy component has supported and facilitated learning in the classroom? To make this assessment, librarians need to be proactive and ask to attend presentations, read and see students' final products, and try to gather feedback from the faculty on how visual literacy was integrated in student learning.

Summary and Conclusion

As information evolves, literacy skills will need to adapt to these changes. Today, the use of visuals has expanded in ways that were perhaps unthinkable to us thirty years ago. Librarians are asked how to cite information from Flickr, how to find examples of the best uses of graphics in advertising, and how to find text fonts that cannot be found in Microsoft Word. As visual sources become more complex and predominant, teaching visual literacy should be the next evolving step of information literacy.

The concept of visual literacy has been prevalent since 1968, when Fransecky and Debes constructed the first definition.[43] It has been established that visual and information literacies have the common goals of developing critical-thinking skills. From that original definition, many others followed, each one reflecting the changes of time. During this time, scholars have always made a connection between visual literacy and media and information literacies, as is evident from the types of skills that qualify one as visually literate. The operational definition of visual literacy that I used in this chapter reflects the current needs of the students and faculty at my institution. This definition is not static but will change as resources and the needs of the patrons change in time. This fluid definition is a guide to help me determine what is important to assess in learning and how to go about teaching visual literacy.

It is evident that even though visual literacy tends to be subject-dependent, there are four common characteristics: how the information is presented, how images can be manipulated with technology, how knowledge of the principles of design affect the message in the image, and how social and personal experiences can influence understanding and communicating with images.

Students have the ability to find what they need according to what technology is available. Students' preference for online resources to find images makes sense: they can search, limit by keyword or image size, preview, and select what they need in one sitting. Long are gone the times of using indexes to find pictures in books or magazines only to end up with images that may be of poor quality or not what one wants. It does make sense for librarians to teach students how to finesse skills they already have. Teaching students how to successfully use the Web or online databases will be an ongoing quest since, as we well know, technology is constantly changing. However, students will also need to refine their visual skills. Learning how to cite visual information, how to use it ethically, and how to interpret its subtle messages are essential skills to have. This task cannot be done by librarians alone, but must be done in collaboration with faculty.

As time goes on, librarians will find themselves more involved with visual literacy and will need to find ways to teach their students how to understand images in order to develop critical-thinking skills, not only with text, but also with images. Because of the many similarities, it makes sense that librarians modify the ACRL *Information Literacy Competency Standards* to assess students' level of knowledge about visual information. Using qualitative methods, librarians can develop questions that will help them to better understand how visual literacy can fit within their role as educators of *all* forms of information. Students and faculty need to be shown that the two literacies are related to each other and, as such, should be taught and learned together. Education strives to develop analytical facility by pushing students to make connections among disciplines, this symbiosis also needs to appear between visual and information literacy. When text and images are used together, a synergy of learning is created.

Notes

1. Marylin Adams, *Learning to Read: Thinking and Learning about Print* (Cambridge, MA: MIT Press, 1990); Maureen Crago and Hugh Crago, *Prelude to Literacy: A Preschool Child's Encounter with Picture and Story* (Carbondale: Southern Illinois University Press, 1983); Lee Galda and Kathy Lee, "Visual Literacy: Exploring Art and Illustration in Children's Books," *Reading Teacher* 46, no. 6 (1993): 506–16; Barbara Kiefer, *The Potential of Picturebooks: From Visual Literacy to Aesthetic Understanding* (Englewood Cliffs, NJ: Merrill, 1995).

2. Allan Paivio, *Imagery and Verbal Processes* (New York: Holt, Rinehart and Winston, 1971); Russell Carney and Joel Levin, "Pictorial Illustrations Still Improve Student's Learning from Text," *Educational Psychology Review* 14, no. 1 (2002): 5–26.

3. Elin Keene and Susan Zimmerman, *Mosaic of Thought: Teaching Comprehension in a Reader's Workshop* (Portsmouth, NH: Heinemann, 1997), 129.

4. Benjamin Harris, "Visual Information Literacy via Visual Means: Three Heuristics," *Reference Services Review* 34, no. 2 (2006): 218.

5. American Library Association, Association of College and Research Libraries (ACRL) *Information Literacy Competency Standards for Higher Education* (Chicago: ACRL, 2000), http://www.ala.org/ala/mgrps/divs/acrl/standards/informationliteracycompetency.cfm.

6. At Hunter Library, imbedded librarians are defined as providing more than one information literacy session for the same course in the same semester. Imbedded librarians collaborate with faculty to determine where the library session will be most appropriate and closely assist faculty and students in their teaching and learning.

7. Paul Messaris, "Visual Culture," in *Culture in the Communication Age,* ed. James Lull (New York: Rutledge, 2001), 180.

8. John Berger, *Ways of Seeing* (New York: Viking Press, 1975), 9.

9. Pierre Bourdieu, *The Field of Cultural Production* (Cambridge: Polity, 1993), 215.

10. Donis A. Donis, *A Primer of Visual Literacy* (Cambridge, MA: MIT Press, 1973); Paul Lester, *Visual Communication: Images with a Message* (Belmont, CA: Wadsworth Publishing, 2000); Paul Messaris, *Visual "Literacy": Image, Mind, and Reality* (Boulder, CO: Westview Press, 1994).

11. P. Wend, "The Language of Pictures," in *The Use and Misuse of Language,* ed. S. I. Hayakawa, 175–86 (New York: Premier Books, 1943).

12. Kerry Freedman and Fernando Hernandez, eds., *Curriculum, Culture and Art Education: Contemporary Perspectives* (New York: State University of New York Press, 1998), 183.

13. Paul Duncum, "Editorial: A Special Issue on Visual Culture," *Visual Arts Research* 28, no. 2 (2002): 1–3.

14. Rudolf Arnheim, *Visual Thinking* (Berkeley: University of California Press, 1969), 18.

15. Paivio, *Imagery and Verbal Processes*; Rune Pettersson, *Visual Information* (Englewood Cliffs, NJ: Educational Technology, 1993); Messaris, *Visual "Literacy."*

16. Jon Callow, "Images, Politics and Multiliteracies: Using a Visual Metalanguage," *Australian Journal of Language & Literacy* 29, no. 1 (2006): 7–23; Bryan Alexander, "Web 2.0 and Emergent Multiliteracies," *Theory unto Practice* 47, no. 2 (2008): 150–60.

17. Kerry Freedman, "Interpreting Gender and Visual Culture in Art Classrooms," *Studies in Art Education* 35, no. 3 (1994): 157–70.

18. International Visual Literacy Association, http://www.ivla.org.

19. Richard Sinatra, *Visual Literacy Connections to Thinking, Reading and Writing* (Springfield, IL: Charles C. Thomas, 1986); Martin Dworkin, "Towards an Image Curriculum: Some Questions and Cautions," in *Proceeding of the First National Conference on Visual Literacy,* ed. C. Williams and J. Debes (New York: Pittman Publishing, 1970), 28–35; Deborah Curtiss, *Introduction to Visual Literacy: A Guide to the Visual Arts and Communication* (Englewood Cliffs, NJ: Prentice-Hall, 1987); R. Braden and J. Hortin, "Identifying the Theoretical Foundations of Visual Literacy," *Journal of Visual/Verbal Languaging* 2, no. 2 (1982): 37–51; Ralph Wileman, *Visual Communicating* (Englewood Cliffs, NJ: Educational Technology, 1993).

20. Roger Fransecky and John Debes, *Visual Literacy: A Way to Learn—A Way to Teach* (Washington, DC: Association for Educational Communications and Technology, 1972), 7.

21. J. Brill, D. Kim and R. Branch, "Visual Literacy Defined: The Results of a Delphi Study—Can IVLA (Operationally) Define Visual Literacy?" in *Exploring the Visual Future: Art Design, Science and Technology,* ed. R. Griffen, V. Williams, and J. Lee (Blacksburg, VA: International Visual Literacy Association, 2001), 9.

22. B. A. Chauvin, "Visual or Medial Literacy?" *Journal of Visual Literacy* 23, no. 2 (2003): 119–28.

23. Michael Streibel, "Visual Literacy, Television Literacy, Computer Literacy: Some Parallels and a Synthesis," *Journal of Visual/Verbal Languaging* 5, no. 2 (1985): 5–14.

24. Jerry Christopherson, "The Growing Need for Visual Literacy at the University," in *VisionQuest: Journeys toward Visual Literacy. Selected Reading from the Annual Conference of the International Visual Literacy Association (28th, Cheyenne, Wyoming, October, 1996)* ed. Robert E. Griffin, J. Mark Hunter, Carole B. Schiffman, and William J. Gibbs (IVLA, 1997), 169–74; John Debes, "The Loom of Visual Literacy: An Overview," in *Proceeding of the First National Conference on Visual Literacy,* ed. C. Williams and J. Debes (New York: Pitman Publishing, 1970), 1–16.

25. ACRL, *Information Literacy Competency Standards.* Definition: "Information literacy is a set of abilities requiring individuals to recognize when information is needed and have the ability to locate, evaluate, and use effectively the needed information."

26. David Considine, "Media Literacy: National Developments and International Origins," *Journal of Popular Film & Television* 30, no. 1 (2002): 7–15; Sonia Livingstone, "Media Literacy and the Challenge of New Information and Communication Technologies," *Communication Review* 7, no. 1 (2004): 3–14.

27. Erik Forrest, "Art Education and the Language of Art," *Studies in Art Education* 26, no. 1 (1984): 27–33; Mia Johnson, "A Comparative Study of Terms Used in Art Education and Computer Graphics to Describe the Visual

Properties of Images," *Studies in Art Education* 37, no. 3 (1996): 184–92; Rachael De Sousa Vianna, "Art Education and Urban Aesthetics," *Leonardo* 35, no. 3 (2002): 255–61.

28. John Dewey, *How We Think* (Lexington, MA: D.C. Heath, 1933); David Mosley, Vivienne Baumfield, Julian Elliott, Maggie Gregson, Steven Higgins, Jennifer Miller, and Douglas Newton, *Frameworks for Thinking: A Handbook for Teaching and Learning* (New York: Cambridge University Press, 2006); Robert J. Sternberg, *Thinking Styles* (New York: Cambridge University Press, 1997).

29. Maria Avgerinou, "Re-viewing Visual Literacy in the 'Bain d' Images' Era," *TechTrends: Linking Research and Practice to Improve Learning* 53, no. 2 (March 1, 2009): 28–34; Jon Callow, "Show Me: Principles for Assessing Students' Visual Literacy," *Reading Teacher* 61, no. 8 (May 1, 2008): 616–26; Harris, "Visual Information Literacy," 213–21.

30. Stacy Ulbig, "Engaging the Unengaged: Using Visual Images to Enhance Students' 'Poli Sci 101' Experience," *PS: Political Science and Politics* 42, no. 2 (April 1, 2009): 385–91; Jane Charlton, "'Behind the Lines and Lines and Lines': Student Studio Solutions to Projects That Facilitate the Exploration of Visual and Textual Languages within Fine Arts Practice," *Journal of Writing in Creative Practice* 1, no. 3 (Nov. 2008): 237–59; T. Ariga and T. Watanabe, "Teaching Materials to Enhance the Visual Expression of Web Pages for Students Not in Art or Design Majors," *Computers & Education* 51, no. 2 (Sept. 1, 2008): 815–28; Susan E. Metros, "The Educator's Role in Preparing Visually Literate Learners," *Theory into Practice* 47, no. 2 (April 1, 2008): 102–9; Kate Rawlinson, Susan Nelson Wood, and Mark Osterman, "Thinking Critically about Social Issues through Visual Material," *Journal of Museum Education* 32, no. 2 (June 1, 2007): 155–74; Callow, "Show Me"; Natalie Selden Barnes, "Hands-on Writing: An Alternative Approach to Understanding Art," *Art Education* 62, no. 3 (May 1, 2009): 40–46.

31. Catherine Marshall and Gretchen Rossman, *Designing Qualitative Research* (Thousand Oaks, CA: Sage, 1999), 194.

32. John Creswell, *Research Design: Qualitative, Quantitative and Mixed Methods Approaches*, 2nd ed. (Thousand Oaks, CA: Sage, 2003).

33. Gary Gorman and Peter Clayton, *Qualitative Research for the Information Professional*, 2nd ed. (London: Facet Publishing, 2005), 5.

34. Philipp Mayring, "Qualitative Content Analysis," *Forum: Qualitative Social Research* 1, no. 2 (2000), http://www.qualitative-research.net/index.php/fqs/article/view/1089/2385; Michael Quinn Patton, *Qualitative Research & Evaluation Methods* (Thousand Oaks, CA: Sage, 2002); James Mahoney and Dietrich Rueschemeyer, eds., *Comparative Historical Analysis in the Social Sciences* (New York: Cambridge University Press, 2003).

35. Sharan Merriam, *Qualitative Research and Case Study Applications in Education* (San Francisco: Jossey-Bass, 1998); Marylin Dosam White and Emily E. Marsh, "Content Analysis: A Flexible Methodology," *Library Trends* 55, no. 1 (2006): 22–45.

36. Steinar Kvale, *InterViews: An Introduction to Qualitative Research Interviewing* (Thousand Oaks, CA: Sage, 1996).

37. Stephanie Huffman, "The Missing Link: The Lack of Citations and Copyright Notices in Multimedia Presentations," *TechTrends: Linking Research and Practice to Improve Learning* 54, no. 3 (May 1, 2010): 38–44.

38. Mary Kalantzis, Bill Cope, and Andrew Harvey, "Assessing Multiliteracies and the New Basics," *Assessment in Education: Principles, Policy & Practice* 10, no. 1 (2003): 15.

39. Jacqueline Diane Coursol Lewis and Lutfa Khan, "College students@tech.edu: A Study of Comfort and the Use of Technology," *Journal of College Student Development* 42, no. 6 (Nov/Dec 2001): 625–31; Steve Jones, Sarah Millermaier, and Francisco Seoane Pérez, "U.S. College Students' Internet Use: Race, Gender and Digital Divides," *Journal of Computer-mediated Communication* 14, no. 2 (Jan. 2009): 244–64.

40. Barbara R. Jones-Kavalier and Suzanne L. Flannigan, "Connecting the Digital Dots: Literacy of the 21st Century," *EDUCAUSE Quarterly* 29, no. 2 (2006): 8–10; Reynol Junco and Gail A. Cole-Avent, "An Introduction to Technologies Commonly Used by College Students," *New Directions for Student Services*, no. 124 (Winter 2008): 3–17.

41. James Marcum, "Beyond Visual Culture: The Challenge of Visual Ecology," *portal: Libraries and the Academy* 2, no. 2 (2002): 189–206.

42. Carol Goman, "Communicating for a New Age," *Strategic Communication Management* 10, no. 5 (2006): 8.

43. Fransecky and Debes, *Visual Literacy*.

Collective Action: Qualitative Methods for Library Collection Development

LeRoy Jason LaFleur

Abstract. Collection development is a holistic practice that involves the selection of library materials as well as the building, management, and organization of library collections. Both qualitative and quantitative research methods play a significant role in this process by allowing librarians to assess the utility and value of library collections. This chapter highlights areas of collection development practice that readily lend themselves to the application of qualitative research methods and reviews the use of such methods in the development and assessment of library collections. The author provides a general introduction to the topic of collection development, a review of historical and contemporary issues involved in the management of library collections, and a discussion of the benefits and practical applications of qualitative methods to collection development practice. In doing so, the use of qualitative research methods puts a key emphasis on the importance of user needs and involvement in the collection development process.

Introduction

As a librarian charged with identifying and purchasing materials in support of a number of academic departments, I am regularly faced with the challenge of selecting materials that best meet the needs of the library patrons I serve. The fact that I have been doing this job for some time can be considered either a help or a hindrance. That is to say that one's perceived understanding or expertise in knowing the needs of any given department or group of individuals may in fact color one's ability to openly listen to the needs of those groups. Librarians as selectors and bibliographers must monitor these needs closely because research and reading interests are constantly changing.

Librarians experienced with the practice of collection development gain familiarity both with collections and with the primary user groups over time. They develop a level of knowledge regarding reading and research trends in a given discipline or topical area or among select populations. They use this information to predict and anticipate the needs of users and to recommend or suggest new directions of inquiry through their material selection decisions. "Collection Development is sometimes called both an art and a science. It combines creativity with empirical knowledge," states author Peggy Johnson in *Fundamentals of Collection Development and Management*.[1] The artistic elements come from the ability of librarians to use their judgment and understanding of readers and resources to identify needs before they are needed and uses before they are useful. The scientific aspects emanate from the different modes of inquiry, qualitative and quantitative, that libraries and librarians employ to better analyze their collections and user communities.

Both qualitative and quantitative approaches have quite a bit to offer library selectors who are hoping to gain a better understanding of the needs of their users and the use of their library's collection. Indeed, there are many times when the two approaches should most effectively be used in tandem. This chapter will focus primarily on the application of qualitative methods for assessing library collections, using real-world examples of challenges we face at my library. I will begin by reviewing some background concepts related to collection development practice and highlight some specific uses of qualitative research methods for managing library collections.

Collection Development in Theory and Practice

Authors Curley and Broderick make the claim that "there is no task in librarianship that requires more time, effort, and intelligence than sound collection development."[2] The practice of collection development has many different forms and organizational configurations depending on the institutions themselves. In some libraries, this work is done primarily by bibliographers or librarians dedicated to selecting materials by disciplines or formats or for distinctive populations of users. In others it is not done by librarians at all, but instead by selected stakeholders outside of the library. Increasingly this work is done by professional librarians who are also responsible for other areas of library outreach, including reference and instruction work.

As a field of practice, collection development is a holistic process by which libraries identify and select materials for inclusion based on a number of predetermined criteria. Over the past few decades, the collection development role has grown to encompass any number of decision-making responsibilities that involve the long-term maintenance and support of

library collections. While book selection or *collection building* is perhaps the act most often associated with collection development, this aspect is but one of the processes that make up this function. "Collection development was understood to cover several activities related to the development of library collections, including selection, the determination and coordination of selection policy, assessment of the needs of users and potential users, collection use studies, collection analysis, budget management, identification of collection needs, community and user outreach and liaison, and planning for resource sharing," states Johnson in her review of the evolution of the field.[3] Other areas sometimes found under the collection development rubric are archiving and preservation, weeding and deselection initiatives, digitization and format conversion, physical collection shifts, and policy development.

Increasingly paired with or substituted for the term *collection management*, library collection development work spans the life cycle of materials in the library collection. Collection development librarians are responsible for managing funds and budgets and evaluating materials both before and after they become part of the library collection. Through the selection process, these librarians identify appropriate materials for inclusion in the collection and later make recommendations for off-site storage and withdrawal of materials. Once the materials are on site, collection development librarians monitor the needs of collection users (patrons) and use patterns of materials in the collection. They also establish and maintain a variety of policy and procedural documents that detail and govern many of these elements. In this regard, collection development librarians must heighten their understanding of how the collection is used and functions as well as their ability to answer questions regarding which materials do and do not circulate and whether select items should be moved to off-site storage or weeded from the collection altogether.

Lastly, the work of collection development then rests squarely at the intersection of library collections and their users. In the user-centered library, users are what should drive acquisitions and the provision of access to library materials. Selectors are buying and acquiring material for both current and future users, which means that they also need to be able to anticipate trends and research interests as and before they develop. For this aspect of their work, collection development practitioners need to be both very aware of and very in touch with the user populations they serve. "Collection development and management in all types of libraries requires close contact with users, and this may be reflected in the assignment of selection responsibilities."[4]

Qualitative Methods for Collection Development

Collection development work requires much decision making, and within the world of libraries, decision making often requires or warrants much data. It is common for library selectors to seek refuge in numbers, circulations statistics, and volume counts in order to better make sense of the work they are doing and the nature of the collections they are building. There are other ways, however, for librarians to gain insight into the use of collections and the needs of collection users. Beyond more traditional forms of statistical analysis, qualitative methods of inquiry offer librarians an opportunity to put library use and users in context.

The choice between qualitative and quantitative methods will often depend on the needs of the library and the kind of information one is trying to achieve. While the use of quantitative methods in collection development is far more prevalent, qualitative methods often provide a greater level of insight than other approaches. On many occasions the two methods of inquiry are used in conjunction, as qualitative approaches rely heavily on perceptions and contextual association, which can be a useful for further exploring and explaining some of the phenomenon discovered through quantitative analysis.

The *Encyclopedia of Social Measurement* states that "qualitative research methods include any techniques, except those focused primarily on counting, measuring, and analyzing statistical data, to study any social phenomenon.[5] Gorman and Clayton offer a longer, more specific definition, indicating that "qualitative research is a process of enquiry that draws data from the context in which events occur, in an attempt to describe these occurrences, as a means of determining the process in which events are embedded and the perspectives of those participating in the events, using induction to derive possible explanations based on observed phenomena."[6] These definitions illustrate that there are seemingly a number of different ways that qualitative methods can be interpreted and defined, which also leaves room for creativity and experimentation.

Quantitative methods are generally considered to be useful for collecting and analyzing numeric data on a given topic or issue and tend to use numerical representations for subjects rather than the subjects themselves. These approaches are often useful for tracking trends, counting numbers of items and transactions, and finding frequencies. Qualitative methods, however, can be useful for exploratory research—to learn or understand more about something, or simply to make determinations on things or in ways that are not easily quantifiable. Qualitative methods inherently attempt to get at a *quality* of service or material in a way that requires the researcher to be directly involved with the items, individuals, or issue in question.

For collection development, quantifiable measures like circulation or reshelving statistics can be useful for ascertaining how often materials are being checked out or pulled off of the shelves. Qualitative techniques, however, like interviews and focus groups, will help librarians to better understand what it is users are doing and hoping to do with library materials in a way that other methods may not.

In practice there are three primary areas in which qualitative approaches tend to be used for collection development work. The first is to assess the quality of a library collection, the second is to ascertain the needs and interests of a user population, and the third is to gain broader insight on collection development processes and procedures.

Library Collection Assessments

Librarians perform collection development functions in a variety of different ways. Selectors use book reviews, publisher catalogs, and vendor approval plans as traditional ways of identifying newly or recently published materials. Another common means of identifying new and needed materials is recommendations from patrons for things they would either like to use or feel that the library should have.

Librarians who want to gain greater insight into the use of library collections regularly perform what is known as a *collection analysis*. These evaluations are conducted in order to gain a greater understanding of how the collection is functioning, by analyzing its contents and use. As far back as 1982, Futas stated, "There are two types of collection evaluations that are currently being done across the nation: quantitative and qualitative. The more common one is the qualitative analysis."[7] Today, quantitative approaches are commonly employed as part of this process, specifically for collection-focused data on the size, breadth, and growth of library collections. Qualitative approaches, however, can be valuable for the user-focused elements of this process, examining who is using the material, and how well they are being served by it. As Johnson so aptly writes:

> The goal of qualitative analysis is to determine collection strengths, weakness and non-strengths (which reflect conscious decisions not to collect). Qualitative analysis depends on the opinion of selectors and external experts and the perceptions of users. Even when collections are checked against external lists these lists are themselves the result of informed opinion about what constitutes a good collection or what characterizes a collection designated at a specific collecting level or appropriate for a specific user group.[8]

In the late 1980s the Research Library Group (RLG) Conspectus project was a large-scale initiative to conduct a qualitative analysis of numerous research library collections. In addition to quantitative methods (shelf list measurements, circulation counts, etc.) previously employed as the root of analysis projects, the conspectus methodology relied on librarians' ability, knowledge, and understanding of their collections in order to identify strengths and weaknesses.[9] The process allowed librarians to assign collecting levels for subject areas in their respective collections. The method also allowed libraries to identify and evaluate past collecting effort and to comparatively benchmark their collections with others institutions.

Aguilar highlights a number of qualitative and quantitative techniques for assessing collections, with the added mention of the more subjective nature of qualitative methods.[10] His review of the literature references two specific methods of qualitative collection evaluation: impressionistic and list checking. The impressionistic method relies on the expertise of a given librarian in order to evaluate the quality of a collection. In addition to its highly subjective nature, this method may be time-consuming, requiring expert evaluators, and costly, "particularly if the evaluators are brought into the institution for the occasion."[11] The list-checking method employs the use of catalogs, bibliographies, or other specialized listings of *quality* collection materials as a benchmarking tool. Two particular concerns arising from the use of this approach are that such lists are rarely comprehensive and that they have a relatively short life span as new materials of value continue to be produced.

Lastly, the development of collection development policies is another key way in which librarians are able to employ aspects of qualitative research. These documents detail what a given library collects and why, in a way that both provides guidelines for prospective library selectors and explanations for non-librarians hoping to better understand the decision-making process with regard to library collections. The creation of a good collection policy requires understanding the current state of the collection, but often includes information regarding its history, scope, and intended audiences. A key step in developing such policies involves meeting with a stakeholder from the user population to collect feedback and to verify that the library is on target as it grows the collection. This meeting often takes the form of an interview, in which the librarian poses a series of questions to a faculty or board member regarding areas of library collections or desired areas of focus. Afterwards this data can be analyzed and incorporated into the final document.

User Needs Assessments

In the user-centered library, users (patrons, faculty, students, clients, etc.) play a significant role in determining what goes into the library collection. There are a number of qualitative methods that librarians can use to collect input from library patrons that can be useful for understanding the context of their interactions and use. Common qualitative techniques include focus groups, observations, and interviews with particular user groups and stakeholders. Johnson provides additional insight on pursuing this approach:

> When selectors gather and analyze primary data through observation, interview, and surveys, they seek specific answers that help guide collection development. Questions may address why an individual does or does not use a library resource, if a resource is easy to use or not, what the individual needed or wanted and was unable to obtain, how long he or she is willing to wait for the resource, and preference for formats.[12]

Focus groups are coordinated sessions in which a researcher or librarian convenes a discussion session with a selection of library patrons and users. The librarian facilitates a discussion among the participants on topics related to a specific area of inquiry. The conversation is guided in a way that should generate open feedback and responses from the participants about their resource needs, how and why they use the library collection, and their perceptions about its utility and quality. Notes and other data generated from the session are generally analyzed afterwards in order to identify themes and directions for action and improvement. Often themes that emerge from focus groups may be further explored through the use of a survey.

Observations can be used by librarians/researchers to collect data on how individual users satisfy information needs in a variety of different ways. For collection development, this process can be useful for gaining an understanding of how library patrons identify and make decisions about what materials in the collection to use. Often these types of observations are prearranged in the sense that the researcher assigns a task for the user to engage in

and then observes the user in action for some duration of time. Collection development librarians may observe which print or electronic resources a patron uses first or what kind of keywords a patron selects to search the library catalog. Regardless of the specific topic or issue, the process of observation can be particularly informative by providing a window into the actions and decision-making patterns of library users.

Interviews are another technique commonly used by those seeking a qualitative approach to gathering data. The use of focused interviews with members of the library user community is another means of gaining insight into the wants and needs of these individuals in order to better understand the strengths and weaknesses of the library collection. Interviews are commonly used as part of the process of developing collection development policies. Many collection development policies contain a narrative portion that describes the library collection and its use by the primary user populations. This data, collected through interviews with patrons and other library stakeholders, can be used to generate the narratives and to verify that current collecting strategies are on target for the needs of library users.

Assessing Collection Development

The practice of collection development itself has not escaped the purview of researchers seeking to understand the variety of mitigating factors that play a role in how library collections evolve. Qualitative methods of inquiry provide a good tool for doing this task, and a number of research studies attempt to explore this arena. Lee examines the ways in which the process of library selection is influenced by factors both within and outside of the library itself. Lee's study, in particular, looks at the "collection development process and analyzes the personal viewpoints and actions, in an institutional context, that can dominate and guide institution discourse with regard to the development of collection."[13]

As part of the research Lee used a historical case study method focused on collection development for women's studies in a university setting.[14] The study relied on archival records, grey literature documentation, and personal interviews to identify and understand the social elements (personal and institutional) that impact the process of collecting library materials, specifically in the field of women's studies. Lee interviewed twenty university administrators, librarians, and faculty about their involvement in this specific field. The majority of these interviews were conducted in person and recorded for later transcription and analysis. She also considered using observation as a method in the study but deemed it impractical due to the longitudinal nature of her research. The results of her study presented collection development as a social process that involves numerous interactions between different parties. In discussing her choice of methods, Lee highlighted that one of the benefits of using archival records in this study was the availability of many materials on the topic and the permanence of these documents. Interviews allowed her to collect new data to supplement those found in the archival records. While Lee stated that her research was not intended to be generalized, there are perhaps common elements from this study that could be used for other fields and by other collection development librarians.

In a similar vein, Chu's research relied on interviews conducted with librarians and instructional faculty in an academic setting.[15] Like Lee,[16] Chu also began his study by reviewing archival documents and other related materials prior to the interviews in order to develop an appropriate set of questions. The data Chu collected from the focused interviews were later analyzed and used as the basis for the theories he set out to further explore.

Chu's work examined the relationship between academic faculty and librarians and the role that each plays as part of the collection development process.[17] His study highlighted a great deal of ambiguity regarding the involvement of faculty and the language used to describe their expected participation in library collection development. Collection development is ultimately a collaborative process, which relies on a series of communications between librarians and teaching faculty, and between faculty and their departmental colleagues. Chu used interviews as a qualitative method in order to better understand the perspectives of those involved in collection development work and to reveal a number of difficulties related to communication and feedback.

Case and Context at George Mason University's Arlington Campus Library

My current institution is a multicampus university, with libraries located on three separate campuses. The library in which I work is situated on a campus that largely provides services for students in graduate-level professional master's degree programs. While these programs range in subject and discipline, almost all of them focus on training practitioners in applied social science fields, including education, public policy, and the management of business, government, and nonprofit organizations. Clear among our priorities is the importance of meeting the needs of the academic units and departments that teach courses on our campus. From the collection development perspective, however, there are a number of challenges we face in meeting this objective.

George Mason University Libraries employ a liaison-based structure in order to best meet the needs of its academic constituents. Along these lines, each department has a dedicated librarian who works closely with faculty and students on matters related to research and collection development. Each library is staffed with librarians who are matched to the different academic programs it serves. However, when academic programs move between campuses, this issue must be addressed by hiring new liaisons or redistributing the disciplinary or program-based responsibilities of a given liaison. My library has three liaison librarians, each focused on the needs of our primary campus departments: Public Policy, Conflict Resolution, Nonprofit Management, Business, Education, and Social Work. In recent semesters, however, the library staff has noted an increasing number of Arts Management classes being taught on campus. The master of arts management program focuses on training students to take on leadership and administrative roles in arts-related agencies, including galleries and the-aters. While this program and its respective liaison librarian are headquartered on a different campus, the department has begun to offer several classes on my campus each semester, and we are increasingly seeing more of their students at the reference desk.

Our current collection, specifically tailored to meet the needs of our regular departments, does not really support arts-related research. While there are some clear areas of overlap between the needs of this group and the nonprofit and business management programs we already support, some likely resources are not being included as part of our regular col-lection development efforts. A number of questions may immediately come to mind. Is this a group that would like to find resources on our campus, or are students content with using resources on other cam-puses? What sorts of materials are most needed for arts management? Are there specific arts subject materials that are important for their research, or are standard business and management publications adequate? Is there a need for specific reference resources, books, and other print resources to be housed on our campus, or do they more heavily rely on journal articles that can be accessed electroni-cally? Is there a general preference for print or elec-tronic materials? As a library selector, it is helpful for me to know if our library collection can meet the needs of these students.

Qualitative methods provide a number of options for addressing this kind of issue. As a first step, I made a point of reviewing the library's holdings to see what our arts-related holdings were. I did this by conducting catalog searches and physically going through the library's reference collection and cir-culating stacks areas in related call number ranges (N: Arts). Based on the results of those reviews, I was able to generate a list of not only what we had in our campus collection, but also what com-parable materials were housed in the collection on our main campus. Using a modified version of this strategy, I also searched our regional consortium catalog to see what titles might be available to us that way. I was curious to learn a bit more about the broader universe of publications in the field, so I conducted a variety of database and Web searches

to look for articles and other documents related to the field. Additionally, I searched the Web sites of both Amazon and Barnes and Noble for new titles in the area of arts management in addition to look-ing for bibliographies on the topic. Through these approaches I found a number of available titles that we did not have either in the library system or on my campus. From this list, I then I was able to identify and select a small core collection of arts manage-ment and arts-related titles to add to the collection.

In the aforementioned process, I opted to use a more qualitative approach to information gather-ing that relied on my knowledge of literature research methods in order to collect data in the form of subject-appropriate resources. While this approach proved to be both adequate and useful in this situa-tion, there are a variety of other qualitative methods that I also could have employed. One option would have been to contact the department administra-tors and set up a meeting to discuss the program and their collection needs. Through this approach I could have conducted interviews with the adminis-trators and faculty members who teach the courses to discuss their research and teaching needs as related to the collection. I could have conducted focus groups with students in the program about their impressions of the existing library collections, recommendations, and perceived needs. I could also have conducted a survey of the members of the Graduate Arts Management Society student group in order to gather data on their interests and preferences. Looking toward the future, some of these possible approaches would be excellent project ideas for us to explore and develop in conjunction with the Art & Visual Technology Liaison Librarian on our main campus.

Another collection-related challenge is decid-ing when to add additional copies of titles that are owned in one of our other library locations. The university libraries have traditionally considered themselves to be building one library collection geo-graphically distributed among different campuses. The result is that we are generally encouraged not to duplicate titles held at other campus libraries unless absolutely necessary. To facilitate this policy, the university libraries have put into place a robust system for delivering books and other documents between campus locations. Nonetheless, there are times when it makes sense to have permanent copies of certain materials at multiple locations. There are a number of interdisciplinary programs at the university, many of which require and recommend the same texts to their students. Additionally there are some key interdisciplinary materials that have a clear place in the different subject-related collections we are attempting to build on different campuses. A quantitative approach might suggest a review of circulation statistics in order to identify the items that are most frequently browsed or checked out as a determining factor for duplication. That would be an entirely appropriate approach; however, qualitative methods can provide another means of making such decisions.

One technique I use is to conduct periodic reviews of our document delivery hold shelves in order to survey the items that have arrived through the myriad of delivery services we offer. For this process I set aside time to review the document delivery holdings shelf by shelf, making note of newer titles and those that I do not recognize as being part of my library's collection. Once I have a list of titles, I search them in my library's OPAC in order to determine whether they are owned by my library or elsewhere within the library system. Many of these items turn out to be books that are already owned at my location but happen to have been checked out at the time of the request. Occasionally, however, I am unable to identify unique titles that we do not have either in the collection at Mason or among our consortial partners. For those items being borrowed from other campus libraries but not owned by my location, I am generally able to use my knowledge of the existing library collection, campus research interests, and departmental synergies to make a determination as to when it would be useful to add an additional copy at my location.

A third challenge we encounter at my library is keeping abreast of materials being recommended to students by faculty. Despite our proactive efforts of establishing vendor approval plans and searching publisher catalogs, we often discover the existence of these titles when students arrive at the library ask-

ing for them. In order to address this issue, I have found that reviewing faculty syllabi in advance of the semester can be a useful mechanism for identifying new material that will soon be in demand. A few of our departments attempt to make all course syllabi available on their Web sites. While the university libraries do not systematically purchase all course-related texts, many of these materials do in fact make excellent additions to the collection. Furthermore, having these items listed in the catalog, ensures that even if these texts are not available for checkout, library staff can verify citation information and refer patrons to the appropriate locations for borrowing. A periodic review of course syllabi, then, is not only an excellent way to enhance the library collection, but also a useful way to gain a greater connection with what faculty are teaching and expecting students to learn in the classroom. Procedurally, once I have access to a given syllabus, I read through the document in order to identify the recommended and required readings for the course. Then I will search each of these titles in the catalog to see if they are held within the university library system. If it turns out that the title is at a different campus location, as discussed above, I determine whether the title is worth duplicating. If the title is not owned by the libraries at all, then I need to decide whether it would make a useful addition to the collection based on subject scope of the work, my knowledge of student and faculty research, and the nature of the collection itself.

Taken together, these examples represent some of the more subtle and simple ways that qualitative techniques can be employed in support of library collection development efforts. While there are a number of different ways any of these challenges could be addressed, each of them can be used to illustrate the ways in which we regularly use qualitative approaches to examine and inform our actions and decision making in libraries.

Critiques and Recommendations for Reflection and Action

While there are many obvious benefits to the use of qualitative approaches of inquiry in collection development, these methods tend to take a backseat to the more popular use of quantitative techniques. Quantitative methods continue to account for the most commonly used approaches in collection development research, in part due to the kinds of quantifiable data they produce and popular support for the scientific paradigms that enable them. Additionally, the increasing sophistication of library management systems and database programs has made it a relatively simple endeavor to collect quantitative data and run statistics on different aspects of the collection, which makes those techniques all the more attractive. Relatedly, the use of qualitative methods for collection development can require additional efforts, planning, and resources on the part of the librarian and library. Librarians planning to utilize qualitative methods for collection development research should determine which qualitative approaches work best for their needs. It is also realistic to consider using multiple approaches, both quantitative and qualitative, as part of a larger study.

General critiques of qualitative methods include suggestions that the results of these techniques are too subjective, not scientific enough, and possibly less accurate than their quantitative counterparts. In reality, however, qualitative methods are equally scientific, and concerns regarding subjectivity and accuracy in any study, whether qualitative or quantitative, largely fall to the role of the researcher. As in any area of social scientific research, librarian-researchers need to be both aware and cautious of the influence they bring to the research project. Each researcher has his or her own perspectives and biases that impact the way the research is conducted and the expected outcomes. If not accounted for, these elements can have a notable and negative effect on the quality of the research. With regard to collection development research, the perspectives and biases of the library selector, too, can have an unwanted influence on selection patterns and decisions. Johnson referenced this concept with her statement that "the new selector working with mental models of how to develop and manage a collection must attempt to identify the assumptions he or she is making and the skills and competencies that guide them."[18] Evans and Saponaro added to this idea, remarking that

"a periodic review of the selector's personal biases and their effects on the selection process is the best check against developing a collection that reflects personal interests rather than user interests."[19]

Moreover, the breadth of definitions as to what constitutes as qualitative research could potentially be problematic for those seeking to better grasp some of these ideas. While focus groups, observations, and interviews are more universally accepted in this regard, techniques such as list checking (reviewing bibliographies and core collection lists), open-ended questions on surveys, and content-based analyses of historical documents are commonly considered qualitative approaches as well.

Conclusion

As previously discussed, qualitative methods allow the librarian-researcher to explore the more contextual aspects of service that can provide new ways of understanding his or her work. Beyond the basic collection of statistics and circulation data, the use of qualitative research methods can help librarians to gain a greater level of understanding about the value of library collections to patrons and contribute to the overall decision-making process.

Technological developments and the growing emphasis on virtual collections are one area that will continue to have an influence on collection development work, with particular reference to the selection and evaluation of electronic resources. As more electronic resources are added to the library collection, librarians will increasingly need to consider new ways of evaluating the utility of these materials. Use statistics including site visits, page views, and other collected data can go a long way toward answering these questions but may overlook the viewpoints of users. Furthermore, as libraries continue to add to the number of electronic databases, books, journals, and reference resources in the collection, how we make decisions about the relocation and deaccessioning of print materials is another area that warrants attention. How will library users feel about decisions to cancel print journal subscriptions? Do certain user communities prefer print books to electronic texts? Should older reference resources be moved into the circulating stacks for future use or weeded from the collection all together? Again, numerical usage data drawn from library management systems and vendor websites may provide part of the picture. Librarians seeking feedback on their digital library initiatives, however, should also turn to traditional qualitative methods, which can be equally useful for assessing the value of both print and electronic resources.

Focus groups with select groups of users—faculty, students, community and board members—can be a good opportunity to hear from these audiences about specific issues related to electronic resources, access, and use. These sessions can be used to explain the library's position on a variety of collection-related matters before decisions are made so that patron perspectives can be properly taken into consideration. Likewise, other methods, such as field observations, can take on new relevance with reference to online materials. Librarians who are interested in understanding how patrons are using electronic resources can set up sessions in which library users are recruited to navigate a database, catalog, or library Web page while under observation. This method of field observation and any resulting notes can provide the librarian with important and otherwise difficult-to-obtain data on how users perceive and use the library's electronic resources. Librarians can then use this information in making determinations about the specifications for electronic resources that are purchased, subscribed to, or developed by the library.

Lastly, the concept of the *collection* has begun to shift as technology has become more interactive and integrated into the daily lives of users. The current conception of the library collection includes materials owned, borrowed, and subscribed to by the library. Patrons are able to build and customize their own personal collections by using combinations of materials from print and digital libraries, including resources they have created themselves, alongside those found on the World Wide Web. Portable media, increased storage capacity, and perpetual Internet access means that many patrons are more easily able to create, maintain, and update their own personal information libraries of files, documents, and media. They are able to share materials with one another in real time and without regard to physical or geographic boundaries. How librarians interact with these patrons and these collections will undoubtedly have an impact on the future of collection development work. At the conclusion of her 2000 article "What Is a Collection?" author Hur-Li Lee suggested that "to serve new generations of users, collections must reflect users' choices of information resources, whether printed materials or electronic documents, owned by one organization or distributed on separate computer servers that are thousands of miles apart."[20] How users perceive and make sense of these customized collections vis-à-vis the library collection continues to open up new avenues of exploration for the use qualitative research methods in collection development.

Notes

1. Peggy Johnson, *Fundamentals of Collection Development and Management*, 2nd ed. (Chicago: American Library Association, 2009), 45.
2. Arthur Curley and Dorothy M. Broderick, *Building Library Collections*, 6th ed. (Metuchen, NJ: Scarecrow Press, 1985), 10.
3. Johnson, *Fundamentals of Collection Development*, 2.
4. Ibid., 47.
5. Kevin G. Barnhurst, "Qualitative Analysis, Political Science," in *Encyclopedia of Social Measurement*, ed. Kimberly Kempf-Leonard (Oxford, UK: Elsevier Academic Press, 2005), 225.
6. G. E. Gorman and Peter Clayton, *Qualitative Research for the Information Professional: A Practical Handbook*, 2nd ed. (London: Facet, 2005), 3.

7. Elizabeth Futas, "Issues in Collection Development: Collection Evaluation," *Collection Building* 4, no. 1 (1982): 54.

8. Johnson, *Fundamentals of Collection Development*, 230.

9. Association of Research Libraries, *Qualitative Collection Analysis: The Conspectus Methodology*, SPEC Kit 151 (Washington, D.C: Association of Research Libraries, Office of Management Services, 1989).

10. William Aguilar, "The Application of Relative Use and Interlibrary Demand in Collection Development," *Collection Management* 8, no. 1 (1986): 15.

11. Ibid., 16.

12. Johnson, *Fundamentals of Collection Development*, 206.

13. Hur Li Lee, "Collection Development as a Social Process," *The Journal of Academic Librarianship* 29, no. 1 (Feb. 2003): 23.

14. Ibid.

15. Felix T. Chu, "Librarian-faculty Relations in Collection Development," *Journal of Academic Librarianship* 23, no. 1 (1997): 15–20.

16. Lee, "Collection Development."

17. Chu, "Librarian-faculty Relations."

18. Johnson, *Fundamentals of Collection Development*, 45.

19. G. Edward Evans and Margaret Zarnosky Saponaro, *Developing Library and Information Center Collections*, 5th ed. (Westport, CT: Libraries Unlimited, 2005), 16.

20. Hur-Li Lee, "What Is a Collection?" *Journal of the American Society for Information Science* 51, no. 12 (2000): 1112.

An Enduring Epistemology of Practice

David Carr

Librarians dwell easily in a culture of questions, though perhaps less easily when the questions are their own. Knowledge is our workplace, and the activities of knowing are the primary forces that flow through it. We are nearly always driven by the problems, inquiries, and tasks of others. We construct bridges with them and urge their inquiries toward completion. We invite them back for more. If we do our work well, we assist people toward entirely new inquiries and fresh ideas. We help them to find new possibilities in the unfinished cycles of striving that compose research. As we do this, our own unknowns—the unknowns of practice, conscience, and ethics—can become more distant, less compelling, and less formidable. As we serve the unfinished issues that move others forward, our own reflective moments are diminished, more removed, and less likely to drive our work. We often need reminding. In the deep practices of librarianship, we are most often driven by routines that mask the challenges and complexities of our tasks. Such routines also keep us from systematic inquiry about what happens in libraries and—perhaps more important—in the cognitive lives of professional librarians.

Our work is evident. We serve, at times, invisibly. Asked or unasked, a question is always the pulsing heartbeat of librarianship. As librarianship appears to me, however, it is our less visible actions and the hidden parts of our collections—our connective themes and resonant consistencies—that most

affect the excellence of librarianship and the experiences of scholarship we guide. Our internal rules of practice, rarely articulated, lead us in what we do. What assumptions drive the quality of practice? What heuristic do we use to review our performance? We know that nothing transformative happens in libraries without a need, an inquiry, or a question spoken, a gap needing to be filled, or an inchoate concept struggling to emerge. Our own needs, inquiries, questions, gaps, and unformed concepts abound: we carry these with us as we work, as we practice. What shapes our conversations and acts with users? How do the user's experiences lead to success, failure, indifferent silence, help—or self-rescue? What promise draws us every day, wherever we work, to live up to the acts we recognize as professional expertise?

Our places and our tools are well-known: they surround us, and we are their advocates every day. Our processes are less evident. We listen and diagnose. We analyze and consider the words of others. We consider what may be unspoken and what large themes are concealed in the question or the concept posed. We consider the depths and paths of our collection. We develop possible strategies; we recommend first steps. We know that there are ideas that cannot be articulated by the user, lacking words. We know that there are some processes we cannot describe, also beyond words. And this is where we are: the effects of our most important forms of service may be invisible, even to us. If you have come through this book, arriving here at the afterword with unabated hope for conclusive ideas about inquiry and the deep, gradual processes that give weight and dimension to particular kinds of knowledge, there is little to offer. (In fact, let's fold up that hope and file it with *the paperless society* and *the great information superhighway*.) One thing you may have seen in these pages is that (1) we are beyond definitive ideals. Another might be that (2) this is a good thing. As the helpful mall or airport map tells us, *you are here*, in a living situation, a fluid world, and an evolving relationship with knowledge and ignorance. The first insight a researcher might cultivate is an appreciation for the ambiguity and transience—the fluidity—in our work. This book prepares you for an immersion in the flow. Sidestroke works best for the long swim, kicking and gliding, head craning out of the water to see slow progress made against that sinking feeling. Kick. Glide. Kick. Glide. Research, if it will matter to the profession at all, is an artifact of long immersion and patient daily practice of the kick and glide.

Observations deepen the shallows of everyday experiences. We live in a flowing, floating world, rough with variables, accidents, shadows, and rocks. We look for patterns and signs, but the sunlight moves and the clear way disappears. We enter the flow again and again, as we must, thinking and acting amid impermanence as our work requires of us. It is an indicator of optimism and hope to ask questions about human behaviors and their implications for practice and service; it is positive and brave to assume that our inquiries and empirical experiences, if they are not pedestrian and reductive, will make a difference. What differences do we want to see in our libraries, in our communities of service, and our practices in the flowing, floating world? How might our experiences have meaning if we think of them as data, as eyewitness news? All experiences, as John Dewey wrote, move us forcefully when we are minding the details, attuned to their implications and lessons. But even the most forceful knowledge and experiences will not change our institutions or our communities, unless, as they

flow through our mindful place in the living world, our experiences change us. In this volume we see that part of our purpose as inquirers is to interrupt the flow and change the situation so that we might see something new, document its signs, evaluate their meanings for practice, and clarify new policies or approaches to our work.

The concept of flow is best understood through components identified by Mihalyi Csikszentmihalyi: in states of flow our experiences are immersive and concentrated, intensely focused on tasks and goals, so that our actions and knowledge become merged and, in a sense, we disappear into our experiences, as actors do. Immersive experiences are direct, optimally challenging (we feel we are capable, but not overwhelmed by the problem), and under our control. When we consider the situation of our work, we find that it flows with abundant strands: the experiences of other humans, the events and circumstances surrounding us beyond the library, the evolving collections of tools and resources at hand, the proliferation of technical devices, the flow of our community and its aspirations. The situation we dwell in is also our problem; progressive acts and responses follow from the lives we live, not only the skills we apply to our jobs. Were I to define "mind in practice"—meaning the totality of our consciousness as librarians—my definition would include our experiences, perspectives, and contexts; our language skills and our cognitive strengths; the actions we take and our ability to revise and reflect on them immediately; our ability to be reflective and communicative with others; and the constraints that limit all these things.

Mind in the practice of librarianship, as I understand it, is expansive, generative, exploratory, transparent, inductive and generally practical; it resists patterns; it is not reductive or simplistic, rarely conclusive, always open to revision or diversion; and it is deeply guided by unarticulated theories. Libraries embody theories of democracy, community, learning, literacy, and human development. Every professional act is informed by theory, carries the influence of every preceding act, and causes invisible changes in other lives. Library work depends on so many invisible factors, in fact, that it is difficult to consider them all. Here are just five variable elements that alter our ability to think like researchers as we act professionally:

- the local climate of value, assessment, and accountability
- the general capacity of leaders to think about policy and practice
- opportunities for reflective conversations with users and peers
- opportunities to document incidents, experiences, and variations in library use and service
- a situation conducive to experimentation and breaking through stasis

The most important among all of these variables is the least visible; we might call it *the motive to know more*. We keep a question strong and vital, constantly refining its unfinished elements, seeing it from alternative perspectives, and striving to document our experiences systematically (through field notes, interviews, reading, writing) whatever elusive evidence we can capture. The essays in this collection offer examples, models, successes, and even errors, which rigorously cultivate and sustain our unknowns.

Every question, of course, seeks a different kind of unknown, and it is useful to be clear about what it might be so that it is recognizable if it should appear before us. How unknowns differ, and how the difference matters, seems to be an elementary concept, but it is often given brief attention in the rush to gather data. We may simply seek to define something: who, what, when, where, how, how many, how much, how big, how frequent, how it looks, yes or no. We may want to find a cause, asking variations of "Why?" We may seek to describe a quality, a value, a relative worth, a purpose, a virtue—or its opposite. Or we are after something more complex: a relationship, comparison, condition, expectation, consequence, process, surprise, feeling, or response. Or we want to know what we should do, what would you do, what do you feel? As librarians know better than others, every question starts a process, every question leads somewhere—and sometimes to answers. What else do we know about questions?

- Questions express need, fear, prediction, anticipation, knowledge, misunderstanding, hope; they rarely indicate ignorance or emptiness.
- We respect a question when we recognize it as a bridge, understand the distance across, envision the engineering of that span, and disregard the height of the suspension.
- Some exploratory questions set the field for other questions. (Is it bigger than a breadbox?) Some are immediate. (Where's the fire?) Some are context-related. (Do you know how to swim?) We need to know when to ask what kind of question.
- A question is a sentence that expresses knowledge and its opposite simultaneously. Questions comprise language, values, assumptions, conditions, and unknowns. Each variable makes a difference to the question. We are able to ask only questions that we have the vocabulary to say.
- Good questions appear, disappear, reappear. The words may be the same, but the question is new because we have become different in its absence. Good questions stay near, hovering and spinning. A single question implies a constellation—or merely a small set—of other, necessary, related questions. What rare question can stand alone? What rare question does not require renewal and variation?
- The more we ask a question, the greater our awareness of what a useful response would mean. Then we feel challenged to live up to the question. We don't ask, "What's the answer?" We ask, "Is an answer possible? If so, what difference would an answer make?" What parts of the question are hidden from us? What does the question cause to happen to us?
- A question is the result of an imaginative, creative, ambiguous, stimulating, unfinished experience. A question inevitably moves toward complexity. As it evolves, so do we.

We also know that it's important to prepare for complexity, to embrace a more critical kind of thinking, leavened by flexibility and maturity; we understand more and reject absolutism. When our world is opened by a complex inquiry, our concepts become more flexible, less ironclad, less arbitrary. Conditions become part of the process, part of our observations.

In the practice of research, one way to prepare for complexity is to look at the unknown, look at the conditions, look at the questions you know and have addressed already. In Polya's *How to Solve It,* we find a heuristic, an unchanging set of questions we can use to describe the problem we want to solve and to assert a systematic protocol as we work on it. Consider the question as a mechanism. What is the unknown? Look at the unknown. What does it look like? Have we ever seen something like this before? What are the conditions of a useful response? How will we recognize it when we find it? How does the question itself suggest the qualities of the unknown? What kind of response will satisfy the unknown? What kind of evidence will be useful in reducing the unknown? What is the best source of evidence? In what situation or context will we find it? Will it be reliable? Will we understand it? Some questions are rhetorical or awe-inspired, and unanswerable. But some questions imply a set of steps and must be asked in a sequence as the evidence accrues, inducing fresh insights that might not appear immediately. No question should be asked before the proper, most useful time. Often the best questions (in my naïve view) are naïve questions, asked in a simulation of innocence and unknowing, in an effort to clear away previous discussion and start from a fresh perspective.

My grounding in research did not begin with problems, techniques, methods, or statistics. It began with theory. I saw my first data three years after reading *The Conduct of Inquiry* by Abraham Kaplan, two years after reading *Theory in Practice* by Chris Argyris and Donald A. Schön, one year after reading *The Discovery of Grounded Theory* by Barney Glaser and Anselm Strauss. When I revisit Kaplan now, it is like a guidebook to dreaming or fiction akin to Calvino's masterpiece *Invisible Cities.* In

1975 *The Conduct of Inquiry* described a parallel world of invisible dwellings or domains where vital concepts—logic, models, theories, concepts, values— still shape valid human discovery. From that preliminary reading and thinking, I drew small ideas about approaching my dissertation, but I also drew the unimaginably vast (and intimidating) ideas of open thinking, transparency of method, the logics of empiricism, respect for informants and their evidence, systematic thinking, the likelihood of error, the need to revise, revise, and revise. These ideas have never left me. I also came to learn that the value of empirical evidence tends to increase insofar as it is local and directly provided to the researcher by the informant; that it is dangerous to close the inquiry prematurely; and that reductive thinking is narrow, constrained, rarely useful thinking. (See above: "A question inevitably moves toward complexity.") What I read at the beginning helped me to define my style, and helped me to see how the world might make tentative sense in my eyes.

The unknowns that draw me now continue to expand toward the unfinished issues in adult lives, toward the ways we have of speaking with each other in public forums, and toward the possibilities of experience in cultural institutions, all part of my original work as a doctoral student more than thirty years ago. When I do research, I talk to people; I listen, and write down or record what they say. Then I think about it for a long time until I am ready to write. (As I conclude this afterword, I am looking at notebooks I kept during the decade between 1983 and 1993, when I did extensive observations in museums. It is time to write about that period and how it changed me.) Observing in libraries and museums, I continue to be informed by the processes that inform this book. In our situations of practice, I ask, what can be observed here? How should we reflect on what we observe, and the data we gather? What acts or changes can we consider in our situation, in our practice? (In his vital and timeless book, *The Reflective Practitioner,* Donald Schön calls these acts "moves.")

Readers of this book might see it as an invitation to devise for themselves the ways that empirical inquiry will fit into everyday librarianship, as we give service to people across the life span, build collections that advance aspirations and journeys, and conduct essential, informing processes for the growth of a community. As our everyday work continues to flow in its evolving ways, we are free to re-imagine and refresh it. Every profession needs an enduring epistemology of practice, a way to clarify what it can do to understand itself, despite constraints. Embedded in nascent clarity and understanding are the promises that lead us on: that we can become different practitioners; that we can make differences by breaking through the boundaries of convention and assumption; and that we can strive to reduce our unknowns by asking difficult questions of ourselves.

Notes

1. Here I am thinking of the extraordinary paintings and prints of nineteenth-century Japan known as ukiyo-e, "pictures of the floating world." See, for example, Gian Carlo Calza, *Ukiyo-e* (London: Phaidon, 2005) and Timothy Clark and others, *The Dawn of the Floating World, 16501765* (London: Royal Academy of Arts, 2001). These are subtle and complex images of the everyday dramas of social interaction and personal observation.
2. John Dewey, *Experience and Education* (New York: Collier Books, 1963 [1938]).
3. Mihalyi Csikszentmihalyi, *Flow: The Psychology of Optimal Experience* (New York: Harper and Row, 1990).
4. See G. Polya, *How to Solve It: A New Aspect of Mathematical Method* (Princeton, NJ: Princeton University Press, 2004 [1945]).
5. Later I read Robert Stake on the case study, Bronowski on the origins of knowledge and imagination, the fine little blue volumes of the Sage series on qualitative research, Norman Denzin on the research act, Robert Nisbet on sociology as an art form, and Walter Wallace's book, *The Logic of Science in Sociology*, where I first read Karl Popper's words, "The demand for scientific objectivity makes it inevitable that every scientific statement must remain tentative forever."

Contributors

EDITORS

Douglas Cook, DEd, is Instruction/Reference Librarian and Professor at Shippensburg University of Pennsylvania. He received his MLS from the University of Maryland and his doctorate from the Pennsylvania State University. He has recently co-edited three books. With Tasha Cooper, *Teaching Information Literacy Skills to Social Science Students and Practioners*, (Chicago: ACRL, 2006). With Ryan Sittler, *Practical Pedagogy for Library Instructors*, (Chicago: ACRL, 2008). And also with Ryan Sittler, *The Library Instruction Cookbook*, (Chicago: ACRL, 2009). His current research interests are Web-centered pedagogy and library assessment. When he is not out taking his Garmin GPS unit and his Canon digital camera for a walk in Michaux Forest he may be contacted by e-mail at dlcook@ship.edu.

Lesley Farmer, EdD, Professor at California State University Long Beach, coordinates the Librarianship program. She earned her master in library science at the University of North Carolina Chapel Hill, and received her doctorate in Adult Education from Temple University. Dr. Farmer has worked as a teacher-librarian in K-12 school settings as well as in public, special and academic libraries. She chaired the Education Section of the Special Libraries Association, and is the International Association of School Librarianship Vice-President of Association Relations. A frequent presenter and writer for the profession, Dr. Farmer's research interests include information literacy, collaboration, and educational technology. Dr. Farmer's most recent book is *Technology Management Handbook for School Library Media Centers*, co-authored with Marc McPhee and published by Neal-Schuman in 2010. She may be contacted at lfarmer@csulb.edu.

AUTHORS

Mariaelena Bartesaghi, PhD, is Assistant Professor of Communication at the University of South Florida. She received both her MA and doctoral degrees from the Annenberg School for Communication at the University of Pennsylvania. As a social construction communication scholar and a discourse analyst, she has published both empirical and theoretical work in book chapters and journals such as *Discourse Studies*, *Communication Yearbook*, and *Communication and Medicine*. Her research studies talk in institutional settings. She can be reached at mbartesaghi@usf.edu.

Penny Beile, PhD, is interim head of Research and Information Services and head of the Curriculum Materials Center at the University of Central Florida. She received her MLS and MEd from the University of Kentucky and her doctorate from the University of Central Florida. She is co-author, with David Boote, of the article "Scholars before Researchers: On the Centrality of the Dissertation Literature Review in Research Preparation," which appeared in *Educational Researcher* in 2005. This highly acclaimed article is required reading in courses taught around the world. Penny's publications and presentations generally focus on some aspect of information literacy and its assessment. When not traveling or gardening she enjoys spending time with her husband, Thomas O'Neil, on their farm. Penny can be reached at pbeile@mail.ucf.edu.

Patricia Bender, MALS, is a Research/Grant Specialist in the Office of Sponsored Research at Rutgers, the State University of New Jersey, Campus at Newark. Ms. Bender has taught writing at Rutgers University, and has offered community writing workshops both nationally and internationally for more than twenty years. A National Writing Project consultant, she founded and directed the Writing Center at Rutgers, Newark (1998 -2008), and she has earned certification in workshop leadership through Amherst Writers and Artists. Most recently her poetry appeared in *LIPS*, and she was awarded the Editor's Choice Award in the 2009 Allen Ginsburg Poetry Contest from the Paterson Poetry Center. She may be contacted at pbender@andromeda.rutgers.edu.

Robin Brown, MA, MLS, is Information Literacy Librarian and Assistant Professor at Borough of Manhattan Community College. She received her MLS from Rutgers University, New Brunswick and her MA in history from Rutgers University, Newark. Her current research interests include e-books, multi-disciplinary collaboration and information literacy instruction, and New Jersey history and historiography. She can be contacted by email at rbrown@bmcc.cuny.edu.

David Carr, PhD. After teaching, observing and practicing in cultural institutions for four decades, David is now a writer and consultant. He holds degrees from Drew, Teachers College - Columbia, and Rutgers Universities, and has taught librarianship at Rutgers and the University of North Carolina at Chapel Hill. He has published two collections of essays, *The Promise of Cultural Institutions* and *A Place Not a Place: Reflection and Possibility in Museums and Libraries.* His most recent essays have appeared in *Curator, The Museum Journal* ("Confluence" in v. 51, n. 3, and "An Aspect of the Infinite: New Zealand Talks" in v. 53, n. 1). His next book will be titled *Open Conversations,* about libraries and museums as instruments of democracy. He may be contacted at wildon.carr@gmail.com.

Carolyn L. Cook, PhD, is Assistant Professor of Education at Mount St. Mary's University in Emmitsburg, Maryland. She received her MEd in reading from Shippensburg University and her doctorate in curriculum and instruction in language and literacy from the Pennsylvania State University. She teaches graduate and undergraduate reading courses. Her research interests include teacher talk and writing instruction, critical literacy and children's literature, and oral storytelling and writing with English language learners. Reading, hiking, and traveling are her favorite pastimes. She may be contacted by email at cook@msmary.edu.

Aaron Dobbs, MSLS, MSM, is Systems and Electronic Resources Librarian, and Assistant Professor at Shippensburg University of Pennsylvania. He received his master of management from Austin Peay State University and his MSLS from the University of Tennessee. The author of several professional book chapters, Aaron is lead editor for a book under contract with Neal-Schuman tentatively titled *LibGuides: Making Dynamic Web Design and Management Simple for Non Web-designers*. Aaron is also heavily involved in ALA as Councilor-at-Large, Chair of the ALA Website Advisory Committee, an ACRL Legislative Advocate, and a member of the LITA Board of Directors. Aaron's current professional interest is in creating student-centered library Web sites, particularly with LibGuides. When Aaron isn't driving around the country collecting counties he may be contacted at awdobbs@ship.edu.

Thomas Scott Duke, PhD, is an Associate Professor of Education at the University of Alaska Southeast, where he coordinates graduate programs in special education and teaches courses in special education, multicultural education, and qualitative research methods. He earned a doctorate in special education from the University of Hawaii-Manoa. His recent publications include a meta-synthesis of the international literature on LGBTQ youth with disabilities, a meta-synthesis of the international literature on preparing information literate teachers (with Jennifer Ward), and a review of the literature on LGBTQ issues in early childhood education programs in the U.S. (with Kathrin McCarthy). His current research interests include LGBTQ issues in P-12 educational contexts and the preparation of information literate teachers. He can be reached by e-mail at thomas.duke@uas.alaska.edu.

Robert Flatley, MLA, MLS, is Electronic Resources and Periodicals Librarian at Kutztown University of Pennsylvania. He received his MLS from Clarion University. Robert is the author of numerous articles in peer-reviewed journals including the *Journal of Academic Librarianship* and *Library Philosophy and Practice*. His research interests are evaluating electronic resources, the information commons model, and conducting focus groups to improve library services and resources. Outside of the library Robert's interests center on cooperative living and environmental activism. He may be contacted by email at flatley@kutztown.edu.

Isabelle Flemming, MA, MLS, is a Reference/Computer Specialist Librarian and Instructor at the Ela Area Public Library in Lake Zurich, Illinois. She received her MLS from the University of Illinois and MA in history from the University of Florida. She has recently had articles published in the *Encyclopedia of Time: Science, Philosophy, Theology, & Culture*, (Los Angeles: Sage, 2009), and chapters in *21st Century Anthropology: a Reference Handbook*, (Thousand Oaks, CA: SAGE Publications, 2010), editor, H. James Birx. Her short stories have been published in a local newspaper, and a short story was published in the *New England Writers' Network* periodical. She is a member of the American Library Association and three of its divisions and currently serves on the History Committee for RUSA. Her research interests lie in the related fields of the history of culture and ideas and in how humans organize and process Information. These culminate in a special interest in the future of virtual worlds and their impact on society. When she is not following her many hobbies she may be contacted by e-mail at iflemming@eapl.org.

Ardis Hanson, MALIS, is the head of the Research Library at the Louis de la Parte Florida Mental Health Institute at the University of South Florida (USF) and an adjunct instructor at USF. Senior editor of *Building a Virtual Library*, she co-authored the monograph *Integrating Geographic Information Systems into Library Services* and a recent book chapter, entitled "Power and Trust in the Virtual Workplace: Team Development as Communities-of-Practice." A doctoral candidate in the Department of Communication at USF, she is studying the discourse of public policy. She can be reached at hanson@fmhi.usf.edu.

Janice Krueger, EdD, is currently an Assistant Professor and Chair of the Library Science department at Clarion University of Pennsylvania. She has a doctorate in education, specializing in curriculum and instruction, and has varied library experience in academic, public, and special libraries. Her most challenging work as a librarian was in an academic library where she engaged in reference, collection development, instruction, technical services, electronic resources, and systems work. She has been teaching undergraduate and graduate students at Clarion since 2006. She also has experience as a middle school teacher and has worked for the government in both a civilian and military capacity. She may be reached at jkrueger@clarion.edu.

LeRoy Jason LaFleur, MLIS, MS, is the Head of the Arlington Campus Library at George Mason University, where he oversees library collections and services for a variety of academic and professional programs. His background includes extensive experience in academic library collection development and public services, with a particular focus on applied social sciences research and scholarship. LeRoy is an active member of the American Library Association, the Association of College and Research Libraries, and the Black Caucus of the American Library Association. He has written and presented on a number of topics related to library outreach and practice including information literacy, diversity, and recruitment. LeRoy received his MLIS from the University of Wisconsin-Madison, and a master of science degree in organization development and knowledge management from George Mason University. He lives several miles from the Pentagon, in Arlington, VA with his wife, son, and two cats. He may be contacted at llafleur@gmu.edu.

David A. Nolfi, MLS, AHIP, is Health Sciences Librarian and chair of the Library Assessment Committee at Duquesne University. He received his MLS from the University of Pittsburgh and has been recognized as a Distinguished member of the Academy of Health Information Professionals. He has served as the Library and Information Sciences editor for *Doody's Review Service* since 2003. Together with colleagues, he has presented on several topics such as librarians as leaders and electronic resource decision making. He is active in several university-wide committees including outcomes assessment and faculty grievance. His email address is nolfi@duq.edu.

Marie L. Radford, PhD, is an Associate Professor at Rutgers, the State University of New Jersey's School of Communication & Information. Previously, she was Acting Dean of Pratt Institute's School of Information and Library Science in NYC. She holds a PhD from Rutgers and an MSLS from Syracuse University. Her research interests are in qualitative methods, interpersonal communication aspects of reference/information services (both traditional and virtual), cultural studies, and media stereotypes of librarians. Her latest co-authored books include *Reference Renaissance* (Neal-Schuman 2010) and *Conducting the Reference Interview,* (Neal-Schuman, 2009). She is the 2010 recipient of the Isadore Gilbert Mudge Award for distinguished contributions to reference librarianship given by the American Library Association, Reference and User Services Association. She may be reached at mradford@rutgers.edu.

Judi Repman, PhD, is Professor and Coordinator of the Instructional Technology Program at Georgia Southern University, Statesboro, GA. She received her MLS and doctoral degree from Louisiana State University, Baton Rouge. Prior to serving on the faculty at Georgia Southern, she was on the faculty at Texas Tech University, Lubbock, TX. In her current position she teaches school library preparation courses online. With Gail Dickinson, she is the editor of *School Library Management,* 6th ed. (Worthington, OH: Linworth Publishing, 2007). Her research interests include information literacy, the impact of Web 2.0 on teaching and learning, and online instruction. When she is not traveling, reading or trying out new web tools, she can be contacted by e-mail at jrepman@georgiasouthern.edu.

Laverna M. Saunders, EdD, is University Librarian at Duquesne University. She received her MLS from Rutgers University, MA from Drew University, and EdD at UNLV. She chairs the University Library Committee and Academic Integrity Committee at Duquesne and is a member of the PALCI Board. She is active in LLAMA BES and has served on various ACRL committees. She is a book reviewer for *Technicalities*, serves on the editorial board of *Technical Services Quarterly*, and has written articles and edited three books on the evolution of the virtual library. Her email address is lsaunders@duq.edu.

Karla M. Schmit, MLIS, MS, is an Education and Behavioral Sciences Librarian and Assistant Director of the Pennsylvania Center for the Book at the Pennsylvania State University. She received her MS in reading education from Minnesota State University, Moorhead and her MLIS from the University of Southern Mississippi. She is currently a PhD candidate at the Pennsylvania State University. The heart of her research interests are embedded in the concept of multiliteracies within a sociocultural context. Her article, "America's Game: When Media Representations Influence Children's Responses to Literature" was chosen to be a presented paper at the 2008 ALA annual conference, (*Issues in Librarianship: Presented Papers at the ALA 2008 Annual Conference,* Chicago: ALA, 2008). She can be contacted at kms454@psu.edu.

Roberta L. Tipton, MBA, MLS, is Business Librarian, Information Literacy Coordinator, and School of Public Affairs and Administration (SPAA) Librarian at The John Cotton Dana Library, Rutgers, the State University of New Jersey, Campus at Newark. She has worked in government, medical, corporate, and academic libraries for more than thirty years. Ms. Tipton is a 2001 graduate of the ACRL Institute for Information Literacy immersion program and winner of the 1990 New Jersey Library Association Research Award. Her research interests include information literacy, organization management, and the research/writing process. She may be contacted at tipton@andromeda.rutgers.edu.

Willis Walker, MLS, is Librarian for the Levy Economics Institute of Bard College and Economics, Finance and Statistics Librarian for Bard College. After over twenty-five years in the professional and reference branch of the publishing industry, he earned his MLS from Rutgers University. His academic interests lie in information and statistical literacy, the history of the book, and digital libraries. He can be contacted at wwalker@levy.org.

Jennifer Diane Ward, MLIS, is Outreach Services Librarian and Associate Professor of Library Science at the University of Alaska Southeast (UAS) in Juneau, Alaska. She graduated from the University of Hawaii at Manoa LIS Program (2001) and has worked at UAS since 2002. Recent publications include a meta-synthesis of the international literature on preparing information literate teachers (with Thomas Duke) and a book chapter on training critically conscious, information literate teachers for Alaska's schools (with Duke and Burkert). Her professional interests include information literacy instruction and distance education and library services. Jennifer enjoys learning about and discussing qualitative research methods and ponders a future in a doctoral degree program and world travel. Contact her at jennifer.ward@uas.alaska.edu.

Michael Weber, MS, MLn, has served as a professional librarian for twenty-four years. He started his professional career in 1986 when he obtained his master's degree in librarianship from Emory University. In the years that followed Michael held positions at Emory University's Crawford Long Hospital, Morehouse School of Medicine, and Alvernia College in Reading, PA. For the past nine years he has served as a Technical Services Librarian at Kutztown University's Rohrbach Library. In 2005 Michael began to study the use of focus groups in library research. To date he has co-written several articles on the subject. Michael's other areas of interest include science librarianship, authority control, web design, and digitization. He may be reached at weber@kutztown.edu.

Alessia Zanin-Yost, MA, MLIS, is a Research and Instruction Librarian/Visuals and Performing Arts Liaison at Western Carolina University (WCU) in North Carolina. She holds an MA in art history from UC Davis, and her MLIS is from San Jose State University. Her field of research is art librarianship, information, media, and visual literacy. Her writings have appeared in *C&RL News*, *Library Philosophy and Practice*, *Art Documentation*, and *Bibliotime*, an Italian peer-review journal for librarians. She is the author of several book chapters, among them "Liaison for the Visual Arts: Responding to the Needs of Diverse Demands" for the recently published book, *The Handbook of Art and Design Librarianship*. She has presented nationally and internationally on the topic of visual and information literacy. Alessia is actively involved with ACRL/Arts, ARLISNA/SE, and with the ACRL Image Resources Interest Group on developing Visual Literacy Competency Standards for Higher Education. Alessia can be contacted at azaniny@wcu.edu.

Cordelia Zinskie, EdD, is Professor of Educational Research and Chair of the Department of Curriculum, Foundations, and Reading at Georgia Southern University, Statesboro, GA. She received her MS and her doctorate from the University of Memphis. In addition to her department chair responsibilities, she teaches research methods courses and serves as a methodologist on a number of dissertation committees. Along with Judi Repman and Elizabeth Downs, she recently published a chapter on institutional factors that impede implementation of e-learning 2.0 on university campuses in *Collective Intelligence and E-Learning 2.0* (H. H. Yang & S. C. Yuen, Hershey, PA: Information Science Reference, 2010). Her research interests include administrative roles in higher education, strategies for teaching research methods, and online instruction. When she is not taking her latest Caribbean cruise, she may be contacted by e-mail at czinskie@georgiasouthern.edu.

Index